! I ♥ TY Bear !

2011
Songwriter's
Market

34TH ANNUAL EDITION

FROM THE EDITORS OF WRITER'S DIGEST BOOKS

You're
Cute !

WD
WRITER'S DIGEST
BOOKS

WritersDigest.com
Cincinnati, Ohio

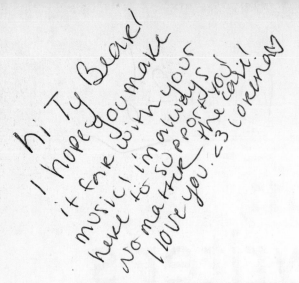

hi Ty Bear!
I hope you make
it far with your
music! I'm always
here to support you!
No matter the earth!
I love you. <3 (oremas)

Publisher & Community Leader, Writing Communities: Phil Sexton

Writer's Market website: www.writersmarket.com
Writer's Digest website: www.writersdigest.com
Writer's Digest Bookstore: www.writersdigestshop.com

Distributed in Canada by Fraser Direct
100 Armstrong Avenue
Georgetown, ON, Canada L7G 5S4
Tel: (905) 877-4411

Distributed in the U.K. and Europe by David & Charles
Brunel House, Newton Abbot, Devon, TQ12 4PU, England
Tel: (+44) 1626 323200, Fax: (+44) 1626 323319
E-mail: mail@davidandcharles.co.uk

Distributed in Australia by Capricorn Link
Loder House, 126 George Street
Windsor, NSW 2756 Australia
Tel: (02) 4577-3555

ISSN: 0161-5971
ISBN-13: 978-1-58297-954-0
ISBN-10: 1-58297-954-5

Cover design by Claudean Wheeler
Interior Design by Clare Finney
Production coordinated by Greg Nock

media

Contents

GETTING STARTED

How to Use Songwriter's Market 1

Where Should I Send My Songs? 4

Demo Recordings 8

How Do I Submit My Demo? 10

How Do I Avoid the Rip-Offs? 15

Submission Strategies 19

MUSIC BIZ BASICS

Royalties 23

What About Copyright? 28

Career Songwriting 31

What About Contracts? 33

ARTICLES & INTERVIEWS

No Rules
Crafting Opportunities as a Songwriter, by Lauren Jonik 37

Alternative Outlets
Writing Songs in a Digital World, by Anders Bylund 44

Scoring Songs for TV, Film & Commercials
by David McPherson 49

Mark Mothersbaugh
Whipping Up Scores, by Anders Bylund 54

Baby Boomers & Songwriting
by Doris Bloodsworth 59

The Poetry of the Song
Using Rhyme, Rhythm & Refrain, by Mary Harwell Sayler 66

Even Stevens
BMI Songwriter of the Century, by Hilary Kanter 71

Writing for Placement
Step-by-Step Guide to Placing Songs in Films, TV and Other Projects,
by Patrick J. Walsh 77

The New Deal
A New Approach to Selling CDs Based on Public Trust, by Grant Peeples 83

Richard Flowhil
Marketing Advice from a Seasoned Promoter, by David McPherson.................... 88

Get the Most Out of Songwriting Workshops
by Kerry Dexter 92

MARKETS

Music Publishers 97

Record Companies 130

Record Producers 169

Managers & Booking Agents 186

Music Firms 209

Play Producers & Publishers 216
    Play Producers 218
    Play Publishers... 226

Classical Performing Arts 231

Contests & Awards 253

RESOURCES

Organizations... 267

Workshops & Conferences 288

Retreats & Colonies... 300

State & Provincial Grants... 305

Publications of Interest 310

Websites of Interest 317

Glossary 324

INDEXES

Category Indexes 333
    Music Publishers 333
    Record Companies 336
    Record Producers 340
    Managers & Booking Agents 342

Openness to Submissions Index 346

Film & TV Index 350

Geographic Index 351

General Index 355

How To Use *Songwriter's Market*

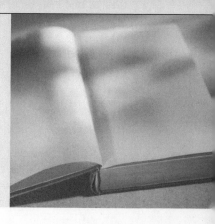

Before you dive into the *Songwriter's Market* listings and start submitting songs willy-nilly, it's a good idea to take the time to read the following information. By educating yourself on how to best use this book, you'll be better prepared when you actually do send off your tape or CD.

Let's take a look at what is actually inside *Songwriter's Market*, why these articles were put into the book in the first place and why they can actually help you in your career.

THE LISTINGS

Beyond the articles, there are 11 sections in the book, from Music Publishers and Record Companies to Contests & Awards. Each section begins with an introduction detailing how the different types of companies function—what part of the music industry they work in, how they make money, and what you need to think about when approaching them with your music.

These listings are the heart of *Songwriter's Market*. They are the names, addresses and contact information of music biz companies looking for songs and artists, as well as descriptions of the types of music they are looking for.

So how do I use *Songwriter's Market*?

The quick answer is that you should use the indexes to find companies who are interested in your type of music, then read the listings for details on how they want the music submitted. For support and help of all sorts, join a songwriting or other music industry association. Read everything you can about songwriting. Talk to other songwriters. That's a good start.

How does *Songwriter's Market* 'work'?

The listings in *Songwriter's Market* are packed with a lot of information. It can be intimidating at first, but they are put together in a structured way to make them easy to work with. Take a few minutes to get used to how the listings are organized, and you'll have it down in no time. For more detailed information about how the listings are put together, skip ahead to "Where Should I Send My Songs?" on page 4.

The following are general rules about how to use the listings:

1. **Read the entire listing** to decide whether to submit your music. Please do not use this book as a mass mailing list. If you blindly mail out demos by the hundreds, you'll waste a lot of money on postage, annoy a lot of people, and your demos will wind up in the trash anyway.

2. **Pay close attention to the "Music" section in each listing.** This will tell you what kind of music the company is looking for. If they want rockabilly only and you write heavy metal, don't submit to that company. That's just common sense.

3. **Pay close attention to submission instructions** shown under "How to Contact" and follow them to the letter. A lot of listings are very particular about how they want submissions packaged. Pay close attention. If you do not follow their instructions, they will probably throw your submission in the garbage. If you are confused about their directions, contact the company for clarification.

4. **If in doubt, contact the company for permission to submit.** This is a good general rule. Many companies don't mind if you send an unsolicited submission, but some will want you to get special prior permission from them. Contacting a company first is also a good way to find out their latest music needs. This is also a chance to briefly make contact on a personal level.

5. **Be courteous, be efficient and always have a purpose** to your personal contact. Do not waste their time. If you call, always have a reason for making contact—permission to submit, checking on guidelines, following up on a demo, etc. These are solid reasons to make personal contact, but once you have their attention, do not wear out your welcome. Always be polite.

6. **Check for a preferred contact.** A lot of listings have a designated contact person shown after a bolded "Contact" in the heading. This is the person you should contact with questions or to whom you should address your submission.

7. **Read the "Tips" section.** This part of the listing provides extra information on how to submit or what it might be like to work with the company. This is just the beginning. For more detailed information about the listings, see "Where Should I Send My Songs?" on page 4 and the sidebar with the sample listing called "A Sample Listing Decoded" on page 7.

FREQUENTLY ASKED QUESTIONS
How do these companies get listed in the book anyway?

No company pays to be included—all listings are free. The listings come from a combination of research the editor does on the music industry and questionnaires requested by companies who want to be listed (many of them contact us to be included). All questionnaires are screened for known sharks and to make sure they meet our requirements.

Why aren't other companies I know about listed in the book?

We may have sent them a questionnaire, but they did not return it, were removed for complaints, went out of business, specifically asked not to be listed, could not be contacted for an update, etc.

What's the deal with companies that don't take unsolicited submissions?

In the interest of completeness, the editor will sometimes include listings of crucial music companies and major labels he thinks you should be aware of. We want you to at least have some idea of what their policies are.

A company said in their listing they take unsolicited submissions. My demo came back unopened. What happened?

Some companies' needs change rapidly and may have changed since we contacted them for this edition of the book. This is another reason why it's often a good idea to contact a company before submitting.

So that's it. You now have the power in your fingertips to go out and become the professional songwriter you always wanted to be. Let us know how you're doing. Drop us a line at marketbooks@fwmedia.com and tell us about any successes you have had because you used the materials found in this book.

Where Should I Send My Songs?

I t depends a lot on whether you write mainly for yourself as a performer, or if you only write and want someone else to pick up your song for their recording (usually the case in country music, for example). *Are you mainly a performing songwriter or a non-performing songwriter?* This is important for figuring out what kind of companies to contact, as well as how you contact them. (For more detail, skip to Submission Strategies on page 19.)

What if I'm a non-performing songwriter?

Many well-known songwriters are not performers in their own right. Some are not skilled instrumentalists or singers, but they understand melody, lyrics and harmony and how they go together. They can write great songs, but they need someone else to bring it to life through skilled musicianship. A non-performing songwriter will usually approach music publishers first for access to artists looking for songs, as

Types of Music Companies

- **Music Publishers**—evaluate songs for commercial potential, find artists to record them, finds other uses for the songs such as film or TV, collects income from songs, protects copyrights from infringement

- **Record Companies**—sign artists to their labels, finance recordings, promotion and touring, releases songs/albums to radio and TV

- **Record Producers**—works in the studio and records songs (independently or for a record company), may be affiliated with a particular artist, sometimes develop artists for record labels, locates or co-writes songs if an artist does not write their own

- **Managers & Booking Agents**—works with artists to manage their careers, finds gigs, locates songs to record if the artist does not write their own well as artists' managers, their producers and their record companies. On the flip side, many incredibly talented musicians can't write to save their lives and need someone else to provide them with good songs to perform. (For more details on the different types of companies and the roles they play for performing songwriters, see the section introductions for Music Publishers on page 97, Record Companies on page 130, Record Producers on page 169, and Managers & Booking Agents on page 186. Also see Submission Strategies on page 19.)

What if I am a performing songwriter?

Many famous songwriters are also famous as performers. They are skilled interpreters of their own material, and they also know how to write to suit their own particular talents as musicians. In this case, their intention is also usually to sell themselves as a performer in hopes of recording and releasing an album, or they have an album and want to find gigs and people who can help guide their careers. They will usually approach record companies or record producers first, on the basis of recording an album. For gigs and career guidance, they talk to booking agents and managers.

A smaller number also approach publishers in hopes of getting others to perform their songs, much like non-performing songwriters. Some music publishers in recent years have also taken on the role of developing artists as both songwriters and performers, or are connected to a major record label, so performing songwriters might go to them for these reasons. (For more details on the different types of companies and the roles they play for performing songwriters, see the section introductions for Music Publishers on page 97, Record Companies on page 130, Record Producers on page 169, and Managers & Booking Agents on page 186. Also see Submission Strategies on page 19.)

How do I use *Songwriter's Market* to narrow my search?

Once you've identified whether you are primarily interested in getting others to perform your songs (non-performing songwriter) or you perform your own songs and want a record deal, etc., there are several steps you can then take:

1. **Identify what kind of music company you wish to approach.** Based on whether you're a performing or non-performing songwriter, do you want to approach a music publisher for a publishing deal? Do you want to approach a record producer because you need someone to help you record an album in the studio? Maybe you want to approach a producer in hopes that an act he's producing needs songs to complete their album. Also see "Submission Strategies" on page 19 and the Section Introductions for Music Publishers on page 97, Record Companies on page 130, Record Producers on page 169, and Managers & Booking Agents on page 186.

2. **Check for companies based on location.** Maybe you need a manager located close by. Maybe you need to find as many Nashville-based companies as you

Additional Resources

For More Info

Songwriter's Market lists music publishers, record companies, producers and managers (as well as advertising firms, play producers and classical performing arts organizations) along with specifications on how to submit your material to each. If you can't find a certain person or company you're interested in, there are other sources of information you can try.

The Recording Industry Sourcebook, an annual directory published by Norris-Whitney Communications, lists record companies, music publishers, producers and managers, as well as attorneys, publicity firms, media, manufacturers, distributors and recording studios around the U.S. Trade publications such as *Billboard* or *Variety*, available at most local libraries and bookstores, are great sources for up-to-date information. These periodicals list new companies as well as the artists, labels, producers and publishers for each song on the charts.

CD booklets can also be valuable sources of information, providing the name of the record company, publisher, producer and usually the manager of an artist or group. Use your imagination in your research and be creative—any contacts you make in the industry can only help your career as a songwriter. See Publications of Interest on page 310.

can because you write country and most country publishers are in Nashville. In this case, start with the Geographic Index on page 351. You can also tell Canadian and Foreign listings by the icons in the listing (see "A Sample Listing Decoded" on page 7).

3. **Look for companies based on the type of music they want.** Some companies want country. Some record labels want only punk rock. Check the Category Indexes on page 333 for a list of music companies broken down by the type of music they are interested in.

4. **Look for companies based on how open they are to beginners.** Some companies are more open than others to beginning artists and songwriters. Maybe you are a beginner and it would help to approach these companies first. Some music publishers are hoping to find that wild card hit song and don't care if it comes from an unknown writer. Maybe you are just starting out looking for gigs or record deals, and you need a manager willing to help build your band's career from the ground up. Check the Openness to Submissions Index on page 346.

For more information on how to read the listings, see "A Sample Listing Decoded" on page 7.

A SAMPLE LISTING DECODED
What do the little symbols at the beginning of the listing mean?

Those are called "icons," and they give you quick information about a listing with one glance. Here is a list of the icons and what they mean:

Openness to submissions

☐ means the company is open to beginners' submissions, regardless of past success

◐ means the company is mostly interested in previously published songwriters/ well-established acts*, but will consider beginners

◑ these companies do not want submissions from beginners, only from previously published songwriters/well-established acts*

⊘ companies with this icon only accept material referred by a reputable industry source**

(*) Well-established acts are those with a following, permanent gigs or previous record deal

(**) Reputable industry sources include managers, entertainment attorneys, performing rights organizations, etc.

Other icons

⊙ means the listing is Canadian means the listing is based overseas (Europe, Britain, Australia, etc.)

⊞ indicates a listing is new to this edition

Ⓝ means there has been a change in the contact information: contact name, phone number, fax, e-mail or website

$ is for companies who have won an industry award of some sortshows a company places songs in films or television

▦ shows (excluding commercials)

EASY-TO-USE REFERENCE ICONS

TERMS OF AGREEMENT

Ⓝ⊙▦▥ **METAL BLADE RECORDS** 2828 Cochran St., Suite 302, Simi Valley CA 93065. (805)522-9111. Fax: (805)522-9380. E-mail: metalblade@metalblade.com. Website: www.metalblade.com. Record company. Estab. 1982. Releases 20 LPs, 2 EPs and 20 CDs/year. Pays negotiable royalty to artists on contract.

DETAILED SUBMISSION GUIDELINES

WHAT THEY'RE LOOKING FOR

How to Contact Submit demo CD by mail. Unsolicited submissions are OK. CD with 3 songs. Does not return material. Responds in 3 months.

Music Mostly **heavy metal** and **industrial**; also **hardcore, gothic** and **noise.** Released "Gallery of Suicide," recorded by Cannibal Corpse; "Voo Doo," recorded by King Diamond; and "A Pleasant Shade of Gray," recorded by Fates Warning, all on Metal Blade Records. Other artists include As I Lay Dying, The Red Chord, The Black Dahlia Murder, and Unearth.

INSIDER ADVICE

Tips "Metal Blade is known throughout the underground for quality metal-oriented acts."

Demo Recordings

What is a "demo"?

The demo, shorthand for *demonstration recording*, is the most important part of your submission package. They are meant to give music industry professionals a way to hear all the elements of your song as clearly as possible so they can decide if it has commercial potential.

Should I send a cassette or a CD?

More and more music industry people want CDs, although the cassette may still be accepted. A few companies want demos sent on CD only. It's getting cheaper and easier all the time to burn recordings, so it is worth the investment to buy a burner or borrow one. Other formats such as DAT ("Digital Audio Tape") are rarely requested.

What should I send if I'm seeking management?

Some companies want a video of an act performing their songs. Check with the companies for specific requirements.

How many songs should I send, and in what order and length?

Most music industry people agree that three songs is enough. Most music professionals are short on time, and if you can't catch their attention in three songs, your songs probably don't have hit potential. Also, put three *complete songs* on your demo, not just snippets. Make sure to put your best, most commercial song first. An up-tempo number is usually best. If you send a cassette, *put all the songs on one side of the cassette and cue the tape to the beginning of the first song so no time is wasted fast-forwarding or rewinding.*

Should I sing my own songs on my demo?

If you can't sing well, you may want to find someone who can. There are many places to check for singers and musicians, including songwriter organizations, music stores, and songwriting magazines. Some aspiring professional singers will sing on demos in exchange for a copy they can use as a demo to showcase their singing.

Should I use a professional demo service?

Many songwriters find professional demo services convenient if they don't have time or the resources to put together musicians on their own. For a fee, a demo service will produce your songs in their studio using in-house singers and musicians (this is pretty common in Nashville). Many of these advertise in music magazines, songwriting newsletters and bulletin boards at music stores. Make sure to hear samples of work they've done in the past. Some are mail-order businesses—you send a rough tape of your song or the sheet music, and they produce and record a demo within a month or two. Be sure you find a service that will let you have some control over how the demo is produced, and tell them exactly how you want your song to sound. As with studios, look around for a service that fits your needs and budget. (Some will charge as low as $300 for three songs, while others may go as high as $3,000 and boast a high-quality sound—*shop around and use your best judgment!*)

Should I buy equipment and record demos myself?

If you have the drive and focus to learn good recording technique, yes. If not, it might be easier to have someone else do it. Digital multi-track recorders are now easily available and within reasonable financial reach of many people. For performing songwriters in search of record deals, the actual sound of their recordings can often be an important part of their artistic concept. Having the "means of production" within their grasp can be crucial to artists pursuing the independent route. But, if you don't know how to use the equipment, it may be better to go into a professional studio.

How elaborate and full should the demo production be if I'm a non-performing songwriter?

Many companies in *Songwriter's Market* tell you what they prefer. If in doubt, contact them and ask. In general, country songs and pop ballads can often be demoed with just a vocal plus guitar or piano, although many songwriters in those genres still prefer to get a more complete recording with drums, guitars and other backing instruments. Up-tempo pop, rock and dance demos usually need a more full production.

What kind of production do I need if I'm a performing songwriter?

If you are a band or artist looking for a record deal, you will need a demo that is as fully produced as possible. Many singer/songwriters record their demos as if they were going to be released as an album. That way, if they don't get a deal, they can still release it on their own. Professionally pressed CDs are also now easily within reach of performing songwriters, and many companies offer graphic design services for a professional-looking product.

How Do I Submit My Demo?

You have three basic options for submitting your songs: submitting by mail, submitting in person and submitting over the Internet (the newest and least widely accepted option at this time).

SUBMITTING BY MAIL

Should I call, write or e-mail first to ask for permission or submission requirements?

This is always a good idea, and many companies ask you to contact them first. If you call, be polite, brief and specific. If you send a letter, make sure it is typed and to the point. Include a typed SASE they can use to reply. If you send an e-mail, again be professional and to the point. Proofread your message before you send it, and then be patient. Give them some time to reply. Do not send out mass e-mails or otherwise spam their e-mail account.

What do I send with my demo?

Most companies have specific requirements, but here are some general pointers:

- Read the listing carefully and submit *exactly* what they ask for, in the exact way they describe. It's also a good idea to call first, just in case they've changed their submission policies.
- Listen to each demo to make sure they sound right and are in the right order (see Demo Recordings: What Should I Know? on page 8).
- If you use cassettes, make sure they are cued up to the beginning of the first song.
- Enclose a *brief*, typed cover letter to introduce yourself. Tell them what songs you are sending and why you are sending them. If you are pitching your songs to a particular artist, say so in the letter. If you are an artist/songwriter looking for a record deal, you should say so. Be specific.
- Include *typed* lyric sheets or lead sheets, if requested. Make sure your name, address and phone number are on each sheet.

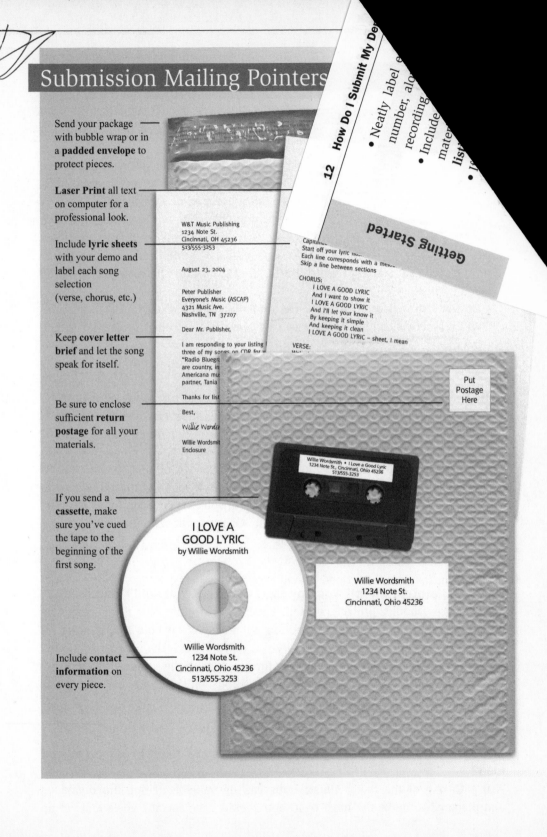

Submission Mailing Pointers

Send your package with bubble wrap or in a **padded envelope** to protect pieces.

Laser Print all text on computer for a professional look.

Include **lyric sheets** with your demo and label each song selection (verse, chorus, etc.)

Keep **cover letter brief** and let the song speak for itself.

Be sure to enclose sufficient **return postage** for all your materials.

If you send a **cassette**, make sure you've cued the tape to the beginning of the first song.

Include **contact information** on every piece.

- Neatly label e...
  number, alo...
  recording...
- Include...
  mater...
  list...

Getting Started

Capitaliz...
Start off your lyric...
Each line corresponds with a melo...
Skip a line between sections

CHORUS:
I LOVE A GOOD LYRIC
And I want to show it
I LOVE A GOOD LYRIC
And I'll let you know it
By keeping it simple
And keeping it clean
I LOVE A GOOD LYRIC – sheet, I mean

VERSE:

W&T Music Publishing
1234 Note St.
Cincinnati, OH 45236
513/555-3253

August 23, 2004

Peter Publisher
Everyone's Music (ASCAP)
4321 Music Ave.
Nashville, TN 37207

Dear Mr. Publisher,

I am responding to your listing...
three of my songs on CDR for...
"Radio Bluegr...
are country, in...
Americana mu...
partner, Tania

Thanks for list...

Best,

Willie Words...

Willie Wordsmit...
Enclosure

Put Postage Here

I LOVE A GOOD LYRIC
by Willie Wordsmith

Willie Wordsmith
1234 Note St.
Cincinnati, Ohio 45236
513/555-3253

Willie Wordsmith • I Love a Good Lyric
1234 Note St., Cincinnati, Ohio 45236
513/555-3253

Willie Wordsmith
1234 Note St.
Cincinnati, Ohio 45236

ach tape or CD with your name, address, e-mail and phone
ng with the names of the songs in the order they appear on the

a SASE with sufficient postage and large enough to return all your
ials. **Warning: Many companies do not return materials, so read each
ing carefully!**

If you submit to companies in other countries, include a self-addressed envelope
(SAE) and International Reply Coupon (IRC), available at most post offices.
Make sure the envelope is large enough to return all of your materials.

- Pack everything neatly. Neatly type or write the company's address and your
return address so they are clearly visible. Your package is the first impression a
company has of you and your songs, so neatness counts!
- Mail first class. Stamp or write "First Class Mail" on the package and the SASE
you enclose.
- **Do not use registered or certified mail unless requested!** Most companies
will not accept or open demos sent by registered or certified mail for fear of
lawsuits.
- Keep records of the dates, songs and companies you submit to.

Is it OK to send demos to more than one person or company at a time?

It is usually acceptable to make simultaneous submissions. One exception is when
a publisher, artist or other industry professional asks to put your song "on hold."

What does it mean when a song is "on hold"?

This means they intend to record the song and don't want you to give the song to
anyone else. This is not a guarantee, though. Your song may eventually be returned
to you, even if it's been on hold for months. Or it may be recorded and included
on the album. If either of these happens, you are free to pitch your song to other
people again.

How can I protect myself from my song being put "on hold" indefinitely?

You can, and should, protect yourself. Establish a deadline for the person who
asks for the hold (for example, "You can put my song on hold for [number of]
months."), or modify the hold to specify you will still pitch the song to others but
won't sign another deal without allowing the person with the song on hold to make
you an offer. Once you sign a contract with a publisher, they have exclusive rights
to your song and you may not pitch it to other would-be publishers.

SUBMITTING IN PERSON

Is a visit to New York, Nashville or Los Angeles to submit in person a good idea?

A trip to one of the major music hubs can be valuable if you are organized
and prepared to make the most of it. You should have specific goals and set up

appointments before you go. Some industry professionals are difficult to see and may not feel meeting out-of-town writers is a high priority. Others are more open and even encourage face-to-face meetings. By taking the time to travel, organize and schedule meetings, you can appear more professional than songwriters who submit blindly through the mail.

What should I take?

Take several copies of your demo and typed lyric sheets of each of your songs. More than one company you visit may ask you to leave a copy for them to review. You can expect occasionally to find a person has cancelled an appointment, but want you to leave a copy of your songs so they may listen and contact you later. (Never give someone the only or last copy of your demo if you absolutely want it returned, though.)

Where should I network while visiting?

Coordinate your trip with a music conference or make plans to visit ASCAP, BMI, or SESAC offices while you are there. For example, the South by Southwest Music Conference in Austin and the NSAI Spring Symposium often feature demo listening sessions, where industry professionals listen to demos submitted by songwriters attending the seminar. ASCAP, BMI, and SESAC also sometimes sponsor seminars or allow aspiring songwriters to make appointments with counselors who can give them solid advice.

How do I deal with rejection?

Many good songs have been rejected simply because they were not what the publisher or record company was looking for at that particular point. Do not take it personally. If few people like your songs, it does not mean they are not good. On the other hand, if you have a clear vision for what your particular songs are trying to get across, specific comments can also teach you a lot about whether your concept is coming across as you intended. If you hear the same criticisms of your songs over and over—for instance, the feel of the melody isn't right or the lyrics need work—give the advice serious thought. Listen carefully and use what the reviewers say constructively to improve your songs.

SUBMITTING OVER THE INTERNET
Is it OK to submit over the Internet?

It can be done, but it's not yet widely accepted. There can still be problems with audio file formats. Although e-mail is more common now if you look through the listings in *Songwriter's Market*, not all music companies are necessarily equipped with computers or Internet access sufficient to make the process easy. But it shows a lot of promise for the future. Web-based companies like Tonos.com or TAXI, among many others are making an effort to connect songwriters and industry professionals over the Internet. The Internet is proving important for networking. Garageband.

com has extensive bulletin boards and allow members to post audio files of songs for critique. Stay tuned for future developments.

If I want to try submitting over the Internet, what should I do?

First, send an e-mail to confirm whether a music company is equipped to stream or download audio files properly (whether mp3 or real audio, etc.). If they do accept demos online, one strategy becoming common is build a website with audio files that can be streamed or downloaded. Then, when you have permission, send an e-mail with links to that website or to particular songs. All they have to do is click on the link and it launches their Web browser to the appropriate page. Do not try to send mp3s or other files as attachments. They are often too large for the free online e-mail accounts people commonly use, and they may be mistakenly erased as potential viruses.

How Do I Avoid the Rip-Offs?

The music industry has its share of dishonest, greedy people who will try to rip you off by appealing to your ambition, by stroking your ego, or by claiming special powers to make you successful—for a price, of course. Most of them use similar methods, and you can prevent a lot of heartbreak by learning to spot them and stay away.

What is a "song shark"?

"Song sharks," as they're called, prey on beginners—songwriters unfamiliar with how the music industry works and what the ethical standards are. Two general signs of a song shark are:

- Song sharks will take *any* songs—quality doesn't count.
- They're not concerned with future royalties, since they get their money up front from songwriters who think they're getting a great deal.

What are some of the more blatant rip-offs?

A request for money up front is the most common element. Song sharks may ask for money in the form of submission fees, an outright offer to publish your song for a fee or an offer to re-record your demo for a sometimes hefty price (with the implication that they will make your song wildly successful if you only pay to have it re-demoed in *their studio*). There are many variations on this theme.

Here is a list of rules that can help you avoid a lot of scams:

- **DO NOT SELL YOUR SONGS OUTRIGHT!** It's unethical for anyone to offer such a proposition. If your song becomes successful after you've sold it outright, you will never get royalties for it.
- **Never pay any sort of "submission fees," "review fees," "service fees," "filing fees," etc.** Reputable companies review material free of charge. If you encounter a company in this book who charges to submit, report them to the editor. If a company charges "only" $15 to submit your song, consider this: *if*

"only" 100 songwriters pay the $15, this company has made an extra $1,500 just for opening the mail!

- **Never pay to have your songs published.** A reputable company interested in your songs assumes the responsibility and cost of promoting them, in hopes of realizing a profit once the songs are recorded and released. If they truly believe in your song, they will accept the costs involved.

- **Do not pay a company to pair you with a collaborator.** It's much better to contact a songwriting organization that offers collaboration services to their members.

- **Never pay to have your lyrics or poems set to music.** This is a classic rip-off. "Music mills"—for a price—may use the same melody for hundreds of lyrics and poems, whether it sounds good or not. Publishers recognize one of these melodies as soon as they hear it.

- **Avoid "pay-to-play" CD compilation deals.** It's totally unrealistic to expect this will open doors for you. These are mainly a money-maker for the music company. CDs are cheap to manufacture, so a company that charges $100 to include your recording on a CD is making a killing. They claim they send these CDs to radio stations, producers, etc., but they usually wind up in the trash or as drink coasters. Music industry professionals have no incentive to listen to them. Everybody on the CD paid to be included, so it's not like they were carefully screened for quality.

- **Avoid "songpluggers" who offer to "shop" your song for an upfront fee or retainer.** This practice is not appropriate for *Songwriter's Market* readers, many of whom are beginners and live away from major music centers like Nashville. Professional, established songwriters in Nashville are sometimes known to work on a fee basis with song-pluggers they have gotten to know over many years, *but the practice is controversial even for professionals.* Also, the songpluggers used by established professionals are very selective about their clients and have their own reputation to uphold. Companies who offer

If You Write Lyrics, But Not Music

- **You must find a collaborator.** The music business is looking for the complete package: music plus lyrics. If you don't write music, find a collaborator who does. The best way to find a collaborator is through songwriting organizations. Check the Organizations section (page 267) for songwriting groups near you.

- **Don't get ripped-off.** "Music mills" advertise in the back of magazines or solicit you through the mail. For a fee they will set your lyrics or poems to music. The rip-off is that they may use the same melody for hundreds of lyrics and poems, whether it sounds good or not. Publishers recognize one of these melodies as soon as they hear it.

you these services but barely know you or your work are to be avoided. Also, contracting a songplugger by long distance offers little or no accountability— you have no direct way of knowing what they're doing on your behalf.

- **Avoid paying a fee up front to have a publisher make a demo of your song.** Some publishers may take demo expenses out of your future royalties (a negotiable contract point usually meant to avoid endless demo sessions), but avoid paying up front for demo costs. Avoid situations where it is implied or expressed that a company will publish your song in return for you paying up front to use their demo services.

- **No record company should ask you to pay them or an associated company to make a demo.** The job of a record company is to make records and decide which artists to sign *after* listening to demo submissions.

- **Read all contracts carefully before signing.** And don't sign any contract you're unsure about or that you don't fully understand. It is well worth paying an attorney for the time it takes him to review a contract if you can avoid a bad situation that may cost you thousands of dollars.

- **Before entering a songwriting contest, read the rules carefully.** Be sure what you're giving up in the way of entry fees, etc., is not more than what you stand to gain by winning the contest. See the Contests & Awards section on page 253.

- **Verify any situation about an individual or company if you have any doubts at all.** Contact the company's Performing Rights Society—ASCAP, BMI, SESAC, or SOCAN (in Canada). Check with the Better Business Bureau in the company's town, or contact the state attorney general's office. Contact professional organizations you're a member of and inquire about the reputation of the company.

- **If a record company or other company asks you to pay expenses up front, be careful.** Record producers commonly charge up front to produce an artist's album. Small indie labels sometimes ask a band to help with recording costs (but seek less control than a major label might). It's up to you to decide whether or not it is a good idea. Talk to other artists who have signed similar contracts before you sign one yourself. Research companies to find out if they can deliver on their claims, and what kind of distribution they have. Visit their website, if they have one. Beware of any company that won't let you know what it has done in the past. If a company has had successes and good working relationships with artists, it should be happy to brag about them.

I noticed record producers charge to produce albums. Is this bad?

Not automatically. Just remember what your goals are. If you write songs, but do not sing or perform, you are looking for publishing opportunities with the producer instead of someone who can help you record an album or CD. If you are a performing artist or band, then you might be in the market to hire a producer,

How Do I File a Complaint?

Write to the *Songwriter's Market* editor at: 4700 E. Galbraith Rd., Cincinnati OH 45236. Include:

• A complete description of the situation, as best you can describe it.

• Copies of any materials a company may have sent you that we may keep on file.

If you encounter situations similar to any of the "song shark" scenarios described above, let us know about it.

in which case you will most likely pay them up front (and possibly give them a share in royalties or publishing, depending on the specific deal you negotiate). For more information see the Record Producers section introduction on page 169 and Royalties: Where Does the Money Come From? on page 23.

Will it help me avoid rip-offs if I join a songwriting organization?

Yes. You will have access to a lot of good advice from a lot of experienced people. You will be able to research and compare notes, which will help you avoid a lot of pitfalls.

What should I know about contracts?

Negotiating a fair contract is important. You must protect yourself, and there are specific things you should look for in a contract (see What About Contracts? on page 33).

Are companies that offer demo services automatically bad?

No, but you are not obligated to make use of their services. Many music companies have their own or related recording studios, and with good recording equipment becoming so cheap and easy to use in recent years, a lot of them are struggling to stay afloat. This doesn't mean a company is necessarily trying to rip you off, but use your best judgment. In some cases, a company will submit a listing to *Songwriter's Market* for the wrong reasons—to pitch their demo services instead of finding songs to sign—in which case you should report them to the *Songwriter's Market* editor.

Submission Strategies

NON-PERFORMING SONGWRITERS

Here's a short list of avenues non-performing songwriters can pursue when submitting songs:

1. Submit to a music publisher. This is the obvious one. Look at the information under "**Music**" in the listing to see examples of a publisher's songs and the artists they've found cuts with. Do you recognize the songs? Have you heard of the artists? Who are the writers? Do they have cuts with artists you would like to get a song to?

2. Submit to a record company. Are the bands and artists on the record company's roster familiar? Do they tend to use outside songs on their albums? When pursuing this angle, it often helps to contact the record company first. Ask if they have a group or artist in development who needs material.

3. Submit to a record producer. Do the producer's credits in the listings show songs written by songwriters other than the artist? Does he produce name artists known for using outside material? Be aware that producers themselves often write with the artists, so your song might also be competing against the producer's songwriting.

4. Submit to an artist's manager. If an artist needs songs, their manager is a prime gateway for your song. Contact the manager and ask if he has an act in need of material.

5. Join a songwriting organization. Songwriting organizations are a good way to make contacts. You'll discover opportunities through the contacts you make that others might not hear about. Some organizations can put you in direct contact with publishers for song critique sessions. You can increase your chances of a hit by co-writing with other songwriters. Your songs will get better because of the feedback from other members.

6. Approach Performing Rights Organizations (PROs). PROs like ASCAP and BMI have writer relations representatives who can sometimes (if they think you're

...eference to a music company. This is one of the favored routes ...Nashville music scene.

...NG SONGWRITERS

...more complicated, because there are a lot of different avenues

...a record deal

This is often a performing songwriter's primary goal—to get a record deal and release an album. Here are some possible ways to approach it:

1. Approach a record company for a record deal. This is another obvious one. Independent labels will be a lot more approachable than major labels, who are usually deluged with demos. Independent labels give you more artistic freedom, while major labels will demand more compromise, especially if you do not have a previous track record. A compromise between the two is to approach one of the "fake indie" labels owned by a major. You'll get more of the benefits of an indie, but with more of the resources and connections of a major label.

2. Approach a record producer for a development deal. Some producers sign artists, produce their album and develop them like a record company, and then approach major labels for distribution deals. This has advantages and drawbacks. For example, the producer gives you guidance and connections, but it can also be harder to get paid because you are signed to the producer and not the label.

3. Get a manager with connections. The right manager with the right connections can make all the difference in getting a record deal.

4. Ask a music publisher. Publishers are taking on more and more of a role of developing performing songwriters as artists. Many major publishers are sister companies to record labels and can shop you for a deal when they think you're ready. They do this in hopes of participating in the mechanical royalties from an album release, and these monies can be substantial when it's a major label release.

5. Approach an entertainment attorney. Entertainment attorneys are a must when it comes to negotiating record contracts, and some moonlight by helping artists make connections for record deals (they will get their cut, of course).

6. Approach PROs. ASCAP and BMI can counsel you on your career and possibly make a referral. They also commonly put on performance showcases where A&R ("artist and repertoire") people from record labels attend to check out new artists.

Finding a producer to help with your album

Independently minded performing songwriters often find they need help navigating the studio when it comes time to produce their own album. In this case, the producer often works for an upfront fee from the artist, for a percentage of the royalty when the album is released and sold (referred to as "points," as in "percentage points"), or a combination of both.

Things to keep in mind when submitting a demo to a producer on this basis:

1. Is the producer known for a particular genre or "sound"? Many producers have a signature sound to their studio productions and are often connected to specific genres. Phil Spector had the "Wall of Sound." Bob Rock pioneered a glossy metal sound for Metallica and The Cult. Daniel Lanois and Brian Eno are famous for the atmospheres they created on albums by U2. Look at your favorite CDs to see who produced. Use these as touchstones when approaching producers to see if they are on your wavelength.

2. What role does a particular producer like to take in the studio? The "Tips" section of *Songwriter's Market* Record Producers listings often have notes from the producer about how they like to work with performing songwriters in the studio. Some work closely as a partner with the artist on developing arrangements and coaching performances. Some prefer final authority on creative decisions. Think carefully about what kind of working relationship you want.

Finding a manager

Many performing songwriters eventually find it necessary to find a manager to help with developing their careers and finding gigs. Some things to keep in mind when looking:

1. Does the manager work with artists in my genre of music? A manager who typically works with punk rock bands may not have as many connections useful to an aspiring country singer-songwriter. A manager who mainly works with gospel artists might not know what to do with a hedonistic rock band.

2. How big is the manager's agency? If a manager is working with multiple acts, but has a small (or no) staff, you might not get the attention you want. Some of the listings have information in the heading about the agency's staff size.

3. Does the manager work with acts from my region? You can check the Geographic Index on page 351 to check for management agencies located near your area. Many of the listings also have information in their headings provided by the companies describing whether they work with regional acts only or artists from any region.

4. Does the manager work with name acts? A manager with famous clients could work wonders for your career. Or you could get lost in the shuffle. Use your best judgment when sizing up a potential manager and be clear with yourself about the kind of relationship you would like to have and the level of attention you want for your career.

5. If I'm a beginner, will the manager work with me? Look in the Openness to Submissions Index on page 346 to find companies open to beginners. Some may suggest extensive changes to your music or image. On the other hand, you may have a strong vision of what you want to do and need a manager who will work with you to achieve that vision instead of changing you around. Decide for yourself how much you are willing to compromise in good faith.

Remember that a relationship between you and a manager is a two-way street. You will have to earn each other's trust and be clear about your goals for mutual success.

Royalties

Where Does the Money Come From?

NON-PERFORMING SONGWRITERS

How do songwriters make money?

The quick answer is that songwriters make money through rights available to them through the copyright laws. For more details, keep reading and see the article "What About Copyright?" on page 28.

What specific rights make money for songwriters?

There are two primary ways songwriters earn money on their songs: Performance Royalties and Mechanical Royalties.

What is a performance royalty?

When you hear a song on the radio, on television, in the elevator, in a restaurant, etc. the songwriter receives royalties, called "Performance Royalties." Performing Rights Organizations (ASCAP, BMI and SESAC in the U.S.A.) collect payment from radio stations, television, etc. and distribute those payments to songwriters (see below).

What is a mechanical royalty?

When a record company puts a song onto a CD, cassette, etc. and distributes copies for sale, they owe a royalty payment to the songwriter for each copy they press of the album. It is called a "mechanical royalty" because of the mechanical process used to mass produce a copy of a CD, cassette or sheet music. The payment is small per song (see the "Royalty Provisions" subhead of the Basic Song Contract Pointers sidebar on page 34), but the earnings can add up and reach massive proportions for songs appearing on successful major label albums. ****Note: This royalty is totally different from the artist royalty on the retail price of the album.****

Who collects the money for performance and mechanical royalties?

Performing Rights Organizations collect performance royalties. There are three organizations that collect performance royalties: ASCAP, BMI and SESAC.

Music Publishing Royalties

These organizations arose many years ago when songwriters and music publishers gathered together to press for their rights and improve their ability to collect fees for the use of their songs. ASCAP, BMI and SESAC collect fees for the use of songs and then pass along the money to their member songwriters and music publishers.

Mechanical rights organizations collect mechanical royalties. There are three organizations that collect mechanical royalties: The Harry Fox Agency (HFA), The American Mechanical Rights Agency (AMRA) and The Songwriters Guild of America (SGA). These three organizations collect mechanical royalties from record companies of all sizes—major labels, mid-size and independents—and pass the royalties along to member music publishers and songwriters.

How do songwriters hook up with this system to earn royalties?

For **Performance Royalties**, individual songwriters **affiliate** with a Performing Rights Organization of their choice, and register their songs in the PRO database. Each PRO has a slightly different method of calculating payment, different ownership, and different membership structure, so choosing a PRO is an individual choice. Once a songwriter is affiliated and has registered their songs, the PROs then collect fees as described above and issue a check to the songwriter.

For **Mechanical Royalties**, three different things can happen:

1. The songwriter is signed to a publisher that is affiliated with The Harry Fox Agency. The Harry Fox Agency collects the mechanical royalties and passes them along to the publisher. The publisher then passes these along to the songwriter within 30 days. This case usually happens when a songwriter is signed to a major publisher and has a song on a major label album release.

2. The songwriter is not signed to a publisher and owns exclusive rights to his songs, and so works with AMRA or The Songwriters Guild of America, who cut a check directly to the songwriter instead of passing them to the publisher first.

3. They are signed to a publisher, but the songs are being released on albums by independent labels. In this case, the songwriter often works with AMRA since they have a focus on the independent music publishing market.

PERFORMING SONGWRITERS/ARTISTS

How do performing songwriters make money?

Performing songwriters and artists (if they write their own songs) make money just like non-performing songwriters, as described above, but they also make money through royalties made on the retail price of an album when it is sold online, in a store, etc.

What about all the stories of performing songwriters getting into bad deals?

The stories are generally true, but if they're smart, performing songwriters usually can hold on to the money they would be owed as songwriters (performing and mechanical royalties). But when it comes to retail sale royalties, all they will usually see is an "advance"—essentially a loan—which must then be paid off from record sales. You will not see a royalty check on retail sales until you're advance is paid off. If you are given a $600,000 advance, you will have to pay back the record company $600,000 out of your sales royalties before you see any more money.

Do performing songwriters and artists get to keep the advance?

Not really. If you have a manager who has gotten you a record deal, he will take his cut. You will probably be required in the contract to pay for the producer and studio time to make the album. Often the producer will take a percentage of subsequent royalties from album sales, which comes out of your pocket. Then there are also music video costs, promotion to radio stations, tour support, paying sidemen, etc. Just about anything you can think of is eventually paid for out of your advance or out of sales royalties. There are also deductions to royalties usually built in to record company contracts that make it harder to earn out an advance.

What should a performing songwriter wanting to sign with a major label do?

Their best option is to negotiate a fair contract, get as big of an advance as possible, and then manage that advance money the best they can. A good contract will keep the songwriting royalties described above completely separate from the flow of sales royalties, and will also cut down on the number of royalty deductions the record company builds into the contract. And because of the difficulty in earning out any size advance or auditing the record company, it makes sense to get as much cash up front as you can, then to manage that as best you can. You will need a good lawyer.

RECORD COMPANIES, PRODUCERS AND MANAGERS & BOOKING AGENTS
How do music publishers make money?

A publisher works as a songwriter's agent, looks for profitable commercial uses for the songs he represents, and then takes a percentage of the profits. This is typically 50% of all earning from a particular song—often referred to as the *publisher's share*. A successful publisher stays in contact with several A&R reps, finding out what upcoming projects are in need of new material, and whether any songs he represents will be appropriate.

How do record companies make money?

Record companies primarily make their money from profits made selling CDs, cassettes, DVDs, etc. Record companies keep most of the profit after subtracting manufacturing costs, royalties to recording artists, distribution fees and the costs of promoting songs to radio (which for major labels can reach up to $300,000 per song). Record companies also usually have music publishing divisions that make money performing all the functions of publishers.

How do record producers make money?

Producers mostly make their money by charging a flat fee up front to helm a recording project, by sharing in the royalties from album sales, or both. A small independent producer might charge $10,000 (or sometimes less) up front to produce a small indie band, while a "name" producer such as Bob Rock, who regularly works with major label bands, might charge $300,000. Either of these might also take a share in sales royalties, referred to as "points"—as in "percentage points." A producer might say, "I'll produce you for $10,000 and 2 points." If an artist is getting a 15% royalty on album sales, then two of those percentage points will go to the producer instead. Producers also make money by co-writing with the artists to get publishing royalties, or they may ask for part of the publishing from songs written by outside songwriters.

How do managers make money?

Most managers make money by taking a percentage commission of their clients' income, usually 10-25%. If a touring band finishes a show and makes a $2,000 profit, a manager on 15% commission would get $300. If an artist gets a $40,000 advance from a mid-size label, the manager would get $6,000. Whether an artist's songwriting income is included in the manager's commission comes down to negotiation. *The commission should give the manager incentive to make things happen for your career, so avoid paying flat fees up front.*

What About Copyright?

How am I protected by the copyright laws?

Copyright protection applies to your songs the instant you put them down in fixed form—a recording, sheet music, lead sheet, etc. This protection lasts for your lifetime plus 70 years (or the lifetime of the last surviving writer, if you co-wrote the song with somebody else). When you prepare demos, place notification of copyright on all copies of your song—the lyric sheets, lead sheets and labels for cassettes, CDs, etc. The notice is simply the word "copyright" or the symbol © followed by the year the song was created (or published) and your name: © 2005 by John Q. Songwriter.

What parts of a song are protected by copyright?

Traditionally, only the melody line and the lyrics are eligible for copyright. Period. Chords and rhythm are virtually never protected. An incredibly original arrangement can sometimes qualify. Sound recordings can also be copyrighted, but this applies strictly to the actual sounds on the recording, not the song itself (this copyright is usually owned by record companies).

What songs are not protected?

Song titles or mere ideas for music and lyrics cannot be copyrighted. Very old songs in the "public domain" are not protected. You could quote a melody from a Bach piece, but you could not then stop someone else from quoting the same melody in their song.

When would I lose or have to share the copyright?

If you *collaborate* with other writers, they are assumed to have equal interests unless you state some other arrangement, in writing. If you write under a *work-for-hire* arrangement, the company or person who hired you to write the song then owns the copyright. Sometimes your spouse may automatically be granted an interest in your copyright as part of their *spousal rights*, which might then become important if you got divorced.

Should I register my copyright?

Registering your copyright with the Library of Congress gives the best possible protection. Registration establishes a public record of your copyright—even though a song is legally protected whether or not it is registered—and could prove useful in any future court cases involving the song. Registration also entitles you to a potentially greater settlement in a copyright infringement lawsuit.

How do I register my song?

To register your song, request government form PA from the Copyright Office. Call the 24-hour hotline at (202)707-9100 and leave your name and address on the messaging system. Once you receive the PA form, you must return it, along with a registration fee and a CD (or tape) and lead sheet of your song. Send these to the Register of Copyrights, Copyright Office, Library of Congress, Washington DC 20559. It may take several months to receive your certificate of registration from the Copyright Office, but your songs are protected from the date of creation (the date of registration will reflect the date you applied). For more information, call the Copyright Office's Public Information Office at (202)707-3000 or visit their website at www.copyright.gov.

How likely is it that someone will try to steal my song?

Copyright infringement is very rare. But, if you ever feel that one of your songs has been stolen—that someone has unlawfully infringed on your copyright—you must prove that you created the work and that the person you are suing had access to your song. Copyright registration is the best proof of a date of creation. You *must* have your copyright registered in order to file a lawsuit. Also, it's helpful if you keep your rough drafts and revisions of songs, either on paper or on tape.

Government Resources

For More Info

The Library of Congress's copyright website is your best source for current, complete information on the subject of copyright. Not only can you learn all you could possibly wish to know about intellectual property rights and U.S. copyright law (the section of the U.S. Code dealing with copyright is reprinted there in its entirety), but you can also download copyright forms directly from the site. The site also includes links to other copyright-related web pages, many of which will be of interest to songwriters, including ASCAP, BMI, SESAC, and the Harry Fox Agency. Check it out at www.copyright.gov.

Music Biz Basics

Why did song sharks begin soliciting me after I registered my song?

This is one potential, unintended consequence of registering your song with the Library of Congress. The copyright indexes are a public record of your songwriting, and song sharks often search the copyright indexes and mail solicitations to songwriters who live out away from major music centers such as Nashville. They figure these songwriters don't know any better and are easy prey. *Do not allow this possibility to stop you from registering your songs!* Just be aware, educate yourself, and then throw the song sharks' mailings in the trash.

What if I mail a tape to myself to get a postmark date on a sealed envelope?

The "poor man's copyright" has not stood up in court, and is not an acceptable substitute for registering your song. If you feel it's important to shore up your copyright, register it with the Library of Congress.

Career Songwriting

What Should I Know?

What career options are open to songwriters who do not perform?

The possibilities range from a beginning songwriter living away from a music center like Nashville who lands an occasional single-song publishing deal, to a staff songwriter signed to a major publishing company. And then there are songwriters like Desmond Child who operate independently, have developed a lot of connections, work with numerous artists, and have set up their own independent publishing operations.

What is "single-song" songwriting about?

In this case, a songwriter submits songs to many different companies. One or two songs gain interest from different publishers, and the songwriter signs separate contracts for each song with each publisher. The songwriter can then pitch other songs to other publishers. In Nashville, for instance, a single-song contract is usually the first taste of success for an aspiring songwriter on his way up the ladder. Success of this sort can induce a songwriter to move to a music center like Nashville (if they haven't already), and is a big boost for a struggling songwriter already living there. A series of single-song contracts often signals a songwriter's maturing skill and marketability.

What is a "staff songwriter"?

A staff songwriter usually works for a major publisher and receives a monthly stipend as an advance against the royalties he is likely to earn for the publisher. The music publisher has exclusive rights to everything the songwriter writes while signed to the company. The publisher also works actively on the writer's behalf to hook him or her up with co-writers and other opportunities. A staff songwriting position is highly treasured by many because it offers a steady income, and in Nashville is a sign the songwriter has "arrived."

What comes after the staff songwriting position?

Songwriters who go to the next level have a significant reputation for their ability to write hit songs. Famous artists seek them out, and they often write actively in several markets at once. They often write on assignment for film and television, and commonly keep their own publishing companies to maximize their income.

As my career grows what should I do about keeping track of expenses, etc.?

You should keep a ledger or notebook with records on all financial transactions related to your songwriting—royalty checks, demo costs, office supplies, postage, travel expenses, dues to organizations, class and workshop fees, plus any publications you purchase pertaining to songwriting. You may also want a separate checking account devoted to your songwriting activities. This will make record keeping easier and help to establish your identity as a business for tax purposes.

What should I know about taxes related to songwriting income?

Any royalties you receive will not reflect taxes or any other mandatory deductions. It is your responsibility to keep track of income and file the correct tax forms. For specific information, contact the IRS or talk to an accountant who serves music industry clients.

What About Contracts?

CO-WRITING

What kind of agreements do I need with co-writers?

You may need to sign a legal agreement between you and a co-writer to establish percentages you will each receive of the writer's royalties. You will also have to iron out what you will do if another person, such as an artist, wants to change your song and receive credit as a cowriter. For example, in the event a major artist wants to cut your song for her album—but also wants to rewrite some lyrics and take a share of the publishing—you and your co-writer need to agree whether it is better to get a song on an album that might sell millions (and make a lot of money) or pass on it because you don't want to give up credit. The situation could be uncomfortable if you are not in sync on the issue.

When do I need a lawyer to look over agreements?

When it comes to doing business with a publisher, producer, or record company, you should always have the contract reviewed by a knowledgeable entertainment attorney. As long as the issues at stake are simple, the co-writers respect each other, and they discuss their business philosophies before writing a song together, they can probably write up an agreement without the aid of a lawyer.

SINGLE-SONG CONTRACTS

What is a single-song contract?

A music publisher offers a single-song contract when he wants to sign one or more of your songs, but doesn't want to hire you as a staff songwriter. You assign your rights to a particular song to the publisher for an agreed-upon number of years, so that he may represent the song and find uses profitable for both of you. This is a common contract and will probably be the first you encounter in your songwriting career.

What basic elements should every single-song contract contain?

Every contract should have the publisher's name, the writer's name, the song's title, the date, and the purpose of the agreement. The songwriter also declares the

Basic Song Contract Pointers

Tip

The following list, taken from a Songwriters Guild of America publication, enumerates the basic features of an acceptable songwriting contract:

1 **Work for Hire.** When you receive a contract covering just one composition, you should make sure the phrases "employment for hire" and "exclusive writer agreement" are *not* included. Also, there should be no options for future songs.

2 **Performing Rights Affiliation.** If you previously signed publishing contracts, you should be affiliated with either ASCAP, BMI, or SESAC. All performance royalties must be received directly by you from your performing rights organization and this should be written into your contract.

3 **Reversion Clause.** The contract should include a provision that if the publisher does not secure a release of a commercial sound recording within a specified time (one year, two years, etc.), the contract can be terminated by you.

4 **Changes in the Composition.** If the contract includes a provision that the publisher can change the title, lyrics or music, this should be amended so that only with your consent can such changes be made.

5 **Royalty Provisions.** You should receive fifty percent (50%) of all publisher's income on all licenses issued. If the publisher prints and sells his own sheet music, your royalty should be ten percent (10%) of the wholesale selling price. The royalty should not be stated in the contract as a flat rate ($.05, $.07, etc.).

6 **Negotiable Deductions.** Ideally, demos and all other expenses of publication should be paid 100% by the publisher. The only allowable fee is for the Harry Fox Agency collection fee, whereby the writer pays one half of the amount charged to the publisher for mechanical rights. The current mechanical royalty collected by the Harry Fox Agency is 9.1 cents per cut for songs under 5 minutes; and 1.75 cents per minute for songs over 5 minutes.

7 **Royalty Statements and Audit Provision.** Once the song is recorded, you are entitled to receive royalty statements at least once every six months. In addition, an audit provision with no time restriction should be included in every contract.

8 **Writer's Credit.** The publisher should make sure that you receive proper credit on all uses of the composition.

9 **Arbitration.** In order to avoid large legal fees in case of a dispute with your publisher, the contract should include an arbitration clause.

10 **Future Uses.** Any use not specifically covered by the contract should be retained by the writer to be negotiated as it comes up.

Music Biz Basics

song is an original work and he is creator of the work. The contract *must* specify the royalties the songwriter will earn from various uses of the song, including performance, mechanical, print and synchronization royalties.

How should the royalties usually be divided in the contract?

The songwriter should receive no less than 50% of the income his song generates. That means the songwriter and publisher split the total royalties 50/50. The songwriter's half is called the "writer's share" and the publisher's half is called the "publisher's share." If there is more than one songwriter, the songwriters split the writer's share. Sometimes, successful songwriters will bargain for a percentage of the publisher's share, negotiating what is basically a co-publishing agreement. For a visual explanation of how royalties are collected and flow to the songwriter, see the chart called Music Publishing Royalties on page 23.

What should the contract say about a "reversion clause"?

Songwriters should always negotiate for a "reversion clause," which returns all rights back to the songwriter if some provision of the contract is not met. Most reversion clauses give a publisher a set amount of time (usually one or two years) to work the song and make money with it. If the publisher can't get the song recorded and released during the agreed-upon time period, the songwriter can then take his song to another publisher. The danger of *not* getting some sort of reversion clause is that you could wind up with a publisher sitting on your song for the entire life-plus-70-years term of the copyright—which may as well be forever.

Is a reversion clause difficult to get?

Some publishers agree to it, and figure if they can't get any action with the song in the first year or two, they're not likely to ever have much luck with it. Other publishers may be reluctant to agree to a reversion clause. They may invest a lot of time and money in demoing and pitching a song to artists and want to keep working at it for a longer period of time. Or, for example, a producer might put a song on hold for a while and then go into a lengthy recording project. A year can easily go by before the artist or producer decides which songs to release as singles. This means you may have to agree to a longer time period, be flexible and trust the publisher has your best mutual interests in mind. Use your best judgment.

What other basic issues should be covered by a single-song contract?

The contract should also address these issues:
- will an advance be paid, and if so, how much will the advance be?
- when will royalties be paid (annually or semiannually)?
- who will pay for demos—the publisher, songwriter or both?
- how will lawsuits against copyright infringement be handled, including the cost of lawsuits?

- will the publisher have the right to sell its interest in the song to another publisher without the songwriter's consent?
- does the publisher have the right to make changes in a song, or approve changes by someone else, without the songwriter's consent?
- the songwriter should have the right to audit the publisher's books if he feels it is necessary and gives the publisher reasonable notice.

Where else can I go for advice on contracts?

The Songwriters Guild of America has drawn up a Popular Songwriter's Contract which it believes to be the best minimum songwriter contract available (see the Basic Song Contract Pointers sidebar above). The Guild will send a copy of the contract at no charge to any interested songwriter upon request (see the Songwriters Guild of America listing in the Organizations section on page 267). SGA will also review—free of charge—any contract offered to its members, and will check it for fairness and completeness. Also see these two books published by Writer's Digest Books: *The Craft and Business of Songwriting, 3rd Edition*, by John Braheny and *The New Songwriter's Guide to Music Publishing, 3rd Edition*, by Randy Poe.

When Does 50% Equal 100%?

NOTE: the publisher's and songwriter's share of the income are sometimes referred to as each being 100%—for 200% total! You might hear someone say, "I'll take 100% of the publisher's share." **Do not be needlessly confused!** If the numbers confuse you, ask for the terms to be clarified.

No Rules

Crafting Opportunities as a Songwriter

by Lauren Jonik

One of the most challenging and potentially rewarding opportunities any songwriter will encounter is how to unite one's creative craft with the art of commerce. This is especially true for artists who are performers as well and who endeavor to make both a living and a life from their work. While many elements working in concert with each other form a career, there are two in any songwriter's life that are key: writing quality songs and ensuring that they are heard. The beauty and the burden is that there are no rules, no guarantees that lead to success, but by observing and learning from what others have done and listening to the ever-present inner guidance, it is possible to find one's unique path to not only bring forth songs into the world, but to create a life that feels authentic.

Pursue the crazy road

Most artists find it easy to sit in one room alone and create, to revel in the process and the journey of blending music and lyrics together into a song. But, there are distinct rewards that only come when one pushes to emerge outside of the cocoon of creation and to allow the fruits of what is often solitary labor to be heard.

As New York City-based singer/songwriter Hugh Colocott explains, "You could be the best unknown writer, the best unknown songwriter in the world, but it is much more satisfying if people can hear your work." Colocott, whose career in music has spanned over 20 years and whose songs have been featured in numerous television shows and movies, embraces a strong work ethic and finds both joy and solace in being dedicated and focused.

It is an approach echoed by Modern Vintage recording artist Misty Boyce. "I can't lie, pursuing music is hard. But I would say that the most beneficial thing is that this path makes me face myself every day. Whatever else I chose to do in my life, I'll come to it with an assurance and awareness that I've developed by first pursuing this crazy road."

LAUREN JONIK is a freelance music journalist and photographer with more than 10 years experience.

Photo credit: Deborah Lopez.

Hugh Colocott says, "Collaborating is the greatest thing in the world. It brings out the best in you."

Indeed, creating a solid body of work and being willing to devote time, energy and effort to a career in songwriting is only part of the equation. It becomes imperative that the songs are heard, but there are many different avenues that can lead to how that happens, including performing locally, touring regionally, nationally or internationally at music venues, playing at house concerts, utilizing the internet and collaborating with other musicians. Though it may not always appear to be so, the business of being a songwriter offers as wide a spectrum of ways to be creative as the act of songwriting itself—and can be equally as important.

Singer/songwriter Amber Rubarth explains that for independent artists being open to navigating one's own journey is crucial. "So many things in music are changing; I don't think anyone knows what the 'path' is. The business exists just in order to get your songs across. The ultimate result is that you want to be writing more or you want to be creating more and you want people to hear it. I don't usually find too much trouble in enjoying the business part of things, especially as an independent musician in this time period. There are so many creative things you can do." Rubarth, who tours regularly throughout the United States and Europe, has released several albums including her latest, Good Mystery, and makes her living full-time as a musician.

Photo credit: Shawn Boyle.

Danielle Gasparro believes that songwriters who honestly promote themselves will find success.

Create and be heard

In a business that is continuing to evolve at a rapid pace, the bottom line for a performing songwriter remains the same: create and be heard. As a long-time New York City resident, singer/songwriter Danielle Gasparro found herself at a crossroads at the start of the recession. No longer employed by the day job she had held while continuing to perform throughout the city, Gasparro made an active choice to leave New York in order to reduce expenses and pursue what she most wanted. "Making the conscious decision to follow my bliss has changed my life in that I have a very profound daily sense that if you do your best and don't resist what life is handing you, then things will align for you at a more rapid pace and will provide you with the people, places and things that are going to take you to the next level of opportunity, awareness, intellect and creativity."

Gasparro soon embarked on her first house concert tour, an emerging niche, which allows for just that—concerts in people's homes. Typically, a host will provide the space such as a living room or backyard and invite guests to an evening of live music. By charging a small fee of each guest, the host is able to pay the performer a pre-arranged, guaranteed amount. House concerts can enhance the connection between audience and performer by the sheer intimacy of the setting and as Gasparro explains, "There are an unlimited number of venues in a way.

Julia Brown advises songwriters to take their "deepest wishes and dreams seriously and act on them however you can."

Photo credit: Michael Benabib.

When you do house concerts, you are taking away all of the hype that surrounds a venue owner. The bottom line at a club is how many drinks can you sell, whereas at a house concert, it's how many drinks can we share under the starry night sky."

Brooklyn, NY singer/songwriter Julia Brown also offers this advice when planning house concerts, "Find friends who know the target areas well, or who know people in the area. Don't be afraid to set rules for the concerts, like the minimum number of people or the minimum donation." While booking house concerts requires effort, Gasparro suggests first starting in your local area before expanding into doing a full house concert tour. "If someone is an artist that already has established an audience, they just have to get the information to the people and make it easy for them to sign on. That takes a little savvy as you don't want to bombard people. But, the truth is the house concerts speak for themselves, so it's just coming up in your own language and voice about how to pitch to people."

And, when taking the next step and booking and playing in unfamiliar areas, both Gasparro and Brown suggest using the internet to make needed connections. But, as Brown who released her second album Strange Scars in Summer 2008 notes, promotion of house concerts is primarily the responsibility of the host. "The hosts of the shows spread the word about the concerts, mostly. I did put out the word via normal gig promotion channels like social networking sites to draw in other people to the shows."

Used with permission.

The Dig's lead singer Emile Mosseri believes much of their success comes from working hard at songwriting and promotion.

Build lasting relationships

The power of the internet as a tool for songwriters to find opportunities and to cultivate a fanbase can not be underestimated, but it is vital to nurture those connections mindfully. Boyce explains, "I've had to learn to write really good e-mails to sell myself. I try to play places where I know a guy who knows a guy who's played such-and-such venue, that way I can name-drop and have an 'in.'" Gasparro concurs, "If how you promote yourself is an honest reflection of who you are, you'll find opportunity."

Whether it is on a national level and through e-mail or promoting a local gig at a small venue by handing out flyers in person, it is key to offer something memorable that is associated with your music. Emile Mosseri, lead singer of the New York City-based rock band The Dig, remembers the beginning days of spreading the word. "The hands-on approach to promoting your band is very limited in what you can do, but it is important to do it especially in the early stages. For every single show we played, we got a thousand flyers printed up and hundreds of posters. We got out there in the street and put in the face time with people and tried to build up a following that way." And, in order to make their flyers stand out, The Dig used the artwork of artist Allessandra Greco. "She was really helpful. It was always a good talking point to hand someone a piece of art and not just hand them a flyer."

The promotional efforts of The Dig have been successful and they now have graduated to playing some of New York City's medium to higher level venues, as well as touring nationally as a supporting act. Their determination captured the attention not only of future fans, but of people in the industry. "We were able to work our way up to getting booked at Mercury Lounge and Bowery Ballroom and I feel like a lot of people respected our work ethic," says Mosseri about two of the city's well-known rock venues. "The promoters and people who worked for Bowery Presents were very helpful and good to us and they knew that if they booked us, we would bust our ass to get people to the show."

Photo credit: Deborah Lopez.

Amber Rubarth follows her passion and advises others to do the same.

Every step forward builds on itself. Mosseri continues, "Now, we're going all over the country and we're selling ourselves to different audiences every night."

Collaborate to find success

Whether it is about promotion or finding unique opportunities for touring and performing, the benefits of hard work are compounded by joining forces to varying degrees and in different ways with others who are on a similar path. Of songwriting itself, Colocott enthuses, "Collaborating is the greatest thing in the world. It brings out the best in you."

He continues, "Not to mention, on a business level it helps too. If two people are shopping a song, it's much better than one person shopping the song because they've got their sources and the things they've done with their career. They can bring to the table what they've got, which is one thing to be aware of when you co-write with people."

Though some people are at their best when writing alone, for others finding a compatible songwriting partner is worth its weight in gold. Colocott, who most frequently co-writes with pop/country singer/songwriter Amber Rhodes and with songwriter Jimmy Santis, with whom he has begun Vortex Music, a writing and production company, most recently has placed songs in "All My Children," and in an animated Disney movie.

Similarly, Rubarth has discovered the good that can come with collaboration. In addition to having written with well-established artists like Adam Levy, Rubarth is part of the duo The Paper Raincoat with Alex Wong and she recently joined forces with composer Paul Brill for the documentary Joan Rivers: A Piece of Work, which received acclaim at the Sundance and Tribeca Film Festivals.

Make your passion the path

Rubarth has witnessed the steady evolution of her career after adhering to a piece of advice she received several years ago while working as a wood sculptor right

Misty Boyce has had to learn the art of e-mail communication to find success.

Photo credit: Ruth Du.

out of high school. "The most important thing that I've learned in my entire life is that you have to follow your number one passion—you're only going to be great if you do that. And, if you're not truly great, you're not serving your purpose in the world. To go above and beyond, you have to be passionate about something and fully dedicate yourself to it," she emphasizes.

However the path beckons, Boyce reminds, "The only way to survive and thrive in anything, but especially as an artist, which will try you like nothing else, is to love it so much that you wouldn't be half as happy doing something else. And then, try to live inside every minute of it. Don't look back. Don't look forward. Don't do it for fame. Don't do it for money. Do it because you have to. You need to."

As much as one creates a song, it is embracing one's own artistry and moving forward with it that shapes a life—yours and others. Perhaps, Julia Brown summarizes it best, "No matter where you are in life, no matter what's going on, take your deepest wishes and dreams seriously and act on them however you can—they are not going to go away."

Alternative Outlets

Writing Songs in a Digital World

by Anders Bylund

Songwriters today have more options available than ever before. Gone are the days when you absolutely had to live and work in a music Mecca like Nashville, Los Angeles or New York in order to launch a career; the relentless March of Progress has opened a plethora of brand-new avenues for the aspiring lyricist, melody maker, and singer/songwriter.

It's a small world

Once upon a time, songwriters absolutely had to live close to the action. You were nobody without lunch dates with record producers, and the shortest route to independent success was to take a nine-to-five-ish staff writer job with a record label, writing music on a "work for hire" basis. That's still a valid career path, but hardly the only one anymore. Welcome to the digital era.

Yes, it's the Internet that's changing yet another time-tested business model. The Web is studded with valuable resources for the aspiring songwriter and absolutely packed with the information you need in order to get the job done. Put it all together, and you can get a real career going without so much as visiting Nashville.

Information everywhere

You can start by using the Internet as an information resource. The book in your hands right now is a great place to start: most of the record companies, producers, and agents you'll find here will have a website with tons of information specific to that company or music professional.

This is where you get to know what they stand for and what they're looking for right now. Look over their artist rosters to find a good fit for your material, and then find quick and easy ways to make first contact. E-mail has become an accepted way of doing business. Many companies even accept digital sound files in lieu of mailed CDs, text files instead of neatly typed lyric sheets. Going the all-electronic route can

ANDERS BYLUND is a freelance journalist and skilled poet. He can be followed on Twitter @TMFZahrim (http://twitter.com/tmfzahrim).

shorten response times and start long-distance conversations at whatever pace is comfortable for the professionals you're dealing with.

Getting your feet wet

Dip your toe in the musical waters by entering songwriting contests. If you believe in your songs, this is a great way to stand out in a crowd—and it never hurts to have a few awards to parade in your cover letters. For example, the *American Songwriter* magazine runs a monthly lyric contest with generous prizes and a high-profile publishing venue for the winners. And the best way to enter is online, through the americansongspace.com site.

While you're there, take a look around. You can post songs here without entering any contests, forming a searchable database for publishers and acts in search of new material. American Songspace also lets artists and producers issue calls for submissions from independent songwriters. The service has a track record of placing independent music with big-name artists like Keith Urban, Tim McGraw, and Darius Rucker, and it's all thanks to a free-flowing two-way exchange of ideas and opportunities across the Internet.

Independent A&R company TAXI does the same thing on a larger scale, minus the songwriting contests. A quick online search for something like "songwriter artist connect" will unearth a veritable goldmine of opportunities for the enterprising writer.

Sing it!

So far, we have been looking at digital opportunities for pure writers. If you have your own band or fall in the singer/songwriter tradition, whole new online vistas open up.

YouTube is becoming the new Star Search. Post an amazing video there and watch the fan base building. Justin Beiber wouldn't have a record deal without the online video service. Clips by 12-year-old Greyson Chance wowed Ellen DeGeneres into starting a record label. YouTube now commands over 2 billion video views every day and music videos are a very large part of that traffic.

Starting a YouTube account in a vacuum won't do you much good, because nobody would know how to find you in those deep, dark waters. Both Chance and Beiber became viral sensations by covering well-known songs from artists like Lady Gaga and Usher, showing the power of mixing in something familiar with your own material. Once the masses know your name in passing, the original clips in your YouTube channel will benefit from the increased attention.

Anything you can do to funnel traffic to your videos—originals and covers alike—will help. You'll need a Facebook page and a Twitter account, and don't be shy about updating both of them early and often. Got a new tune on the 'Tube? Let the world know right away. MySpace was once the preferred medium for this type of viral marketing, and is still worth a look. Commission a starving hacker to create a you-themed iPhone/iPad application featuring your music and ways to buy more of it. Don't forget the up-and-coming Android mobile media market, either. Start a blog to connect with your fans on a more personal level. Eventually, one of those fans, iPhone app customers, or Twitter contacts will be a record producer, an A&R rep, or an artist looking for some fresh tunes.

Or you can go indie, like Radiohead and Nine Inch Nails did in 2007. Not everyone can sell truckloads of CD boxes and digital downloads to fans who could simply grab the music files and walk away for free, as Radiohead did with "In Rainbows," but distribution services like CD Baby, TuneCore, and Apple iTunes now make it possible to make a living from recorded music sales without having a record label taking a cut of the revenue. Studies have shown that it takes as many as 25 retail sales through a low-end record label royalty deal to return as much money to the artist and songwriter as a label-free CD Baby release. You're on your own with marketing, but the volume you need in order to make a living is much smaller.

Playing games with your art

Why constrain yourself to direct music markets? The grass may actually be greener elsewhere.

Worldwide recorded music sales added up to $17 billion in 2009, according to industry group IFPI. That's a large market, but it pales next to the $30 billion in global box office receipts reported by the MPAA. Film music is another valid career option for the aspiring musician, whether you're looking to land a song on the soundtrack of a blockbuster hit or scoring an entire film. (Mark Mothersbaugh dives deeper into these waters on page 54). But even Hollywood isn't the biggest entertainment market today.

That distinction belongs to video games. Market research firm DFC Intelligence reports that global sales of computer games and video games racked up an astonishing $60 billion in 2009, and the market is expected to grow to $70 billion by 2015.

Like Hollywood, the gaming industry needs music that fits the product. Games range from big-budget blockbusters like "Grand Theft Auto IV" and "Red Dead Redemption" to small-time titles such as "Portal" or the three-person project "World of Goo." You have spaghetti westerns and science fiction adventures, drama and romance, tie-ins to movie titles and TV shows, and everything in between. Whatever style of music you work in, someone is working on a video game somewhere that could use it.

Video game music is a beast all its own, as any sector veteran will tell you. James Hannigan, who has scored such hits as the "Command and Conquer" series from Electronic Arts, explains:

"There are stark differences between the various mediums in terms of the approach taken to composition. Not only in terms of how music is organized and prepared for use in games (e.g. getting music to loop, layer up or comply with some sort of interactive music system) but in terms of its function. Music for film and television exists for a passive audience and mostly supports an existing narrative, often synched to picture. The game player is both 'audience to' and 'participant in' the events of the game—existing in a sort of filmic reality rather than a cold, sterile 3D virtual reality. So you don't want your music to push them out of the immersing virtual reality experience by treating them as just an audience looking on, but you also want to manipulate their emotions and entertain them, put their actions into some kind of emotional context. Apart from in scripted sequences or 'cut scenes' you don't always know exactly when certain events will take place in a game or how long players will spend in a given area, and that has a knock on effect for music as you don't want it to sound disconnected or detached from the game. Very often, music seems to set out to create a specific emotional state going with an activity."

OK, I'm in. What's next?

If that sounds exciting to you, you'll be heartened to know that there are many ways into this blistering opportunity. While big studios like EA and Activision-Blizzard tend to keep a stable of star composers on hand, a plethora of smaller game development houses have lower barriers to entry. A track record in the music industry certainly helps, but "that doesn't mean someone couldn't become the composer on a game for another, perhaps smaller, studio that then gets taken up by a big publisher," notes Mr. Hannigan. "It's worth remembering that companies like EA, Ubisoft, Activision and so on are also publishers."

One way in is to have fans in the game studio. After playing a gig in Seattle, Jonathan Coulton met with people from the Valve studio and agreed to write a song for one of their upcoming games. Still Alive, which plays during the end credits to Valve's "Portal," is now arguably Coulton's biggest claim to fame as well as a selling point for the game itself.

Or, you can work your way into the market. Before scoring and performing in hits like "Dragon Age: Origins," award-winning game music virtuoso Aubrey Ashburn was representing other composers as an agent for the Soundelux Design Music Group. Then she fell in love with what her clients were doing. She was "pleasantly surprised to find that music for games is up to film quality in all aspects. Of course I jumped in there where I could and got my first opportunity with EA's 'Lord of the Rings: Battle For Middle Earth II,' and it's been an evolving path ever since."

Ms. Ashburn's advice to aspiring video game composers is to "read up on the industry, even the stuff that seems boring or irrelevant. Learn the language and the key players and of course listen to soundtracks and see if you think your stuff would fit. Go in educated and familiar with the types of games you want to do and be brave, send in your material to anyone with the title Audio Director."

Video games aren't all wine and roses, though. "The bad news about games is, you usually don't get residuals," says Devo's Mark Mothersbaugh, who has scored a dozen video games. "They usually don't honor royalties of any kind, including things like ASCAP, BMI, SESAC—they don't let you collect with their success, you know? They just pay you a fee up front and then they own your music."

Even so, it's an exciting market, abounding with opportunity. "If you're a songwriter and you're excited about writing music, either songs or score, I'd go there, just check it out," Mothersbaugh continues. "That's the most growing area and you know, everybody's exploitable, so you might as well find out what it's all about."

Onward and upward!

The digital age has opened new doors to musicians of all stripes. Don't be afraid to poke your head into cyberspace and look around. From video games to self-publishing resources to a cornucopia of information and contact methods, computers are rewiring the inner workings of the music industry machine. You need to take advantage of the digital revolution.

Scoring Songs for TV, Film & Commercials

by David McPherson

Friday night. You are slumped back on the couch watching your favorite sitcom; the end credits roll, and there's one of your songs. Every songwriter's dream right? The thinking among musicians used to be you were "selling out" if one of your songs was used to sell product in a commercial on TV. Who can forget Neil Young's cheeky song and video, "This Notes for You."

Today, though, the music business is tougher than ever for artists to crack and get their songs heard by the masses, so looking for alternative avenues to find new audiences such as TV, film and commercials is totally acceptable. So, how does one land songs in these media markets? Ask a bunch of seasoned songwriters and the advice is endless. Here follows tips from a handful of musicians who have had luck placing their songs in TV and films.

Royal Wood

Royal Wood is a Toronto-based songwriter. According to the bio on his website: "His approach to writing harkens back to traditions of song crafting that go straight to the heart of the relationship an artist creates with an audience. As great songwriting defies the whimsies of a trend, Royal's classic songs explore the architecture of emotions upon which our most cherished relationships are built. Named an iTunes Songwriter of the Year in 2008, Royal's music shares an emotional immediacy with the listener that creates a lingering feeling of intimacy with his recordings and live performances."

In 2008, Wood had his song "A Mirror Without" from his disc *A Good Enough Day*, air on the smash TV show *Grey's Anatomy*. His songs have also been featured on HBO programs and on CBC Television in Canada.

DAVID MCPHERSON *is a Toronto-based freelance writer with more than 17 years experience writing about music. A graduate of the University of Western Ontario, with a Masters in Journalism, David has published thousands of articles in daily newspapers, consumer magazines, and websites across North America, including Bluegrass Unlimited, Paste, American Songwriter, Performing Songwriter to name a few. His website is: www.davidmcpherson.ca.*

The songsmith says he's never actively tried to pitch his songs. He advises to start by making contact with a licenser and approach them about trying to represent you for one record. Also, as an indie artist, a lot of indie films will contact you.

"It then goes from there," Wood says. "The more music you are making the more options people have to choose one of your songs. If you try to randomly pitch your songs to ABC television, for example, you are never going to get the right person. I have been at radio interviews or at some record label's office and I see these massive boxes in the corner filled with yellow, unopened manila envelopes.

"People are constantly taking that shot hoping someone is going to open up their package, but the sad reality is that there is so much music out there and so many people out there trying to make a living at it, that they need these filters to direct things to them...you are in a sea of artists/would be artists, to find a place to take a deep breath takes a long time." Once you get one song in though, Wood says it often snowballs from there.

"The more records I put out the more songs I had to pass around. Eventually I got a licenser who worked solely for me trying to place songs. He pitches songs, travelling back and forth to LA...that's his job. He gets tips of what types of songs producers are looking for and he pitches things to the director and producer that he thinks would fit."

Troy Campbell

"Take the words out," advises the Austin-based musician.

Campbell, originally from Ohio, was a past member of bands The Highwaymen and Loose Diamonds. Today, between performing solo and writing songs, he works as a music supervisor; he offers songwriters advice garnered from both sides of the table.

"I make a terrible supervisor because when a director says 'I would really like to use this song,' since I know what it costs, I immediately say 'You can't afford it.' and they get really broken hearted," he says.

Joking aside, Campbell's best advice to songwriters looking to land their creations in TV, film and commercials, is to strip out the vocals.

"I tell friends who are songwriters such as Gurf Morlix and Ray Wylie Hubbard, when making your records, make instrumental versions too since it increases your odds by 50 percent," Campbell says. "I would venture even more than 50 percent sometimes based on what I've seen and the way I've been able to pick something for somebody. Give me copies without the vocals. A lot of the songwriters, especially singer-songwriters, have distinct voices. During the course of a movie, or on the end credits of *Grey's Anatomy*, that's beneficial because it's impactful. But if you are in the middle of the show, your voice is going to jar against the dialogue, so you have a lesser chance of getting your song in.

"My theory is your music is great, emotional and cool and they like you, but your voice is more of a distraction," he says. "So give me an instrumental version...just pull the vocals out when making your record."

Campbell says another option is to do what Gurf Morlix did for a recent movie project.

"He just put in other things and made a whole new record," he explains. "His song, which I co-wrote with him, 'Killing Time in Texas,' we recently put an instrumental version in a documentary called *Happiness Is*—a documentary about the pursuit of happiness in America...whatever that means. We put four tracks of Gurf's in the film because it just worked. It opens him up to a bigger audience."

Another piece of advice Campbell offers is to put yourself in the music supervisor's shoes.

"As an independent, you are going to get my attention if you consider what I have to do," he explains. "A lot of times, I'm just under stress to come up with options and I really want to use my favorite people and independents, but a lot of time it's a hassle to get them to send me things."

Josh Finlayson

Co-founder, guitarist, and one of the chief songwriters for Canadian roots band The SkyDiggers, says, in a lot of cases, getting your songs on TV and film are the only ways you get exposure for your music today because commercial radio has become so limited in what they play. He also says landing songs in TV and films involves a bit of luck.

"Typically, the way this stuff happens is that there is someone—a director or a producer—someone who works in that arena, who discovers a CD or a song from a band and wants to use it in a movie or a TV show," he explains. "Early on for us, and it continues for our band, there are certain songs people have in their mind for certain scenes."

Finlayson says while there are avenues you can go and "flog your wares," it seems today, TV, film and commercials while once frowned upon, are now seen as a way to get your music out there.

An obvious example is Canadian artist Feist, whose song "1,2,3,4" promoted the launch of Apple's iPod Nano.

"Ten to fifteen years ago, the perception was seen as selling out a bit, but the reality now is although it is very easy to get your music out to the world through the Internet, how do you really make people conscious of it," says Finlayson. "I don't know what role that song played in helping Feist's career, but have to think it was significant."

Findlayson says the other side of the equation is traditionally music publishers played a big role in getting your music into films and onto TV shows, but today they are competing more and more with all kinds of independent people...boutique shops doing the same thing who have built up relationships with production companies and films.

Articles & Interviews

More Tips from Tamara Miller

Songwriter Tamara Miller offers two more tips to help you get your songs placed in TV and movies:

1) Be sure you have an amazing finished product and aside from the actual recording, be sure to conduct as much research as you can about your genre of music and what shows/films are seeking your type of music. There are so many independent film makers out there who are looking for great music. Try the university and college campuses; you never know where that independent film maker will end up. The director might ask you to compose a piece for free, but think about all of the exposure you will receive and what other projects that will lead to...this is key. You also need to find the music supervisors who are responsible for finding that perfect song for film and television. Google is a wonderful thing. Research, research, research. Don't wait until your CD is complete, research ahead of time and work that into your plan.

2) Know your rights. You can make a great living from writing music for a film or television series. If your music gets picked up by the music supervisor based on your own self-promotion, you can obtain both the songwriter's half, referred to as the "writers share" and the publisher's half, referred to as the "publishers share." If your song is selected, you will most likely receive compensation from the company using your music. This is referred to as the license fee or fee for "renting your music" for their show. At least with a song placement in a television agreement, you should be paid both a license fee for your Master and a Synchronization fee (permission for the company to synch your music with picture); this depends on how your song will be used. Before any of this happens, you will most likely encounter a legal agreement/contract between the company and yourself; be sure to have this document reviewed by an entertainment lawyer. It will cost you, but it's worth every penny. The last thing you need to is to have to pay thousands of dollars in court trying to get out of the agreement. Research the company and make sure they are legit. Make sure you are a member of a performing rights organization.

Astrid Young

Astrid Young, Neil Young's half-sister, and a seasoned songwriter, is blunter in her advice, but it rings true; she says the best thing you can do is to "find out who all the music editors are and kiss their asses up and down."

"They're the ones who really call the shots, not the music supervisors or the execs," she says. "If they (the editors) slug something into an edit, it's likely to get in the film—that's the bottom line." Young also advises to get your music into music libraries.

"There is a whole world out there doing music for trailers and other commercials and it pays not bad," she says.

Like Campbell, she also believes cutting a second version of your song, minus the words, is good advice. "Make sure when you mix a song you've always got, in addition to your final mix, an instrumental mix. This goes a long way for versatility. [If one] of these guys ask for an instrumental mix, and if you don't have one, you might be out of luck."

Tamara Miller

The Toronto-based songwriter, who's CD *60 Seconds* was released in April 2008, says it all starts with the song.

"You need to have a belief and a passion that what you have created simply must be heard," she says. "It's something you want to share with the world and you stop at nothing to attain it."

Miller says she always wanted to compose music for film and television.

"I would often sit at the piano for hours and play 'abstract tinkles' on the ivories," she says. "The music took me away to places of possibility. I was told by random people I met while playing piano in a lobby of a hotel or a shopping mall that I should be writing for the screen. The more I heard it, the more I felt it while playing."

Eight months after Miller independently released her disc the title cut was selected for the hit television show, *Degrassi: The Next Generation*.

"I thought my heart was going to jump out of my chest," she recalls. "I just couldn't believe it. I had looked at a goal sheet I set the year before, and it consisted of recording a new CD, having my songs featured on radio, getting press, and having a song selected for TV. These items were all on the list! What I learned was that it was crucial to have a plan. I always had that positive vision, and always believed that anything is possible, even with all the competition out there. But I made sure it was going to happen by being organized and developing a plan. There are so many ways to make it in the music industry…it's just important to be creative both in your music and in the music business."

Articles & Interviews

Mark Mothersbaugh

Whipping Up Scores

by Anders Bylund

You know Mark Mothersbaugh as the lead singer of the post-pop band Devo. But when he doesn't whip it with his bandmates, Mark is also a prolific songwriter and generalist. After getting started with the theme music for "Pee-Wee's Playhouse," the man has written theme songs and scores for "maybe 67 TV series, about 40 feature films, and about a dozen games. And along the way, I've written about 300-400 TV commercials."

Devo isn't dead, as the band released its ninth studio album, "Something for Everybody," in June of 2010. That's just very far from all Mr. Mothersbaugh is doing these days. And he is chock full of advice for the aspiring singer/songwriter.

Your friend Paul Reubens came to you to kick start your first onscreen project. Did you ever go after that kind of opportunity yourself?

Sure. All sorts of things. Once you start doing things, working, then you get a reputation. But there were things along the line that I was specifically interested in, like, I got asked to watch a rough draft of Wes Anderson's first film, his director's cut, and he didn't have any original music in it yet. After I saw that, I really wanted to work with him on it and that was great, so I arranged a meeting and we got together and we did his first four movies together.

When you're writing for a movie, you obviously work from the rough cuts and all that, but what is it that really inspires you when you're working on a score or a soundtrack song?

I wrote one soundtrack song this morning; I got up at three in the morning because I forgot that I have to write a song before I leave town tonight. So I got up at three and I wrote a song for a Muppets movie. I never worked on the Muppets, I always thought they were cool, and kids' stuff is easy for me because I like really visual

---

ANDERS BYLUND is a freelance journalist and skilled poet. He can be followed on Twitter @TMFZahrim (http://twitter.com/tmfzahrim).

film projects. It's usually very colorful and has a lot of great characters, and they are also very interested in all kinds of music styles. When you work on kids' shows, there's a freedom to experiment a lot. You don't always get that when you're working in pop music. Pop music is so much about relating to what's currently hip and what people are currently paying attention to, and you don't have those restraints in film and TV programming, usually.

Used with permission.

Mark Mothersbaugh may be most famous for his affiliation with Devo, but he's very successful as a result of writing scores.

I mean, sometimes you do. Sometimes it's very specific what they're asking for, but with kid material it's an area where you can mix banjo music with, like, Chinese computer rock and you can come up with something interesting and kids will like it. They don't say "What's that? That's strange. I don't understand." So in some ways, it's more fun to work on kids' projects than it is with MTV things or radio things or pop music.

How are video games different?

Video games are interesting because it's very complicated how you write music for them. You have to write a piece of music, maybe it's for one scene or maybe it's a character, maybe it's Homer Simpson running around a food court collecting junk foods from all the different stores and he has to stack up so much food and then you get to go to the next thing or whatever.

You have to write your music so it starts off kind of very minimal, and if you're recording an orchestra—oftentimes with games you write the music as one big piece but you cut the orchestra into fourths. Maybe use the basses and low winds and play the slowest, most legato lines, and then when Homer does something and there's a reward, or the stakes get higher, then the next section of the music kicks in along with it. But it has to work in each of these four steps, so when it's bass the melody line has to be there, the movement has to all be there, but then the next layer with maybe the rest of the strings comes in and it picks up energy and picks up speed and intensity, and the next level with, like, brass comes in. It has to be seamless—the kid can sit there for three minutes and then make the move, or they can learn the game and they can get right to that next area in only ten seconds, you know? So the music has to be able to change at any point when the player accomplishes something in the game.

So you keep upping the intensity but at the same time it's still the same piece of music and it seamless and it's interesting. Then you record the orchestra in four passes. You have to have the players play each pass so that when it gets mixed down to stereo you have four stereo pairs that are then used by the game builders so that they can all make sense. So games are kind of fun, they're kind of crazy in a way.

Articles & Interviews

The bad news about games is, you usually don't get residuals. They usually don't honor royalties of any kind, including things like ASCAP, BMI, SESAC—they don't let you collect with their success, you know? They just pay you a fee up front and then they own your music.

Would you say that the game market is something a beginning songwriter should be thinking about or do you need to establish yourself elsewhere before you go there?

I would go there. If you're a songwriter and you're excited about writing music, either songs or score, I'd go there, just check it out. That's the most growing area and you know, everybody's exploitable, so you might as well find out what it's all about.

Some games, you can do it all electronically. They all have different needs, you know, it's pretty wide. They have as much variation in music styles for games as you do in films, so I'd go to games. The trick is figuring how to get in.

So is it what you know or who you know that matters?

It's both. Unfortunately, in the entertainment industry it's a lot of who you know that sometimes outweighs what you know. So that makes it hard to get a start. On the other hand, now there are so many people who are up-and-coming directors that are getting their start and just about every college town has a film department, so it's easy to find people.

There's film festivals where more and more directors are coming to show their films, and it's easy to meet these people yourself and not have to wait for an agent that wants to pick you up and handle you. I'd just go to them and no matter what the film is—if the film's a piece of crap—still do it anyhow and just say, you know what? The film isn't very good but I'm going to make music that's so good that people are gonna hear it and go, "Wow! The movie wasn't very good but I love the score!"

If you do that, it's a good way to go from being nameless, faceless in the entertainment world to people taking notice, because even small, little dumpy films, there's people paying attention to them and they're making references and they're looking for ideas, and they're looking for new people to work with—either actors or directors or composers, you know? So you don't have to live in Hollywood or New York to break into scoring.

Let me tell you what I think is the best way to break into getting a song in a movie, for anybody who has a great song and doesn't know how to get it in front of people and wants to do it as inexpensively as possible. I'll tell you what I think, and this is the truth: I would go to the Internet, probably IMDB, find a list of every picture editor and every music editor and every—don't even bother with music supervisors, they're so inundated with CDs and new music every day that they can't even listen to it. They don't listen to it. Some of these people open up their mail and they have 30 or 40 new CDs every single day of the week so they just dump 'em in the trash or they just put them in boxes and they eventually take them to Amoeba Records for a quarter apiece.

But I think the way to do it is take it to picture editors, especially, for movies and commercials. I'll tell you why; because they're the first people in the chain, usually, now that everybody's using Avid digital editing tools. In the old days this wasn't easy to do because you had to cut film by hand and you had a magneto-optical audio track and there was a gap between the time when the picture got cut and the music got put on.

Now that everyone is doing picture-cutting on Avid, these guys have their own music libraries. And they go, "Hmm. Who do I want to cut to for this? I'm looking at this, I need something that inspires me."

So they'll go and pull out something that they like out of their record library, and maybe it's just a Danny Elfman track or an Aerosmith song, but oftentimes they know the director doesn't want that song and they know they can't afford it, so they're like, "Why would we put in an Aerosmith song that's gonna cost $700,000 and we won't be able to afford that? Somebody sent me this great CD and I listened to it on the way home from work the other day and it's got a really great song on it that would actually be good to cut to."

So they cut to your song. Once they cut to your song, that's where the director comes in and he goes, "Okay, I like the way this is going," and he's talking about the picture. They don't even really address music right away; they just talk about the picture. But as the picture gets tightened up and everything, they're doing it to your song. Then they go out and the music supervisor tries to find something that the director likes as much, and he's in love with this obscure song. I've seen it happen dozens of times: a picture editor brings in a song to a film or a TV show, he cuts to it, and anything else anybody else brings in, it doesn't really cut the same way. He's cutting to where the cymbal crash is or where the drums and bass kick in together for the chorus or something, and the director goes, "Wow, these other songs by big-name bands just don't fit as good as that—what was that song I was just listening to?"

And I kid you not, because as a composer there are so many times when I'm in the other position, where I have to write music to replace something that the editor did. Sometimes it takes a long time to get there; sometimes they go back and they still want the other music just because he cut to that and that's the best music that they should have for the film.

So I would take my song and send it to the picture editor for every film that I like and that I think my music would fit into, go online and look up the credits and get an address for them. Just send them a CD with a letter on it so it's more than just a nameless thing that comes in, because CDs are like herpes sores or something, there are so many of them, nobody wants them, you can't even look at them anymore. But if you put a letter in it or something personal to this person, compliment them on some movies that they edited, and then send them the music, then they're gonna say, "Oh! This guy knows who I am."

They're crazy—they're like composers, just sitting by themselves with the picture to work on it day after day, so if somebody writes them a letter and compliments their work, they love that. Do that a hundred times.

That's advice I've never heard before.

People don't want to tell you that! Composers, you know what they're thinking? They're thinking, "If I really help these guys, they're gonna take over my job!" Hey, I'm 60 years old, so...you can have my job. I got to have a really great time in this business. I have two little kids so I still gotta stay here for a while, but you know, I've got job security so I'm okay.

But I'm serious, I feel so bad when I think of all the—'cause I remember how I was when I was a kid, I had absolutely no concept of how to make a record. I had no concept what a record company was, what a recording studio was, and we didn't have all the great gear that you can buy now, so it took me so long to get to that point and I wrote songs that I didn't know what to do with them. And I just wish I would have had advice back then when I was younger, advice that I never got. I just had to learn it the slow, hard-knocks way.

So try that, see if it works for you. If it does, you have to send me a copy of the movie! Or no, send me a copy of the letter you sent to the editor so I know that it worked.

You've been doing this for a long time now—what do you credit for your longevity in this business? A lot of people in your shoes would have burned out decades ago.

Oh, I think for me it was just the fact that I was lucky enough that I could move around and ... if I could just do commercials, it takes a part of your creative brain and it burns a hole in it like a laser. And the same with movies, the same with TV shows; you can just get a hole burnt right in your brain in some area, but because I got to jump around, it's a totally different animal to score a movie than it is to write a song for Devo, and I'm the singer of the band so I was lucky there. I could not think about the keyboards or the guitar for a while, I can just go and sing stuff when I write it. I don't know, I think it's just being able to bounce around instead of just wearing a hole in the sole of my soul.

Baby Boomers & Songwriting

by Doris Bloodsworth

It's only natural that the generation that came of age between Elvis Presley and Woodstock would make up a growing number of new songwriters. Born between 1946 and 1964, these men and women are finding new outlets for their passion and talents. And many are finding success.

Lots of baby boomers say that with childrearing and career-building behind them, they finally have the time and disposable income to pursue their long-dormant talents. Some say a health crisis, divorce or other life-changing event pushed them into songwriting as a way to cope.

Jack Speer, a 59-year-old Florida building project manager, says he had enjoyed writing songs for a band he founded during his teen years. But music took a backseat as he took on college, career and family responsibilities. It wasn't until the death of his parents several years ago that he turned again to songwriting as a catharsis. "Now I can't imagine a day when I'm not in my home studio working on a song," he says.

Like their younger counterparts, baby boomers are tapping the Internet for its wealth of "how-to" information on everything from writing lyrics to researching copyright laws to connecting with music publishers. These silver-haired songwriters have their own websites, MySpace and Facebook pages and stay in touch with the latest trends through music-industry message boards and e-newsletters—tools that have brought Nashville into homes across the country and around the world.

By day, these Beatle-generation composers are teachers, cops, engineers and grandparents. They rush home, eager to work on the latest melody or lyrics and spend hours at their computers and keyboards. Through networking groups, they find support, critiques, collaborators, mentors and friends.

DORIS BLOODSWORTH *is a Pulitzer-nominated writer, author and president of Crosswords Communications in Orlando, Fla. She is a former reporter for the Wall Street Journal and currently covers Florida federal courts for Bloomberg News in addition to freelance writing. Bloodsworth graduated from the University of Florida with highest honors and is a member of the Florida Writers Association.*

Steve Desjardins, 61, was a Rhode Island police officer who grew up with no musical training. A chance meeting with songwriter Jimmie Crane, who wrote "If I Give My Heart to You" and "Hurt" among other hits, sparked Desjardins' interest in music. At age 35, when his friends were buying sports cars, Desjardins took his first piano lesson and started writing songs with Crane acting as mentor.

"He taught me about becoming the character in the song," Desjardins says. "He taught me to write lyrics that were clever and surprised people."

In 2003, Desjardins entered the Nashville Song Search Contest and earned an honorable mention. In 2006, his song "When He Comes Home to Her" was voted the top country song for Billboard's World Songwriting Contest. A mutual friend introduced him to legendary country singer and publisher Mel Tillis who listened to Desjardins' CD and signed a contract to publish four songs.

Although Desjardins is still waiting to have one of his songs recorded by a "Music Row" artist, several of his songs have been recorded by up-and-coming singers; and one of his songs was picked up for a movie with Jerry Springer.

Although some baby boomers gain satisfaction in just sharing their music on a local level, it is success stories such as Desjardin's that have others hoping their next song could be "the one."

What follow are tips—culled from dozens of interviews with baby boomer songwriters and industry professionals—that have proven helpful for aspiring newbies as well as veteran musicians.

How to get started

It is important to find a support system as soon as possible. That might mean one-on-one coaching from a professional mentor or more often it's a group of fellow songwriters who encourage each other and offer feedback on songs. One of the most popular networks is the Nashville Songwriters Association International (NSAI), which sponsors peer critique groups around the world.

Although composing melodies and writing lyrics may be a solitary effort for many, experts encourage songwriters to join a support group, such as the NSAI, to become better educated about the music industry, to form connections to publishers and to get audience feedback. In smaller towns or rural areas, people can start their own group by posting a notice in the local paper, on community billboards, on songwriting forums or by contacting the music faculty at community colleges.

During the NSAI local meetings, the leader usually shares songwriting tips or the latest news from the music industry. Members then have an opportunity to get feedback on their latest songs. They bring a recording and copies of the lyrics for other members to review. After the song is played, fellow songwriters share their opinions on what they liked or thought could be improved. The emphasis is on being positive but frank.

Members also have an opportunity to forward their songs to the NSAI group in Nashville for further objective feedback.

Whether songwriting is a hobby or a more serious pursuit, the songwriter will need to make an investment. A typical startup would include an instrument, such as a piano or guitar, a computer with sequencing software, a microphone, speakers and a headphone.

Sequencing software allows the songwriter to create, record, edit and mix vocals and instruments. Popular systems include Pro Tools, Cubase and Cakewalk, among others.

The Internet offers a wealth of free resources, such as rhymezone.com, which helps songwriters think of rhyming words and phrases. The NSAI and other trade industry sites, such as ASCAP.com, can help educate songwriters about copyrighting, licensing and other business issues so that they can protect and earn revenue for their efforts.

All roads lead to Nashville

Los Angeles, New York and a few other cities have major recording studios. But Nashville is still the center of the musical universe for most songwriters—not just for country music but for all genres.

Some songwriters who want to pursue the craft professionally move to Nashville. Tim Buppert, 50, spent 12 years on the road playing clubs from Florida to Pennsylvania before moving to Nashville to become a songwriter. Buppert has had several hits by some of the top recording artists, including a No. 1 single by Kevin Sharp, "She's Sure Taking It Well."

"I wish I'd moved here sooner," Buppert says. "It's a network-driven town and business. You have to be here so that if Kenny Chesney is going into the studio tomorrow and needs one more song, you'll be here to hear about it."

For many baby boomers, moving is not an option. After all, they have often invested decades in their day jobs and aren't close enough to retirement to pull up stakes. Music insiders say in that case, songwriters need to come to Nashville as often as possible. There are many opportunities, such as Tin Pan South, Songposium and NSAI's spring training. Songwriters have an opportunity to get professional critiques and to form relationships with Nashville's top publishers and song pluggers—people who pitch to the studios and artists throughout the year.

Desjardins, the retired cop turned songwriter, says he endeared himself to a number of music industry insiders, including a top executive at Warner Bros. Records, when he flew from Central Florida to Nashville every week for two months to take part in a songwriting camp.

"If you can't live there, then spend your money there," says Desjardins, who spends around $1,000 each time he gets professional demos of his songs made.

NSAI lists success stories on its website that show how trips to Nashville can pay off. Alice Lankford, 52, from Sapulpa, Okla., attended a symposium. A Banner Music executive heard Lankford's music at a critique session and ended up signing her to a contract.

Helpful Resources

For More Info

Organizations

- **Nashville Songwriters Association International (NSAI)**—A premiere site for songwriters for all genres and levels of experience. NSAI is the headquarters for local support groups around the world and features numerous educational and networking opportunities, including Tin Pan South, NSAI Spring Training, Songposium and weekly song camps in Nashville.

- **The American Society of Composers, Authors and Publishers (ASCAP)**—An association for U.S. songwriters, composers, lyricists and music publishers dedicated to protecting the rights of its members through licensing and distributing royalties.

- **Broadcast Music Inc. (BMI)**—BMI collects license fees from businesses that use music and then distributes the royalties to songwriters, composers and publishers.

Websites

- **Allmusicindustrycontacts.com**—One-stop website with explanations of who to contact in the music industry. The site includes the names of companies and executives for top label A&Rs, managers, producers and publishers.

- **Songwriterstipjar.com**—Tips and creative songwriting ideas from songwriters for songwriters. It includes an e-newsletter and discussion forums.

- **Paulreisler.com**—Reisler features several popular songwriting camps set in some of North America's most beautiful locations.

- **Nashvillesongwriters.com**—The website for one of the top educational and networking organizations for songwriters. Members can access Webcasts that explain all aspects of the music industry.

- **Ascap.com**—The website for ASCAP, which includes a portal for songwriters that has numerous resources, such as "Playback Magazine" and advice on a variety of music-related topics.

- **Bmi.com**—User friendly explanations for songwriters about copyrighting and royalties.

- **Cdbaby.com**—Touts itself as the world's largest online distributor of independent music. Especially useful for songwriters who also are singers and want to market their music to download retailers, such as iTunes, Rhapsodiy and eMusic.

- **Broadjam.com**—Includes opportunities to blog and to expose music to indie music fans.

Articles & Interviews

Helpful Resources, cont.

For More Info

- **Indieheaven.com**—A resource for independent Christian musicians and songwriters with numerous services available to members. The online music store promises to pay members 100 percent for the gross sales of their music.

- **Sesac.com**—A performing rights organization that represents songwriters and publishers. It includes a section on "getting started."

- **Musesmuse.com**—A songwriting resource for all levels of experience. It includes news, a message board and a reference guide for frequently used terms in songwriting.

- **Songu.com**—An online connection to courses, coaching, people who will plug your songs to the music industry and collaborators.

- **Musicsubmit.com**—Get help getting your music submitted to online music directories, blogs, podcasts and radio stations.

- **Billboard.com**—Delivers the latest news on the music industry, including artists, songs and trends.

- **Bbhq.com**—Baby Boomers Headquarters includes a music page with a lyrics library.

- **Berkleemusic.com**—For those who want to polish their skills and earn a songwriting certificate online and connect to the renowned faculty at the college whose alumni include songwriting legends Melissa Etheridge, John Mayer, Donald Fagen and composer Quincy Jones. The site also has numerous blogs with insights about the latest software and cutting-edge songwriting opportunities, such as video games.

- **Songpluggers.net**—A host of services, including a link to highly rated song pluggers, who pitch songs to the recording studios and artists.

- **Taxi.com**—Touts itself as the world's leading independent artist and repertoire (A&R) company. The company helps songwriters connect to record companies, publishers and others shopping for music, such as filmmakers. The site includes practical tips for songwriters, such as how to avoid clichéd lyrics and the importance of contrast.

E-newsletters

- **ASCAP Daily Brief**—dailyref@ascap.com. Information about music, copyright and new technology affecting the music industry.

Books and Magazines

- *Songwriter's Market*
- *The Craft of Lyric Writing*, by Sheila Davis
- *Writing Better Lyrics*, by Pat Pattison

Articles & Interviews

New opportunities are emerging

Although it's true that CD sales are shrinking and the music industry is struggling, it's also just as true that new opportunities are evolving for songwriters—regardless of their age. Songwriters can open up their own virtual music shops online, pitch to indie labels, film studios, television and radio in addition to new outlets, such as video games and greeting cards.

Here is just a sample of baby boomer songwriters who have found success without leaving their hometowns:

- **Ed Kliman**, 55, of Austin, Texas, (TexasMusicForge.com), has won a couple of songwriting awards and had his music licensed for radio and television in the United States and Canada in addition to writing music for musical theater.
- **Leon Olguin**, 51, and **Sheryl Olguin**, 50, of Cocoa, Fla., (SoloCreativeMedia. com), have had songs published and recorded in the United States and the United Kingdom. Leon Olguin's "White as Snow," has been recorded more than 100 times and has earned a reputation as a classic praise song. His wife, Sheryl, has written themes for local radio and TV shows. "Having lived 50 years, I've experienced a lot that has added depth to what I write," Sheryl Olguin says. "This is the really helpful part of being a midlife boomer."
- **Terry Kitchen**, 50, of Boston, Mass., (TerryKitchen.com), has won numerous awards including first place in the USA Songwriting Competition. He has recorded about 100 songs and released them on his private label. Some of his songs have been used in documentary films. "Being a baby boomer is helpful in that much of my audience has the same cultural and musical landmarks that I have," Kitchen says.
- **Jeffrey Bosworth**, 47, of Altamonte Springs, Fla., (Bozmusic.com and ieminvest. com), runs a marketing company by day but spends his nights at the recording studio creating songs for his Island Estuary label. Bosworth's vision is to create a venue near the Walt Disney World and Universal Studios theme parks that would give more songwriters and artists a chance to share their music. "Being a bit older gives us a real demographic who love music and loved it through the '60s into the '90s when music was made more for art than money," Bosworth says.

Writing for younger audiences

Jack Perricone, chair of the songwriting department at renowned Berklee College of Music in Boston, says baby boomers have to adapt in order to get their songs published for today's younger consumers.

"Melodic rhythms of today's music are more complex," Perricone says. "Rhythms are faster and there are more words—both in pop and country, probably because of the influence of rap."

Perricone suggested baby boomers study the songs that are getting the most airplay on radio. Online courses are another way to prepare for a professional

career in contemporary music. Berklee was the first college to offer a co
songwriting degree.

Debbie Cavalier, dean of the continuing education online school Berkleemusic.
com, says the number of baby boomers enrolling in the school's online songwriting
program has been rising.

"They say they are finally getting back to something they always wanted to do,"
she says.

Even veteran songwriters are struggling to compete in an industry in which new
stars are teens, such as Taylor Swift and Miley Cyrus. Swift writes many of her own
songs.

"As much as I hate to admit it, I don't have a clue what a 15-year-old girl thinks,"
says Buppert, who records demos for aspiring songwriters in addition to writing
and performing his own songs.

NSAI boomer songwriter Robert Wagener of Belleville, Ill., says he thinks age
neither helps nor hurts. "Age means nothing to the process," he says.

Boom

Bruce Springsteen, "The Boss," turned 60 and graced the cover of *AARP* in its
September-October 2009 edition. The multitalented actor and songwriter, Jeff
Daniels, 54, pokes fun at baby boomers in the songs he's written for his one-man
road show. Both have found no shortage of audiences.

At 75 million strong, U.S. baby boomers have too big an impact on the economy
to be ignored—as songwriters or song buyers.

Passionate boomer songwriters, such as Desjardins, are not easily dissuaded. He
says on one of his early trips a well-known Nashville executive says, "Kiddo, what
you're trying to do—the chances are a million to one," to which Desjardins says, "I
believe I am that one in a million."

He encourages his peers to believe in themselves, believe in their songs and
believe in their songwriting.

"Don't get discouraged," he says. "Enjoy the ride. Sometimes the journey is better
than the destination."

INTERVIEWS

Poetry
he Song

Using Rhyme, Rhythm & Refrain

by Mary Harwell Sayler

Songwriting and poetry writing often sound discordant notes in the length, imagery, and terminology used to discuss techniques, and the variations that work well for one might not for the other. However, both song lyrics and poetry can hit a high note with each of the three R's: Rhyme, Rhythm, and Refrain.

WRITING A REFRAIN

Whether you write song lyrics or a traditional form of poetry that relies on repetition, try taking it from the flip side and start with a refrain. This might consist of a single sentence or a line or two, but regardless of the length, the refrain needs to be worth repeating. If you think about something that's important to you, chances are, other people will care about it too. The trick then is to hold that thought in a clear, conversational way so people can readily identify with what you sing or say.

Although a well-written refrain usually steers clear of clichés, you can put those old phrases to use before discarding them. Just list a few of your favorite expressions then keep playing with the words or thoughts until you find an unusual twist or view.

For example, I wanted to write a villanelle, which is a traditional form of poetry with a complex pattern repeat. I also wanted to tie the poem to the timely but timeless subject of the aftermath of war, so I started jotting down thoughts, such as, "We come along and tell them what to do, but who knows what is right for them or true?" I liked that thought and could see several possibilities for developing the idea. However, to keep in line with the form I'd chosen, I had to split the sentence in two, insert a variation, and weave each line back and forth until both came together at the end. By then the thought had progressed enough to change "them"

MARY HARWELL SAYLER *has authored over two dozen books of fiction and nonfiction and placed many poems in periodicals and anthologies. Since 1983, she's worked with other poets and writers, first through home study courses then her critique service and website, www.poetryofcourse.com.*

to "us," which gave the initial idea a little twist as well as a stronger connection between the "us" and "them" of this world.

To do something similar with song lyrics, just refresh an old thought or phrase to fit your lines to the cultural times. With songwriting you also have the advantage of musical timing to refresh a common theme or ordinary subject. For example, the flat statements, "You are so beautiful" and "I want to hold your hand," or the rather plainly put question, "Didn't we almost make it this time?" scored high with music-lovers because of the musical emphasis that accentuated each word and made familiar thoughts outstanding.

USING TRUE & SLANT RHYME

Besides musical emphasis, the naturally-occurring sound echoes of the spoken word can be used to emphasize your important thoughts. Since the most resounding echoes arise with the ring of true rhymes, those words will usually provide your strongest emphasis in writing song lyrics and poems. I say "usually" because all true rhymes do not have the same quality of freshness or strength of meaning. For example, notice the contrast between the true-ringing but cliché-singing pair of rhymes *of* / *above* and the stronger rhymes that typically occur with nouns *hand* / *sand* or active verbs, *give* / *live* or a combination of the two, *bird* / *heard*.

Generally, true rhymes are easy to recognize as you hear a single sound repeated in the last syllable of two or more words, each of which begins with a different letter of the alphabet, for example, *word* / *stirred*. As that example also demonstrates, spelling may vary, while the sound remains the same.

Compared to other languages, English offers relatively few choices for creating true rhymes. However, you can increase your sound options by using other types of echoes, such as those found in slant rhyme and alliteration. The words *summer/ simmer* provide an example of both since those words echo the consonants and almost rhyme, but don't.

Words beginning with the same letter of the alphabet create the sound effect known as alliteration, which, carried to extreme, can create humor, twist the tongue, and make a song almost impossible to sing. So as you write and revise your song lyrics, experiment with the effects you most want to hear. For instance, you might like the subtle sound of assonance, a form of alliteration that focuses the vocals on the vowels, such as those found in *blue* / *moon* and *alone* / *own*. Notice, too, how those long vowels act similarly to a held note, which means the musical timing can increase the emphasis even more.

How will you know such things? Experiment—experiment as you write but, even more so, as you revise. If you find that you still prefer the pure sound of true rhymes, attune your ear to notice which syllables seem most apt to rhyme. For instance, the sounds of such word-ending syllables as *and*, *ate*, *all*, *am* can often be heard in English, but if you listen for a word that rhymes with *orange*, disappointment and strange sounds will surely occur.

More Writing Tips

Tips

- Listen to the lyrics of contemporary songs you like, focusing on their use of the three R's.

- Study, too, song lyrics you don't like, analyzing what makes them less effective.

- Evaluate lyrics you've previously written to see if you have used the three R's well.

- Song lyrics occasionally hum with mystery, but unlike poems that rely on the eye, irony and subtle changes of meaning can be confusing to the ear.

- Let your lyrics be clear in sound and meaning.

- Make your choice of words, phrases, and refrain highly sing-able.

- Allow variation in your use of each of the three R's but have a good reason for any deviation from what the ear normally expects to hear.

- Read aloud or sing each revision to be sure nothing hinders the musicality.

- Revise your lyrics until you're satisfied with the results.

- As you consider the overall effectiveness of sound effects, let your ear be the final judge.

- If you haven't already done so, select a catchy title in keeping with the song's primary subject, mood, and theme.

To help you find your rhyming options more readily, all sorts of rhyming dictionaries have become available online and in bookstores. If, however, you have neither book nor Internet connection, connect the sounds yourself by listing your key words. This can be a fun word game as you run through an alphabet of sounds, listening for potential rhymes that relate to the theme and content of your lyrics. More importantly, perhaps, playing with words, sounds, and meanings can open up unexpected options that you might not have noticed by glancing at a ready-made list instead of relying on your ear.

Once you have assured your mind and ear that you have adequate rhyming options, use those clear notes to establish a rhyme scheme. For example, traditional patterns of rhyme commonly include *abab* or *abba* or *xaxa*, which simply means that the "a" rhyme comes first, the "b" rhyme second, and "x" doesn't rhyme with anything.

As your ear will confirm, an "x" between a rhyming pair of words can soften the ring of true rhymes and make slant rhyme almost imperceptible. To test that artistic effect, sing or read aloud your lyrics. If you want to mix up the sound effects even more, try tossing an occasional rhyme inside a line instead of always plinking away at the end.

FINDING THE RHYTHM

True rhyme, slant rhyme, and alliteration help your listeners to hear the emphasis on each resounding word. These echoes also contribute to the rhythm of your song as the sounds increase or decrease. To hear this for yourself, read your lyrics aloud as you would a poem, listening especially for any off-beat sound or jarring effect that you did not intend. If you notice that a particular word or phrase causes a rough spot in the beat, find a more effective word choice as you revise. For instance, test each potential word replacement against your ear until you like the sound of a synonym that emphasizes other syllables.

Notice, too, the sense of each sound. In poetry, the popular two-syllable iamb ends on an accentuated syllable, making it upbeat, whereas the two-syllable trochee starts on a high note then drops the speaking voice down. Simply knowing this can help a poet to match words with the general tone or feelings, and songwriters can do this too. For instance, if the tempo is downbeat, your lyrics can correspond to that, increasing the effect of the mood. Conversely, an upbeat tune might call for lively lyrics.

That said, once you've mastered the technique of matching sound with sense, experiment. For instance, try using upbeat words in a downbeat song and vice verse, being aware, of course, that this could bring about either totally ridiculous or positively brilliant results. And that's another similarity between poetry writing and songwriting: Something unique and exciting often happens as you play around with words and try out new approaches.

Having a stable, established structure as the springboard for something new is one reason poets continue to write in traditional forms. You can do this, too, as you practice writing new lyrics to the tunes of old ballads, hymns, folk songs, or once-popular melodies now available for public use with, of course, proper acknowledgement but no payment or permission required. To find these songs on the Internet, begin your search with a relevant phrase, such as "music in the public domain" or "songs out of copyright."

As you hum a tune or listen to your favorite "oldies," write down whatever words the melody and refrain suggest to you. Let your thoughts flow without censoring yourself. Later, as you return to revise your work, build the lyrics toward a dramatic conclusion or insightful ending as you might in a poem, saving the best for last.

BEYOND THE R'S

For many people, poetry writing provides an opportunity to explore a visual image through figurative language, comparisons, or word plays, but for me, poems often start with music. Suddenly, a phrase catches my ear, and I write down that small beginning to see where the music might lead. This can happen in songwriting too, especially if you have been given a tune in need of lyrics.

Whatever writing method works for you, each song or poem needs to consider the content as well as the musicality. Depending on your unique blend of interests, this might be an interesting story told in a narrative ballad or lyrical love song. Or you might write a rave in a hard-rocking knock against hypocrisy, complacency, or the absurdity of violence and most fears. Regardless of your overriding emphasis, focus on a single but universal theme that will matter to almost everyone, for instance, life, death, love, war, relationships, or various aspects of change.

If you have not thought about a theme before now, don't worry. That's not uncommon. Poets and songwriters often finish a first draft before detecting the overriding theme that arises from the initial flow of creativity. Also, the song or poem itself can lead you into discovering a main premise, not only for one set of lyrics but major life themes as well.

If those thoughts or beliefs happen to relate to the very people you hope will hear your songs, so much the better. To be heard, cared about, and remembered, well-written song lyrics and poems will speak to and for other people. Then, with skillful use of each of the three R's, you just might have a poetic hit on your hands.

Even Stevens

BMI Songwriter of the Century

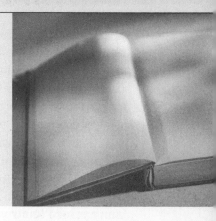

by Hillary Kanter

Mention the name Even Stevens in Nashville, and the first reaction you will get, is that of total respect. After all, over the many years of his career, the man has garnered 26 #1 Country Awards, 14 Pop Awards, and if that weren't enough, 13 BMI Million-Airplay Awards, (meaning the songs were played over one million times on the radio) many of which, each one, are double, triple, and quadruple awards! Additionally, he was awarded BMI's Songwriter of the Year, for the Eddie Rabbitt hit "Suspicions," ASCAP's Song of the Year for Kenny Rogers called "Love Will Turn You Around," and later went on to be named a BMI Songwriter of the Century.

Even has had songs recorded by a diverse array of artists, including Eddie Rabbit, Tim McGraw, Kenny Rogers, Martina McBride, Kenny Chesney, Ricky Skaggs, Alabama, Dolly Parton, Joe Cocker, The London Symphony, and Julio Iglesias. He is a phenomenon in the world of songwriting today, not simply because of the multitude of hits he has written, but because of his rare ability to sustain writing hits over such a long and illustrious career.

I know you are from Ohio, but how did you wind up in Nashville writing songs?

I came to Nashville on a complete whim. I was living in Ohio, and was preparing myself to attend the Dayton Art Institute, to pursue a career in graphic arts.

One night, I got a call from my long lost uncle Bob, who was living in Nashville, and working as a road drummer and recording engineer. He asked if I was interested in coming down to visit and maybe he could help me meet some people who might be interested in the handful of songs that I had written. I was broke, so I borrowed forty dollars from our next-door neighbor and drove down to Nashville that night in my old beat up mail truck. I arrived around midnight at a dive where my uncle was

HILLARY KANTER is a Nashville songwriter who has recently turned to writing books (fiction and nonfiction). For many years, she was a songwriting partner of Even Stevens. Learn more at her website: www.hillarykanter.com.

playing in a cover country band. While the band was tearing down for the night, I was playing one of my songs on a guitar I found propped up against the wall near the restroom, and a big country star named Web Pierce (who had his heyday in the 1950's) walked by. He said, "You know, that song right there would be perfect for my daughter to record. Are you interested in letting me publish it?" I said, "You bet!" At two in the morning, I signed a publishing agreement.

Well nothing ever happened with that song, but that promise of a dream coming true made me give up art school, and stay in Music City.

It was three long years before I actually got one of my songs recorded.

Many people know you as the co-writer and moving force behind the Eddie Rabbitt phenomenon for fifteen years, starting in the 1970's. How many hits did you two write together?

I think we had around fifteen number one hits, and quite a few releases that made it into the top five as well. Luckily, many of our country chart toppers also crossed over into the pop and adult contemporary charts too.

Songs like "Suspicions," "Driving My Life Away," "I Love a Rainy Night," and so many other mega hits...why do you think these songs with Eddie Rabbitt were so successful?

It's hard to be certain, but we tried to write songs about what people were feeling and experiencing in their everyday lives. Also, we were big believers in rhythm (I think it was Jimi Hendrix who said, "Get them in the crotch, and their hearts will follow.") and the magic of harmony.

You wrote a song, by yourself, called "When You're in Love With a Beautiful Woman," which was a worldwide hit for the group Dr. Hook. Where did you get that idea?

I had a new girlfriend at the time that sang with a rock group, playing at a bar in the Holiday Inn near Vanderbilt University. I was waiting for her to take a break and come over and see me, but she never made it because all the guys in the place were stopping her and hitting on her. That irked me to no end, so I left the club and wrote "When You're in Love With a Beautiful Woman" in the short time it took to drive to my apartment. Art imitating life, so to speak.

You have co-written songs with many other great songwriters like Kenny Rogers, Paul Overstreet, J.D. Souther, Thom Schuyler and the late, great, Shel Silverstein. What is it that makes a great co-writing partner for you, other than their obviously being good writers?

Friendship, usually—as in the case of my teaming up with Eddie Rabbitt. We knew each other for at least six months before we ever wrote a song together.

Ideally, you need to be very comfortable around someone before you can risk making a fool of yourself. I have found that the dumbest lyric idea can eventually lead to something great. The words may suck, but the concept might be brilliant. If you are afraid or embarrassed to blurt it out, the greatness may never be realized.

When you sit down to write a song, do you have a specific singer in mind for the song?

Not that often. I mostly write what I feel and then try to find a home for it. Every time I try to outguess things, it ends up a waste of time. There are exceptions though. "Love Will Turn You Around" was written by request from Kenny Rogers. He wanted a hit song for a movie he had coming out called "Six Pack." We met and he sang us a cool little melody that he had, and within a week it was written and out on the charts. It became ASCAP's most played song of that year and opened up more cuts for me with Kenny.

I know you are asked this a million times, but what comes first...words or music?

Every song starts differently. Quite often, it begins with a concept or title first, but then again, a great melody can truly inspire a lyric, so I guess there is no pat answer to that question.

How long do you decide to work on a song before moving on, if it is just not happening?

Until I become frustrated and depressed. If I still think it is a great idea or title, I may lay it on a songwriting partner and hope he or she has a fresh slant on it, that can save it.

How important is the rewriting process and how long does it usually take?

I am never done writing a song until the very last second of the very last studio mix of the demo. My thinking is: "Take out everything that doesn't sound right until it does sound right."

It is important though, to know when to stop.

Which is more important in songwriting—being artistic or being commercial?

I like a good mixture of both.

What, in your opinion, makes the difference between a "good" song and a "great" song?

I think a great song has what I call "the money line." At least one moment in the song, be it lyric or music, that sticks with the listener and pulls them out of their world and into yours, and hopefully, makes them want to own it. That, to me, is commercial...and commercial is a beautiful word. It means that the most people possible are hearing and liking your song.

Do you think life experience is necessary, in order to write great songs, or can one just use their fantasy?

Life experience lends a quality to your song that connects with other people. After all, aren't we trying to communicate? And how better to communicate, than to be able to relate on a human level?

How many of your songs are written from personal experience? Do you think those songs are better songs?

I would have to say that my favorites are always from personal experience. They just have more "legs" for me. They create an impact for a much longer time.

Must one be a "tortured soul" to write great songs? Is suffering necessary to good writing?

Not at all. There are many examples of revered writers—and artists—whose problems and notoriety outshine their talents by a mile.

How important is the craft of songwriting? How can someone learn the craft? Are there any tools?

You learn it by doing. Out of quantity comes quality. The more you write, the more you can learn "what not to do." As I mentioned earlier, take out the bad stuff until all that is left is the good.

Can someone be taught to write great songs? How much is learned and how much has to be innate talent?

Talent is important. And you learn by doing it. However, what you really need is great passion, and to be utterly obsessed with songwriting, to write great songs.

What is the best way to demo a song to give it the best chance to get recorded? Does it need a lot of instrumentation, or just a piano or guitar?

You have a better chance of a record turning out the way you want it to, if you "mini-produce" your demos to sound like records. However, you can be pleasantly surprised sometimes by the prowess of some producers that take your song to greater heights than you ever imagined. But occasionally, a truly great song, too, can be recorded from a simple guitar or piano.

I guess the best rule of thumb is to make it sound like magic—no matter what you do to it. Just listen to Willie Nelson's cut of "Blue Eyes Crying In The Rain"... simple magic. Just get the goose bumps going.

I heard that someone very well known and successful in the music business once told you that you would never write hit songs. What was that like, and how did you react?

Luckily my ego was of such magnitude that I just thought he was a no-talent idiot, and I went on with my delusions of grandeur.

After so much success writing, do you think there is anything new to learn?

There is always something new to learn in life if you keep your mind open.

Do you think you are a better songwriter today than when you were writing all the Eddie Rabbit hits? How?

Whenever I hear some writer say he or she thinks they are writing the best songs of their career now, my first reaction is, "Oh boy, is this going to stink, or what?" Therefore, I refuse to answer on the grounds that it may incriminate me.

After having written over a thousand songs, are there any new ideas under the sun to write about?

There is only one creator. We are all but imitators. So, imitate away!

Most people do not realize that even very successful songwriters can experience some lean years, and experience rejection. How have you dealt with it? What do you say to yourself, when someone turns down a song?

I remind myself that everyone has an opinion. If they do not like my songs, they might be in a foul mood...or maybe they suffer from the "Van Gogh Disease," you know...they have no ears!

Is there anything you know now that you wish you had known back when you were just getting started?

I actually would not change a thing about my songwriting career. It has been such a wonderful ride. I have had—and continue to have—such a great time. It is always good to appreciate what you've got.

You are still getting songs recorded and having hits. What do you think is the secret to your longevity in a business that constantly changes?

Luck. And I continue to strive to do my best.

If somebody is new in Nashville and does not have any connections in the songwriting world, is there a place they can meet other songwriters or network? How do they go about it?

Some would say that there is a "click" in the Nashville songwriting world, but I do not believe that is the case. If you are really serious about being a professional songwriter, you must live here and commit. You have to become a fixture, put in the time, get yourself noticed, and be in it for the long haul. Play your songs at every opportunity, at every open writer's night you can find and write, write, write... nothing will make it all work better than a fantastic song. Word gets around and it will open every door.

I would also recommend contacting the NSAI. (Nashville Songwriters Association International.) For song evaluations and workshops, info can be found at 615-256-3354 OR 1-800-321-6008.

Writing for Placement

Step-by-Step Guide to Placing Songs in Films, TV and Other Projects

by Patrick J. Walsh

Flip on the TV; what's that song playing behind the local newscast? Pop in a DVD of your favorite indie film; isn't that that band coming out of the radio during the romantic scene? Or maybe go online to see if there's a new episode of your favorite podcast; whose music is that over the opening credits, and how did it get there?

No matter how varied the story of how a particular song has come to turn up in your favorite media—in a film, a TV show, a video game, even a cellphone app—there is in every case an example of how you can learn to get your own music into similar productions, through the magic of music placement.

Whether you are seeking to license your existing music for use in other people's projects or want to start composing specifically for placement, you'll need a little business expertise, some marketing initiative, and a reasonably open-minded approach to other people incorporating your work in their own productions.

In this end-to-end look at the nuts and bolts of song placement, we'll start with some tips for focusing your compositions with an eye toward placement, and then get into the marketing and business aspects of song licensing.

Placement-friendly compositions

There are various ways to get your music into other people's projects: you can license your existing original songs; you can compose music with a readily identifiable mood that can be shopped to music supervisors, directly or via a music placement service; or you can be assigned to write an original score for a given project.

In each case the ultimate goal is to get your work into the hands of the music supervisor—the person who oversees the music selection and licensing process.

PATRICK J. WALSH is the author of two books: the 3-volume Spaceflight: A Historical Encyclopedia (Greenwood Press/ABC-CLIO) and Echoes Among the Stars: A Short History of the U.S. Space Program (M.E. Sharpe, Inc.). He has also written more than 250 paid, bylined articles for a variety of trade press, mass market and general interest magazines, newspapers and online publications.

Those artists who are inclined to license their existing songs are often faced with the dilemma of how to reap the benefits of licensing while still maintaining control of their work.

For Fred Gillen Jr., owner of the independent folk label DYS Records and a long time singer-songwriter who has released seven full length solo albums since 1997, the conflict between creativity and commerce became particularly acute when he began pursuing placement opportunities for his intensely personal songs.

The production team at the ABC-TV soap opera "All My Children" came across Gillen's song "Free" through a music publisher that doubled as a song placement service. They were willing to pay an acceptable fee for the use of the song, but the scope of the license was a point of concern for Gillen, who was worried by the prospect of relinquishing control over his work.

The solution? The publisher simply assigned a new title to the composition—thereby enabling the artist to maintain ownership of his original song.

"That's how they operated," Gillen says. "They would re-title the song, and then have the artist register the new title with the performing rights organization, which in this case was BMI. The re-titled song is basically considered a different song."

In the licensing of original compositions, the song often changes along with the title, when the artist is asked to provide an alternate or custom version.

Writing specifically for placement, meanwhile—writing with a particular use in mind, or composing an original score—can be a daunting prospect for songwriters who are more accustomed to penning songs based on personal experience. in each case, though, the success of a given piece is derived from the same basic skill: the ability to clearly and economically convey emotion through music.

"The similarities are that you have to have an ear for hooks regardless of what you are writing for," says Brian Trim, a post sound engineer and composer who writes electronic instrumental compositions intended for television placement via music libraries. "If you write epic pieces that go nowhere and don't hold interest, then you don't place anything."

Trim began his musical career as a drummer, and then moved into mixing and doing post sound production. His electronic compositions are generally short pieces designed to accompany action or adventure sequences in TV dramas.

The knack of writing for such a specific use requires a delicate sense of mood as well as the musical skill necessary to convey the proper emotion.

"The audience has to feel what they are seeing and hearing. The folks who produce these shows want the perfect thing or they won't even consider you," Trim says. "It has to be awesome."

Getting your work heard by the right people

In several important particulars, the task of getting your music considered for placement by a music supervisor is similar to getting a record label's A&R person to hear your work. It's important to keep in mind that the individuals involved at the other end of each of these transactions are bound by a complex set of business and legal parameters that will largely define the arrangements they make when they want to work with you.

Happily, the changing state of the music industry is making it easier for songwriters to find music supervisors who are open to considering their songs.

"In the past, people focused on licensing work by major label artists, but the playing field is much more open now," says Michele Wernick, executive vice president of music placement and licensing at Secret Road Music Services, Inc. in Hollywood. "Licensing budgets have come down so much, and supervisors want independent artists who are affordable."

Secret Road seeks out placement opportunities for a roster of about 100 artists and some record labels, and also handles music supervision—most notably for the FOX television show "House," and for television commercials.

Wernick has had experience on both the buying and selling side of music supervision, and has also worked in virtually every sector of the music business. Her resume includes work for record labels, music video production, music supervision for films, booking musical guests for the VH1 show "Late World with Zach," and five years of licensing music for musical equipment manufacturer Line Six.

For songwriters looking for placement opportunities, Wernick stresses the importance of learning all you can about the music supervisors you'd like to pitch.

"When you just send stuff cold, most supervisors are not going to listen. Most of the time, people don't want unsolicited material. But if you do your research about the music supervisors you are trying to reach and find out what they are working on, then you can target the right people so you know your music is a good fit for them."

Another avenue to finding projects that are looking for music is to consider submitting your work to a music placement service.

"One benefit of using a program like ours is that your song will be evaluated by people who have had music placed, or who have been music supervisors," says David Harper, director of music services at J4U Entertainment in Pasadena.

Sporting the slogan "Every song has its place," J4U acts as an intermediary for artists seeking placement and productions seeking music. In addition to seeking out conventional placement opportunities, the company also places songs on retail radio playlists—gaining exposure for artists in the music mix one typically hears in stores at the mall. J4U also handled music supervision chores for the 2009 indie film "Hope For A Thorn," providing an original score of vintage-sounding retro 1940s music.

"The filmmakers were in a bind. They needed music, their budget was low, and they had a tough time getting licensing," Harper recalls. "We offered to get them music from the artists in our program. The songwriters delivered eight songs, we had musicians come in and perform them, and we delivered the music."

While the prospect of having a direct pipeline to a film project is obviously attractive, Harper is quick to note that many independent artists who want to work

Articles & Interviews

with a song placement service worry about the specter of being charged large fees or about the service taking a substantial chunk of the licensing fee.

"A lot of placement services will charge you a big yearly fee or take a percentage of your deal. It's better for the songwriter if a company offers the service without taking a percentage, but I think charging a fee is fair if the price is fair," Harper says.

The business of song placement

Once you've put in all that effort to market your existing songs or to create some great placement-friendly compositions, and you've begun to develop a good working relationship with a few music supervisors or a music placement service, you're well on your way to begin licensing your work. There are just a few more steps to setting up your song placement business as a professional venture—and a reliable source of income.

You will first have to get used to the idea of negotiating the terms of a licensing arrangement. And to negotiate well, you need to keep in mind what it is that you are actually selling.

There are two elements of a song that can be licensed—your composition itself, and your recorded performance of the song. If you're already signed to a record label (or you run your own label), the right to use the recording of your performance will most likely be controlled by the record company or the entity you created to distribute your own recordings (which, happily, is likely still controlled by you). The right to use the composition of the song, meanwhile, will likely be controlled by your music publishing company (which again may be you, if you self publish your work or if your songs have not been published and you are the sole copyright owner).

The contractual arrangement creates a license that allows the producer of the project to use your song in a specific manner—for example, the contract may call for your song to become the theme of an independent film, played over the opening and/or closing credits; or it might specify that your work will be used as background music in a given scene.

To arrive at the appropriate value for that license, you will need to know how the song will be used; how and where the project will be distributed; and how long the producer will need to have the right to use your song. Each of these considerations is figured into the budget and the projected market value of the project, and each will in turn give you some idea of how much money is available for purchasing the rights to use your song.

"It's important to know the scope of the project, to determine if there's wiggle room for negotiating," says Wernick, who cautions that the negotiation process may initially be difficult for songwriters to navigate.

"Productions do tend to tier their fees, from independent artists (on the low end) to major label artists," she said. "You don't want to undervalue your copyright, but an independent artist is not really in a position to make a lot of demands. In most cases, the supervisor will quote a particular fee and the artist will basically have to decide whether to take it or leave it."

To get an idea of how music licensing works on the high end, consider the case of a typical big budget Hollywood film. In this scenario, the music supervisor will virtually always seek to acquire the rights to use both your composition and the recording of your performance in all media (including theatrical showings of the film, its broadcast on TV, etc.), in all territories (in the U.S. and in other areas throughout the world), and in perpetuity (meaning that the license will continue to be in effect throughout the copyright life of the film).

Such a big ticket project may include an attractive up front payment for the rights to use the composition and your recorded performance of the song, and a provision defining the amount of royalty payments you would receive for a variety of distribution options such as television airings or home video sales.

In a standard contract, these items will be referred to as the Synchronization License (which conveys the right to use the composition), the Master Use License (covering the use of the recording of your performance), and the Public Performance Royalty (which sets forth the type and amount of royalties due).

On the other end of the licensing spectrum, you might find a far less formal scenario with say, the producer of an online video podcast who wants to use your song to introduce a segment of her show. Assuming a smaller budget and less thorough procedures for accounting for and paying royalties, you might instead agree to an arrangement where a portion of your song might be used, say, once per episode for a flat fee, with a mention of your name and available recordings in the show's credits—in effect giving up royalties you might never see anyway in return for a small but steady income and some free advertising.

In either case, it is important to get all agreements in writing, and to ensure that both parties understand and consent to everything in the contract. To speed the process, you should have all pertinent data about each of your compositions ready in advance—including your name and contact information as it will appear in the contract, song titles (particularly if you're re-titling), the names of anyone else who has any copyright interest in the song, and the song's lyrics, if it has any.

"When an artist has all the paperwork in order, that makes my job easier," says Harper. "If you have a song that a third party wants, you want to be able to give it to them as soon as possible. You want a song that they like, that fits the intended use, and that you can deliver to them quickly."

Once you have progressed to the point where your songs are generating serious interest from potential licensees, you need to make sure that you are properly credited and compensated for your work. Your first resource for keeping track of the use of your licensed compositions is your performing rights organization (PRO; in the U.S., these include ASCAP, BMI, SESAC).

Each of the PROs has an individual who specializes in music licensing, and each organization oversees the payment of royalties for compositions that appear in productions aired on television. In the case of music licensed for use in films, the songwriter's PRO receives a cue sheet from the film's production office that details the exact nature of the song's use in the film—an important factor in determining the proper payment of royalties.

Finally, it's important to remember that the skills you need to succeed at song placement are really just an extension of all the things that make you a good songwriter in the first place. In both cases, it's your vision, technical expertise, and ability to make good choices that will get your music the exposure it deserves.

The New Deal

*A New Approach to Selling CDs
Based on Public Trust*

by Grant Peeples

In the Fall of 2007 I began to develop a new idea about a way to sell CDs of the songs I was writing and recording. It all started as I licked an envelope into which I had just placed a check for $1,200, made out to someone in Hollywood, known to me only as: TellyMan.

Aside from the obviousness of the name, I had no idea who TellyMan was. I never once spoke with him on the phone. As I recall I didn't even have an e-mail address for him. But he had a blond, 1984 Fender Telecaster listed on ebay that fit the criteria of the instrument I had been hunting. And the price was right. After a few question-and-answer transmissions through the enchanting eBay portal of dream and profit, I pulled the trigger. I told TellyMan I wanted the guitar and that the proverbial check was in the mail.

Bam. Welcome to commerce in the 21st Century. It was a pleasure doing business with you. Whoever you are.

Less than two weeks after my check set out on its 2,000 mile journey to TellyMan in California, my new guitar was plugged in to a Fender twin amplifier and I was assaulting the countryside where I live with cranked up twang and liquid reverb.

It would be a little while before I got back to that new idea I had about how to sell those records of mine. The first thing I had to deal with was the deputy sheriff who was coming up the drive. Somebody had called the law on my songs.

The selling of recorded music has changed radically over the last 10 years. The development of MP3s, digital downloading, and the sharing and distribution of music files has done to the corner record store what Henry Ford did to the horse and buggy. There has developed, too, a corresponding ethical disconnect between an artist's proprietary right to his creation and what the public feels it owes him for it.

GRANT PEEPLES *is a touring Americana singer/songwriter out of Tallahassee, Florida. His bio, songs, videos and performance schedule can be found at www.grantpeeples.com.*

This became patently clear to me at a gig last winter in South Florida. After my show I was in the lobby of the club selling CDs at a small table I had set up. I was chatting with two couples who were on their way out when one of the men said to me: "Hey, I don't have your first CD. I should get that now."

He was reaching for his wallet and I was reaching for a CD to hand to him when the female half of the other couple gleefully weighed in. "Oh, you don't need to do that, Les. I already have that one. I'll just burn a copy for you." Though the blood drained from my own face, all four of them were all smiles. It must have seemed like a plausible and sensible idea. It never occurred to any of them that there might be anything improper or unfair or embarrassing—not to mention illegal or unethical—to what the woman had proposed. To them, I guess, this was no different than if she had offered to loan him a copy of a book so that he didn't have to purchase one. And of course one might wonder: what *is* the difference?

Though there is no shortage of arguments for either side of that question, the only really pertinent issue for the independent musician is: can I make a record of my songs and get compensated for my creations and efforts to the extent that I will be able to carry on with my artistic life and...make yet another record at some date in the future?

Making a record—not just any record, but a really good record, with production values equal to what the industry's best studios were issuing 20 years ago—is easier and far less expensive than any of us ever imagined back before the personal computer worked its way into the heart and soul of recording studios. But *selling* a record has never been more challenging than it is today.

(You might have noticed I often use the term "record," when referring to music on a CD. I like to argue that in spite of all the changes in technology, a musical recording is still a "record" of music, a document, and that the CD is merely the conveyor of a creation, like paper or film or canvas or...vinyl.)

Not only have the conventional channels of distribution gone the way of the 8-track tape, virtually anyone who has ever played three chords on a guitar now has a recording of their work. And like any artist worth the eviction notice tacked to his door, they want to share their vision and creations with others. So there's more music out there than there ever has been, but only a fraction remains of the distribution points where it could once be featured and retailed. In other words: there's a sonic log jam in the frothy wake of the Digital Age.

So...what's a Bob Dylan wannabe to do?

Which leads us back (almost) to me licking that envelope I was sending off to TellyMan.

On my first record, my sales approach was...what? Well, to do what everybody else seemed to be doing. I joined CD Baby (www.cdbaby.com), that hugely popular web distribution company for independent artists. I did the same with the behemoth and unwieldy Amazon. I also linked up with PayPal, which enabled me to sell directly from my own website.

I did okay with CD Baby, (they are, in fact, a good company, very user friendly and helpful, and I still distribute through them today) but it cost $30 to join and list the record, and they award themselves four dollars from every CD sold from their site. Additionally, I had to pay the shipping to them in Oregon, where the CDs were stocked. Amazon takes a whopping 50 percent from each sale, which I found, frankly, larcenous, but again—everybody else seemed to be doing it. PayPal took a much smaller cut, (essentially, they are just money collectors, not involved in fulfillment, as are CD Baby and Amazon) but the process was cumbersome. And in all three cases (unless you were a PayPal member with a credit balance), people had to whip out their credit card and type a lot of personal information into little boxes on a computer screen. For my taste, this has always been a loathsome impediment and deterrent when it comes to being excited about buying something new. Moreover, having the ubiquitous PayPal icon there on my web page just seemed tacky. Still, artistic indignation notwithstanding, the biggest issue was that I just wasn't happy with the sales I was getting from my marketing strategy.

It was at this juncture that my dealings with TellyMan cracked open a door for me. And I began to wonder about a new approach to my second record. It began with the redoubtable question: WHAT IF?

What if I just sent out a blast to my e-mail list, (at that time, about a thousand people) and told them I had a new record, and that I had come up with a real easy way for them to get their hands on it. That all they had to do was *tell* me they wanted it, and to give me their mailing address, and that I would mail it to them. And that I would include an envelope, addressed to me, into which they could put their payment to me. In other words, they were to pay for the CD *after* they got it.

And what if I put a banner on my web page that very much said the same thing? Inviting anyone out there is cyber space to request a CD, and leave it up to them and their conscience to pay for it?

What would happen? Would this painless way of requesting and receiving the new record spur sales? And—this was the real kicker—what percentage of people would actually send the payment?

It seemed to me that the somewhat impulsive buyer (with whom, I admit, I am duly sympathetic) would be much more likely to buy the CD than if he had to go through all the rigmarole of pulling out his credit card and laboring through the miasma of an Internet order, which statistics, surely, prove no customer *ever* gets through the first time without having to go back and fix some mistake they made in the process. I figured that if 25 percent of the people did *not* pay me, I would still be way ahead of the game even if the strategy didn't increase the number of purchases, which I could not imagine it not doing. But more than anything, I just liked the idea, the feel, its premise of trusting people out there in the cyber heartland, (most of whom I didn't even know). It felt right making it incumbent upon them to decide whether or not they would live up to the tenets of my original proposition, which I promptly and very unoriginally named: The New Deal.

I bounced it off a few fellow musicians. The consensus was that my idea was interesting but risky. But I think all were curious just how it might pan out, and most seemed to think I didn't have that much to lose. They, too, had been struggling with record sales. They knew.

In any event, when my new CD, "It's Later Than You Think," was delivered by the duplicator in April of 2008, I posted a New Deal banner on my web page, and sent out this blast to my e-mail list:

> **Hey folks, my new record, "It's Later Than You Think," is out. And I think it might be...good. It might even be real good. If you would like a copy, all you have to do is just hit reply and send me your mailing address. I'll send you the new CD, and I'll also include a self-addressed envelope. After you get the CD, stick the money in that envelope and mail it to me. Quick, easy and painless.**

Within 48 hours I had sold 150 CDs at $15 each. (The price included postage.) Fifteen percent of my mailing list had placed an order. I quickly made a run for envelopes and stamps. The living room was soon awash with mailroom clutter.

Sensing I might now be on to something, a week after sending out the blast, I re-sent it, this time with a link to a video I had recently made of one of the songs that was on the record. More than 50 more orders came back.

And then the checks starting arriving at the big rural mail box at the end of my drive. In the parlance of today's Youth: "Swee-eet."

Between May of 2008 and May of 2009 I send out another 20 or so blasts to my e-mail list, which I now worked steadily to broaden and increase in number. No matter what the blast was about—gigs, reviews, radio play, etc.—I always included the New Deal in it, and always got at least a few sales. I made a personal decision that it wasn't overtly unethical to "pirate" an occasional list of e-mail addresses from someone who had sent out a blast of their own without blind copying their recipients. (I always blind copy my own.) But I absolved myself by never forgetting to put a red note at the top of every mailing saying that if the recipient wanted off the list, all they had to do was hit return and say "remove."

During that year I also opened and began to build a Facebook page, reconnecting with old friends and finding new ones whose musical taste and world view jibed with my own. And in the spring of 2009, when my next record, "PawnShop," was ready to be shipped (yes, thanks to the sales through the New Deal I was able to return to the studio), I had 2,700 names on my e-mail list, and 500 Facebook friends. I sent two blasts in 10 days, redesigned my web page with even more emphasis on the New Deal, and sent a note to all my Facebook friends letting them know how they, too, could get the record. The printed copy on the CD packaging also talks about the New Deal and gives the e-mail address to write to should someone want another copy or if they would like to have a copy sent to somebody else. (In th case I send the CD to one address, and the envelope to another.) The first month that "PawnShop" was out I sold more than 400 copies on my own, without paying a nickel's commission to anybody.

Of course the 64-dollar question in all of this is: Did the public live up to their end of the deal? Did they follow through with their commitment and send in their money? To date I have sold more than 1,100 CDs through the New Deal as it is presented through e-mail blasts, my web page and Facebook. And my collection rate is over 95 percent.

Maybe it's just me, but I find that a very revealing number when it comes to how an artist can think about selling his wares these days.

I made a decision early on that if somebody didn't pay, I was not going to chase them down or otherwise play collection agency with them. People often write and ask me for my address, saying they have misplaced the envelope I sent with the CD for remittance. On several occasions I have had people come up to me at gigs and hand me money, saying that they had lost the envelope or had just never gotten around to sending me a check. I find that continuing to send e-mail blasts that mention the New Deal reminds people who might have forgotten that they have not yet paid for the CD they received. Checks seem to just wander in.

At the root of all this, of course, is a fact about us humans that I think we often forget about in our daily interactions with each other—and that is that trust is an empowering thing. To trust someone is to establish a relationship with them, ipso facto. For musicians this is crucial knowledge, because our business is all about establishing relationships, whether it's from the stage, through a pair of speakers, or in the public forum of cyber space. A musical performance itself, at least a good one, balances on the trust the performer has of his audience to hear him out, let him open up his heart to them and have his say. Likewise, it is trust that brings the audience to the performer, trust that he will be honest and forthright and worthy of their time and attention. That's what puts the checks in the mailbox.

hard Flowhil

ng Advice from a
Seasoned Promoter

by David McPherson

Richard Flohil recently turned 75. The grey, shoulder-length wispy hair epitomizes the experience of this Toronto music publicist, promoter and passionate champion of roots music.

Walk through his house in midtown Toronto and immediately you know you are in the midst of a music lover; his shelves—from the bathroom to the living room are lined with more than 11,000 vinyl and CD records, along with hundreds of music books. His electronic Rolodex is 3,500 names and counting.

Catch up with him and you may find him nursing a mild hangover and charming a young songwriter—telling her how to get started in the music biz; then you watch him kill (or reply to) 100 e-mails. Next, he figures out the guest list for that evening's show at Hugh's Room before, as he says, "wrestling" an Ian Tyson biography to the ground.

Flohil emigrated to Canada in 1957; he started out working in journalism for various trade publications before moving into PR in the late 60s. In 1970, Richard Flohil & Associates was born and 39 years later this boutique PR agency that handles publicity for musicians, record companies, concert tours and club gigs is still going strong.

He has promoted concerts for the likes of Muddy Waters, BB King, and k.d. lang over the years. He has worked with the Downchild Blues band for 37 years, Stony Plain Records for 27 years and Loreena McKennitt for 20 years. The Renaissance man has also contributed liner notes to more than 100 albums and written hundreds of bios for musicians.

Here follows some marketing advice for songwriters from this veteran publicist.

GENERAL RULES OF PROMOTING ONESELF

These apply regardless of what media you use. You use media to spread the word faster than word-of-mouth can spread it. Word-of-mouth is still the most reliable,

DAVID MCPHERSON is a Toronto-based freelance writer with more than 17 years experience writing about music. A graduate of the University of Western Ontario, with a Masters in Journalism, David has published thousands of articles in daily newspapers, consumer magazines, and websites across North America, including Bluegrass Unlimited, Paste, American Songwriter, Performing Songwriter to name a few. His website is: www.davidmcpherson.ca.

effective method of making people believe in what you do, your music, and you as a person, but it is impractical to reach a mass audience.

The bio

A certain degree of hyperbole and hype is permitted. Downright lying is not. It's surprising the number of people...they don't really lie, but they exaggerate past the point of no return. If you are writing a bio there are various elements you have to consider. Who are you, what do you do...make these things as objective as possible. You can use them on your MySpace, Facebook, and Sonic Bids pages, but be objective.

Do not say, "I'm Joe Blow, I'm the best singer-songwriter to come out of North America in the last 20 years and I've been compared to Bob Dylan, etc." There is no believability. People turn off instantly. It is perfectly permissible though to carefully use other people's quotes. For example, if the *New York Times* says, "We regard Fred Smith as one of the best folk singers in Ontario." That's OK since it's not you [saying it].

Objective bio material is the first step. If you've got a penchant for writing objectively about yourself, fair enough, you can write it, otherwise get someone to do it. You also need a hook. I helped a client write her bio recently. She has a tattoo on her wrist in Sanskrit or something and I asked "What does that read?" And she said, "Tell the truth." There's your angle.

Good photographs

Do not let your brother-in-law's sister take your picture. There are specific needs for pictures. Good photos are important. I sound like a broken record on this one, especially with photographers I work with who continue to ignore it, but the media needs, likes and gives bigger space to horizontal images, rather than vertical images. A vertical image can very easily be made into a single column shot.

The book

Your music isn't enough. I hate to say that, but to be successful, and you can define success any way you like, making a living is a good way in this climate. Forget about Gold records and multi-million dollar this and that as it probably won't happen. If it does, nice, but don't bang your head against the wall trying to get there.

Apart from the music, you have to be focused and ambitious. You have to go for it. The fact is that most people will screw up parts of their life in search of this golden rainbow. You may screw up your relationships, your family...whatever. It behoves you to go for it, especially if you are young...let the relationships and the other things go by the wall if you want to be successful. If you want a domestic life, terrific, that's your decision, but it's hard to do both. If you are very young, that's a hook.

Learning Never Stops

Flohil Talks with Randy Newman.

"Some people never stop learning," says Richard Flohil.

That point was driven home during an on-stage interview Flohil did with Randy Newman. Here's how he recounts the end of his conversation with the singer-songwriter:

Flohil: You are a recording artist, you've done stuff for movies; is there anything like an average day in your house?

Newman: Yea, I watch the baby, middle of the day I may go for my piano lesson...

Flohill: Wait a minute...

Newman: Yeah, I'm studying classical piano.

Flohill: You play a Beethoven sonata?

Newman: Sure.

When I first started working with Serena Ryder, she was 17 and that was the hook. Yes, she had an amazing voice, but her youth was the hook. Being old is also a hook. I have an e-mail quote from Teddy Thompson, son of Richard Thompson, the line is, "You can be hip until you are 30 and then after that there is a period of limbo and then after 60 you can be a legend."

The music itself is not so much a hook, although that's what grabs new listeners. When I was working with k.d. lang, I did the very first dates in Toronto at a blues bar and she was doing her neo-country thing at the time, so that was an interesting experiment. Take music out of its normal context and put it somewhere else. You have to be careful because if it's too over the top, or too artificial or too manufactured, media people in particular spot it, unless it is so bizarre they have to cover it. Think in country music: Garth Brooks, black hat, never seen without it, Dolly Parton's wigs and her enhanced figure, never seen without it. Because it is so over the top it's incredibly likeable. Longevity is a hook for some people: think Gordon Lightfoot.

Join together

I think this is self-evident, but any successful artist, no matter what stage in their career, needs a team around them. When Serena Ryder was 16 she had a friend who did her press and hyped her to the local media and sent out cassettes to people like me saying, "What do you think?" My response was it's astonishing, amazing, can I help? Part of that help was I introduced her to Hawksley Workman who produced her first real record. Hawksley introduced her to her manager who is still on the scene. Building a team is important. I think this works universally throughout North America and Europe.

When you are looking for a manager or agent and you are still a very baby artist, you are going to be lucky to find one because those parts of the music industry by tradition, by custom and by practice are based on a percentage of your earnings. If you are not earning anything, why would you expect a manager or agent to invest time and money working with you when the income is non-existent or very small. Find a friend to get involved in an evangelical way...it's called looking for a believer. You may find an experienced manager or agent who susses you out and thinks you have an unusual talent and signs you; it does happen, but not very often. The first person on your team would be a family member or a friend. Sooner or later that has to give way to someone with more connections.

As a publicist who has been at the business for a long time, we don't want a percentage, we want a fee. It may be that your first professional team member in your search for a believer is somebody like myself who have music industry contacts, we didn't lie too many times, so we have credibility attached to what we say. And, on our part, as a sidebar, we are very careful about who we take on... don't want to take on a turkey as their reputation rests on you and you on them.

Get out & play

A newcomer has to hone the art of the act. Any acoustic artist should look for work in the folk festivals, regardless of the dubious image of the "f" word because you can be exposed to huge audiences who didn't expect to see you; if you are good you will surprise them. If you are going to be doing a showcase, don't expect media to come unless there is a hook. Where you hold it is a hook. The act has to be together and you have to pack it with friends, relatives, uncles, whoever, so it gives the appearance to the handful of media you might entice out, they go "Oh my god!" Have to have the songs down, new strings on your guitar if need be and pace your set.

THESE RULES WERE MADE TO BE BROKEN

The other thing about the music industry is that it's covered and covered with layers and layers of rules, the biggest of which is that there are no rules. Anything that is a standard practice or normal can be broken, can be different or changed. Learn the rules, but once you know them, it's like writing songs, once you have them down, you can break them and make better songs maybe or different songs. One person I know learned to play piano so she could write songs on piano instead of guitar because they would come out different than ones she created on guitar.

Get the Most Out of Songwriting Workshops

by Kerry Dexter

Perhaps you're just beginning to write songs. Maybe you've been at it for a while and band members tell you your songs are great, but you wonder how they'd sound to others. Maybe you've been writing in a certain style but you have ideas that don't seem to fit there. Could be you've got a sheaf of songs you know are great and you wonder how to get them recorded. Maybe you want to brush up on your playing skills to take your songwriting further. Could be you know you're a good writer but you've hit roadblocks in writing your songs or getting people to listen to them. Maybe you're wondering if your writing could be a career. Maybe your situation doesn't fit any of these scenarios. If you're considering taking a workshop, though—your first or your fifteenth—think about where you are with your songwriting, where you want to be, and how—and what kind—of songwriting workshop could help you get there.

Know yourself and your goals

You'll want to think about how you learn best, and what sort of time and resources you have to invest. Your choices will become more clear as you research what's on offer—there are ideas about that to come. Right now, though:

- What's your favorite way of learning: having someone tell you, having someone show you, or hands on doing it yourself? That's going to vary with what you're learning, of course, but spend time thinking over what the best experiences have been for you so far. Then pair them up with the workshop descriptions you'll find as you research specific programs.
- When you are in a group or class, do you like to sit back and take it all in, talk over things with your classmates, or sit up front and ask questions?

KERRY DEXTER is an independent writer, editor, and photographer in the U.S. and Europe. Her work has appeared in VH1.com, music magazine Dirty Linen, Strings, Symphony, Wandering Educators, and CMT, among others. She's contributed chapters to Ireland and The Americas, The Dictionary of American History, and The Encyclopedia of Counterculture, and writes about the arts at http://musicroad.blogspot.com.

- How confident are you in sharing your music with others? Playing onstage, in class, other workshops, on your own or part of a group?
- How skilled are you at listening, both to musical ideas and in everyday conversation?

There are no right or wrong answers to these questions. They'll get you thinking about your learning styles, though, which will help you as you look at what workshops to take and again when you make your choice and go about learning from your instructor, your fellow musicians, and yourself.

"Choose a format that fits your learning goals," suggests Carrie Newcomer, a folk and Americana songwriter based in Indiana. "Some workshops are presented in a relaxed atmosphere, but still within a classroom method approach. Some workshops are presented more as up close concerts where the artist plays songs and answers songwriting questions. Some workshops focus on critiquing previously written material and learning what happens through listening and discussion. Some workshops focus on developing new tools for the craft and practical application through exercises and group writing experiences."

Research what's out there

If you already have a specific workshop in mind, it's still good to review your choice in light of what you've learned through thinking about the ideas above—that will help you make the most of your time at the workshop. If you're looking around, time, money, distance, length of course, subject matter, instructor style, and level of instruction, and how all this fits with your song writing goals are all things that will influence your choice. You'll find hands-on, talk and interview, lecture, discussion, songwriter in the round, and just about every sort of workshop style in between. "Choose a workshop that focuses on the areas in which you hope to gain new experience," says Carrie Newcomer. California-based bluegrass musician Laurie Lewis points out "How do I know how to get the most out of a particular workshop unless I know how the workshop is being taught?"

Several places to look:

- **Local resources.** Is there a songwriter association in your town? It may offer courses or bring in guest speakers. Adult education programs and community centers are other places to start. Ask your librarian. Ask your musician friends and music teachers for leads. "It's not always the best move to jump to study with the most famous player, who may or may not have the slightest idea how to help other players. It can sometimes be worth taking a little time to gather word-of-mouth recommendations from other students," says Massachusetts-based Shannon Heaton, who composes and plays Celtic music.
- **Nearby colleges, and universities.** Both academic departments (think music, English, education) and student organizations may have workshops or classes you'd like. Summer music schools, such as The Swannanoa Gathering, held on the campus of Warren Wilson College in North Carolina, and Augusta, held on

Articles & Interviews

the campus of Davis Elkins College in West Virginia, sometimes take place on college campuses, too.

- **Music and arts festivals.** Workshops are often part of day time programs at these events. MerleFest in North Carolina, The Montana Irish Festival, and The Florida Folk Festival are just three of the many festivals that regularly offer workshops.

- **Your favorite artist's website.** Many artists teach in formal and informal situations. Check out the online presence of musicians you like, and see what's offered.

- **Online resources.** You've probably been using the Internet to help research all these possibilities, and while you are online, you might want to look into online songwriting workshops. Berkleemusic and SongU are both well respected programs, and there is a range of others out there. The Nashville Songwriters Association (NSAI) offers online and live workshops to its members—and no, they are not all about writing country music. Read over the NSAI, Berklee and SongU sites (see sidebar) as benchmarks to use when evaluating other programs.

Where to Look Online

Three sources for online song writing workshops:

- www.berkleemusic.com

- www.nashvillesongwriters.com [NSAI]

- www.SongU.com

Artists' websites:

- Danny Arena—www.songu.com/pubwhoweare.asp

- Matt Heaton—www.mattandshannonheaton.com

- Shannon Heaton—www.mattandshannonheaton.com

- Corrina Hewat—www.corrinahewat.com

- Laurie Lewis—www.laurielewis.com

- Carrie Newcomer—www.carrienewcomer.com

- John Smith—www.johnsmithmusic.com

- Del Suggs—www.salt

Prepare

Knowing yourself and knowing your goals, you've made your choice. What's next? "Take care of the details ahead of time, so they don't distract you from the actual workshop," says Boston-based guitarist and singer Matt Heaton. Some pre-work you can do:

- Gather the practical details—time, date, place, how to get there, registration information—and have all that ready to take with you.
- If you're bringing your instrument recording device (ask if this is not addressed in the workshop materials), make sure all it is in working order. Check the batteries beforehand. Have it ready to go, so you don't have to ask the teacher to wait while you read the instruction manual.
- Bring a notebook, and more than one pen.
- Be on time.
- If it's a hands-on workshop, tune before you sit down.
- If you're taking a workshop with a specific artist, you may want to listen to his or her work.
- You may want to prepare a few questions. But do not feel you have to ask them.
- Review your goals, both short term and long term.
- Relax.

"I think most people like to come away from a hands-on workshop with a new song or two," says John Smith, a touring songwriter based in Wisconsin. "Of course, this means making a safe environment for fragile new starts."

Focus

Maybe your style is to jump right in, maybe you prefer to scope things out a bit first. Either way, pay attention to the vibe of the class. Be ready to play a song if that's requested or seems appropriate. If you're to give a critique, be thoughtful and honest. Listen to the critiques given to and by others. Listen to all that goes on, record the class if allowed, and take notes. Be courteous and stay focused on the subject matter of the workshop in your comments and questions.

"Participate fully," advises Florida-based singer and songwriter Del Suggs. "Lots of folks want to sit in the back of the class and only take notes. Get involved, volunteer to play your song when the teacher asks."

"Go with the flow," adds Matt Heaton. "Some workshops will not be what you expect them to be. Try to do whatever the teacher asks. If you don't understand something, ask a question. But don't ask questions that are designed to show how much you know. It is tempting, when pushed out of your comfort zone, to try to bolster that comfort zone ('well, I normally don't play this type of music, I play this other type'). A workshop isn't the place for that. When you're at a workshop, you are formally saying that you are there to learn. And you will, if you're open to it."

Scottish composer and singer Corrina Hewat agrees. It's a good idea to research the subject matter of the workshop a bit, she says, and then "Go with an open mind and willingness to try anything. And go with confidence that you can achieve whatever is being asked of you, and what you are asking of yourself."

Follow up

Thank the workshop leader, briefly. Every other workshop participant probably has something to say to the leader too. Keep it brief and cheerful and save longer questions for another time or an e-mail, if offered.

Exchange contact information with other workshop participants if it's natural to do so. "While it's great to chat with the guest speakers and thank them for their time, it's just as important to get to know some of those attending the same workshop or class, whether online or in-person. You just might meet a future major label artist, the future collaborator on your first hit song, or a future Grammy-Award winning record producer who you'll be calling in a few years to listen to your songs," says songwriter and teacher Danny Arena, who is based in Nashville. "Sometimes my song writing group attendees establish an e-mail list and share new songs over the months following the workshop," adds John Smith

Let what you've learned sink in, reflect on all that went on, and review your notes. Put what you've learned into practice in your music.

If things go wrong

Trust you instincts. Maybe a certain workshop, or this leader, isn't right for you, for any number of reasons. Give yourself permission to look for a better fit. Maybe you'll discover that working in a group isn't right for your goals just now.

If that's so, you might benefit from the sort of workshop where an artist plays and talks about his or her songs, rather than one where you play yours. You might also like taking a workshop that's about another area. Learning more about your instrument or looking into the history of a favorite style could inspire you. All of these options—including getting out of a situation that isn't working—are great ways to work on your songwriting goals. "I would say that the most important thing to take away from any workshop situation is the fact that in order to write well, you must *begin* to write," says Laurie Lewis. "Sometimes this is the most difficult thing. Just starting the process."

"You can learn about the components, you can understand how the pieces fit together, you can grasp the nuances of melody and structure. But it's up to you to put all those parts together into a great song," says Del Suggs. "And you can do it— it's a matter of applying what you know and what you learn with what you feel."

"A workshop is a place to try out new ideas and skills. Some of these experiments will be more successful than others, but the point is to jump in the pool and paddle around until you get used to the water," says Carrie Newcomer. "Have fun!"

Take risks, trust yourself, and. keep on learning.

Music Publishers

Music publishers find songs and then get them recorded. In return for a share of the money made from your songs, they work as an agent for you by plugging your songs to recording artists, taking care of paperwork and accounting, setting you up with co-writers (recording artists or other songwriters), and so on.

HOW DO MUSIC PUBLISHERS MAKE MONEY FROM SONGS?

Music publishers make money by getting songs recorded onto albums, Film and TV soundtracks, commercials, etc. and other areas. While this is their primary function, music publishers also handle administrative tasks such as copyrighting songs; collecting royalties for the songwriter; negotiating and issuing synchronization licenses for use of music in films, television programs and commercials; arranging and administering foreign rights; auditing record companies and other music users; suing infringers; and producing new demos of new songs. In a small, independent publishing company, one or two people may handle all these jobs. Larger publishing companies are more likely to be divided into the following departments: creative (or professional), copyright, licensing, legal affairs, business affairs, royalty, accounting and foreign.

HOW DO MUSIC PUBLISHERS FIND SONGS?

The *creative department* is responsible for finding talented writers and signing them to the company. Once a writer is signed, it is up to the creative department to develop and nurture the writer so he will write songs that create income for the company. Staff members often put writers together to form collaborative teams. And, perhaps most important, the creative department is responsible for securing commercial recordings of songs and pitching them for use in film and other media. The head of the creative department—usually called the "professional manager"—is charged with locating talented writers for the company.

HOW DO MUSIC PUBLISHERS GET SONGS RECORDED?

Once a writer is signed, the professional manager arranges for a demo to be made of the writer's songs. Even though a writer may already have recorded his own demo, the publisher will often re-demo the songs using established studio musicians in an effort to produce the highest-quality demo possible.

Once a demo is produced, the professional manager begins shopping the song to various outlets. He may try to get the song recorded by a top artist on his or her next album or get the song used in an upcoming film. The professional manager uses all the contacts and leads he has to get the writer's songs recorded by as many artists as possible. Therefore, he must be able to deal efficiently and effectively with people in other segments of the music industry, including A&R personnel, recording artists, producers, distributors, managers and lawyers. Through these contacts, he can find out what artists are looking for new material, and who may be interested in recording one of the writer's songs.

HOW IS A PUBLISHING COMPANY ORGANIZED?

After a writer's songs are recorded, the other departments at the publishing company come into play.

- The *licensing and copyright departments* are responsible for issuing any licenses for use of the writer's songs in film or TV and for filing various forms with the copyright office.
- The *legal affairs department and business affairs department* works with the professional department in negotiating contracts with its writers.
- The *royalty and accounting departments* are responsible for making sure that users of music are paying correct royalties to the publisher and ensuring the writer is receiving the proper royalty rate as specified in the contract and that statements are mailed to the writer promptly.
- Finally, the *foreign department*'s role is to oversee any publishing activities outside of the United States, to notify sub-publishers of the proper writer and ownership information of songs in the catalogue and update all activity and new releases, and to make sure a writer is being paid for any uses of his material in foreign countries.

LOCATING A MUSIC PUBLISHER

How do you go about finding a music publisher that will work well for you? First, you must find a publisher suited to the type of music you write. If a particular publisher works mostly with alternative music and you're a country songwriter, the contacts he has within the industry will hardly be beneficial to you.

Each listing in this section details, in order of importance, the type of music that publisher is most interested in; the music types appear in **boldface** to make them easier to locate. It's also very important to submit only to companies interested in your level of experience (see A Sample Listing Decoded on page 7). You will also want to refer to the Category Indexes on page 333, which list companies by the type of music they work with. Publishers placing music in film or TV will be proceded by an ⌧ (see the Film & TV Index on page 350 for a complete list of these companies).

Do your research!

It's important to study the market and do research to identify which companies to submit to.

- Many record producers have publishing companies or have joint ventures with major publishers who fund the signing of songwriters and who provide administration services. Since producers have an influence over what is recorded in a session, targeting the producer/publisher can be a useful avenue.
- Since most publishers don't open unsolicited material, try to meet the publishing representative in person (at conferences, speaking engagements, etc.) or try to have an intermediary intercede on your behalf (for example, an entertainment attorney; a manager, an agent, etc.).
- As to demos, submit no more than 3 songs.
- As to publishing deals, co-publishing deals (where a writer owns part of the publishing share through his or her own company) are relatively common if the writer has a well-established track record.
- Are you targeting a specific artist to sing your songs? If so, find out if that artist even considers outside material. Get a copy of the artist's latest album, and see who wrote most of the songs. If they were all written by the artist, he's probably not interested in hearing material from outside writers. If the songs were written by a variety of different writers, however, he may be open to hearing new songs.
- Check the album liner notes, which will list the names of the publishers of each writer. These publishers obviously have had luck pitching songs to the artist, and they may be able to get your songs to that artist as well.
- If the artist you're interested in has a recent hit on the *Billboard* charts, the publisher of that song will be listed in the "Hot 100 A-Z" index. Carefully choosing which publishers will work best for the material you write may take time, but it will only increase your chances of getting your songs heard. "Shotgunning" your demo packages (sending out many packages without regard for music preference or submission policy) is a waste of time and money and will hurt, rather than help, your songwriting career.

Once you've found some companies that may be interested in your work, learn what songs have been successfully handled by those publishers. Most publishers are happy to provide you with this information in order to attract high-quality material. As you're researching music publishers, keep in mind how you get along with them personally. If you can't work with a publisher on a personal level, chances are your material won't be represented as you would like it to be. A publisher can become your most valuable connection to all other segments of the music industry, so it's important to find someone you can trust and feel comfortable with.

Independent or major company?

Also consider the size of the publishing company. The publishing affiliates of the major music conglomerates are huge, handling catalogs of thousands of songs by hundreds of songwriters. Unless you are an established songwriter, your songs probably won't receive enough attention from such large companies. Smaller, independent publishers offer several advantages. First, independent music publishers are located all over the country, making it easier for you to work face-to-face rather than by mail or phone. Smaller companies usually aren't affiliated with a particular record company and are

Icons

For More Info

For more instructional information on the listings in this book, including explanations of symbols (N ✔ ▼ ⟟ ❧ 🌐 ○ ⟁ ◓ ⊘), read the article *How To Use Songwriter's Market* on page 1.

therefore able to pitch your songs to many different labels and acts. Independent music publishers are usually interested in a smaller range of music, allowing you to target your submissions more accurately. The most obvious advantage to working with a smaller publisher is the personal attention they can bring to you and your songs. With a smaller roster of artists to work with, the independent music publisher is able to concentrate more time and effort on each particular project.

SUBMITTING MATERIAL TO PUBLISHERS

When submitting material to a publisher, always keep in mind that a professional, courteous manner goes a long way in making a good impression. When you submit a demo through the mail, make sure your package is neat and meets the particular needs of the publisher. Review each publisher's submission policy carefully, and follow it to the letter. Disregarding this information will only make you look like an amateur in the eyes of the company you're submitting to.

Listings of companies in Canada are preceded by a ❧, and international markets are designated with a 🌐. You will find an alphabetical list of these companies at the back of the book, along with an index of publishers by state in the Geographic Index (see page 351).

PUBLISHING CONTRACTS

Once you've located a publisher you like and he's interested in shopping your work, it's time to consider the publishing contract—an agreement in which a songwriter grants certain rights to a publisher for one or more songs. The contract specifies any advances offered to the writer, the rights that will be transferred to the publisher, the royalties a songwriter is to receive and the length of time the contract is valid.

- When a contract is signed, a publisher will ask for a 50-50 split with the writer. *This is standard industry practice*; the publisher is taking that 50% to cover the overhead costs of running his business and for the work he's doing to get your songs recorded.
- It is always a good idea to have a publishing contract (or any music business contract) reviewed by a competent entertainment lawyer.
- There is no "standard" publishing contract, and each company offers different provisions for their writers.

Make sure you ask questions about anything you don't understand, especially if you're new in the business. Songwriter organizations such as the Songwriters Guild of America (SGA) provide contract review services, and can help you learn about music business language and what constitutes a fair music publishing contract. Be sure to read What About Contracts? on page 33 for more information on contracts. See the Organizations section, beginning on page 267 of this book, for more information on the SGA and other songwriting groups.

When signing a contract, it's important to be aware of the music industry's unethical practitioners. The "song shark," as he's called, makes his living by asking a songwriter to pay to have a song published. The shark will ask for money to demo a song and promote it to radio stations; he may also ask for more than the standard 50% publisher's share or ask you to give up all rights to a song in order to have it published. Although none of these practices is illegal, it's certainly not ethical, and no successful publisher uses these methods. *Songwriter's Market* works to list only honest companies interested in hearing new material. (For more on "song sharks," see How Do I Avoid the Rip-Offs? on page 15.)

ADDITIONAL PUBLISHERS

There are **more publishers** located in other sections of the book! On page 129 use the list of Additional Publishers to find listings within other sections who are also music publishers.

☑ ABEAR PUBLISHING (BMI)/SONGTOWN PUBLISHING (ASCAP)

Nashville TN. E-mail: ronhebert@gmail.com. **Contact:** Ron Hebert, publisher. Estab. 2000. Pays standard royalty.

How to Contact Submit mp3 by e-mail. Unsolicited submissions are OK. Prefers 3 songs with lyric sheets. Responds in 1 week if interested.

Music Mostly **country**, **country/pop**, **pop**, **dance**, and **Christian**.

🌐 ◯ ALL ROCK MUSIC

P.O. Box 1200, 3260 AE Oud Beijerland The Netherlands. (31) 186-604266. Fax: (32) 0186-604366. E-mail: info@collectorrecords.nl. Website: www.collectorrecords.nl. **Contact:** Cees Klop, president. Music publisher, record company (Collector Records) and record producer. Estab. 1967. Publishes 40 songs/year; publishes several new songwriters/year. Staff size: 3. Pays standard royalty.

- Also see the listings for Collector Records in the Record Companies and Record Producers sections of this book.

Affiliates All Rock Music (United Kingdom).

How to Contact Submit demo package by mail. Unsolicited submissions are OK. Prefers cassette. SAE and IRC. Responds in 2 months.

Music Mostly '50s rock, **rockabilly** and **country rock**; also **piano boogie woogie**. Published *Rock Crazy Baby* (album), written and recorded by Art Adams (1950s rockabilly), released 2004; *Marvin Jackson* (album), by Marvin Jackson (1950s rockers), released 2005; *Western Australian Snake Pit R&R* (album), recorded by various (1950s rockers), released 2005, all on Collector Records.

Tips "Send only the kind of material we issue/produce as listed."

📷 ☑ ALPHA MUSIC INC.

Dept. SM, One International Blvd Ste. 212, Mahwah, NJ 07495. (201)335-0005. Fax: (201)335-0004. E-mail: alpha@trfmusic.com. Website: www.trfmusic.com. **Contact:** Michael Nurko. Music publisher. Estab. 1931. Pays standard royalty.Affiliate(s) Dorian Music Publishers, Inc. (ASCAP) and TRF Music Inc.

- Also see listing for TRF Production Music Libraries in the Advertising, Audiovisual & Commercial Music Firms section of this book.

How to Contact "We accept submissions of new compositions. Submissions are not returnable."

Music All categories, mainly **instrumental** and **acoustic** suitable for use as **production music**, including **theme and background music for television and film**. "Have published over 50,000 titles since 1931."

📷 ☑ BIXIO MUSIC GROUP & ASSOCIATES/IDM MUSIC (ASCAP)

111 E. 14th St., Suite 140, New York NY 10003. (212)695-3911. Fax: (212)967-6284. E-mail: info@bixio.com. Website: www.bixio.com and www.idmmusic.com. **General Manager**: Johannes in der Muhlen. Administrator: Miriam Westercappel (all styles). A&R Director:

Office Manager: Courtney Stack-Slutsky. Administrative Assistant: Karlene Evans (soundtracks). Creative Director: Robert Draghi (all styles). Senior Creative Director/Producer: Tomo. A&R: Claudene Neysmith (world/New Age). Music publisher, record company and rights clearances. Estab. 1985. Publishes a few hundred songs/year; publishes 2 new songwriters/year. Staff size: 6. Pays standard royalty.

How to Contact *Does not accept unsolicited material.*

Music Mostly **soundtracks**. Published "La Strada Nel Bosco," included in the TV show *Ed* (NBC); "La Beguine Du Mac," included in the TV show *The Chris Isaac Show* (Showtime); and "Alfonsina Delle Camelie," included in the TV show *UC: Undercover* (NBC).

◻ BRANDON HILLS MUSIC, LLC (BMI)/HEATH BROWN MUSIC (ASCAP)/STEVEN LYNN MUSIC (SESAC)

N. 3425 Searle County Line Rd., Brandon WI 53919. (920)398-3279 or (cell) (920)570-1076. E-mail: marta@dotnet.com. **Contact:** Marsha Brown, president. Music publishers. Estab. 2005. Publishes 4 new songwriters/year. Staff size: 2. Pays standard royalty of 50%.

How to Contact Submit demo package by mail. Unsolicited submissions are OK. Prefers CD with 1-4 songs and cover letter. Does not return submissions. Responds only if interested.

Music Mostly **country (traditional, modern, country rock)**, **contemporary Christian**, **blues**; also **children's** and **bluegrass** and **rap**. Published "Let It Rain," recorded by Steff Nevers, written by Larry Migliore and Kevin Gallarello (Universal Records, Norway); "Do You Like My Body," recorded by Ginger-Ly, written by Nisa McCall (SEI Corp and Big Daddy G Music, CA); "Did I Ever Thank You Lord," recorded by Jacob Garcia, written by Eletta Sias (TRW Records); "Honky Tonk In Heaven," recorded by Buddy Lewis, written by Mike Heath and Bob Alexander (Ozark Records).

Tips "We prefer studio-produced CDs. The lyrics and the CD must match. Cover letter, lyrics, and CD should have a professional look. Demos should have vocals up front and every word should be distinguishable. Please make sure your lyrics match your song. Submit only your best. The better the demo, the better of chance of getting your music published and recorded."

◪ ◲ CHRISTMAS & HOLIDAY MUSIC

26642 Via Noveno, Mission Viejo CA 92691. (949)859-1615. E-mail: justinwilde@christmassongs.com. Website: www.christmassongs.com. **Contact:** Justin Wilde, president. Music publisher. Estab. 1980. Publishes 8-12 songs/year; publishes 8-12 new songwriters/year. Staff size: 1. "All submissions must be complete songs (i.e., music and lyrics)." Pays standard royalty.

Affiliates Songcastle Music (ASCAP).

How to Contact Submit demo CD by mail. Unsolicited submissions are OK. *Do not call. Do not send unsolicited mp3s or links to Web sites.* See website for submission guidelines. "First Class Mail only. Registered or certified mail not accepted." Prefers CD with no more than 3 songs with lyric sheets. Do not send lead sheets or promotional material, bios, etc." Include SASE but does not return material out of the US. Responds only if interested.

Film & TV Places 10-15 songs in TV/year. Published Barbara Streisand's "It Must Have Been the Mistletoe."

Music Strictly **Christmas**, **Halloween**, **Hanukkah**, **Mother's Day**, **Thanksgiving**, **Father's Day** and **New Year's Eve music** in every style imaginable: easy listening, rock, pop, blues, jazz, country, reggae, rap, children's secular or religious. *Please do not send anything that isn't a holiday song.* Published "It Must Have Been the Mistletoe" (single by Justin Wilde/Doug Konecky) from *Christmas Memories* (album), recorded by Barbra Streisand (pop Christmas), by Columbia; "What Made the Baby Cry?" (single by Toby Keith) and "Mr. Santa Claus" (single by James Golseth) from *Casper's Haunted Christmas* soundtrack (album), recorded by Scotty Blevins (Christmas) on Koch International.

Tips "We only sign one out of every 200 submissions. Please be selective. If a stranger can hum your melody back to you after hearing it twice, it has 'standard' potential. Couple that with a lyric filled with unique, inventive imagery, that stands on its own, even without music. Combine the two elements, and workshop the finished result thoroughly to identify weak points. Submit to us only when the song is polished to perfection. Submit positive lyrics only. Avoid negative themes like 'Blue Christmas'."

☑ CHRYSALIS MUSIC GROUP (ASCAP, BMI)

8447 Wilshire Boulevard, Suite 400, Beverly Hills CA 90211. (323)658-9125. Fax: (323)658-8019. E-mail: enquiries@chrysalis.com. Website: chrysalismusicusa.com. **Contact:** Mark Friedman, vice president of A&R. Music publisher. Estab. 1968.

How to Contact *Chrysalis Music does not accept any unsolicited submissions.*

Music Published "Sum 41" (single), written and recorded by OutKast; "Light Ladder" (single), written and recorded by David Gray. Administer, David Lee Roth, Andrea Boccelli, Velvet Revolver, and Johnta Austin.

☑ COME ALIVE COMMUNICATIONS, INC. (ASCAP)

348 Valley Rd., Suite A, P.O. Box 436, West Grove PA 19390-0436. (610)869-3660. Fax: (610)869-3660. E-mail: info@comealivemusic.com. Website: www.comealivemusic.com. Professional Managers: Joseph L. Hooker (pop, rock, jazz); Bridget G. Hylak (spiritual, country, classical). Music publisher, record producer and record company. Estab. 1985. Publishes 4 singles/year. Staff: 7. Pays standard royalty of 50%.

• Come Alive Communications received a IHS Ministries Award in 1996, John Lennon Songwriting Contest winnter, 2003.

How to Contact *Call first to obtain permission to submit a demo.* For song publishing submissions, prefers CD with 3 songs, lyric sheet, and cover letter. Does not return submissions. Responds only if interested.

Music Mostly **pop**, **easy listening**, **contemporary Christian**, and **patriotic**; also **country** and **spiritual**. Does not want obscene, suggestive, violent, or morally offensive lyrics.

Produced "In Search of America" (single) from *Long Road to Freedom* (album), written and recorded by J. Hooker (patriotic), released 2003 on ComeAliveMusic.com; "Our Priests/ Nuestros Sacerdotes," named CMN's official theme song for the Vatican Designated Year of the Priest (2009-10). See www.ourpriests.com.

⊘ COPPERFIELD MUSIC GROUP/PENNY ANNIE MUSIC (BMI)/TOP BRASS MUSIC (ASCAP)/BIDDY BABY MUSIC (SESAC)

1400 South St., Nashville TN 37212. (615)726-3100. E-mail: ken@copperfieldmusic.com. Website: www.copperfieldmusic.com **Contact**: Ken Biddy, president/CEO.

How to Contact Contact first and obtain permission to submit a demo by e-mail only. Does not return submissions or accept phone calls. Responds only if interested.

Music Mostly **country**; also **modern bluegrass**. Does not want rap or heavy/metal/ rock. Recently published "Daddy Won't Sell the Farm" from *Tattoos and Scars* (album), recorded by Montgomery Gentry (country).

◖ CORELLI MUSIC GROUP (BMI/ASCAP)

P.O. Box 2314, Tacoma WA 98401-2314. (253)273-6205. E-mail: JerryCorelli@yahoo.com. Website: www.CorelliMusicGroup.com. **Contact:** Jerry Corelli, owner. Music publisher, record company (Omega III Records), record producer (Jerry Corelli/Angels Dance Recording Studio) and booking agency (Tone Deaf Booking). Estab. 1996. Publishes 12 songs/year; publishes 6 new songwriters/year. Staff size: 3. Pays standard royalty.

Affiliates My Angel's Songs (ASCAP); Corelli's Music Box (BMI).

How to Contact Submit demo by mail. Unsolicited submissions are OK. "No phone calls, e-mails, or letters asking to submit." CD only with no more than 3 songs, lyric sheet and cover letter. *"We DO NOT accept mp3s vie e-mail.* We want love songs with a message and overtly Christian songs. Make sure all material is copyrighted. *You MUST include SASE or we DO NOT respond!"* Responds in 2 months

Music Mostly **contemporary Christian**, **Christian soft rock** and **Christmas**; also **love songs**, **ballads** and **new country**. Does not want songs without lyrics or lyrics without music. Published "I'm Not Dead Yet" (by Jerry Corelli), "Fried Bologna" (by Jerry Corelli), and "His Name is Jesus" (by Jerry Corelli), all from *I'm Not Dead Yet* (album), released 2010 on Omega III Records.

Tips "Success is obtained when opportunity meets preparation! If a SASE is not sent with demo, we don't even listen to the demo. Be willing to do a rewrite. Don't send material expecting us to place it with a Top Ten artist. Be practical. Do your songs say what's always been said, except differently? Don't take rejection personally. Always send a #10 self-adhesive envelope for your SASE."

⊘ THE CORNELIUS COMPANIES/GATEWAY ENTERTAINMENT, INC. (BMI, ASCAP, SESAC)

9 Music Square South, Suite 92, Nashville TN 37203. (615)321-5333. E-mail: corneliuscomps@bellsouth.net. Website: www.gatewayentertainment.com. **Contact:**

Ron Cornelius, owner/president. Music publisher and record producer (Ron Cornelius). Estab. 1986. Publishes 60-80 songs/year; publishes 2-3 new songwriters/year. Occasionally hires staff writers. Pays standard royalty.

Affiliates RobinSparrow Music (BMI), Strummin' Bird Music (ASCAP) and Bridgeway Music (SESAC).

How to Contact *Contact by e-mail or call for permission to submit material.* Submit demo package by mail. Unsolicited submissions are OK. "Send demo on CD format only with 2-3 songs." Include SASE. Responds in 2 months.

Music Mostly **country** and **pop**; also **positive country**, **gospel** and **alternative**. Published songs by Confederate Railroad, Faith Hill, David Allen Coe, Alabama and over 50 radio singles in the positive Christian/country format.

Tips "Looking for material suitable for film."

⊕ CRINGE MUSIC (PRS, MCPS)

The Cedars, Elvington Lane, Folkestone Kent CT18 7AD United Kingdom. (01)(303)893-472. Fax: (01)(303)893-833. E-mail: info@cringemusic.co.uk. Website: www.cringemusic.co.uk. **Contact:** Christopher Ashman. Music publisher and record company (Red Admiral Records). Estab. 1979. Staff size: 2.

How to Contact Submit demo package by mail. Unsolicited submissions are OK. CD only with unlimited number of songs and lyric sheet, lead sheet. Submission materials are not returned. Responds if interested.

Music All styles.

DEFINE SOMETHING IN NOTHING MUSIC (ASCAP)

11213 W. Baden Street, Avondale AZ 85323. (360)421-9225. E-mail: definesinm@gmail.com. **Contact**: Jaime Reynolds, president. Estab. 2008. Music agency. Staff Size: 5. Pays 75% of gross revenue.

How to Contact Prefers MP3s sent to e-mail only. "Please do not contact for permission, just send your music." Does not return submissions. Responds in 2 weeks if interested.

Music Interested in all styles. "We welcome everything all over the world."

Tips "Please e-mail a zip file via yousendit.com. No phone calls or mail, no CDs or cassettes."

⊠ ☑ THE EDWARD DE MILES MUSIC COMPANY (BMI)

10573 W. Pico Blvd., #352, Los Angeles CA 90064-2348. (310)948-9652. Fax: (310)474-7705. E-mail: info@edmsahara.com. Website: www.edmsahara.com. **Contact:** Professional Manager. Music publisher, record company (Sahara Records), record producer, management, bookings and promotions. Estab. 1984. Publishes 50-75 songs/year; publishes 5 new songwriters/year. Hires staff songwriters. Pays standard royalty.

- Also see the listings for Edward De Miles in the Record Producers and Managers & Booking Agents sections, and Sahara Records And Filmworks Entertainment in the Record Companies section of this book.

How to Contact *Write first and obtain permission to submit.* Prefers CD with 1-3 songs and lyric sheet. Does not return material. Reponds in 1 month.

Music Mostly **top 40 pop/rock**, **R&B/dance** and **country**; also **musical scores for TV, radio, films** and **jingles**. Published "Dance Wit Me" and "Moments" (singles), written and recorded by Steve Lynn; "Games" (single), written and recorded by D'von Edwards (jazz), all on Sahara Records. Other artists include Multiple Choice.

Tips "Copyright all materials before submitting. Equipment and showmanship a must."

DISNEY MUSIC PUBLISHING (ASCAP, BMI)

500 S. Buena Vista St., Burbank CA 91521-6182. (818)567-5069. Website: home.disney. go.com/music/. **Contact:** Ashley Saunig, DMP creative department. Affiliate(s) Seven Peaks Music and Seven Summits Music.

• Part of the Buena Vista Music Group.

How to Contact *"We cannot accept any unsolicited material."*

DUNSDON MUSIC PUBLISHING

P.O. Box 635, Montvale NJ 07645. (212)400-7662. Fax: (201)426-2366. E-mail: info@ dunsdonmusic.com. Website: www.dunsdonmusic.com. **Contact**: Ian Dunsdon. Estab. 2006. Published 3 songs in the last year; published 2 new songwriters in the last year. Staff size: 2. Hires staff writers. Pays standard royalty of 50%.

Affiliates Newave Music Publishing (BMI).

How to Contact Contact first and obtain permission to submit a demo. Include CD or e-mail a download link, lyric sheet, and cover letter. Does not return submissions. Responds only if interested.

Film & TV Placed 3 songs in film/year. Recently published "Pennyless," "Already Know by Now," and "Coming Down" by Mark Mullane, recorded by The Misery Loves, in *Jumping Up and Down* (film) (Pragma Records).

Music Mostly **rock/pop, hip hop**, and **dance**; also **country** and **alternative**.

EMI CHRISTIAN MUSIC PUBLISHING (ASCAP, BMI, SESAC)

P.O. Box 5084, Brentwood TN 37024. (615)371-4300. Website: www.EMICMGPublishing. com. Music publisher. Publishes more than 100 songs/year. Represents more than 35,000 songs and over 300 writers. Hires staff songwriters. Pays standard royalty.

Affiliates Birdwing Music (ASCAP), Sparrow Song (BMI), His Eye Music (SESAC), Ariose Music (ASCAP), Straightway Music (ASCAP), Shepherd's Fold Music (BMI), Songs of Promise (SESAC), Dawn Treader Music (SESAC), Meadowgreen Music Company (ASCAP), River Oaks Music Company (BMI), Stonebrook Music Company (SESAC), Bud John Songs, Inc. (ASCAP), Bud John Music, Inc. (BMI), Bud John Tunes, Inc. (SESAC), WorshipTogether Songs, ThankYou Music, Thirst Moon River.

How to Contact *"We do not accept unsolicited submissions."*

Music Published Chris Tomlin, Toby Mac, David Crowder, Jeremy Camp, Stephen Curtis Chapman, Delirious, Tim Hughes, Matt Redman, Demon Hunter, Underoath, Switchfoot, Third Day, Casting Crowns, and many others.

Tips "Do what you do with passion and excellence and success will follow; just be open to new and potentially more satisfying definitions of what 'success' means."

☑ EMI MUSIC PUBLISHING

75 Ninth Ave., 4th Floor, New York NY 10011. (212)492-1200. Fax: (212)492-1865. Website: www.emimusicpub.com. Music publisher.

How to Contact *EMI does not accept unsolicited material.*

Music Published "All Night Long" (by F. Evans/R. Lawrence/S. Combs), recorded by Faith Evans featuring Puff Daddy on Bad Boy; "You" (by C. Roland/J. Powell), recorded by Jesse Powell on Silas; and "I Was" (by C. Black/P. Vassar), recorded by Neal McCoy on Atlantic.

Tips "Don't bury your songs. Less is more—we will ask for more if we need it. Put your strongest song first."

☑ EMSTONE MUSIC PUBLISHING (BMI)

Box 398, Hallandale FL 33008. (305)936-0412. E-mail: michael@emstonemusic publishing.com. Website: www.emstonemusicpublishing.com. **Contact:** Michael Gary, creative director. President: Mitchell Stone. Vice President: Madeline Stone. Music publisher. Estab. 1997. Pays standard royalty.

How to Contact Submit demo CD by mail with any number of songs. Unsolicited submissions are OK. Does not return material. Responds only if interested. "Also check our sister company at SongwritersBestSong.com."

Music All types. Published *Greetings from Texas* (2009) (album), by Greetings From Texas; "Gonna Recall My Heart" (written by Dan Jury) from *No Tears* (album), recorded by Cole Seaver and Tammie Darlene, released on CountryStock Records; and "I Love What I've Got" (single by Heather and Paul Turner) from *The Best of Talented Kids* (compilation album) recorded by Gypsy; "My Christmas Card to You" (words and music by Madeline and Mitchell Stone); and "Your Turn to Shine" (words and music by Mitchell Stone).

Tips "Keep the materials inside your demo package as simple as possible. Just include a brief cover letter (with your contact information) and lyric sheets. Avoid written explanations of the songs; if your music is great, it'll speak for itself. We only offer publishing contracts to writers whose songs exhibit a spark of genius. Anything less can't compete in the music industry."

FATT CHANTZ MUSIC (BMI)

2535 Winthrope Way, Lawrenceville GA 30044.Estab. 2009. (770)982-7055. Fax: (770)982-1882. E-mail: hitcd@bellsouth.net. Website: www.jeromepromotions.com. Contact: Bill

Jerome, president and CEO. Music Publisher. Estab. 2009. Staff size: 3. Pays standard royalty of 50%.

How to Contact Contact first and obtain permission to submit a demo. Include CD or mp3 and cover letter. Does not return submissions. Responds in 1 week.

Music Top 40, **alt country**. Also **alternative**, crossover **R&B** and **hip-hop**. Does not want rap, gospel, country. Published "She's My Girl," written by Lefkowith/Rogers, recorded by Hifi on Red/Generic (2009).

◻ FIFTH AVENUE MEDIA, LTD. (ASCAP)

8 Alden Rd., East Rockaway NY 11518. (212)691-5630. Fax: (212)861-6001. E-mail: thefirm@thefirm.com. Website: www.thefirm.com. Professional Managers: Bruce E. Colfin(rootsy bluesy rock/reggae, Jam bands, alternative rock/heavy metal); Jeffrey E. Jacobson (hip-hop/R&B/dance). Music publisher and record company (Fifth Avenue Media, Ltd.). Estab. 1995. Publishes 2 songs/year. Staff size: 4. Pays standard royalty.

Music Published "Analog" (single by Paul Byrne) from Paul Byrne & the Bleeders (album), recorded by Paul Byrne (pop rock), released 2001 on Independent.

⊕ ▣ ◻ FIRST TIME MUSIC (PUBLISHING) U.K.

Sovereign House, 12 Trewartha Road, Praa Sands, Penzance, Cornwall TR20 9ST United Kingdom. (01736)762826. Fax: (01736)763328. E-mail: panamus@aol.com. Website: www.digimixrecords.com. **Contact:** Roderick G. Jones, CEO. Music publisher, record company (Digimix Records Ltd www.digimaxrecords.com, Rainy Day Records, Mohock Records, Pure Gold Records). Estab. 1986. Publishes 500-750 songs/year; 20-50 new songwriters/year. Staff size: 6. Hires staff writers. Pays standard royalty; "50-60% to established and up-and-coming writers with the right attitude."

Affiliates Scamp Music Publishing, Panama Music Library, Musik Image Library, Caribbean Music Library, PSI Music Library, ADN Creation Music Library, Promo Sonor International, Eventide Music, Melody First Music Library, Piano Bar Music Library, Corelia Music Library, Panama Music Ltd, Panama Music Productions, Digimix Worldwide Digital Distribution Services.

How to Contact Submit demo package by mail. Unsolicited submissions are OK. Submit on CD only, "of professional quality" with unlimited number of songs/instrumentals and lyric or lead sheets. Responds in 1 month. SAE and IRC required for reply.

Film & TV Places 200 songs in film and TV/year. "Copyrights and phonographic rights of Panama Music Limited and its associated catalogue idents have been used and subsist in many productions broadcasts and adverts produced by major and independent production companies, television, film/video companies, radio broadcasters (not just in the UK, but in various countries world-wide) and by commercial record companies for general release and sale. In the UK & Republic of Ireland they include the BBC networks of national/regional television and radio, ITV network programs and promotions (Channel 4, Border TV, Granada TV, Tyne Tees TV, Scottish TV, Yorkshire TV, HTV, Central TV, Channel TV, LWT, Meridian TV, Grampian TV, GMTV, Ulster TV, Westcountry TV, Channel TV, Carlton

TV, Anglia TV, TV3, RTE (Ireland), Planet TV, Rapido TV, VT4 TV, BBC Worldwide, etc.), independent radio stations, satellite Sky Television (BskyB), Discovery Channel, Learning Channel, National Geographic, Living Channel, Sony, Trouble TV, UK Style Channel, Hon Cyf, CSI, etc., and cable companies, GWR Creative, Premier, Spectrum FM, Local Radio Partnership, Fox, Manx, Swansea Sound, Mercury, 2CRFM, Broadland, BBC Radio Collection, etc. Some credits include copyrights in programs, films/videos, broadcasts, trailers and promotions such as *Desmond's*, *One Foot in the Grave*, *EastEnders*, *Hale* and *Pace*, *Holidays from Hell*, *A Touch of Frost*, *999 International*, and *Get Away*."

Music All styles. Published "I Get Stoned" (hardcore dance), recorded by AudioJunkie & Stylus, released by EMI records (2009) on *Hardcore Nation 2009*; "Long Way to Go" (country/MOR) on *Under Blue Skies*, recorded by Charlie Landsborough, released on Rosette Records (2008); "Mr Wilson" (folk) from *Only the Willows are Weeping*, released on Digimix Records (2009); "Blitz" (progressive rock/goth rock), recorded by Bram Stoker on *Rock Paranoia*, released by Digimix Records and many more.

Tips "Have a professional approach—present well produced demos. First impressions are important and may be the only chance you get. Writers are advised to join the Guild of International Songwriters and Composers in the United Kingdom (www.songwriters-guild.co.uk and www.myspace.com/guildofsongwriters)."

◘ ○ FRESH ENTERTAINMENT

1315 Joseph E. Boone Blvd. NW, Suite 5, Atlanta GA 30314. E-mail: whunter1122@yahoo.com. **Contact:** Willie W. Hunter, managing director. Music publisher and record company. Publishes 5 songs/year. Staff size: 4. Hires staff songwriters. Pays standard royalty.

Affiliates !Hserf Music (ASCAP), Blair Vizzion Music (BMI), Santron Music (BMI), G.I. Joe Muzick Publishing (BMI), and Bing-O Productions.

How to Contact Submit demo package by mail. Unsolicited submissions are OK. Prefers cassette or videocassette with 3 songs and lyric sheet. "Send photo if available." Include SASE. Responds in 6 weeks.

Film & TV Places 1 song in TV/year. Published the theme song for BET's *Comic Vue* (by Charles E. Jones), recorded by Cirocco.

Music Mostly **rap**, **R&B** and **pop/dance**. Published *Ancestral Spirits* (album), written and recorded by Robert Miles (jazz), released 2004 on Sheets of Sound/Fresh Entertainment; *My Life My Hustle* (album), written and recorded by Jamal Smith (rap/hip-hop), released 2004 on Vision Vibe/Fresh Entertainment; "Go Sit Down" (single), by Maceo, released 2005 on Quick Flip/Fresh Entertainment; Bob Miles' *Nubian Woman* 2009; Lissen (R&B/hip hop); "As the World Turns" by Kaz & Kardi (Bing-O Productions).

○ GLAD MUSIC CO.

14340 Torrey Chase, Suite 380, Houston TX 77014. (281)397-7300. Fax: (281)397-6206. E-mail: hwesdaily@gladmusicco.com. Website: www.gladmusicco.com. **Contact:** Wes Daily, A&R Director (country). Music publisher, record company and record producer.

Estab. 1958. Publishes 3 songs/year; publishes 2 new songwriters/year. Staff size: 2. Pays standard royalty.

Affiliates Bud-Don (ASCAP), Rayde (SESAC), and Glad Music (BMI).

How to Contact Submit via CD or mp3 with 3 songs maximum, lyric sheet and cover letter. Lyric sheet should be folded around CD and submitted in a rigid case and secured with rubber band. Does not return material. Responds in 6 weeks. SASE or e-mail address for reply.

Music Mostly **country**. Does not want weak songs. Published **Love Bug** (album by C. Wayne/W. Kemp), recorded by George Strait, released 1995 on MCA; *Walk Through This World With Me* (album), recorded by George Jones; and *Race Is On* (album by D. Rollins), recorded by George Jones, both released 1999 on Asylum.

G MAJOR PUBLISHING

P.O. Box 3331, Fort Smith AR 72913-3331. E-mail: Alex@gmajor.org. Website: www. GMajorPublishing.com. Professional Managers: Alex Hoover. Music publisher. Estab. 1992. Publishes 10 songs/year; publishes 2 new songwriters/year. Staff size: 2. Pays standard royalty.

How to Contact *No unsolicited submissions*. Submit inquiry by mail with SASE. Prefers CD or mp3. Submit up to 3 songs with lyrics. Include SASE. Responds in 4-6 weeks.

Music Mostly **country** and **contemporary Christian**. Published *Set The Captives Free* (album by Chad Little/Jeff Pitzer/Ben Storie), recorded by Sweeter Rain (contemporary Christian), for Cornerstone Television; "Hopes and Dreams" (single by Jerry Glidewell), recorded by Carrie Underwood (country), released on Star Rise; and "Be Still" (single by Chad Little/Dave Romero/Bryan Morse/Jerry Glidewell), recorded CO3 (contemporary Christian), released on Flagship Records.

Tips "We are looking for 'smash hits' to pitch to the Country and Christian markets."

GOODNIGHT KISS MUSIC (BMI, ASCAP)

10153½ Riverside Dr. #239, Toluca Lake CA 91602. (831)479-9993. Website: www. goodnightkiss.com. **Contact:** Janet Fisher, managing director. Music publisher, record company and record producer. Estab. 1986. Publishes 6-8 songs/year; publishes 4-5 new songwriters/year. Pays standard royalty.

• Goodnight Kiss Music specializes in placing music in movies and TV.

Affiliates Scene Stealer Music (ASCAP).

How to Contact "Check our website or subscribe to newsletter (www.goodnightkiss. com) to see what we are looking for and to obtain codes. Packages must have proper submission codes, or they are discarded." Only accepts material that is requested on the website. Does not return material. Responds in 6 months.

Film & TV Places 3-5 songs in film/year. Published "I Do, I Do, Love You" (by Joe David Curtis), recorded by Ricky Kershaw in Road Ends; "Bee Charmer's Charmer" (by Marc Tilson) for the MTV movie *Love Song*; "Right When I Left" (by B. Turner/J. Fisher) in the movie *Knight Club*.

Music All modern styles. Published and produced Addiction: *Highs & Lows* (CD), written and recorded by various artists (all styles), released 2004; *Tall Tales of Osama Bin Laden* (CD), written and recorded by various artists (all styles parody), released 2004; and *Rythm of Honor* (CD), written and recorded by various artists (all styles), slated release 2005, all on Goodnight Kiss Records.

Tips "The absolute best way to keep apprised of the company's needs is to subscribe to the online newsletter. Only specifically requested material is accepted, as listed in the newsletter (what the industry calls us for is what we request from writers). We basically use an SGA contract, and there are never fees to be considered for specific projects or albums. However, we are a real music company, and the competition is just as fierce as with the majors."

❐ L.J. GOOD PUBLISHING (ASCAP)

33 Appleway Rd., Okanogan WA 98840. (509)422-1400. Fax: (509)267-8611. E-mail: lonnie@ljgood.com. Website: www.wingsforchrist.com. **Contact:** Lonnie Good, president. Music publisher. Estab. 2006. Publishes 5 songs/year. Publishes 1 new songwriters/year. Staff size: 1. Pays standard royalty of 50%.

Affiliates L.J. Good Publishing (ASCAP).

How to Contact Prefers CD or mp3 with 3 songs and lyric sheet, cover letter. Does not e-mailed mp3s. Does not return submissions.

Music Mostly **country**, **blues**, **soft rock**, **contemporary Christian/Praise and Worship**.

❐ R L HAMMEL ASSOCIATES, INC.

"Consultants to the Music, Recording & Entertainment Industries," P.O. Box 531, Alexandria IN 46001-0531. E-mail: info@rlhammel.com. Website: www.rlhammel. com. **Contact:** A&R Department. President: Randal L. Hammel. Music publisher, record producer and consultant. Estab. 1974. Staff size: 3-5. Pays standard royalty.

Affiliates LADNAR Music (ASCAP) and LEMMAH Music (BMI).

How to Contact Submit demo package and brief bio by mail. Unsolicited submissions are OK. Prefers CD, DAT or VHS/8mm videocassette with a maximum of 3 songs and typed lyric sheets. "Please notate three (3) best songs—no time to listen to a full project." Does not return material. Responds ASAP. "No fixed timeline."

Music Mostly **pop**, **R&B** and **Christian**; also **MOR**, **light rock**, **pop country** and **feature film title cuts**. Produced/arranged *The Wedding Collection Series* for WORD Records. Published *Lessons For Life* (album by Kelly Hubbell/Jim Boedicker) and *I Just Want Jesus* (album by Mark Condon), both recorded by Kelly Connor, released on iMPACT Records.

⊕ 🖼 ⊘ HEUPFERD MUSIKVERLAG GMBH

Ringwaldstr. 18, Dreieich 63303. Germany. E-mail: heupferd@t-online.de. Website: http://www.heupferd-musik.de. **Contact:** Christian Winkelmann, general manager.

Music publisher and record company (Viva La Difference). GEMA. Publishes 30 songs/ year. Staff size: 3. Pays "royalties after GEMA distribution plan."

Affiliates Song Buücherei (book series). "Vive La Difference!" (label).

How to Contact *Does not accept unsolicited submissions.*

Film & TV Places 1 song in film/year. Published "El Grito Y El Silencio" (by Thomas Hickstein), recorded by Tierra in *Frauen sind was Wunderbares* .

Music Mostly **folk**, **jazz** and **fusion**; also **New Age**, **rock** and **ethnic music**. Published "Mi Mundo" (single by Denise M'Baye/Matthias Furstenberg) from *Havana—Vamos A Ver* (album), recorded by Havana (Latin), released 2003 on Vive La Difference. Printed *Andy Irvine: Aiming For the Heart—Irish Song Affairs*, released in 2007.

☐ HOME TOWN HERO'S PUBLISHING (BMI)

112 West Houston, Leonard TX 75452. E-mail: hometownheroes1@verizon.net. Website: www.myspace.com/hometownherospublishing1. **Contact:** Tammy Wood, owner. Music publisher. Estab. 2003. Staff size: 2. Pays standard royalty.

How to Contact Submit demo by mail. Unsolicited submissions are OK. Prefers CD with 3-6 songs, lyric sheet, and cover letter. Does not return submissions. Responds only if interested.

Music Mostly **country (all styles)**, **pop**, **Southern rock**; also **ballads**, **gospel**, and **blues**. Does not want heavy metal and rap.

Tips "Most of all, believe in yourself. The best songs come from the heart. Don't get discouraged, be tough, keep writing, and always think positive. Songwriters, no calls please. I will contact you if interested. Send me your best."

IAMA (INTERNATIONAL ACOUSTIC MUSIC AWARDS)

2881 E. Oakland Park Blvd., Fort Lauderdale FL 33306.(954)537-3127. E-mail: info@ inacoustic.com. Website: www.inacoustic.com.

IDOL PUBLISHING

P.O. Box 720043, Dallas TX 75372.Estab. 1992. (214)321-8890. E-mail: info@idolrecords. com. Website: www.IdolRecords.com. **Contact:** Erv Karwelis, president. Record publisher. Estab. 1992. Releases 30 singles, 80 LPs, 20 EPs and 10-15 CDs/year. Pays negotiable royalty to artists on contract; negotiable rate to publisher per song on record.

How to Contact See website at www.IdolRecords.com for submission policy. No phone calls or e-mail follow-ups.

Music Mostly **rock**, **pop**, and **alternative**; also some **hip-hop**. Released *The Boys Names Sue-The Hits Vol. Sue!* (album), The O's - *We are the Os* (album), Little Black Dress — *Snow in June (album)*, *The Man*, recorded by Sponge (alternative); *Movements* (album), recorded by Black Tie Dynasty (alternative); In Between Days (album), recorded by Glen Reynolds (rock), all released 2006/2006 on Idol Records. Other artists include Flickerstick, DARYL, Centro-matic, The Deathray Davies, GBH, PPT, The Crash that Took Me, Shibboleth, Trey Johnson.

⊞ 🖼 ⊘ INTOXYGENE SARL

283 Fbg St. Antoine, Paris 75011 France. 011(33)1 43485151. Fax: 011(33)1 43485753. Website: www.intoxygene.com or www.intoxygene.net. E-mail: infos@intoxygene.com. **Contact:** Patrick Jammes, managing director. Music publisher and record company. Estab. 1990. Staff size: 1. Publishes 30 songs/year. Pays 50% royalty.

How to Contact *Does not accept unsolicited submissions.*

Film & TV Places 3/5 songs in film and in TV/year.

Music Mostly **new industrial** and **metal**, **lounge**, **electronic**, and **ambient**. Publisher for Peepingtom (trip-hop), Djaimin (house), Missa Furiosa by Thierry Zaboitzeff (progressive), The Young Gods (alternative), Alex Carter, Love Motel, Steve Tallis, and lo'n, amongst others.

▢ IVORY PEN ENTERTAINMENT (ASCAP)

P.O. Box 1097, Laurel MD 20725. Fax: (240)786-6744. E-mail: ivorypen@comcast.net. Professional Managers: Steven Lewis (R&B, pop/rock, inspirational); Sonya Lewis (AC, dance) Wandaliz Colon (Latin, Ethnic); Cornelius Roundtree (gospel/inspirational). Music publisher. Estab. 2003. Publishes 10 songs/year. Staff size: 4. Pays standard royalty.

How to Contact E-mail electronic press kit or mp3 no less than 128k. Unsolicited submissions are OK. Prefers CD with 3-5 songs and cover letter. Does not return material. Responds in 4 months. "Don't forget contact info with e-mail address for faster response! Always be professional when you submit your work to any company. Quality counts."

Music Mostly **R&B**, **dance**, **pop/rock**, **Latin**, **adult contemporary**, and **inspirational**. Published Ryan Vetter (single), writer recorded by Alan Johnson (/pop/rock), released on Ivory Pen Entertainment; and "Mirror" (single), by Angel Demone, on Vox Angel Inc./Ivory Pen Entertainment.

Tips "Learn your craft. Always deliver high quality demos. 'Remember, if you don't invest in yourself, don't expect others to invest in you. Ivory Pen Entertainment is a music publishing company that caters to the new songwriter, producer, and aspiring artist. We also place music tracks (no vocals) with artists for release."

▢ JANA JAE MUSIC

P.O. Box 35726, Tulsa OK 74153. (918)786-8896. Fax: (918)786-8897. E-mail: janajae@janajae.com. Website: www.janajae.com. **Contact:** Kathleen Pixley, secretary. Music publisher, record company (Lark Record Productions, Inc.) and record producer (Lark Talent and Advertising). Estab. 1980. Publishes 5-10 songs/year; publishes 1-2 new songwriters/year. Staff size: 8. Pays standard royalty.

How to Contact Submit demo by mail. Unsolicited submissions are OK. Prefers CD or DVD with 3-4 songs and typed lyric and lead sheet if possible. Does not return material. Responds only if accepted for use.

Music Mostly **country**, **bluegrass**, **jazz** and **instrumentals** (**classical** or **country**). Published *Mayonnaise* (album by Steve Upfold), recorded by Jana Jae; and *Let the Bible Be Your Roadmap* (album by Irene Elliot), recorded by Jana Jae, both on Lark Records.

◻ KAYSARAH MUSIC (ASCAP, BMI)

P.O. Box 1264, 6020 W. Pottstown Rd., Peoria IL 61654-1264. (309)673-5755. Fax: (309)673-7636. E-mail: jerryhanlon33@yahoo.com. Website: www.unitedcyber.com and www.myspace.com/jerryhanlon. **Contact:** Jerry Hanlon, owner/producer. Music Publisher, record company (UAR Records), and record producer. Estab. 2000. Publishes 2 new songwriters/year. Staff size: 3. Pays standard royalty.

- lso see the listing for Jerjoy Music in this section and UAR Records in the Record Companies section of this book.

Affiliates Jerjoy Music (BMI); Abilite Music (BMI).

How to Contact *Write first and obtain permission to submit.* "WE DO NOT RESPOND TO TELEPHONE CALLS. Unsolicited submissions are OK, but be sure to send SASE and/or postage or mailing materials if you want a reply and/or a return of all your material. WE DO NOT OFFER CRITIQUES OF YOUR WORK UNLESS SPECIFICALLY ASKED." Prefers CD with 4 songs and lyric sheet and cover letter. Include SASE. Responds in 2 weeks.

Music Mostly **traditional country** and **country gospel**; also **Irish country**, **Irish ballads** and **Irish folk/traditional**.

Tips "Be honest and self-critical of your work. Make every word in a song count. Attempt to create work that is not over 2:50 minutes in length. Compare your work to the songs that seem to be what you hear on radio. A good A&R person or professional recording artist with a creative mind can determine the potential value of a song simply by hearing a melody line (guitar or keyboard) and the lyrics. DON'T convince yourself that your work is outstanding if you feel that it will not be able to compete with the tough competition of today 's market."

◻ LITA MUSIC (ASCAP)

2831 Dogwood Place, Nashville TN 37204. (615)269-8682. Fax: (615)269-8929. Website: www.songsfortheplanet.com. **Contact:** Justin Peters, president. Music publisher. Estab. 1980.

Affiliates Justin Peters Music, Platinum Planet Music and Tourmaline (BMI).

How to Contact Submit demo package by mail. Unsolicited submissions are OK. Prefers CD with 5 songs and lyric sheet. Does not return material. "Place code '2011' on each envelope submission."

Music Mostly **country**, **classic rock**, **Southern rock**, **inspirational AC Pop**, **Southern gospel/Christian,** and **worship songs**. Published "The Bottom Line" recorded by Charley Pride on Music City Records (written by Art Craig, Drew Bourke, and Justin Peters); "No Less Than Faithful" (single by Don Pardoe/Joel Lyndsey), recorded by Ann Downing on Daywind Records, Jim Bullard on Genesis Records and Melody Beizer (#1 song) on Covenant Records; "No Other Like You" (single by Mark Comden/Paula Carpenter), recorded by Twila Paris and Tony Melendez (#5 song) on Starsong Records; "Making A New Start" and "Invincible Faith" (singles by Gayle Cox), recorded by Kingdom Heirs on Sonlite Records; "I Don't Want To Go Back" (single by Gayle Cox), recorded by Greater

Vision on Benson Records; and "HE HAD MERCY ON ME" (by Constance and Justin Peters) recorded by Shining Grace.

⬭ M & T WALDOCH PUBLISHING, INC. (BMI)

4803 S. Seventh St., Milwaukee WI 53221. (414)482-2194. VP, Creative Management (rockabilly, pop, country): Timothy J. Waldoch. Professional Manager (country, top 40): Mark T. Waldoch. Music publisher. Estab. 1990. Publishes 2-3 songs/year; publishes 2-3 new songwriters/year. Staff size: 2. Pays standard royalty.

How to Contact Submit demo package by mail. Unsolicited submissions are OK. Prefers CD with 3-6 songs and lyric or lead sheet. "We will also accept a studio produced demo tape." Include SASE. Responds in 3 months.

Music Mostly **country/pop**, **rock**, **top 40 pop**; also **melodic metal**, **dance**, **R&B**. Does not want rap. Published "It's Only Me" and "Let Peace Rule the World" (by Kenny LePrix), recorded by Brigade on SBD Records (rock).

Tips "Study the classic pop songs from the 1950s through the present time. There is a reason why good songs stand the test of time. Today's hits will be tomorrow's classics. Send your best well-crafted, polished song material."

⬭ MAUI ARTS & MUSIC ASSOCIATION/SURVIVOR RECORDS/TEN OF DIAMONDS MUSIC (BMI)

PMB 208, P.O. Box 79-1540, Paia HI 96779. (808)874-5900. E-mail: mamamaui@mac. com. Website: www.dreammaui.com. Professional Manager: Greta Warren (pop). Director: Jason Schwartz. Music publisher and record producer. Estab. 1974. Publishes 1-2 artists/year. Staff size: 2. Pays standard royalty.

How to Contact *Prefers that submitters send a sound file submission via e-mail, maximum of 5 minutes in length.*

Music Mostly **pop**, **country**, **R&B**, and **New Age**. Does not want rock. Published "In the Morning Light" (by Jack Warren), recorded by Jason (pop ballad); "Before the Rain" (by Giles Feldscher), recorded by Jason (pop ballad), both on Survivor; and "Then I Do" (single), written and recorded by Lono, released on Ono Music.

Tips "Looking for a great single only!"

⬭ MCCLURE & TROWBRIDGE PUBLISHING, LTD (ASCAP, BMI)

P.O. Box 148548, Nashville TN 37214. (615)902-0509. Website: www.TrowbridgePlanetEarth. com. Contact: Miig Miniger, director of marketing. Music publisher, and record label (JIP Records) and production company (George McClure, producer). Estab. 1983. Publishes 35 songs/year. Publishes 5 new songwriters/year. Staff size: 8. Pays standard royalty of 50%.

How to Contact *Follow directions ONLINE ONLY—obtain Control Number to submit a demo via US Mail.* Requires CD with 1-5 songs, lyric sheet, and cover letter. Does not return submissions. Responds in 3 weeks if interested.

Music Pop, **country**, **gospel**, **Latin** and **swing**. Publisher of Band of Writers (BOW) series. Published "Experience (Should Have Taught Me)" album 2010 on JIP Records; "The Lights Of Christmas" album; "Playboy Swing," released 2008 on JIP Records; "Miles Away" (single) on Discovery Channel's "The Deadliest Catch"; and "I'm A Wild One" (single), recorded by Veronica Leigh, released 2006 on Artist Choice CD.

☐ JIM MCCOY MUSIC (BMI)

25 Troubadour Lane, Berkeley Springs WV 25411. (304)258-9381 or (304)258-8314. E-mail: mccoytroubadour@aol.com. Website: www.troubadourlounge.com. **Contact:** Bertha and Jim McCoy, owners. Music publisher, record company (Winchester Records) and record producer (Jim McCoy Productions). Estab. 1973. Publishes 20 songs/year; publishes 3-5 new songwriters/year. Pays standard royalty.

Affiliates New Edition Music (BMI).

How to Contact Submit demo by mail with lyric sheet. Unsolicited submissions are OK. Prefers cassette or CD with 6 songs. Include SASE. Responds in 1 month.

Music Mostly **country**, **country/rock** and **rock**; also **bluegrass** and **gospel**. Published *Jim McCoy and Friends Remember Ernest Tubb*; "She's the Best" recorded by Matt Hahn on Troubadour Records (written by Jim McCoy); "Shadows on My Mind" recorded by Sandy Utley (written by Jim McCoy), "Rock and Roll Hillbilly Redneck Girl" recorded by Elaine Arthur (written by Jim McCoy), released in 2007.

▨ ☑ MIDI TRACK PUBLISHING (BMI)

P.O. Box 1545, Smithtown NY 11787. (718)767-8995. E-mail: info@allrsmusic.com. Website: www.allrsmusic.com. **Contact:** Renee Silvestri-Bushey, president. F.John Silvestri, founder; Leslie Migliorelli, director of operations. Music publisher, record company (MIDI Track Records), music consultant, artist management, record producer. Voting member of NARAS/National Academy of Recording Arts and Sciences (The Grammy Awards), voting member of the Country Music Association (CMA Awards); SGMA/Southern Gospel Music Association, SGA/Songwriters Guild of America (Diamond Member). Estab. 1994. Staff size: 6. Publishes 3 songs/year; publishes 2 new songwriters/year. Pays standard royalty. Affiliate(s) ALLRS Music Publishing Co. (ASCAP).

How to Contact "Write or e-mail first to obtain permission to submit. We do not accept unsolicited submissions." Prefers CD with 3 songs, lyric sheet and cover letter. Does not return material. Responds in 6 months only if interested.

Film & TV Places 1 song in film/year. Published "Why Can't You Hear My Prayer" (single by F. John Silvestri/Leslie Silvestri), recorded by Iliana Medina in a documentary by Silvermine Films.

Music Mostly **country**, **gospel**, **top 40**, **R&B**, **MOR** and **pop**. Does not want showtunes, jazz, classical or rap. Published "Why Can't You Hear My Prayer" (single by F. John Silvestri/Leslie Silvestri), recorded by eight-time Grammy nominee Huey Dunbar of the group DLG (Dark Latin Groove), released on MIDI Track Records (including other multiple releases); "Chasing Rainbows" (single by F. John Silvestri/Leslie Silvestri/Darin

Kelly), recorded by Tommy Cash (country), released on MMT Records (including other multiple releases); "Because of You" (single by F. John Silvestri/Leslie Silvestri), recorded by Iliana Medina, released 2002 on MIDI Track Records (including other multiple releases also recorded by Grammy nominee Terri Williams, of Always, Patsy Cline, Grand Ole Opry member Ernie Ashworth), released on KMA Records and including other multiple releases; "My Coney Island" (single by F. John Silvestri/Leslie Silvestri), recorded by eight-time Grammy nominee Huey Dunbar, released 2005-2009 on MIDI Track Records.

Tips "Attend workshops, seminars, and visit our blog on our website for advise, tips, and info on the music industry."

☑ MUST HAVE MUSIC (ASCAP, BMI)

P.O. Box 361326, Los Angeles CA 90036-1326. (323)932-9524. E-mail: info@ musthavemusic.com. Website: www.musthavemusic.com. **Contact:** Kenneth R. Klar, managing director. Music publisher and music library. Estab. 1990. Pays standard royalty.

Affiliates Must Have More Music (ASCAP); Must Have Music (BMI).

How to Contact Submit demo by mail with a personal e-mail address included for directors response. Unsolicited submissions are OK. Prefers CD with lyric sheet and cover letter. Does not return submissions. Responds in 2 months.

Film & TV Music supervisor: Ken Klar, managing director.

Music Mostly **pop/R&B**, **pop/country** and **rock**; also **AAA**, **adult contemporary**, and **contemporary Christian/gospel**. Does not want instrumental music. "We only work with completed songs with lyric and vocal."

Tips "Write what you know and what you believe. Then re-write it!"

⊕ ◻ NERVOUS PUBLISHING

5 Sussex Crescent, Northolt, Middlesex UB5 4DL United Kingdom. +44(020) 8423 7373. Fax: +44(020) 8423 7773. E-mail: info@nervous.co.uk. Website: www.nervous.co.uk. **Contact:** Roy Williams, owner. Music publisher, record company (Nervous Records) and record producer. MCPS, PRS and Phonographic Performance Ltd. Estab. 1979. Publishes 100 songs/year; publishes 25 new songwriters/year. Pays standard royalty; royalties paid directly to US songwriters.

- Nervous Publishing's record label, Nervous Records, is listed in the Record Companies section.

How to Contact Submit demo by mail. Unsolicited submissions are OK. Prefers CD with 3-10 songs and lyric sheet. "Include letter giving your age and mentioning any previously published material." SAE and IRC. Responds in 3 weeks.

Music Mostly **psychobilly, rockabilly** and **rock** (impossibly fast music—e.g.: Stray Cats but twice as fast); also **blues, country, R&B** and **rock** ('50s style). Published *Trouble* (album), recorded by Dido Bonneville (rockabilly); *Rockabilly Comp* (album), recorded by various artists; and *Nervous Singles Collection* (album), recorded by various artists, all on Nervous Records.

Tips "Submit *no* rap, soul, funk—we want *rockabilly.*"

☑ NEWBRAUGH BROTHERS MUSIC (ASCAP, BMI)

228 Morgan Lane, Berkeley Springs WV 25411-3475. (304)261-0228. E-mail: Nbtoys@verizon.net. **Contact:** John S. Newbraugh, owner. Music publisher, record company (NBT Records, BMI/ASCAP). Estab. 1967. Publishes 124 songs/year. Publishes 14 new songwriters/year. Staff size: 1. Pays standard royalty.

Affiliates NBT Music (ASCAP) and Newbraugh Brothers Music (BMI).

How to Contact Submit demo by mail. Unsolicited submissions are OK. Prefers cassette or CD with any amount of songs, a lyric sheet and a cover letter. Include SASE. Responds in 6 weeks. "Please don't call for permission to submit. Your materials are welcomed."

Music Mostly **rockabilly**, **hillbilly**, **folk** and **bluegrass**; also **rock**, **country**, and **gospel**. "We will accept all genres of music except songs with vulgar language." Published Released *"Ride the Train Series Vol. 25; Layin' It On the Line* by Night Drive (2009); "Love Notes" The Sisters Two; "The Country Cowboy" by Jack Long; "Original Praise Songs" by Russ and Donna Miller.

Tips "Find out if a publisher/record company has any special interest. NBT, for instance, is always hunting 'original' train songs. Our 'registered' trademark is a train and from time to time we release a compilation album of all train songs. We welcome all genres of music for this project."

☑ A NEW RAP JAM PUBLISHING (BMI)

P.O. Box 683, Lima OH 45802. E-mail: just_chilling_2002@yahoo.com. Professional Managers: William Roach (rap, clean); James Milligan (country, 70s music, pop). **Contact:** A&R Dept. Music publisher and record company (New Experience/Faze 4 Records, Pump It Up Records, and Rough Edge Records). Estab. 1989. Publishes 40 songs/year; Grind Blocc Rec Touch Tone Recording publishes 2-3 new songwriters/year. Hires staff songwriters. Staff size: 6. Pays standard royalty.

Affiliates Party House Publishing (BMI), Creative Star Management, and Rough Edge Records. Distribution through NER/The Orchard/Interscope Digital, and other distribution services.

How to Contact *Write first to arrange personal interview or submit demo CD by mail.* Unsolicited submissions are OK. Prefers CD with 3-5 songs and lyric or lead sheet. Include SASE. Responds in 6-8 weeks. "Visit www.NewExperienceRecords.com for more information."

Music Mostly **R&B**, **pop**, **blues** and **rock/rap** (clean); also **contemporary**, **gospel**, **country** and **soul**. Published "Lets Go Dancing" (single by Dion Mikel), recorded and released 2006 on Faze 4 Records/New Experience Records; "The Broken Hearted" (single) from The Final Chapter (album), recorded by T.M.C. the milligan connection (R&B/gospel); James Jr.: Girl Like You feat. Terry Zapp Troutman, additional appearances by Kurtis Blow, King MC, Sugarfoot Lead Singer (Ohio Players) Level Jackson 2009/10 on

New Experience/Pump It Up Records. Other artists include singer-songwriter James, Jr. on Faze 4 Records/Rough Edge Records/Moiko Rec Grind Blocc Rec.

Tips "We are seeking hit artists 70s, 80s, and 90s who would like to be signed, as well as new talent and female solo artists. Send any available information supporting the group or act. We are a label that does not promote violence, drugs or anything that we feel is a bad example for our youth. Establish music industry contacts, write and keep writing and most of all believe in yourself. Use a good recording studio but be very professional. Just take your time and produce the best music possible. Sometimes you only get one chance. Make sure you place your best song on your demo first. This will increase your chances greatly. If you're the owner of your own small label and have a finished product, please send it. And if there is interest we will contact you. Also be on the lookout for new artists on Rough Edge Records. now reviewing material. Please be aware of the new sampling laws and laws for digital downloading. It is against the law. People are being jailed and fined for this act. Do your homework. Read the new digital downloading contracts carefully or seek legal help if need be. Good luck and thanks for considering our company for your musical needs."

N ● ☻ PEGASUS MUSIC

1 Derwent Street, Oamaru 9400, Otago, New Zealand. E-mail: peg.music@xtra.co.nz. Website: www.pegasusmusic.biz. Professional Managers: Errol Peters (country, rock); Ginny Peters (gospel, pop). Music publisher and record company. Estab. 1981. Publishes 20-30 songs/year; publishes 5 new songwriters/year. Pays standard royalty.

How to Contact Submit demo package by mail. Unsolicited submissions are OK. Prefers CD with 3-5 songs and lyric sheet. SAE and IRC. Responds in 1 month.

Music Mostly **country**; also **bluegrass**, **easy listening** and **top 40/pop**. Published "Beyond the Reason," written and recorded by Ginny Peters (Pegasus Records); "I Only See You," written by Ginny Peters, recorded by Dennis Marsh (Rajon Records, New Zealand); "The Mystery of God," written and recorded by Ginny Peters (NCM Records, England).

Tips "Get to the meat of the subject without too many words. Less is better."

☻ PERLA MUSIC (ASCAP)

134 Parker Av., Easton PA 18042-1361. (212)957-9509. Fax: (917)338-7596. E-mail: PM@PMRecords.Org. Website: www.PMRecords.org. **Contact:** Gene Perla (jazz). Music publisher, record company (PMRecords.org), record producer (Perla.org), studio production (TheSystemMSP.com) and Internet Design (CCINYC.com). Estab. 1971. Publishes 5 songs/year. Staff size: 5. Pays 75%/25% royalty.

How to Contact *E-mail first and obtain permission to submit.*

Music Mostly **jazz** and **rock**.

☐ JUSTIN PETERS MUSIC (BMI)

P.O. Box 40251, Nashville TN 37204. (615)269-8682. Fax: (615)269-8929. Website: www. songsfortheplanet.com. **Contact:** Justin Peters, president. Music publisher. Estab. 1981.

Affiliates Platinum Planet Music(BMI), Tourmaline (BMI) and LITA Music (ASCAP).

How to Contact Submit demo package by mail. Unsolicited submissions are OK. Prefers CD with 5 songs and lyric sheet. Does not return material. "Place code '2010' on each envelope submission."

Music Mostly **pop**, **reggae**, **country** and **comedy**. Published "Saved By Love" (single), recorded by Amy Grant on A&M Records; "From the Center of my Heart," by Shey Baby on JAM Records; "A Gift That She Don't Want" (single), recorded by Bill Engvall on Warner Brother Records; "The Bottom Line," recorded by Charley Pride on Music City Records, cowritten by Justin Peters; "Heaven's Got to Help Me Shake These Blues" (single), written by Vickie Shaub and Justin Peters, recorded by B.J. Thomas; "Virginia Dreams" and "Closer to You" (Jimmy Fortune/Justin Peters), recorded by Jimmy Fortune.

◪ PIANO PRESS (ASCAP)

P.O. Box 85, Del Mar CA 92014-0085. (619)884-1401. Fax: (858)755-1104. E-mail: pianopress@pianopress.com. Website: www.pianopress.com. **Contact:** Elizabeth C. Axford, M.A., owner. Music publisher and distributor. Publishes songbooks & CD's for music students and teachers. Estab. 1998. Licenses 32-100 songs/year; publishes 1-24 new songwriters/year. Staff size: 5. Pays standard print music and/or mechanical royalty; songwriter retains rights to songs.

How to Contact *E-mail first to obtain permission to submit.* Prefers CD with 1-3 songs, lyric and lead sheet, cover letter and sheet music/piano arrangements. "Looking for children's songs for young piano students and arrangements of public domain folk songs of any nationality." Currently accepting submissions for various projects. Include SASE. Responds in 2-3 months.

Music Mostly **children's songs**, **folk songs** and **holiday songs**; also **teaching pieces**, **piano arrangements**, **lead sheets with melody, chords and lyrics** and **songbooks**. Published *My Halloween Fun Songbook* and CD and *My Christmas Fun Songbook* series, *The Holiday Fun* series, *The Pieces for Piano* series, *The Piano Composers* series, and *The Kidtunes* series.

Tips "Songs should be simple, melodic and memorable. Lyrics should be for a juvenile audience and well-crafted."

▢ PLATINUM PLANET MUSIC, INC. (BMI)

2831 Dogwood Place, Nashville TN 37204. (615)269-8682. Fax: (615)269-8929. Website: www.songsfortheplanet.com. **Contact:** Justin Peters, president. Music publisher. Estab. 1997.

Affiliates Justin Peters Music (BMI), Tourmaline (BMI) and LITA Music (ASCAP).

How to Contact Submit demo package by mail. Unsolicited submissions are OK. Prefers CD with 5 songs and lyric sheet. Does not return material. "Place code '2011' on each envelope submission."

Music Mostly **R&B**, **reggae**, **sports themes**, **dance** and **country**; also represents many **Christian** artists/writers. Published "Happy Face" (single by Dez Dickerson/Jordan

Dickerson), recorded by Squirt on Absolute Records; "Buena Vida" (Daron Glenn and Justin Peters), recorded by Daron Glenn on PPMI; "Love's Not A Game" (single), written by Art Craig and J. Peters and recorded by Kashief Lindo on Heavybeat Records; "Place Called Heaven" written by Armond Morales and Kevin Wicker and released by the Imperials, "Love Won't Let Me Leave" (Art Craig and Justin Peters), recorded by Jason Rogers on Independent; and "Loud" (single), written and recorded by These Five Down on Absolute Records.

☑ POLLYBYRD PUBLICATIONS LIMITED (ASCAP, BMI, SESAC)

P.O. Box 261488, Encino CA 91426. (818)506-8533. Fax: (818)506-8534. E-mail: pplzmi@ aol.com. Website: www.pplzmi.com. Branch office: 468 N. Camden Drive Suite 200, Beverly Hills CA 90210. **Contact:** Dakota Hawk, vice president. Professional Managers: Cisco Blue (country, pop, rock); Tedford Steele (hip-hop, R&B). Music publisher, record company (PPL Entertainment) and Management firm (Sa'mall Management). Estab. 1979. Publishes 100 songs/year; publishes 25-40 new songwriters/year. Hires staff writers. Pays standard royalty.

Affiliates Kellijai Music (ASCAP), Pollyann Music (ASCAP), Ja'Nikki Songs (BMI), Velma Songs International (BMI), Lonnvanness Songs (SESAC), PPL Music (ASCAP), Zettitalia Music, Butternut Music (BMI), Zett Two Music (ASCAP), Plus Publishing and Zett One Songs (BMI).

How to Contact *Write first and obtain permission to submit.* No phone calls. Prefers CD, cassette, or videocassette with 4 songs and lyric and lead sheet. Include SASE. Responds in 2 months.

Music Published "Return of the Players" (album) by Juz-Cuz 2004 on PPL; "Believe" (single by J. Jarrett/S. Cuseo) from *Time* (album), recorded by Lejenz (pop), released 2001 on PRL/Credence; *Rainbow Gypsy Child* (album), written and recorded by Riki Hendrix (rock), released 2001 on PRL/Sony; and "What's Up With That" (single by Brandon James/Patrick Bouvier) from *Outcast* (album), recorded by Condottieré; (hip-hop), released 2001 on Bouvier.

Tips "Make those decisions—are you really a songwriter? Are you prepared to starve for your craft? Do you believe in delayed gratification? Are you commercial or do you write only for yourself? Can you take rejection? Do you want to be the best? If so, contact us—if not, keep your day job."

☑ ◌ QUARK, INC.

P.O. Box 452, Newtown, CT 06470. (917)687-9988. E-mail: quarkent@aol.com. **Contact:** Curtis Urbina, manager. Music publisher, record company (Quark Records) and record producer (Curtis Urbina). Estab. 1984. Publishes 12 songs/year; 2 new songwriters/year. Staff size: 4. Pays standard royalty.

Affiliates Quarkette Music (BMI), Freedurb Music (ASCAP), and Quark Records.

How to Contact Prefers CD only with 2 songs. No cassettes. Include SASE. Responds in 2 months.

Film & TV Places 10 songs in film/year. Music Supervisor: Curtis Urbina.
Music Pop. Does not want anything short of a hit.

◪ ◪ ◻ RANCO MUSIC PUBLISHING

(formerly Lilly Music Publishing) 61 Euphrasia Dr., Toronto ON M6B 3V8 Canada. (416)782-5768. Fax: (416)782-7170. E-mail: panfilo@sympatico.ca. **Contact:** Panfilo Di Matteo, president. Music publisher and record company (P. & N. Records). Estab. 1992. Publishes 20 songs/year; publishes 8 new songwriters/year. Staff size: 3. Pays standard royalty.
Affiliates San Martino Music Publishing and Paglieta Music Publishing (CMRRA).
How to Contact Submit demo by mail. Unsolicited submissions are OK. Prefers CD (or videocassette if available) with 3 songs and lyric and lead sheets. "We will contact you only if we are interested in the material." Responds in 1 month.
Film & TV Places 12 songs in film/year.
Music Mostly **dance**, **ballads** and **rock**; also **country**. Published "I'd Give It All" (single by Glenna J. Sparkes), recorded by Suzanne Michelle (country crossover), released 2005 on Lilly Records.

☑ ◻ RED SUNDOWN MUSIC (BMI)

1920 Errel Dowlen Rd., Pleasant View TN 37146. (615)746-0844. E-mail: rsdr@bellsouth. net. **Contact:** Ruby Perry.
How to Contact *Does not accept unsolicited submissions.* Submit CD and cover letter. Does not return submissions.
Music Country, **rock**, and **pop**. Does not want rap or hip-hop. Published "Take A Heart" (single by Kyle Pierce) from *Take Me With You* (album), recorded by Tammy Lee (country) released in 1998 on Red Sundown Records.

◻ SABTECA MUSIC CO. (ASCAP)

P.O. Box 10286, Oakland CA 94610. (510)465-2805. Fax: (510)832-0464. Professional Managers: Sean Herring (pop, R&B, jazz); Lois Shayne (pop, R&B, soul, country). **Contact:** Duane Herring, president. Music publisher and record company (Sabteca Record Co., Andre Romare). Estab. 1980. Publishes 8-10 songs/year; 1-2 new songwriters/year. Pays standard royalty.
Affiliates Toyiabe Publishing (BMI).
How to Contact *Write first and obtain permission to submit.* Prefers cassette with 2 songs and lyric sheet. Include SASE. Responds in 1 month.
Music Mostly **R&B**, **pop** and **country**. Published "Walking My Baby Home" (single by Reggie Walker) from *Reggie Walker* (album), recorded by Reggie Walker (pop), 2002 on Andre Romare Records/Sabteca; "Treat Me Like a Dog" (single by Duane Herring/ Thomas Roller), recorded by John Butterworth (pop), released 2004 Sabteca Music Co; "Sleeping Beauty", recorded by C Haynace, released 2008, Sabteca Music Co.
Tips "Listen to music daily, if possible. Keep improving writing skills."

☐ SANDALPHON MUSIC PUBLISHING (BMI)

P.O. Box 542407, Grand Prairie TX 75054. (972)333-0876. E-mail: rotey01@gmail.com. **Contact:** Ruth Otey, president. Music publisher, record company (Sandalphon Records), and management agency (Sandalphon Management). Estab. 2005. Staff size: 2. Pays standard royalty of 50%.

How to Contact Submit demo by mail. Unsolicited submissions are fine. Prefers CD with 1-5 songs, lyric sheet, and cover letter. Include SASE or SAE and IRC for outside United States. Responds in 6-8 weeks.

Music Mostly **rock**, **country**, and **alternative**; also **pop**, **blues**, and **gospel**.

⊕ ☐ SINUS MUSIK PRODUKTION, ULLI WEIGEL

Geitnerweg 30a, D-12209, Berlin Germany. +49-30-7159050. Fax: +49-30-71590522. E-mail: ulli.weigel@arcor.de. Website: www.ulli-weigel.de. **Contact:** Ulli Weigel, owner. Music publisher, record producer and screenwriter. Wrote German lyrics for more than 500 records. Member: GEMA, GVL. Estab. 1976. Publishes 20 songs/year; publishes 6 new songwriters/year. Staff size: 3. Pays standard royalty.

Affiliates Sinus Musikverlag H.U. Weigel GmbH.

How to Contact Submit demo package by mail. Prefers CD or cassette with up to 10 songs and lyric sheets. If you want to send mp3 attachments, you should contact me before. Attachments from unknown senders will not be opened. Responds in 2 months by email. "If material should be returned, please send 2 International Reply Coupons (IRC) for cassettes and 3 for a CD. No stamps."

Music Mostly **rock**, **pop** and **New Age**; also **background music for movies and audio books**. Published "Simple Story" (single), recorded by MAANAM on RCA (Polish rock); *Die Musik Maschine* (album by Klaus Lage), recorded by CWN Productions on Hansa Records (pop/German), "Villa Woodstock" (film music/comedy) Gebrueder Blattschuss, Juergen Von Der Lippe, Hans Werner Olm (2005).

Tips "Take more time working on the melody than on the instrumentation. I am also looking for master-quality recordings for non-exclusive release on my label (and to use them as soundtracks for multimedia projects, TV and movie scripts I am working on)."

☐ SME PUBLISHING GROUP (ASCAP, BMI)

P.O. Box 1150, Tuttle OK 73089. (405)381-3754. Fax: (405)381-3754. E-mail: smemusic@juno.com. Website: www.smepublishinggroup.com. Professional Managers: Cliff Shelder (southern gospel); Sharon Kinard (country gospel). Music publisher. Estab. 1994. Publishes 6 songs/year; publishes 2 new songwriters/year. Staff size: 2. Pays standard royalty.

Affiliates Touch of Heaven Music (ASCAP) and SME Music (BMI).

How to Contact Submit demo package by mail. Unsolicited submissions are OK. Prefers CD with 3 songs and lyric sheet. Make sure tapes and CDs are labeled and include song title, writer's name, e-mail address, and phone number. Do not send SASE. Does not return or critique material. Responds only if interested.

Music Mostly **Southern gospel**, **country gospel** and **Christian country**. Does not want Christian rap, rock and roll, and hard-core country. Released "I Love You Son" (single), by Jeff Hinton and Quint Randle, from *My Oasis* (album), recorded by the Crist Family (Southern gospel) on Crossroads Records; "Look Who's in the Ship" (Single by Mike Spanhanks) from *How I Picture Me* (album), recorded by the Skyline Boys (Southern Gospel) on Journey Records; "My Oasis" from *My Oasis* (album), recorded by the Crist Family (Southern gospel) on Crossroads Records.

Tips "Always submit good quality demos. Never give up."

⊘ SONY/ATV MUSIC PUBLISHING (ASCAP, BMI, SESAC)

8 Music Square W., Nashville TN 37203. (615)726-8300. Fax: (615)242-3441. E-mail: info@sonyatv.com. Website: www.sonyatv.com. **Santa Monica**: 10635 Santa Monica Blvd., Suite 300, Los Angeles CA 90025. (310)441-1300. **New York**: 550 Madison Ave., 5th Floor, New York NY 10022. (212)833-7730.

How to Contact *Sony/ATV Music does not accept unsolicited submissions.*

⊡ ◻ THISTLE HILL (BMI)

P.O. Box 707, Hermitage TN 37076. (615)889-7105. E-mail: billyherzig@hotmail.com. **Contact:** Arden Miller.

How to Contact Submit demo by mail. Unsolicited submissions OK. Prefers CD with 3-10 songs. *No* lyric sheets. Responds only if interested.

Music Country, **pop**, and **rock**; also **songs for film/TV**. Published "Angry Heart " (single) from *See What You Wanna See* (album), recorded by Radney Foster (Americana); and "I Wanna be Free" (single) from *I Wanna be Free* (album), recorded by Jordon MyCoskie (Americana), released 2003 on Ah! Records; "Que Vamos Hacer" (single) from *Rachel Rodriguez* (album), recorded by Rachel Rodriguez.

⊘ TOURMALINE MUSIC, INC. (BMI)

2831 Dogwood Place, Nashville TN 37204. (615)269-8682. Fax: (615)269-8929. Website: www.songsfortheplanet.com. **Contact:** Justin Peters, president. Music publisher. Estab. 1980.

Affiliates Justin Peters Music (BMI), LITA Music (ASCAP) and Platinum Planet Music (BMI).

How to Contact Submit demo package by mail. Unsolicited submissions are OK. Prefers CD with 5 songs and lyric sheet. Does not return material. "Place code '2011' on each envelope submissions."

Music Mostly **rock and roll**, **classy alternative**, **adult contemporary**, **classic rock**, **country**, **Spanish gospel**, and some **Christmas music**. Published "Making War In The Heavenlies," written by George Searcy, recorded by Ron Kenoly (Integrity); "The Hurt is Worth The Chance," by Justin Peters/Billy Simon, recorded by Gary Chapman on RCA/BMG Records, and "The Bottom Line," by Art Craig, Drew Bourke, and Justin Peters, recorded by Charley Pride (Music City Records).

⊕ ⬚ ⊘ TRANSAMERIKA MUSIKVERLAG KG

Wilhelmstrasse 10, Bad Schwartau 23611 Germany. (00) (49) 4512 1530. E-mail: transamerika@online.de. Website: www.TRANSAMERIKAmusik.de. General Manager: Pia Kaminsky. License Dept: Cubus Medienverlag GMGH. **Hamburg**: Knauerstr 1, 20249 Hamburg, Germany.Phone: 0049-40-46 06 3394. License Manager: Kirsten Jung. Member: GEMA, KODA, NCB. Music publisher and administrator. Estab. 1978. Staff size: 3. Pays 50% royalty if releasing a record; 85% if only administrating.

Affiliates Administrative agreements with: German Fried Music, Rock and Roll Stew Music, Cas Music Edition, MCI Music Publishing (UK), Native Tongue Music Pty. (Australia and New Zealand), Sinless Music (USA), Sinpays Publishing (USA), Pacific Electric Music Publishing (USA), Evolution Music Partners (USA), Justin Faye (composer), and Don Crouse (composer) (USA).

How to Contact "We accept only released materials—no demos!" Submit CD or MP3. Does not return material. Responds only if interested.

Film & TV administration.

Music Mostly **pop**; also **rock**, **country**, **reggae**, and especially **film music**.

Tips "We are specializing in administering (filing, registering, licensing and finding unclaimed royalties, and dealing with counter-claims) publishers worldwide."

⬚ TRANSITION MUSIC CORPORATION (ASCAP, BMI, SESAC)

P.O. Box 2586, Toluca Lake CA 91610. (323)860-7074. Fax: (323)860-7986. E-mail: onestopmus@aol.com. Website: www.transitionmusic.com. Creative Director: Todd Johnson. Chief Administrator: Mike Dobson. Music publisher. Estab. 1998. Publishes 250 songs/year; publishes 50 new songwriters/year. Variable royalty based on song placement and writer.

Affiliates Pushy Publishing (ASCAP), Creative Entertainment Music (BMI) and One Stop Shop Music (SESAC).

How to Contact Address submissions to: New Submissions Dept. Unsolicited submissions are accepted. Prefers CD with no more than 3 songs per. **Responses will not be given due to the high volume of submissions daily. Please do not call/email to inquire about us receiving your submission. TMC will only Contact who they intend on signing.**

Film & TV "TMC provides music for all forms of visual media. Mainly Television." Music-all styles.

Tips "Supply master quality material with great songs."

⊘ TRIO PRODUCTIONS, INC/SONGSCAPE MUSIC, LLC

1026 15th Ave. S., Nashville TN 37212. (615)726-5810. E-mail: info@trioproductions.com. Website: www.trioproductions.com. **Contact:** Robyn Taylor-Drake.

Affiliates ASCAP, BMI, SESAC, Harry Fox Agency, CMA, WMBA, IPA

How to Contact Contact first by e-mail to obtain permission to submit demo. *Unsolicited material will not be listened to or returned.* Submit CD with 3-4 songs and lyric sheet. Submit via mp3 once permission to send has been received. Include a lyric sheet.

Music Country, pop, and **Americana**.

UNIVERSAL MUSIC PUBLISHING (ASCAP, BMI, SESAC)

2220 Colorado Av., Santa Monica CA 90404. (310)235-4700. **New York**: 1755 Broadway, 3rd Floor, New York NY 10019. (212)841-8000. **Tennessee**: 1904 Adelicia St., Nashville TN 37212. (615)340-5400. Website: www.umusicpub.com or www.synchexpress.com.

- In 1999, MCA Music Publishing and PolyGram Music Publishing merged into Universal Music Publishing.

How to Contact *Does not accept unsolicited submissions.*

VAAM MUSIC GROUP (BMI)

P.O. Box 29550, Hollywood CA 90029-0550. E-mail: pmarti3636@aol.com. Website: www.VaamMusic.com. **Contact**: Pete Martin, president. Music publisher and record producer (Pete Martin/Vaam Productions). Estab. 1967. Publishes 9-24 new songs/year. Pays standard royalty.

- Also see the listings for Blue Gem Records in the Record Companies section of this book and Pete Martin/Vaam Music Productions in the record Producers section of this book.

Affiliates Pete Martin Music (ASCAP).

How to Contact Send CD with 2 songs and lyric sheet. Include SASE. Responds in 1 month. "Small packages only."

Music Mostly **top 40/pop**, **country**, and **R&B**. "Submitted material must have potential of reaching top 5 on charts."

Tips "Study the top 10 charts in the style you write. Stay current and up-to-date with today's market."

WARNER/CHAPPELL MUSIC, INC.

10585 Santa Monica Blvd., Third Floor, Los Angeles CA 90025. (310)441-8600. Fax: (310)441-8780. **New York**: 1290 Avenue of the Americas, 23rd floor, New York NY 10104. (212)707-2600. Fax: (212)405-5428. **Nashville**: 20 Music Square E., Nashville TN 37203. (615)733-1880. Fax: (615)733-1885. Website: www.warnerchappell.com. Music publisher.

How to Contact *Warner/Chappell does not accept unsolicited material.*

WILCOM PUBLISHING (ASCAP)

B248 Deano Rd, Branson MO 65616. (4170)559-5256. Fax: (870)847-1721. E-mail: william@wilcompublishing.com. **Contact**: William Clark, owner. Music publisher. Estab. 1989. Publishes 10-15 songs/year; publishes 1-2 new songwriters/year. Staff size: 2. Pays standard royalty.

How to Contact *Write or call first and obtain permission to submit.* Prefers CD with 1-2 songs and lyric sheet. Include SASE. Responds in 3 weeks.

Music Mostly **R&B**, **pop** and **rock**; also **country**. Does not want rap. Published "Girl Can't Help It" (single by W. Clark/D. Walsh/P. Oland), recorded by Stage 1 on Rockit Records (top 40). Also produced a cover of "D'yer M'aker" by Mylo Bigsby on MGL Records.

☑ YOUR BEST SONGS PUBLISHING (ASCAP)

1402 Auburn Way N, Suite 396, Auburn WA 98002. (877)672-2520. **Contact:** John Markovich, general manager. Music publisher. Estab. 1988. Publishes 1-5 songs/year; publishes 1-3 new songwriters/year. Query for royalty terms.

How to Contact *Write first and obtain permission to submit.* Prefers CD with 1-3 songs and lyric sheet. "Submit your 1-3 best songs per type of music. Use separate CDs per music type and indicate music type on each CD." Include SASE. Responds in 3 months.

Music Mostly **country**, **rock/blues**, and **pop/rock**; also **progressive**, **A/C**, some **heavy metal** and **New Age**.

Tips "We just require good lyrics, good melodies and good rhythm in a song. We absolutely do not want music without a decent melodic structure. We do not want lyrics with foul language or lyrics that do not inspire some form of imaginative thought."

A

Ariana Records 136

Atlan-Dec/Grooveline Records 137

Avita Records 137

B

Blue Gem Records 138

Blues Alley Records 172

C

Cambria Records & Publishing 138

Celt Musical Services, Jan 173

Chattahoochee Records 139

Cherry Street Records 139

Collector Records 140

Cosmotone Records 140

D

DaVinci's Notebook Records 174

F

Final Mix Inc. 176

Fresh Entertainment 144

H

Hailing Frequency Music Productions 176

Hardison International Entertainment Corporation 194

Heart Consort Music 176

Heart Music, Inc. 145

Hottrax Records 146

K

Kuper Personal Management/Recovery Recordings 195

L

L.A. Entertainment, Inc. 177

M

O

On

P

Panama Music Group of Companies, The 152

R

Ranco Records 154

RAVE Records, Inc. 154

Riohcat Music 200

Robbins Entertainment LLC 156

Roll On Records 157

S

Sahara Records and Filmworks Entertainment 158

T

Tangent® Records 160

Tas Music Co./Dave Tasse Entertainment 204

U

UAR Records 163

W

Warner Productions, Cheryl K. 205

Winterland Entertainment Management & Publishing 206

Music Publishers

Record companies release and distribute records, cassettes and CDs—the tangible products of the music industry. They sign artists to recording contracts, decide what songs those artists will record, and determine which songs to release. They are also responsible for providing recording facilities, securing producers and musicians, and overseeing the manufacture, distribution and promotion of new releases.

MAJOR LABELS & INDEPENDENT LABELS

Major labels and independent labels—what's the difference between the two?

The majors

As of this writing, there are four major record labels, commonly referred to as the "Big 4":

- **The EMI Group** (Capitol Music Group, Angel Music Group, Astralwerks, Chrysalis Records, etc.)
- **Sony BMG** (Columbia Records, Epic Records, RCA Records, Arista Records, J Records, Provident Label Group, etc.)
- **Universal Music Group** (Universal Records, Interscope/Geffen/A&M, Island/Def Jam, Dreamworks Records, MCA Nashville Records, Verve Music Group, etc.)
- **Warner Music Group** (Atlantic Records, Bad Boy, Asylum Records, Warner Bros. Records, Maverick Records, Sub Pop, etc.)

Each of the "Big 4" is a large publicly-traded corporation beholden to shareholders and quarterly profit expectations. This means the major labels have greater financial resources and promotional muscle than a smaller "indie" label, but it's also harder to get signed to a major. A big major label may also expect more contractual control over an artist or band's sound and image.

As shown in the above list, they also each act as umbrella organizations for numerous other well-known labels—former major labels in their own right, well-respected former independent/boutique labels, as well as subsidiary "vanity" labels fronted by successful major label recording artists. Each major label also has its own related worldwide product distribution system, and many independent labels will contract with the majors for distribution into stores.

The Case for Independents

Tip

If you're interested in getting a major label deal, it makes sense to look to independent record labels to get your start. Independent labels are seen by many as a stepping stone to a major recording contract. Very few artists are signed to a major label at the start of their careers; usually, they've had a few independent releases that helped build their reputation in the industry. Major labels watch independent labels closely to locate up-and-coming bands and new trends. In the current economic atmosphere at major labels—with extremely high overhead costs for developing new bands and the fact that only 10% of acts on major labels actually make any profit—they're not willing to risk everything on an unknown act. Most major labels won't even consider signing a new act that hasn't had some indie success.

But independents aren't just farming grounds for future major label acts; many bands have long term relationships with indies, and prefer it that way. While they may not be able to provide the extensive distribution and promotion that a major label can (though there are exceptions), indie labels can help an artist become a regional success, and may even help the performer to see a profit as well. With the lower overhead and smaller production costs an independent label operates on, it's much easier to "succeed" on an indie label than on a major.

If a label is distributed by one of these major companies, you can be assured any release coming out on that label has a large distribution network behind it. It will most likely be sent to most major retail stores in the United States.

The independents

Independent labels go through smaller distribution companies to distribute their product. They usually don't have the ability to deliver records in massive quantities as the major distributors do. However, that doesn't mean independent labels aren't able to have hit records just like their major counterparts. A record label's distributors are found in the listings after the **Distributed by** heading.

Which do I submit to?

Many of the companies listed in this section are independent labels. They are usually the most receptive to receiving material from new artists. Major labels spend more money than most other segments of the music industry; the music publisher, for instance, pays only for items such as salaries and the costs of making demos. Record companies, at great financial risk, pay for many more services, including production, manufacturing and promotion. Therefore, they must be very selective when signing new talent. Also, the continuing fear of copyright infringement suits has closed avenues to getting new material heard by the majors. Most don't listen to unsolicited submissions, period. Only songs recommended by attorneys, managers and producers who record company employees trust and respect are being heard by A&R people at major labels (companies with a referral policy have a ⊘ preceding their listing). But that doesn't mean all major labels are closed to new artists. With a combination of a strong local following, success on an independent label (or strong sales of an independently produced and released album) and the right connections, you could conceivably get an attentive audience at a major label.

But the competition is fierce at the majors, so you shouldn't overlook independent labels. Since they're located all over the country, indie labels are easier to contact and can be important in building a local base of support for your music (consult the Geographic Index at the back of the book to find out which companies are located near you). Independent labels usually concentrate on a specific type of music, which will help you target those companies your submissions should be sent to. And since the staff at an indie label is smaller, there are fewer channels to go through to get your music heard by the decision makers in the company.

HOW RECORD COMPANIES WORK

Independent record labels can run on a small staff, with only a handful of people running the day-to-day business. Major record labels are more likely to be divided into the following departments: A&R, sales, marketing, promotion, product management, artist development, production, finance, business/legal and international.

- The *A&R department* is staffed with A&R representatives who search out new talent. They go out and see new bands, listen to demo tapes, and decide which artists to sign. They also look for new material for already signed acts, match producers with artists and oversee recording projects. Once an artist is signed by an A&R rep and a record is recorded, the rest of the departments at the company come into play.
- The *sales department* is responsible for getting a record into stores. They make sure record stores and other outlets receive enough copies of a record to meet consumer demand.
- The *marketing department* is in charge of publicity, advertising in magazines and other media, promotional videos, album cover artwork, in-store displays, and any other means of getting the name and image of an artist to the public.
- The *promotion department*'s main objective is to get songs from a new album played on the radio. They work with radio programmers to make sure a product gets airplay.
- The *product management department* is the ringmaster of the sales, marketing and promotion departments, assuring that they're all going in the same direction when promoting a new release.
- The *artist development department* is responsible for taking care of things while an artist is on tour, such as setting up promotional opportunities in cities where an act is performing.
- The *production department* handles the actual manufacturing and pressing of the record and makes sure it gets shipped to distributors in a timely manner.
- People in the *finance department* compute and distribute royalties, as well as keep track of expenses and income at the company.
- The *business/legal department* takes care of contracts, not only between the record company and artists but with foreign distributors, record clubs, etc.

Icons

For More Info

For more instructional information on the listings in this book, including explanations of symbols (N ✔ �‏▽ ☛ ✤ ⊕ ◯ ◌ ◑ ∅), read the article *How To Use Songwriter's Market* on page 1.

• And finally, the *international department* is responsible for working with international companies for the release of records in other countries.

LOCATING A RECORD LABEL

With the abundance of record labels out there, how do you go about finding one that's right for the music you create? First, it helps to know exactly what kind of music a record label releases. Become familiar with the records a company has released, and see if they fit in with what you're doing. Each listing in this section details the type of music a particular record company is interested in releasing. You will want to refer to the Category Index on page 333 to help you find those companies most receptive to the type of music you write. You should only approach companies open to your level of experience (see A Sample Listing Decoded on page 7). Visiting a company's website can also provide valuable information about a company's philosophy, the artists on the label and the music they work with.

Networking

Recommendations by key music industry people are an important part of making contacts with record companies. Songwriters must remember that talent alone does not guarantee success in the music business. You must be recognized through contacts, and the only way to make contacts is through networking. Networking is the process of building an interconnecting web of acquaintances within the music business. The more industry people you meet, the larger your contact base becomes, and the better are your chances of meeting someone with the clout to get your demo into the hands of the right people. If you want to get your music heard by key A&R representatives, networking is imperative.

Networking opportunities can be found anywhere industry people gather. A good place to meet key industry people is at regional and national music conferences and workshops. There are many held all over the country for all types of music (see the Workshops and Conferences section for more information). You should try to attend at least one or two of these events each year; it's a great way to increase the number and quality of your music industry contacts.

Creating a buzz

Another good way to attract A&R people is to make a name for yourself as an artist. By starting your career on a local level and building it from there, you can start to cultivate a following and prove to labels that you can be a success. A&R people figure if an act can be successful locally, there's a good chance they could be successful nationally. Start getting booked at local clubs, and start a mailing list of fans and local media. Once you gain some success on a local level, branch out. All this attention you're slowly gathering, this "buzz" you're generating, will not only get to your fans but to influential people in the music industry as well.

SUBMITTING TO RECORD COMPANIES

When submitting to a record company, major or independent, a professional attitude is imperative. Be specific about what you are submitting and what your goals are. If you are strictly a songwriter and the label carries a band you believe would properly present your song, state that in your cover letter. If you are an artist looking for a contract, showcase your strong points as a performer. Whatever your goals are, follow submission guidelines closely, be as neat as possible and include a top-notch demo. If you need more information concerning a company's requirements, write or call for more details. (For more information on submitting your material, see the article Where Should I Send My Songs? on page 4 and Demo Recordings on page 8.)

RECORD COMPANY CONTRACTS

Once you've found a record company that is interested in your work, the next step is signing a contract. Independent label contracts are usually not as long and complicated as major label ones, but they are still binding, legal contracts. Make sure the terms are in the best interest of both you and the label. Avoid anything in your contract that you feel is too restrictive. It's important to have your contract reviewed by a competent entertainment lawyer. A basic recording contract can run from 40-100 pages, and you need a lawyer to help you understand it. A lawyer will also be essential in helping you negotiate a deal that is in your best interest.

Recording contracts cover many areas, and just a few of the things you will be asked to consider will be: What royalty rate is the record label willing to pay you? What kind of advance are they offering? How many records will the company commit to? Will they offer tour support? Will they provide a budget for video? What sort of a recording budget are they offering? Are they asking you to give up any publishing rights? Are they offering you a publishing advance? These are only a few of the complex issues raised by a recording contract, so it's vital to have an entertainment lawyer at your side as you negotiate.

ADDITIONAL RECORD COMPANIES

There are **more record companies** located in other sections of the book! On page 168 use the list of Additional Record Companies to find listings within other sections who are also record companies.

🌐 4AD

Beggar's Group, 17-19 Alma Road, London UK SW18 1AA. 020 8870 9912. E-mail: 4AD@4AD.com. Website: www.4ad.com.

How to Contact Submit demo (CD or vinyl only) by mail, attention A&R, 4AD. "Sadly, there just aren't enough hours in the day to respond to everything that comes in. We'll only get in touch if we really like something."

Music Mostly rock, indie/alternative. Current artists include Blonde Redhead, Bon Iver, Camera Obscura, The Breeders, The National, TV On The Radio, and more.

◪ ALTERNATIVE TENTACLES

Attn: New Materials, P.O. Box 419092, San Francisco CA 94141. (510)596-8981. Fax: (510)596-8982. E-mail: jello@alternativetentacles.com. Website: www.alternativetentacles.com.

Contact: Jello Biafra. Estab. 1979. Staff size: 4. Releases 15-20 albums/year.

Distributed By Lumberjack/Mordam Records.

How to Contact Unsolicited submissions OK. Prefers CD or cassette. Does not return material. Responds only if interested. " *We accept demos by postal mail ONLY! We do not accept mp3s sent to us.* We will not go out and listen to your mp3s on Web sites. If you are interested in having ATR hear your music, you need to send us a CD, tape or vinyl. We cannot return your demos either, so please don't send us your originals or ask us to send them back. Sometimes Jello replies to people submitting demos; sometimes he doesn't. There is no way for us to check on your 'status', so please don't ask us."

Music Mostly **punk rock**, **spoken word**, **Brazilian hardcore**, **bent pop**, **faux-country**, and **assorted rock & roll**. Released *It's Not the Eat, It's the Humidity* (album), recorded by the Eat (punk); *Fuck World Trade* (album), recorded by Leftover Crack (punk); *Live from the Armed Madhouse* (album), recorded by Greg Palast (spoken word); *Dash Rip Rock* (album), recorded by Hee Haw Hell (southern country punk); *Homem Inimigo Do Homem* (album), recorded by Ratos De Parao (Brazilian hardcore). Other artists include Jello Biafra, The (International) Noise Conspiracy, Subhumans, Butthole Surfers, Dead Kennedys, DOA, Pansy Division, and Melvins.

◪ AMERICAN RECORDINGS

8920 Sunset Blvd., 2nd Floor, W. Hollywood CA 90069. (310)288-5300. Website: www.columbiarecords.com. A&R: Dino Paredes, George Drakoulias, Antony Bland, Brendon Mendoza. Labels include Too Pure, Infinite Zero, UBL, Venture and Onion. Record company. American Recordings is a subsidiary of Sony BMG, one of the "Big 4" major labels.

Distributed By Sony.

How to Contact Submit demo by mail. Unsolicited submissions are OK. Prefers CD, cassette or videocassette with lyric and lead sheet.

Music Released *Unchained*, recorded by Johnny Cash, released on American Recordings. Other artists include Slayer, System of a Down, The Jayhawks, Rahat Feteh Ali Khan, Paloalto, Noise Ratchet, and The (International) Noise Conspiracy.

⊘ ANGEL RECORDS

150 Fifth Ave., 6th Floor, New York NY 10011. (212)786-8600. Website: www.angelrecords. com. Record company. Labels include EMI Classics, Manhattan Records, and Virgin Classics.

- Angel Records is a subsidiary of the EMI Group, one of the "Big 4" major labels. EMI is a British-based company.

Distributed By EMI Music Distribution.

How to Contact *Angel/EMI Records does not accept unsolicited submissions.*

Music Artists include Sarah Brightman, Sir Paul McCartney, and Bernadette Peters.

◓ ARIANA RECORDS

1312 S. Avenida Polar, Tucson AZ 85710. Website: www.arianarecords.net. **Contact:** James M. Gasper, president. Vice President (pop, rock): Tom Dukes. Partners: Tom Privett (funk, experimental, rock); Scott Smith (pop, rock, AOR). Labels include Smart Monkey Records, The MoleHole Studio, Chumway Studios. Record company, music publisher (Myko Music/BMI) and record producer. Estab. 1980. Releases 5 CDs a year and 1 compilation/year. Pays negotiable rates.

Distributed By LoneBoy Records London, The Yellow Record Company in Germany, and Groovetune Music distributors in Alberta, Canada.

How to Contact "Send finished masters only. No demos! Unsolicited material okay."

Music Mostly **rock**, **funk**, **jazz**, **anything weird**, **strange**, or **lo-fi** (must be mastered to CD). Released "Rustling Silk (electronic) by BuddyLoveBand; "PornMuzik 2" (ambient); "T.G.I.F4" (electronica); "UnderCover Band"; "2010" (pop rock and funk); "Catch the Ghost" (hard rock).

Tips "Keep on trying."

◓ ASTRALWERKS

ATTN: A&R Dept. 150 5th Ave, New York NY 10011. E-mail: A&R@astralwerks.net. Website: www.astralwerks.com. **Contact:** A&R. Record company. Estab. 1979. Releases 10-12 12" singles and 100 CDs/year. Pays varying royalty to artists on contract; statutory rate to publisher per song.

- Astralwerks is a subsidiary of the EMI Group, one of the "Big 4" major labels. EMI is a British-based company.

How to Contact Send submissions to: "A&R Dept." to address above. No unsolicited phone calls please. Prefers CD. "Please include any pertinent information, including your group name, track titles, names of members, bio background, successes, and any contact info. Do not send e-mail attachments."

Music Mostly **alternative/indie/electronic**. Artists include VHS or BETA, Badly Drawn boy, The Beta Band, Chemical Brothers, Turin Breaks, and Fatboy Slim.

Tips "We are open to artists of unique quality and enjoy developing artists from the ground up. We listen to all types of 'alternative' music regardless of genre. It's about the aesthetic and artistic quality first. We send out rejection letters so do not call to find out what's happening with your demo."

☐ ATLAN-DEC/GROOVELINE RECORDS

2529 Green Forest Court, Snellville GA 30078-4183. (770)985-1686. Fax: (877)751-5169. E-mail: atlandec@prodigy.net. Website: www.ATLAN-DEC.com. President/Senior A&R Rep: James Hatcher. A&R Rep: Wiletta J. Hatcher. Record company, music publisher and record producer. Estab. 1994. Staff size: 2. Releases 3-4 singles, 3-4 LPs and 3-4 CDs/year. Pays 10-25% royalty to artists on contract; statutory rate to publisher per song on record.

Distributed By C.E.D. Entertainment Dist.

How to Contact Submit demo package by mail. Unsolicited submissions are OK. Prefers CD with lyric sheet. Does not return material. Responds in 3 months.

Music Mostly **R&B/urban**, **hip-hop/rap**, and **contemporary jazz**; also **soft rock**, **gospel**, **dance**, and **new country**. Released "Temptation" by Shawree, released 2004 on Atlan-Dec/Grooveline Records; *Enemy of the State* (album), recorded by Lowlife (rap/hip-hop); *I'm The Definition* (album), recorded by L.S. (rap/hip-hop), released 2007; "AHHW" (single), recorded by LeTebony Simmons (R&B), released 2007. Other artists include Furious D (rap/hip-hop), Mark Cocker (new country), and Looka, "From the Top" (rap/hip-hop) recorded in 2008.

🎵 ⊘ ATLANTIC RECORDS

1290 Avenue of the Americas, New York NY 10104. (212)707-2000. Fax: (212)581-6414. Website: www.atlanticrecords.com. **New York:** 1290 Avenue of the Americas, New York, NY 10104. **Los Angeles:** 3400 W. Olive Ave., 3rd Floor, Burbank CA 91505. (818)238-6800 Fax: (310)205-7411. **Nashville:** 20 Music Square East, Nashville TN 37203. (615)272-7990. Labels include Big Beat Records, LAVA, Nonesuch Records, Atlantic Classics, and Rhino Records. Record company. Pays negotiable royalty to artists on contract; negotiable rate to publisher per song on record.

- Atlantic Records is a subsidiary of Warner Music Group, one of the "Big 4" major labels.

Distributed By WEA.

How to Contact *Does not accept unsolicited material.* "No phone calls please."

Music Artists include Missy Elliott, Simple Plan, Lupe Fiasco, Phil Collins, Gnarls Barkley, and Metallica.

⊘ AVITA RECORDS

P.O. Box 764, Hendersonville TN 37077-0764. (615)824-9313. Fax: (615)824-0797. E-mail: tachoir@bellsouth.net. Website: www.tachoir.com. **Contact:** Robert Kayre, manager. Record company, music publisher (Riohcat Music, BMI) and record producer (Jerry Tachoir). Estab. 1976. Staff size: 8. Releases 2 LPs and 2 CDs/year. Pays negotiable royalty to artists on contract; statutory rate to publisher per song on record.

- Also see the listing for Riohcat Music in the Managers & Booking Agents section of this book.

How to Contact *Contact first and obtain permission to submit.* We only accept material referred to us by a reputable industry source. Prefers CD, cassette, or DAT. Does not return materials. Responds only if interested.

Music Mostly **jazz**. Released *Improvised Thoughts* (album by Marlene Tachoir/Jerry Tachoir/Van Manakas), recorded by Jerry Tachoir and Van Manakas (jazz), released 2001 on Avita Records. Other artists include Van Manakas.

⊘ AWARE RECORDS

624 Davis St., 2nd Floor, Evanston IL 60201. (874)424-2000. E-mail: info@awaremusic. com. Website: www.awaremusic.com. **A&R:** Steve Smith. **President:** Gregg Latterman. Record company. Estab. 1993. Staff size: 6. Releases 5 LPs, 1 EP and 3 CDs/year. Pays negotiable royalty to artists on contract; statutory rate to publisher per song on record.

How to Contact *Does not accept unsolicited submissions.*

Music Mostly **rock/pop**. Artists include Mat Kearney and Guster.

⊘ BLACKHEART RECORDS

636 Broadway, New York NY 10012.(212)353-9600. Fax: (212)353-8300. E-mail: blackheart@blackheart.com. Website: www.blackheart.com. **Contact:** Zander Wolff, a&r. Record label. Estab. 1982.

How to Contact Unsolicited submissions are OK. Prefers CD with 1-3 songs and lyric sheets. Include SASE. Responds only if interested.

Music Mostly **rock**. Artists include Joan Jett & the Blackhearts, The Dollyrots, The Vacancies, Girl In A Coma, and The Eyeliners.

☐ BLUE GEM RECORDS

P.O. Box 29550, Hollywood CA 90029. (323)664-7765. E-mail: pmarti3636@aol.com. Website: www.bluegemrecords.com. **Contact:** Pete Martin. Record company, music publisher (Vaam Music Group) and record producer (Pete Martin/Vaam Productions). Estab. 1981. Pays 6-15% royalty to artists on contract; statutory rate to publisher per song on record.

- Also see the listings for Vaam Music Group in the Music Publishers section of this book and Pete Martin/Vaam Music Productions in the Record Producers section of this book.

How to Contact Submit demo by mail. Unsolicited submissions are OK. Prefers CD or cassette with 2 songs. Include SASE. Responds in 3 weeks.

Music Mostly **country** and **R&B**; also **pop/top 40** and **rock**.

☺ CAMBRIA RECORDS & PUBLISHING

P.O. Box 374, Lomita CA 90717. (310)831-1322. Fax: (310)833-7442. E-mail: cambriamus@ aol.com. Website: cambriamus.com. **Contact:** Lance Bowling, director of recording operations. Labels include Charade Records. Record company and music publisher. Estab. 1979. Staff size: 3. Pays 5-8% royalty to artists on contract; statutory rate to publisher for each record sold.

Distributed By Albany Distribution.

How to Contact *Write first and obtain permission to submit.* Prefers cassette. Include SASE. Responds in 1 month.

Music Mostly *classical*. Released *Songs of Elinor Remick Warren* (album) on Cambria Records. Other artists include Marie Gibson (soprano), Leonard Pennario (piano), Thomas Hampson (voice), Mischa Leftkowitz (violin), Leigh Kaplan (piano), North Wind Quintet, and Sierra Wind Quintet.

✪ CAPITOL RECORDS

1750 N. Vine St., Hollywood CA 90028-5274. (323)462-6252. Fax: (323)469-4542. Website: www.hollywoodandvine.com. Nashville: 3322 West End Ave., 11th Floor, Nashville TN 37203. (615)269-2000. Labels include Blue Note Records, Grand Royal Records, Pangaea Records, The Right Stuff Records and Capitol Nashville Records. Record company.

• Capitol Records is a subsidiary of the EMI Group, one of the "Big 4" major labels.

Distributed By EMD.

How to Contact *Capitol Records does not accept unsolicited submissions.*

Music Artists include Coldplay, The Decemberists, Beastie Boys, Liz Phair, Interpol, Lily Allen, and Auf der Maur.

◻ CHATTAHOOCHEE RECORDS

2544 Roscomare Rd., Los Angeles CA 90077. (818)788-6863. Fax: (310)471-2089. E-mail: cyardum@prodigy.net. **Contact:** Robyn Meyers, Music Director/A&R. Music Director: Chris Yardum. Record company and music publisher (Etnoc/Conte). Member NARAS. Releases 4 singles/year. Pays negotiable royalty to artists on contract.

How to Contact : Submit demo by e-mail. Will respond only if interested.

Music Mostly **rock**. Released *Don't Touch It Let It Drip* (album), recorded by Cream House (hard rock), released 2000 on Chattahoochee Records. Artists include DNA, Noctrnl, and Vator.

✪ CHERRY STREET RECORDS

P.O. Box 52626, Tulsa OK 74152. (918)742-8087. Fax: (918)975-9736. E-mail: ryound@ cherrystreetrecords.com. Website: www.cherrystreetrecords.com. President: Rodney Young. Record company and music publisher. Estab. 1990. Staff size: 1. Releases 1 CD/year. Pays 50% royalty to artists on contract; statutory rate to publisher per song on record.

Distributed By Internet.

How to Contact *Write first and obtain permission to submit.* Prefers CD with 4 songs and lyric sheet. Include SASE. Responds in 4 months.

Music Rock, **country**, and **R&B**; also **jazz**. Released *Promised Land* (album), written and recorded by Richard Neville on Cherry Street (rock). Other artists include George W. Carroll and Chris Blevins.

Tips "We sign only artists who play an instrument, sing, and write songs. Send only your best 4 songs."

⊕ ⃝ COLLECTOR RECORDS

P.O. Box 1200, 3260 AE oud beyerland Holland. (31)186 604266. Fax: (31)186 604366. E-mail: info@collectorrecords.nl. Website: www.collectorrecords.nl. **Contact:** Cees Klop, president. Manager: John Moore. Labels include All Rock, Downsouth, Unknown, Pro Forma and White Label Records. Record company, music publisher (All Rock Music Publishing) and record producer (Cees Klop). Estab. 1967. Staff size: 4. Release 25 LPs/year. Pays 10% royalty to artist on contract.

How to Contact Submit demo package by mail. Unsolicited submissions are OK. Prefers cassette. SAE and IRC. Responds in 2 months.

Music Mostly '50s rock, **rockabilly**, **hillbilly boogie** and **country/rock**; also **piano boogie woogie**. Released *Rock Crazy Baby* (album), by Art Adams (1950s rockabilly), released 2005; *Marvin Jackson* (album), by Marvin Jackson (1950s rockers), released 2005; *Western Australian Snake Pit R&R* (album), recorded by various (1950s rockers), released 2005, all on Collector Records. Other artists include Henk Pepping, Rob Hoeke, Eric-Jan Overbeek, and more. "See our website."

⊘ COLUMBIA RECORDS

555 Madison Ave., 10th Floor, New York NY 10022. (212)833-4000. Fax: (212)833-4389. E-mail: sonymusiconline@sonymusic.com. Website: www.columbiarecords.com. **Santa Monica:** 2100 Colorado Ave., Santa Monica CA 90404. (310)449-2100. Fax: (310)449-2743. **Nashville:** 34 Music Square E., Nashville TN 37203. (615)742-4321. Fax: (615)244-2549. Labels include So So Def Records and Ruffhouse Records. Record company.

• Columbia Records is a subsidiary of Sony BMG, one of the "Big 4" major labels.

Distributed By Sony.

How to Contact *Columbia Records does not accept unsolicited submissions.*

Music Artists include Aerosmith, Marc Anthony, Beyonce, Bob Dylan, and Patti Smith.

⊘ COSMOTONE RECORDS

2951 Marina Bay Dr., Ste. 130, PMB 501, League City TX 77573-2733. E-mail: marianland@earthlink.net. Website: www.cosmotonerecords.com. Record company, music publisher (Cosmotone Music, ASCAP) and record producer (Rafael Brom). Estab. 1984.

Distributed By Marianland.com.

How to Contact "Sorry, we do not accept material at this time." Does not return materials.

Music Mostly **Christian pop/rock**. Released *Rafael Brom I*, *Padre Pio* Lord Hamilton, *Dance for Padre Pio*, *Peace of Heart*, *Music for Peace of Mind*, *The Sounds of Heaven*,

The Christmas Songs, Angelophany, The True Measure of Love, All My Love to You Jesus (albums), and *Rafael Brom Unplugged* (live concert DVD), *Life is Good, Enjoy it While You Can, Change,* by Rafael Brom, *Refugee from Socialism* by Rafael Brom, and *Move Your Ass,* by Rafael Brom.

CURB RECORDS

48 Music Square E., Nashville TN 37203. (615)321-5080. Fax: (615)327-1964. Website: www.curb.com. **Contact:** John Ozler, A&R coordinator. Record company.

How to Contact *Curb Records does not accept unsolicited submissions; accepts previously published material only. Do not submit without permission.*

Music Released *Everywhere* (album), recorded by Tim McGraw; *Sittin' On Top of the World* (album), recorded by LeAnn Rimes; and *I'm Alright* (album), recorded by Jo Dee Messina, all on Curb Records. Other artists include Mary Black, Merle Haggard, Kal Ketchum, David Kersh, Lyle Lovett, Tim McGraw, Wynonna, and Sawyer Brown.

DEEP ELM RECORDS

210 N. Church St. #2502, Charlotte NC 28202-2385. E-mail: info@deepelm.com. Website: www.deepelm.com.

How to Contact Accepts unsolicited submissions. DO NOT e-mail sound files. "We are most interested in receiving completed full-length albums (at least 10 songs) that are available for immediate worldwide release. Send a CD or CDR with the BAND NAME, PHONE and E-MAIL directly written on the face of the CD. If the CD has artwork on it, write the information on a label, white sticker or piece of making tape and affix it to the face of the CD. Send your CD in a jewel case or with a piece of cardboard to protect it from breaking. Forget the fancy folders, bios, reviews and photos...we don't need it. It's only the music that matters. Send your CD by Regular Mail ONLY (absolutley no Express Mail, Fedex, DHL, UPS) to: Deep Elm Records - Music Submission, 210 N. Church Street #2502, Charlotte, NC 28202-2385 USA. If we are interested in your music, WE will be in contact with you. PLEASE do not call, e-mail or contact us. Assume we received your package if it has not been returned to you in the mail, as we cannot track unsolicited packages. Sorry, packages cannot be returned and we do not comment on music that we pass on. More details here: www.deepelm.com/submit."

Music Public Radio, Moving Mountains, Nathan Xander, 500 Miles to Memphis, This Drama, Goonies Never Say Die, Latterman, Desoto Jones, Track A Tiger, The Emo Diaries, The Appleseed Cast.

DEEP SOUTH ENTERTAINMENT

P.O. Box 17737, Raleigh NC 27619-7737. (919)844-1515. Fax: (919)847-5922. E-mail: info@ deepsouthentertainment.com. Website: www.deepsouthentertainment.com. Manager: Amy Cox. Record company and management company. Estab. 1996. Staff size: 10. Pays negotiable royalty to artists on contract; statutory rate to publisher per song on record.

Distributed By Redeye Distribution, Valley, Select-O-Hits, City Hall, AEC/Bassin, Northeast One Stop, Pollstar, and Koch International.

How to Contact Submit demo by mail. Unsolicited submissions are OK. Prefers cassette or CD with 3 songs, cover letter, and press clippings. Does not return material. Responds only if interested.

Music Mostly **pop**, **modern rock**, and **alternative**; also **swing**, **rockabilly**, and **heavy rock**. Does not want rap or R&B. Artists include Bruce Hornsby, Little Feat, Mike Daly, SR-71, Stretch Princess, Darden Smith, and Vienna Teng.

◖ DENTAL RECORDS

P.O. Box 20058, New York NY 10017. E-mail: info@dentalrecords.com. Website: www. dentalrecords.com. **Contact:** Rick Sanford, owner. Record company. Estab. 1981. Staff size: 1. Releases occasional material, primarily digitally. Pays negotiable royalty to artists on contract; statutory rate to publisher per song on record.

How to Contact "Check website to see if your material is appropriate." *Not currently accepting unsolicited submissions.*

Music Pop-derived structures, **jazz-derived harmonies**, and **neo-classic-wannabee-pretenses**. Claims no expertise, nor interest, in urban, heavy metal, or hard core. Released *Perspectivism* (album), written and recorded by Rick Sanford (instrumental), released 2003 on Dental Records. Other artists include Les Izmor.

EARACHE RECORDS

4402 11th St., $507A Long Island City, NY 11101. (718)786-1707. Fax: (718)786-1756. E-mail: usaproduction@earache.com. Website: www.earache.com. Estab. 1993 (US).

Music Rock, **industrial**, **heavy metal techno**, **death metal**, **grindcore**. Artists include Municipal Waste, Dillinger Escape Plan, Bring Me the Horizon, Deicide, Oceano, and more.

◙ ELEKTRA RECORDS

75 Rockefeller Plaza, 17th Floor, New York NY 10019. Website: www.elektra.com. Labels include Elektra Records, Eastwest Records, and Asylum Records. Record company.

- Elektra Records is a subsidiary of Warner Music Group, one of the "Big 4" major labels.

Distributed By WEA.

How to Contact *Elektra does not accept unsolicited submissions.*

Music Mostly alternative/modern rock. Artists include Cee Lo, Justice, Little Boots, and *True Blood.*

◙ EPIC RECORDS

550 Madison Ave., 21st Floor, New York NY 10022. (212)833-8870. Fax: (212)833-4054. Website: www.epicrecords.com. Senior Vice Presidents A&R: Ben Goldman, Rose Noone. **Santa Monica:** 2100 Colorado Ave., Santa Monica CA 90404. (310)449-2100 Fax: (310)449-

2848. A&R: Pete Giberga, Mike Flynn. Labels include Epic Soundtrax, LV Records, Immortal Records, and Word Records. Record company.

• Epic Records is a subsidiary of Sony BMG, one of the "Big 4" major labels.

Distributed By Sony Music Distribution.

How to Contact *Write or call first and obtain permission to submit* (New York office only). Does not return material. Responds only if interested. *Santa Monica and Nashville offices do not accept unsolicited submissions.*

Music Artists include Celine Dion, Macy Gray, Modest Mouse, Fuel, Jennifer Lopez, B2K, Incubus, Ben Folds.

Tips "Do an internship if you don't have experience or work as someone's assistant. Learn the business and work hard while you figure out what your talents are and where you fit in. Once you figure out which area of the record company you're suited for, focus on that, work hard at it and it shall be yours."

N ⊘ EPITAPH RECORDS

2798 Sunset Blvd., Los Angeles CA 90026. (213)355-5000. Website: www.epitaph.com. Contact: Brett Gurewitz, founder. Record company. Contains imprints Hellcat Records and Anti. "Epitaph Records was founded by Bad Religion guitarist Brett Gurewitz with the aim of starting an artist-friendly label from a musicians point of view. Perhaps most well known for being the little indie from L.A. that spawned the 90s punk explosion."

How to Contact "Post your demos on-line at one of the many free music portals, then simply fill out the Demo Submission-form" on website.

Music Artists include Social Distortion, Alkaline Trio, Rancid, The Weakerthans, You Me At Six, Bad Religion, Every Time I Die.

EYEBALL RECORDS

P.O. Box 400, Ridgewood NJ 07451. E-mail: info@eyeballrecords.com. Website: www. eyeballrecords.com. **Contact:** A&R.

How to Contact "Familiarize yourself with the bands we work with." Submit demo by mail. "You don't have to call or e-mail us to follow up."

Music New London Fire, Pompeii, The Blackout Pact, United Nations, Wolftron, and more.

FATT CHANTZ RECORDS

2535 Winthrope Way, Lawrenceville GA 30044. (770)982-7055. Fax: (770)982-1882. E-mail: hitcd@bellsouth.net. Website: www.jeromepromotions.com. **Contact**: Bill Jerome, president and CEO. Estab: 2009. Record company. Staff size: 3. Royalties are negotiable.

How to Contact Contact first and obtain permission to submit a demo. Include CD with 5 songs and cover letter. Does not return submissions. Responds in 1 week.

Music Mostly interested in **top 40**, **adult contemporary, hot AC**; also **R&B, alternative,** and **hip-hop crossover**. Does not want rap, country, gospel, hard rock.

FAT WRECK CHORDS

P.O. Box 193690, San Francisco CA 94119. E-mail: mailbag@fatwreck.com. Website: www.fatwreck.com. Contact: Mike.

How to Contact Accepts demos by mail at: Asian Man Records, ATTN: Mike, P.O. Box 35585, Monte Soreno, CA 95030. Responds via e-mail or through the post "in time."

Music Punk, rock, alternative. Artists include NOFX, Rise Against, The Lawrence Arms, Anti-Flag, Me First and the Gimme Gimmes, Propagandhi, Dillinger Four, Against Me, and more.

FEARLESS RECORDS

13772 Goldenwest St. #545, Westminster CA 92683. E-mail: bridget@fearlessrecords. com. Website: www.fearlessrecords.com.

How to Contact Send all demos to mailing address. "Do not e-mail us about demos or with links to mp3s."

Music Alternative, pop, indie, rock, metal. Artists include Plain White T's, At The Drive-in, The Maine, Mayday Parade, Sugarcult, Every Avenue, Alesana, blessthefall, Breathe Carolina, Artist Vs Poet, and more

☐ FRESH ENTERTAINMENT

1315 Joseph E. Boone Blvd., NW, Suite 5, Atlanta GA 30314. E-mail: whunter1122@yahoo.com. **Contact:** Willie W. Hunter, managing director. Record company and music publisher (Hserf Music/ASCAP, Blair Vizzion Music/BMI). Releases 5 singles and 2 LPs/year. Pays 7-10% royalty to artists on contract; statutory rate to publisher per song on record.

Distributed By Ichiban International and Intersound Records.

How to Contact Submit demo package by mail. Unsolicited submissions are OK. Prefers cassette or VHS videocassette with at least 3 songs and lyric sheet. Include SASE. Responds in 2 months.

Music Mostly **R&B**, **rock** and **pop**; also **jazz**, **gospel** and **rap**. Released in 2008: *Nubian Woman* by Bob Miles (Jazz); Lissen (R&B/hip hop); *You Know I'm From the A* by Joe "Da Bingo" Bing (rap); "As the World Turns" by Kaz & Cardi (rap).

FUELED BY RAMEN

P.O. Box 1803, Tampa FL 33601. Website: www.fueledbyramen.com. Contact: Johnny Minardi.

How to Contact Send demos by mail to address above.

Music Alternative, Rock, Indie. Artists include The Academy Is..., Cobra Starship, Cute Is What We Aim For, Gym Class Heroes, The Hush Sound, Panic At the Disco, Paramore, A Rocket to the Moon, This Providence, and more.

☑ ◻ GONZO! RECORDS INC.

5757 E. Erin Ave., Fresno CA 93727. (559)269-2244. E-mail: SangerParanormal@aol.com. Website: SangerParanormalSociety.com. **Contact:** Jeffrey Gonzalez, president. Record company. Estab. 1993. Staff size: 3. Releases 3 singles and 1-6 CDs/year. Pays negotiable royalty to artists on contract; statutory rate to publisher per song on record.

- Gonzo! Records was awarded Best Indie Label, and Full Frequency was awarded Best Techno/Industrial Band at the 1999 Los Angeles Music Awards.

How to Contact Submit demo package by mail. Unsolicited submissions are OK. Prefers cassette or CD. "When submitting, please specify that you got the listing from Songwriter's Market." Does not return material. Responds in 6 weeks.

Music Mostly **commercial industrial**, **dance** and **techno**; also **commercial alternative** and **synth pop**. Released *Hate Breeds Hate* (album), written and recorded by BOL (hard industrial); *Momentum* (album), written and recorded by Full Frequency (commerical industrial); and *Ruth in Alien Corn* (album), written and recorded by Pinch Point (alternative pop), all on Gonzo! Records. Other artists include Turning Keys.

Tips "If you're going to submit music to me, it must be because you love to write music, not because you want to be a rock star. That will eventually happen with a lot of hard work."

☑ ◻ GOTHAM RECORDS

Attn: A&R, P.O. Box 7185, Santa Monica, CA 90406. E-mail: ar@gothamrecords.com. Website: www.gothamrecords.com. Record company. Estab. 1994. Staff size: 3. Releases 8 LPs and 8 CDs/year. Pays negotiable royalty to artists on contract; statutory rate to publisher per song on record. "Gotham Music Placement is Gotham Records' main focus. Gotham Music Placement places recorded material with motion picture, TV, advertising, and video game companies. GMP supervises full feature films and releases full soundtracks, and represents artists from all over the world and all types of genres."

Distributed By Sony RED.

How to Contact Submit demo by mail "in a padded mailer or similar package." Unsolicited submissions are OK. Prefers CD and bios, pictures, and touring information. Does not return material.

Music All genres. Artists include SLANT, Red Horizon, The Day After..., and The Vicious Martinis.

Tips "Send all submissions in regular packaging. Spend your money on production and basics, not on fancy packaging and gift wrap."

⊘ HEART MUSIC, INC.

P.O. Box 160326, Austin TX 78716-0326. (512)795-2375. E-mail: info@heartmusic.com. Website: www.heartmusic.com. **Contact:** Tab Bartling, president. Record company and music publisher (Coolhot Music). "Studio available for artists." Estab. 1989. Staff size: 2. Releases 1-2 CDs/year. Pays statutory rate to publisher per song on record.

How to Contact *Not interested in new material at this time.* Does not return material. Responds only if interested.

Music Mostly **Folk-rock, pop,** and **jazz**; also **blues** and **contemporary folk**. Libby Kirkpatrick's Heroine in early 2011; released *The Fisherman* (album), recorded by Darin Layne/Jason McKensie; released The Fisherman by Darin Layne; Joe LoCascio Woody Witt Seasons Ago In the City of Lost Things (jazz), recorded by Joe LoCascio, both released in 2007; Collaborations (album), recorded by Will Taylor and Strings Attached , featuring Eliza Gilkyson, Shawn Colvin, Patrice Pike, Ian Moore, Guy Forsyth, Ruthie Foster, Libby Kirkpatrick, Jimmy LaFave, Slaid Cleaves, and Barbara K., released 2006; *Goodnight Venus* (album), recorded by Libby Kirkpatrick, released in 2003, and *Be Cool Be Kind* (album), recorded by Carla Helmbrecht (jazz), released January 2001.

☐ HOTTRAX RECORDS

1957 Kilburn Dr., Atlanta GA 30324. (770)662-6661. E-mail: hotwax@hottrax.com. Website: www.hottrax.com. **Contact:** George Burdell, vice president, A&R. Labels include Dance-A-Thon and Hardkor. Record company and music publisher (Starfox Publishing). Staff size: 6. Releases 8 singles and 3-4 CDs/year. Pays 5-15% royalty to artists on contract. Estab. 1975.

- Also see the listing for Alexander Janoulis Productions/Big Al Jano Productions in the Record Producers section of this book.

Distributed By Get Hip Inc., DWM Music and Super D.

How to Contact *E-mail first to obtain permission to submit.* Prefers an e-link to songs and lyrics in the e-mail. Does not return CDs or printed material. Responds in 6 months. "When submissions get extremely heavy, we do not have the time to respond/return material we pass on. We do notify those sending the most promising work we review, however. Current economic conditions may also affect song acceptance and response."

Music Mostly **blues/blues rock**, some **top 40/pop, rock**, and **country**; also **hardcore punk** and **jazz-fusion**. Released *Power Pop Deluxe* (album), by Secret Lover featuring Delanna Protas, *Some of My Best Friends Have the Blues* (album), by Big Al Jano, *Hot to Trot* (album), written and recorded by Starfoxx (rock); *Lady That Digs The Blues* (album), recorded by Big Al Jano's Blues Mafia Show (blues rock); and *Vol. III, Psychedelic Era. 1967-1969* (album), released 2002 on Hottrax. Other artists include Big Al Jano, Sammy Blue, and Sheffield & Webb. Released in 2010: *So Much Love* (album), by Michael Rozakis & Yorgos; Beyond the Shadows—Then and Now, by Little Phil. Scheduled: *Rare Pidgeon* (CD) by Rick Ware.

ℕ ☑ IDOL RECORDS

P.O. Box 720043, Dallas TX 75372. (214)321-8890. E-mail: info@idolrecords.com. Website: www.IdolRecords.com. **Contact:** Erv Karwelis, president. Record company. Estab. 1992. Releases 30 singles, 80 LPs, 20 EPs and 10-15 CDs/year. Pays negotiable royalty to artists on contract; negotiable rate to publisher per song on record.

Distributed By Super D (SDID).

How to Contact See website at www.IdolRecords.com for submission policy. No phone calls or e-mail follow-ups.

Music Mostly **rock**, **pop**, and **alternative**; also some **hip-hop**. Released *The Boys Names Sue-The Hits Vol. Sue!* (album), The O's - *We are the Os* (album), Little Black Dress — *Snow in June (album)*, *The Man*, recorded by Sponge (alternative); *Movements* (album), recorded by Black Tie Dynasty (alternative); In Between Days (album), recorded by Glen Reynolds (rock), all released 2006/2006 on Idol Records. Other artists include Flickerstick, DARYL, Centro-matic, The Deathray Davies, GBH, PPT, The Crash that Took Me, Shibboleth, Trey Johnson.

⚡ ⊘ INTERSCOPE/GEFFEN/A&M RECORDS

2220 Colorado Ave., Santa Monica CA 90404. (310)865-1000. Fax: (310)865-7908. Website: www.interscoperecords.com. Labels include Death Row Records, Nothing Records, Rock Land, Almo Sounds, Aftermath Records, and Trauma Records. Record company.

- Interscope/Geffen/A&M is a subsidiary of Universal Music Group, one of the "Big 4" major labels.

How to Contact *Does not accept unsolicited submissions.*

Music Released *Worlds Apart*, recorded by... And You Will Know Us By The Trail Of Dead; and *Guero*, recorded by Beck. Other artists include U2, M.I.A, Keane, and Marilyn Manson.

⊘ ISLAND/DEF JAM MUSIC GROUP

825 Eighth Ave., 29th Floor, New York NY 10019. (212)333-8000. Fax: (212)603-7654. Website: www.islanddefjam.com. Los Angeles: 8920 Sunset Blvd, 2nd Floor, Los Angeles CA 90069. (310)276-4500. Fax: (310)242-7023. Executive A&R: Paul Pontius. Labels include Mouth Almighty Records, Worldly/Triloka Records, Blackheart Records, Private Records, Slipdisc Records, Thirsty Ear, Blue Gorilla, Dubbly, Little Dog Records, Rounder, and Capricorn Records. Record company.

- Island/Def Jam is a subsidiary of Universal Music Group, one of the "Big 4" major labels.

How to Contact *Island/Def Jam Music Group does not accept unsolicited submissions. Do not send material unless requested.*

Music Artists include Bon Jovi, Fall Out Boy, Kanye West, Rihanna, The Killers, Jay-Z, and Ludacris.

⊘ J RECORDS

745 Fifth Ave., 6th Floor, New York NY 10151. (646)840-5600. Website: www.jrecords. com. Part of Arista Records.

How to Contact *J Records does not accept unsolicited submissions.*

Music Artists include Faithless, Alicia Keys, and Annie Lennox.

◎ KILL ROCK STARS

1526 NE Alberta St. #231, Portland OR 97211. E-mail: krs@killrockstars.com. Website: www.killrockstars.com. **Contact:** Record company. Estab. 1991. Releases 4 singles, 10 LPs, 4-6 EPs and 35 CDs/year. Pays 50% of net profit to artists on contract; negotiated rate to publisher per song on record.

Distributed By Redeye Distribution.

How to Contact *Does not accept or listen to demos sent by mail.* Will listen to links online only if in a touring band coming through Portland. "If you are not touring through Portland, don't send us anything." Prefers link to Web page or EPK. Does not return material.

Music Mostly **punk rock**, **neo-folk** or **anti-folk** and **spoken word**. Artists include Deerhoof, Xiu Xiu, Mary Timony, The Gossip, Erase Errata, and Two Ton Boa.

Tips "We will only work with touring acts, so let us know if you are playing Olympia, Seattle or Portland. Particularly interested in young artists with indie-rock background."

◎ LARK RECORD PRODUCTIONS, INC.

P.O. Box 35726, Tulsa OK 74153. (918)786-8896. Fax: (918)786-8897. E-mail: janajae@janajae.com. Website: www.janajae.com. **Contact:** Kathleen Pixley, vice president. Record company, music publisher (Jana Jae Music/BMI), management firm (Jana Jae Enterprises) and record producer (Lark Talent and Advertising). Estab. 1980. Staff size: 8. Pays negotiable royalty to artists on contract; statutory rate to publisher per song on record.

How to Contact Submit demo by mail. Unsolicited submissions are OK. Prefers CD or DVD with 3 songs and lead sheets. Does not return material. Responds only if interested.

Music Mostly **country**, **bluegrass**, and **classical**; also **instrumentals**. Released "Fiddlestix" (single by Jana Jae); "Mayonnaise" (single by Steve Upfold); and "Flyin' South" (single by Cindy Walker), all recorded by Jana Jae on Lark Records (country). Other artists include Sydni, Hotwire, and Matt Greif.

◎ MAGNA CARTA RECORDS

A-1 Country Club Rd, East Rochester NY 14445. (585)381-5224. Fax: (585)381-0658. E-mail: magcart@aol.com. Website: www.magnacarta.net. **Contact:** Pete Morticelli. Record label.

How to Contact Contact first and obtain permission to submit. *No unsolicited material.*

Music Mostly **progressive metal**, **progressive rock**, and **progressive jazz**.

◎ MATADOR RECORDS

Beggar's Group, 304 Hudson St., New York NY 10013. (212)995-5882. Fax: (212)995-5883. E-mail: webmaster@matadorrecords.com. Website: www.matadorrecords.com. **UK address:** 17-19 Alma Road, London, SW18 1AA United Kingdom.

How to Contact "We are sorry to say that we *no longer accept unsolicited demo submissions.*"

Music Alternative rock. Artists include Lou Reed, Pavement, Belle and Sebastian, Cat Power, Jay Reatard, Sonic Youth, Yo La Tengo, Mogwai, The New Pornographers, and more.

☑ ⊘ MCA NASHVILLE

(formerly MCA Records), 1904 Adelicia St., Nashville TN 37212. (615)244-8944. Fax: (615)880-7447. Website: www.umgnashville.com Record company and music publisher (MCA Music).

- MCA Nashville is a subsidiary of Universal Music Group, one of the "Big 4" major labels.

How to Contact *MCA Nashville cannot accept unsolicited submissions.*

Music Artists include Tracy Byrd, George Strait, Vince Gill, The Mavericks, and Trisha Yearwood.

☐ MEGAFORCE RECORDS

New York office: P.O. Box 1955, New York NY 10113. (212)741-8861. Fax: (509)757-8602. E-mail: gregaforce@aol.com. Website: www.megaforcerecords.com. **Contact:** Robert John, President. General Manager: Missi Callazzo. Record company. Estab. 1983. Staff size: 5. Releases 6 CDs/year. Pays various royalties to artists on contract; ¾ statutory rate to publisher per song on record.

Distributed By Red/Sony Distribution.

How to Contact *Contact first and obtain permission to submit.* Submissions go to the Philadelphia office.

Music Mostly **rock**. Artists include Truth and Salvage, The Meat Puppets, and The Disco Biscuits.

☑ ⊘ METAL BLADE RECORDS

5737 Kanan Rd #143, Agoura Hills CA 91301. (805)522-9111. Fax: (805)522-9380. E-mail: metalblade@metalblade.com. Website: www.metalblade.com. **Contact:** A&R. Record company. Estab. 1982. Releases 20 LPs, 2 EPs and 20 CDs/year. Pays negotiable royalty to artists on contract.

How to Contact Submit demo through website form. Does not accept physical copies of demos. Unsolicited submissions are OK. Response time varies, but "be patient."

Music Mostly **heavy metal** and **industrial**; also **hardcore**, **gothic** and **noise**. Released "Gallery of Suicide," recorded by Cannibal Corpse; "Voo Doo," recorded by King Diamond; and "A Pleasant Shade of Gray," recorded by Fates Warning, all on Metal Blade Records. Other artists include As I Lay Dying, The Red Chord, The Black Dahlia Murder, and Unearth.

Tips "Metal Blade is known throughout the underground for quality metal-oriented acts."

☐ MODAL MUSIC, INC.

P.O. Box 6473, Evanston IL 60204-6473. Phone/Fax: (847)864-1022. E-mail: info@ modalmusic.com. Website: www.modalmusic.com. President: Terran Doehrer. Assistant: J. Distler. Record company and agent. Estab. 1988. Staff size: 2. Releases 1-2 LPs/year. Pays negotiable royalty to artists on contract; negotiable rate to publisher per song on record.

How to Contact Submit demo package by mail. Unsolicited submissions are OK. Prefers CD with bio, PR, brochures, any info about artist and music. Does not return material. Responds in 4 months.

Music Mostly **ethnic** and **world**. Released "St. James Vet Clinic" (single by T. Doehrer/Z. Doehrer) from *Wolfpak Den Recordings* (album), recorded by Wolfpak, released 2005; "Dance The Night Away" (single by T. Doehrer) from *Dance The Night Away* (album), recorded by Balkan Rhythm Band™; "Sid Beckerman's Rumanian" (single by D. Jacobs) from *Meet Your Neighbor's Folk Music*™ (album), recorded by Jutta & The Hi-Dukes™; and *Hold Whatcha Got* (album), recorded by Razzemetazz™, all on Modal Music Records. Other artists include Ensemble M'chaiya™, Nordland Band™ and Terran's Greek Band™.

Tips "Please note our focus is primarily traditional and traditionally-based ethnic which is a very limited, non-mainstream market niche. You waste your time and money by sending us any other type of music. If you are unsure of your music fitting our focus, please call us before sending anything. Put your name and contact info on every item you send!"

☐ NBT RECORDS

228 Morgan Lane, Berkeley Springs WV 25411-3475. (304)261-0228. E-mail: nbtoys@ verizon.net. **Contact:** John S. Newbraugh, owner. Record company, music publisher (Newbraugh Brothers Music/BMI, NBT Music/ASCAP). Estab. 1967. Staff size: 1. Releases 4 singles and 52 CDs/year. Pays negotiable royalty to artists on contract; statutory royalty to publishers per song on record.

Distributed By "Distribution depends on the genre of the release. Our biggest distributor is perhaps the artists themselves, for the most part, depending on the genre of the release. We do have product in some stores and on the Internet as well."

How to Contact Submit demo package by mail. Unsolicited submissions are OK. Prefers CD or cassette with any amount of songs, lyric sheet and cover letter. Include SASE. Responds in 4-6 weeks. "Please don't call for permission to submit. Your materials are welcomed."

Music Mostly **rockabilly**, **hillbilly**, **folk** and **bluegrass**; also **rock**, **country** and **gospel**. Does not want any music with vulgar lyrics. "We will accept all genres of music except songs that contain vulgar language." Released *Ride the Train Series Vol. 25*; "Love Notes" by The Sisters Two; "The Country Cowboy" by Jack Long; "Original Praise Songs" by Russ and Donna Miller.

Tips "We are best known for our rockabilly releases. Reviews of our records can be found on both the American and European rockabilly websites. Our 'registered' trademark is a train. From time to time, we put out a CD with various artists featuring original songs that use trains as part of their theme. We use all genres of music for our train releases. We have received train songs from various parts of the world. All submissions on this topic are welcomed."

⊕ ◻ NERVOUS RECORDS

5 Sussex Crescent, Northolt, Middlesex UB5 4DL England. 44(20)8423 7373. E-mail: nervous@compuserve.com. Website: www.nervous.co.uk. **Contact:** R. Williams, managing director. Record company (Rage Records), record producer and music publisher (Nervous Publishing and Zorch Music). Member: MCPS, PRS, PPL, ASCAP, NCB. Releases 10 CDs/year. Pays 8-12% royalty to artists on contract; statutory rate to publisher per song on records. Royalties paid directly to US songwriters and artists or through US publishing or recording affiliate.

• Nervous Records' publishing company, Nervous Publishing, is listed in the Music Publishers section.

How to Contact Submit demo tape by mail. Unsolicited submissions are OK. Prefers cassette with 4-15 songs and lyric sheet. SAE and IRC. Responds in 3 weeks.

Music Mostly **psychobilly** and **rockabilly**. "No heavy rock, AOR, stadium rock, disco, soul, pop—only wild rockabilly and psychobilly." Released "Extra Chrome", written and recorded by Johnny Black; "It's Still Rock 'N' Roll to Me", written and recorded by The Time. Other artists include Restless Wild and Taggy Tones.

◻ NORTH STAR MUSIC

338 Compass Circle A1, North Kingstown, RI 02852. (401)886-8888 or (800)346-2706. Fax: (401)886-8880. E-mail: info@northstarmusic.com. Website: www.northstarmusic.com. **Contact:** Richard Waterman, president. Record company. Estab. 1985. Staff size: 15. Releases 12-16 LPs/year. Pays 9% royalty to artists on contract; ¾ statutory rate to publisher per song on record.

Distributed By Goldenrod and in-house distribution.

How to Contact Submit demo CD by mail. Unsolicited submissions are OK. Prefers finished CD. Does not return material. Responds in 2 months.

Music Mostly **instrumental, traditional** and **contemporary jazz**, **New Age**, **traditional world (Cuban, Brasilian, singer/songwriter, Hawaiian and Flamenco)** and **classical**. Released *Sacred* (album), written and recorded by David Tolk (inspirational), released 2003; *An Evening In Tuscany* (album), written and recorded by Bruce Foulke/Howard Kleinfeld (contemporary instrumental), released 2004; *Always & Forever* (album), written and recorded by David Osborne (piano), released 2003, all on North Star Music. Other artists include Judith Lynn Stillman, David Osborne, Emilio Kauderer, Gerry Beaudoin, Cheryl Wheeler and Nathaniel Rosen.

☻ OGLIO RECORDS

P.O. Box 404, Redondo Beach CA 90277. (310)791-8600. Fax: (310)791-8670. E-mail: getinfo4@oglio.com. Website: www.oglio.com. Record company. Estab. 1992. Releases 20 LPs and 20 CDs/year. Pays negotiable royalty to artist on contract; statutory rate to publisher per song on record.

How to Contact *No unsolicited demos.*

Music Mostly **alternative rock** and **comedy**. Released *Shine* (album), recorded by Cyndi Lauper (pop); *Live At The Roxy* (album), recorded by Brian Wilson (rock); *Team Leader* (album), recorded by George Lopez (comedy).

☻ OUTSTANDING RECORDS

P.O. Box 2111, Huntington Beach CA 92647. (714)377-7447 E-mail: beecher@outstandingmusic.com Website: www.outstandingmusic.com. **Contact:** Earl Beecher, owner. Labels include Outstanding, Morrhythm (mainstream/commercial), School Band (educational/charity), Church Choir (religious charity), and Empowerment (educational CDs and DVDs). Record company, music publisher (Earl Beecher Publishing/BMI and Beecher Music Publishing/ASCAP) and record producer (Earl Beecher). Estab. 1968. Staff size: 1. Releases 100 CDs/year. Pays $2/CD royalty to artists on contract; statutory rate to publisher per song on record.

Distributed By All full CDs listed on the website can be ordered directly through the website. Most of them are now available via download through iTunes, Napster, Rhapsody, Amazon/mp3, Emusic, or Yahoo. Whenever wholesale distributors contact me for specific orders, I am happy to work with them, especially distributors overseas.

How to Contact Submit demo by mail. Unsolicited submissions are OK. Prefers CD (full albums), lyric sheet, photo and cover letter. Include SASE. Responds in 3 weeks.

Music Mostly **jazz**, **rock** and **country**; also **everything else especially Latin**. Does not want music with negative, anti-social or immoral messages. "View our website for a listing of all current releases."

Tips "We prefer to receive full CDs, rather than just three numbers. A lot of submitters suggest we release their song in the form of singles, but we just can't bother with singles at the present time. Especially looking for performers who want to release their material on my labels. Some songwriters are pairing up with performers and putting out CDs with a 'Writer Presents the Performer' concept. No dirty language. Do not encourage listeners to use drugs, alcohol or engage in immoral behavior. I'm especially looking for upbeat, happy, danceable music."

⊕ ☻ THE PANAMA MUSIC GROUP OF COMPANIES

(formerly Audio-Visual Media Productions), Sovereign House, 12 Trewartha Rd., Praa Sands, Penzance, Cornwall TR20 9ST England. +44 (0)1736 762826. Fax: +44 (0)1736 763328. E-mail: panamus@aol.com. Website: www.songwriters-guild.co.uk and www.panamamusic.co.uk. **Contact:** Roderick G. Jones, CEO, A&R. Labels include Pure Gold Records, Panama Music Library, Rainy Day Records, Panama Records, Mohock Records,

Digimix Records (www.digimixrecords.com and www.myspace.com/digimixrecords). Registered members of Phonographic Performance Ltd. (PPL). Record company, music publisher, production and development company (Panama Music Library, Melody First Music Library, Eventide Music Library, Musik Image Music Library, Promo Sonor International Music Library, Caribbean Music Library, ADN Creation Music Library, Piano Bar Music Library, Corelia Music Library, PSI Music Library, Scamp Music, First Time Music Publishing U.K.), registered members of the Mechanical Copyright Protection Society (MCPS) and the Performing Right Society (PRS) (London, England UK), management firm and record producer (First Time Management & Production Co.). Estab. 1986. Staff size: 6. Pays variable royalty to artists on contract; statutory rate to publisher per song on record subject to deal.

Distributed By Media U.K. Distributors and Digimix Worldwide Digital Distribution.

How to Contact Submit demo package by mail. Unsolicited submissions are OK. CD only with unlimited number of songs/instrumentals and lyric or lead sheets where necessary. "We do not return material so there is no need to send return postage. We will, due to volume of material received only respond to you if we have any interest. Please note: no MP3 submissions, attachments, downloads, or referrals to Web sites in the first instance via e-mail. Do not send anything by recorded delivery or courier as it will not be signed for. If we are interested, we will follow up for further requests and offers as necessary."

Music All styles. Published by Scamp Music: "F*ck Me I'm Famous" written by Paul Clarke & Matthew Dick (film/DVD & single & album track), released worldwide in *Get Him to the Greek*, starring Russell Brand, recorded by Dougal & Gammer, released as an album track by Gut Records Ltd. and as a single by Essential Platinum Records in 2010. Also published "The River" (soul/R&B), recorded by Leonie Parker, released by Diximax Records, Ltd.; "Wait a Second" (hard dance", recorded by DJ Matt Lee, released by TidyTrax Records; "Break It" (hardcore), recorded by Dougal & Gammer, released by Universal Records/All Around the World; Published by Panama Music Library: "I Get Stoned" (hardcore dance) recorded by AudioJunkie & Stylus, released by EMI records on *Hardcore Nation 2009* and more.

PAPER + PLASTICK

Website: paperandplastick.com. **Contact:** through form on website. Paper + Plastick handles both visual artwork and music.

Music Rock, punk, and more. Artists include: Dopamines, Andrew Dost, Coffee Project, Foundation, Gatorface, Blacklist Royals, Landmines, We are the Union, and more.

☑ PARLIAMENT RECORDS

357 S. Fairfax Avenue #430, Los Angeles CA 90036. (323)653-0693. E-mail: parlirec@ aol.com. Website: www.parliamentrecords.com. **Contact:** Ben Weisman, owner. Record company, record producer (Weisman Production Group) and music publisher (Audio Music Publishers, Queen Esther Music Publishing). Estab. 1965. Produces 30 singles/ year. Fee derived from sales royalty when song or artist is recorded.

- Also see the listings for Audio Music Publishers and Queen Esther Music Publishing in the Music Publishers section and Weisman Production Group in the Record Producer section.

How to Contact Submit demo package by mail. Unsolicited submissions are OK. Prefers CD with 3-10 songs and lyric sheet. Include SASE. "Mention Songwriter's Market. Please make return envelope the same size as the envelopes you send material in, otherwise we cannot send everything back." Responds in 6 weeks.

Music Mostly **R&B**, **soul**, **dance**, and **top 40/pop**; also **gospel** and **blues**. Arists include Rapture 7 (gospel), Wisdom (male gospel singers), Chosen Recovery Ministry (female gospel group), Jewel With Love (gospel), Apostle J. Dancy (gospel), Mirac (rap), The Mighty Voices of Joy (Gospel Group) L'nee (R&B/pop artist).

Tips "Parliament Records will also listen to 'tracks' only. If you send tracks, please include a letter stating what equipment you record on—ADAT, Protools or Roland VS recorders."

☑ QUARK RECORDS

P.O. Box 452, Newtown CT, 06470. (917)687-9988. E-mail: quarkent@aol.com. **Contact:** Curtis Urbina. Record company and music publisher (Quarkette Music/BMI and Freedurb Music/ASCAP). Estab. 1984. Releases 3 singles and 3 LPs/year. Pays negotiable royalty to artists on contract; ¾ statutory rate to publisher per song on record.

How to Contact Prefers CD with 2 songs (max). Include SASE. "Must be an absolute 'hit' song!" Responds in 6 weeks.

Music POP and Dance music only.

☒ ☐ RANCO RECORDS

61 Euphrasia Dr., Toronto ON M6B 3V8 Canada. (416)782-5768. Fax: (416)782-7170. E-mail: panfilo@sympatico.ca. **Contact:** Panfilo Di Matteo, president, A&R. Record company, record producer and music publisher (Lilly Music Publishing). Estab. 1993. Staff size: 2. Releases 10 singles, 20 12" singles, 15 LPs, 20 EPs and 15 CDs/year. Pays 25-35% royalty to artists on contract; statutory rate to publisher per song on record.

How to Contact Submit demo by mail. Unsolicited submissions are OK. Prefers CD or videocassette with 3 songs and lyric or lead sheet. Does not return material. Responds in 1 month only if interested.

Music Mostly **dance**, **ballads** and **rock**. Released *Only This Way* (album), written and recorded by Angelica Castro; *The End of Us* (album), written and recorded by Putz, both on P. & N. Records (dance); and "Lovers" (single by Marc Singer), recorded by Silvana (dance), released 2001 on P. and N. Records.

☑ RAVE RECORDS, INC.

Attn: Production Dept., 13400 W. Seven Mile Rd., Detroit MI 48235. E-mail: info@ raverecords.com. Website: www.raverecords.com. **Contact:** Carolyn and Derrick, production managers. Record company and music publisher (Magic Brain Music/ASCAP).

Estab. 1992. Staff size: 2. Releases 2-4 singles and 2 CDs/year. Pays various royalty to artists on contract; statutory rate to publisher per song on record.

Distributed By Action Music Sales.

How to Contact *"We do not accept unsolicited submissions."* Submit demo package by mail. Prefers CD with 3 songs, lyric sheet. "Include any bios, fact sheets, and press you may have. We will contact you if we need any further information." Does not return materials.

Music Mostly **alternative rock** and **dance**. Artists include Cyber Cryst, Dorothy, Nicole, and Bukimi 3.

⊠ ☑ ⊘ RCA RECORDS

550 Madison Ave, New York NY 10022. (212)930-4936. Fax: (212)930-4447. Website: www.rcarecords.com. A&R: Donna Pearce. Beverly Hills: 8750 Wilshire Blvd., Beverly Hills CA 90211. (310)358-4105 Fax: (310)358-4127. Senior Vice President of A&R: Jeff Blue. Nashville: 1400 18th Ave. S., Nashville TN 37212. A&R Director: Jim Catino. Labels include Loud Records, Deconstruction Records and Judgment/RCA Records. Record company.

- RCA Records is a subsidiary of Sony BMG, one of the "Big 4" major labels.

Distributed By BMG.

How to Contact *RCA Records does not accept unsolicited submissions.*

Music Artists include The Strokes, Dave Matthews Band, Anti-Flag, Christina Aguilera, and Foo Fighters.

⊕ RED ADMIRAL RECORDS LLP

The Cedars, Elvington Lane, Folkestone Kent CT18 7AD United Kingdom. Estab. 1979. (01)(303)893-472. Fax: (01)(303)893-833. E-mail: info@redadmiralrecords.com. Website: www.redadmiralrecords.com. **Contact:** Chris Ashman. Registered members of MCPS, PRS, and PPL. Record company and music publisher (Cringe Music (MCPS/PRS)). Estab. 1979.

How to Contact Submit demo package by mail. Unsolicited submissions are OK. Submit CD only with unlimited number of songs. Submission materials are not returned. Responds if interested.

Music All styles. Artists include Crispian St. Peters, Rik Waller, Wim Hautekiet, Mirkwood, David Hay, The Silent Kingdom, Peter Dinsley, Carmen Wiltshire Hardly Mozart, The Sharpee's.

⊡ REDEMPTION RECORDS

P.O. Box 10238, Beverly Hills CA 90213. E-mail: info@redemption.net. Website: www.redemption.net. A&R Czar: Ryan D. Kuper (indie rock, power pop, rock, etc.). Record company. Estab. 1990. Staff size: varies. Releases 2-3 (various)/year. "We typically engage in profit splits with signed artists."

Distributed By GoDigital (digital); misc. (physical).

How to Contact Submit via e-mail with link to digital tracks. Include accomplishments and goals. Responds only if interested.

Music Mostly **indie rock** and **power pop**. Artists include Race For Titles, Vicious Vicious, Motion City Soundtrack, and The Working Title.

Tips "We only sign acts that will tour in support of their releases. Make sure your line-up is secure."

⊘ REPRISE RECORDS

3300 Warner Blvd., 4th Floor, Burbank CA 91505. (818)846-9090. Fax: (818)840-2389. Website: www.repriserecords.com. Labels include Duck and Sire. Record company.

- Reprise Records is a subsidiary of Warner Music Group, one of the "Big 4" major labels.

Distributed By WEA.

How to Contact *Reprise Records does not accept unsolicited submissions.*

Music Artists include Eric Clapton, My Chemical Romance, The Used, Muse, The Distillers, Talking Heads, The Who, Tom Petty, Green Day, Jane's Addiction, and Neil Young.

RISE RECORDS

917 SW Oak Street Suite 422, Portland OR 97205. E-mail: Matthew@RiseRecords.com. Website: www.riserecords.com.

How to Contact E-mail a link to music, either on Purevolume or MySpace. "Please save your money and don't mail a presskit."

Music Rock, metal, alternative. Artists include Dance Gavin Dance; Drop Dead, Gorgeous; Emarose; Oceana; The Devil Wears Prada; Tides of Man, and more.

ROADRUNNER RECORDS

902 Broadway, 8th Floor, New York NY 10010. (212)274-7500. Fax: (212)505-7469. E-mail: roadrunner@roadrunnerrecords.com. Website: www.roadrunnerrecords.com.

How to Contact Submit demo by e-mail at signmeto@roadrunnerrecords.com. Submissions are currently open.

Music Rock, metal, alternative. Artists include Killswitch Engage, The Wombats, Opeth, Nickelback, Biffy Clyro, Lynyrd Skynyrd, Megadeth, Slipknot, and more.

◖ ROBBINS ENTERTAINMENT LLC

35 Worth St., 4th Floor, New York NY 10013. (212)675-4321. Fax: (212)675-4441. E-mail: info@robbinsent.com. Website: www.robbinsent.com. **Contact:** Matt D'Arduini, Manager/A&R. Record company and music publisher (Rocks, No Salt). Estab. 1996. Staff size: 10. Releases 25 singles and 12-14 CDs/year. Pays negotiable royalty to artists on contract; statutory rate to publisher per song on record.

Distributed By Sony/BMG.

How to Contact Accepts unsolicited radio edit demos as long as it's dance music. Prefers CD with 2 songs or less. "Make sure everything is labeled with the song title information and your contact information. This is important in case the CD and the jewel case get separated. Do not call us and ask if you can send your package. The answer is yes."

Music Commercial **dance** only. Released top 10 pop smashes, "Heaven" (single), recorded by DJ Sammy; "Everytime We Touch" (single), recorded by Cascada; "Listen To Your Heart" (single), recored by DHT; as well as Hot 100 records from Rockell, Lasgo, Reina and K5. Other artists include Ian Van Dahl, September, Andain, Judy Torres, Jenna Drey, Marly, Dee Dee, Milky, Kreo and many others.

Tips "Do not send your package 'Supreme-Overnight-Before-You-Wake-Up' delivery. Save yourself some money. Do not send material if you are going to state in your letter that, 'If I had more (fill in the blank) it would sound better.' We are interested in hearing your best and only your best. Do not call us and ask if you can send your package. The answer is yes. We are looking for dance music with crossover potential."

☐ ROLL ON RECORDS

112 Widmar Pl., Clayton CA 94517. (925)833-4680. E-mail: rollonrecords@aol.com. **Contact:** Edgar J. Brincat, owner. Record company and music publisher (California Country Music). Estab. 1985. Pays 10% royalty to artists on contract; statutory rate to publisher per song on record. Member of Harry Fox Agency.

Distributed By Tower.

How to Contact Submit demo package by mail. Unsolicited submissions are OK. "Do not call or write for permission to submit, if you do you will be rejected." Prefers CD with 3 songs and lyric sheet. Include SASE and phone number. Responds in 6 weeks.

Music Mostly **contemporary/country** and **modern gospel**. Released "Broken Record" (single by Horace Linsley/Dianne Baumgartner), recorded by Edee Gordon on Roll On Records; Maddy and For Realities Sake (albums both by F.L. Pittman/Madonna Weeks), recorded by Ron Banks/L.J. Reynolds on Life Records/Bellmark Records.

Tips "Be patient and prepare to be in it for the long haul. A successful songwriter does not happen overnight. It's rare to write a song today and have a hit tomorrow. If you give us your song and want it back, then don't give it to us to begin with."

ℕ ☐ ROTTEN RECORDS

Attn: A&R Dept., P.O. Box 56, Upland CA 91785. (909)920-4567. E-mail: rotten@rottenrecords.com. Website: www.rottenrecords.com. President: Ron Peterson. Promotions/Radio/Video: Andi Jones. Record company. Estab. 1988. Releases 3 LPs, 3 EPs and 3 CDs/year.

Distributed By RIOT (Australia), Sonic Rendezvous (NL), RED (US) and PHD (Canada).

How to Contact Submit demo package by mail. Unsolicited submissions are OK. Prefers CD or MySpace link. Does not return material.

Music Mostly **rock**, **alternative** and **commercial**; also **punk** and **heavy metal**. Released *Paegan Terrorism* (album), written and recorded by Acid Bath; *Kiss the Clown* (album by K. Donivon), recorded by Kiss the Clown; and *Full Speed Ahead* (album by Cassidy/Brecht), recorded by D.R.T., all on Rotten Records.

Record Companies

Tips "Be patient."

🌐 ROUGH TRADE RECORDS

Beggar's Group, 66 Golborne Road, London W10 5PS. +44 020 8960 9888. Fax: +44 020 8968 6715. Website: www.roughtraderecords.com.

How to Contact Demos should be marked for attention of Paul Jones.

Music Alternative. Artists include Super Furry Animals, Jarvis Cocker, The Hold Steady, Emiliana Torrini, British Sea Power, The Libertines, My Morning Jacket, Jenny Lewis, The Strokes, The Mystery Jets, the Decemberists, and more.

🖉 RUSTIC RECORDS

6337 Murray Lane, Brentwood TN 37027. (615)371-0646. Fax: (615)370-0353. E-mail: rusticrecordsinc@aol.com. Website: www.rusticrecordsinc.com. President: Jack Schneider. Executive VP & Operations Manager: Nell Schneider. VP Publishing and Catalog Manager: Amanda Mark. VP Marketing and Promotions: Ross Schneider. Videography, Photography, and Graphic Design: Wayne Hall. Image consultant: Jo Ann Rossi. Independent traditional country music label and music publisher (Iron Skillet Music/ASCAP, Covered Bridge/ BMI, Old Towne Square/ SESAC). Estab. 1979. Staff size: 6. Releases 2-3/year. Pays negotiable royalty to artists on contracts; statutory royalty to publisher per song on record.

Distributed By CDBaby.com and available on iTunes, MSN Music, Rhapsody, and more.

How to Contact Submit professional demo package by mail. Unsolicited submissions are OK. CD only; no mp3s or e-mails. Include no more than 4 songs with corresponding lyric sheets and cover letter. Include appropriately-sized SASE. Responds in 4 weeks.

Music Good combination of traditional and modern **country**. 2008-09 releases: *Ready to Ride* - debut album from Nikki Britt, featuring "C-O-W-B-O-Y," "Do I Look Like Him," "Star in My Car," and "You Happened"; *Hank Stuff* from DeAnna Cox - featuring "I'm a Long Gone Mama," and "I'm so Lonesome I Could Cry."

Tips "Professional demo preferred."

🖿 🖉 SAHARA RECORDS AND FILMWORKS ENTERTAINMENT

10573 W. Pico Blvd., #352, Los Angeles CA 90064-2348. Phone: (310)948-9652. Fax: (310)474-7705. E-mail: info@edmsahara.com. Website: www.edmsahara.com. **Contact:** Edward De Miles, president. Record company, music publisher (EDM Music/BMI, Edward De Miles Music Company) and record producer (Edward De Miles). Estab. 1981. Releases 15-20 CD singles and 5-10 CDs/year. Pays 9½-11% royalty to artists on contract; statutory rate to publishers per song on record.

How to Contact *Does not accept unsolicited submissions.*

Music Mostly **R&B/dance, top 40 pop/rock** and **contemporary jazz**; also **TV-film themes, musical scores and jingles**. Released "Hooked on U," "Dance Wit Me" and "Moments" (singles), written and recorded by Steve Lynn (R&B) on Sahara Records. Other artists include Lost in Wonder, Devon Edwards and Multiple Choice.

Tips "We're looking for strong mainstream material. Lyrics and melodies with good hooks that grab people's attention."

☐ SANDALPHON RECORDS

P.O. Box 542407, Grand Prairie TX 75054. (972)333-0876. E-mail: rotey01@gmail.com. **Contact:** Ruth Otey, president. Record company, music publisher (Sandalphon Music/BMI), and management agency (Sandalphon Management). Estab. 2005. Staff size: 2. Pays negotiable royalty to artists on contract; statutory royalty to publisher per song on record.

Distributed By "We are currently negotiating for distribution."

How to Contact Submit demo packageby mail. Unsolicited submissions are fine. Prefers CD with 1-5 songs with lyric sheet and cover letter. Returns submissions if accompanied by a SASE or SAE and IRC for outside the United States. Responds in 6-8 weeks.

Music Mostly **rock**, **country**, and **alternative**; also **pop**, **gospel**, and **blues**.

SIMPLY GRAND MUSIC INC

P.O. Box 770208, Memphis TN 38177-0208.Estab. 1965. (901)763-4787. Fax: (901)763-4883. E-mail: wahani@aol.com. Website: www.simplygrandmusic.com. **Contact:** Linda Lucchesi, president. Record company (Memphis Town Music) and music publisher (Beckie Publishing Company). Estab. 1965. Staff size: 2. Released 9 CDs last year. Royalties are negotiable.

Distributed By Ace Records and various others.

How to Contact Contact first and obtain permission to submit a demo. Include CD with 1-3 songs and lyric sheet. Returns submissions if accompanied by an SASE with ample postage. Responds in 3 months.

Music Mostly interested in **country**, **soul/R&B**, **pop**; also interested in **top 40**, **soft rock**. Recently published "Can't Find Happiness" written by Charlie Chalmers and Paul Selph, Jr., recorded by Barbara & The Browns (soul) for *Can't Find Happiness* (album) on Ace Records; "Hooked on a Feeling" written by Mark James, recorded by The Ovations feat. Louis Williams (soul) for *One In a Million* (album) on Ace Records; "Love Made a Fool of Me" written by Gary McEwen and Louis Paul, Jr., recorded by Bettye LaVette (soul/R&B) for *Take Another Little Piece of My Heart* (album) on Varese Sarabande Records.

SKELETON CREW

NJ.E-mail: info@skeletoncrewonline.com. Website: www.skeletoncrewonline.com.

How to Contact E-mail or send message through MySpace page for directions on sending material.

Music **Punk**, **indie**, **rock**, **alternative**. Artists include David Costa, Architects, New Tomorrow, The Mean Reds, and more.

▧ SMOG VEIL RECORDS

1658 N. Milwaukee Ave., #284, Chicago IL 60647. (773)706-0450. Fax: (312)276-8519. E-mail: SmogVeil@mac.com. Website: www.smogveil.com. **Contact**: Frank Mauceri. "Smog Veil Records focuses primarily on underground, challenging, unknown, and/or bombastic rock'n'roll."

How to Contact Submit CD or CD-R to Frank Mauceri by mail. Does not accept submissions by e-mail or links to website. Submissions must inlcud a contact, press kit, and plans for touring. Response time is slow. "Note that if your band is playing the Chicago area, we cannot help with booking, but may be interested in seeing you perform live. Therefore, please email gig details. Demo submissions cannot be returned to the submitter."

Music Artists include Batusis, David Thomas, Thor, This Moment in Black History, Butcher Boys, and Prisoners.

⊘ SONY BMG

550 Madison Ave., New York NY 10022. Website: www.sonymusic.com.

• Sony BMG is one of the primary "Big 4" major labels.

How to Contact For specific contact information see the listings in this section for Sony subsidiaries Columbia Records, Epic Records, Sony Nashville, RCA Records, J Records, Arista, and American Recordings.

⊘ SONY MUSIC NASHVILLE

8 Music Square W., Nashville TN 37203-3204. (615)726-8300. Website: www.sonymusic. com. Labels include Columbia Nashville, Arista Nashville, RCA, BNA, and Provident Music Group.

• Sony Music Nashville is a subsidiary of Sony BMG, one of the "Big 4" major labels.

How to Contact *Sony Music Nashville does not accept unsolicited submissions.*

▧ ☑ ⊘ SUGAR HILL RECORDS

E-mail: info@sugarhillrecords.com. Website: www.sugarhillrecords.com. Record company. Estab. 1978.

• Welk Music Group acquired Sugar Hill Records in 1998.

How to Contact *No unsolicited submissions.* "If you are interested in having your music heard by Sugar Hill Records or the Welk Music Group, we suggest you establish a relationship with a manager, publisher, or attorney that has an ongoing relationship with our company. We do not have a list of such entities."

Music Mostly **Americana**, **bluegrass**, and **country**. Artists include Nickel Creek, Allison Moorer, The Duhks, Sonny Landreth, Scott Miller, Reckless Kelly, Tim O'Brien, The Gibson Brothers, and more.

▢ TANGENT® RECORDS

P.O. Box 383, Reynoldsburg OH 43068-0383. (614)751-1962. Fax: (614)751-6414. E-mail: info@tangentrecords.com. Website: www.tangentrecords.com. **Contact**: Andrew

Batchelor, president. Director of Marketing: Elisa Batchelor. Record company and music publisher (ArcTangent Music/BMI). Estab. 1986. Staff size: 3. Releases 10-12 CDs/year. Pays negotiable royalty to artists on contract; statutory rate to publisher per song on record.

How to Contact Submit demo package by mail. Unsolicited submissions are OK. Prefers CD, with minimum of 3 songs and lead sheet if available. "Please include a brief biography/history of artist(s) and/or band, including musical training/education, performance experience, recording studio experience, discography and photos (if available)." Does not return material. Responds if interested.

Music Mostly **artrock** and **contemporary instrumental/rock instrumental**; also **contemporary classical**, **world beat**, **jazz/rock**, **ambient**, **electronic**, and **New Age**.

Tips "Take the time to pull together a quality CD or cassette demo with package/portfolio, including such relevant information as experience (on stage and in studio, etc.), education/training, biography, career goals, discography, photos, etc. Should be typed. We are not interested in generic sounding or 'straight ahead' music. We are seeking music that is innovative, pioneering and eclectic with a fresh, unique sound."

✪ TEXAS ROSE RECORDS

2002 Platinum St., Garland TX 75042. (972)272-3131. Fax: (972)272-3155. E-mail: txrr1@aol.com. Website: www.texasroserecords.com. **Contact:** Nancy Baxendale, president. Record company, music publisher (Yellow Rose of Texas Publishing) and record producer (Nancy Baxendale). Estab. 1994. Staff size: 3. Releases 3 CDs/year. Pays negotiable royalty to artists on contract; statutory rate to publisher per song on record.

Distributed By Self distribution.

How to Contact *E-mail first for permission to submit.* Submit maximum of 2 songs on CD and lyrics. Does not return material. Responds only if interested.

Music Mostly **country**, **soft rock** and **blues**; also **pop**. Does not want hip-hop, rap, heavy metal. Released *Flyin' High Over Texas* (album), recorded by Dusty Martin (country); *High On The Hog* (album), recorded by Steve Harr (country); *Time For Time to Pay* (album), recorded by Jeff Elliot (country); *Double XXposure* (album), recorded by Jeff Elliott and Kim Neeley (country), Pendulum Dream (album) recorded by Maureen Kelly (Americana) and "Cowboy Super Hero" (single) written and recorded by Robert Mauldin.

Tips "We are interested in songs written for today's market with a strong musical hook. No home recordings, please."

✪ TOMMY BOY ENTERTAINMENT LLC

120 Fifth Avenue, 7th Floor, New York NY 10011. (212)388-8300. Fax: (212)388-8431. E-mail: info@tommyboy.com. Website: www.tommyboy.com. Record company. Labels include Penalty Recordings, Outcaste Records, Timber and Tommy Boy Gospel.

Distributed By WEA, Subway Records.

How to Contact E-mail to obtain current demo submission policy.

Music Artists include Chavela Vargas, Afrika Bambaataa, Biz Markie, Kool Keith, and INXS.

◯ TON RECORDS

E-mail: tonmusic@earthlink.net. Website: www.tonrecords.com or www.myspace.com/ tonrecords. Vice President: Jay Vasquez. Labels include 7" collectors series and Ton Special Projects. Record company and record producer (RJ Vasquez). Estab. 1992. Releases 6-9 LPs, 1-2 EPs and 10-11 CDs/year. Pays negotiable royalty to artists on contract; statutory rate to publisher per song on record.

How to Contact Not signing at present time.

Music Mostly **new music**; also **hard new music**. Released *Intoxicated Birthday Lies* (album), recorded by shoegazer (punk rock); *The Good Times R Killing Me* (album), recorded by Top Jimmy, all on Ton Records. Other artists include Why? Things Burn, Sarge, and the Ramblers.

Tips "Work as hard as we do."

◲ TOPCAT RECORDS

P.O. Box 670234, Dallas TX 75367. (972)484-4141. Fax: (972)620-8333. E-mail: info@topcatrecords.com. Website: www.topcatrecords.com or www.myspace.com/ topcatrecords. President: Richard Chalk. Record company and record producer. Estab. 1991. Staff size: 3. Releases 4-6 CDs/year. Pays 10-15% royalty to artists on contract; statutory rate to publisher per song on record.

Distributed By City Hall.

How to Contact *Call first and obtain permission to submit.* Prefers CD. Does not return material. Responds in 1 month.

Music Mostly **blues**, **swing**, **rockabilly**, **Americana**, **Texana** and **R&B**. Released *If You Need Me* (album), written and recorded by Robert Ealey (blues); *Texas Blueswomen* (album by 3 Female Singers), recorded by various (blues/R&B); and *Jungle Jane* (album), written and recorded by Holland K. Smith (blues/swing), all on Topcat. Released CDs: *Jim Suhler & Alan Haynes—Live*; Bob Kirkpatrick *Drive Across Texas*; *Rock My Blues to Sleep* by Johnny Nicholas; *Walking Heart Attack*, by Holland K. Smith; *Dirt Road* (album), recorded by Jim Suhler; *Josh Alan Band* (album), recorded by Josh Alan; *Bust Out* (album), recorded by Robin Sylar. Other artists include Grant Cook, Muddy Waters, Big Mama Thornton, Big Joe Turner, Geo. "Harmonica" Smith, J.B. Hutto and Bee Houston. "View our website for an up-to-date listing of releases."

Tips "Send me blues (fast, slow, happy, sad, etc.) or good blues oriented R&B. No pop, hip-hop, or rap."

TOUCH AND GO/QUARTERSTICK RECORDS

P.O. Box 25520, Chicago IL 60625. Phone/Fax: (773)388-8888. E-mail: info@tgrec.com. Website: www.touchandgorecords.com. Quarterstick Records: P.O. Box 25342, Chicago, IL 60625.

How to Contact Mail to one or the other (staffed by same people, no need to send to both labels). "Demos are listened to by any and all staffers who want to or have time to listen to them. Do not call or e-mail us about your demo." Do not e-mail mp3s or web URLs.
Music All Styles. Artists include Therapy?, TV on the Radio, Pinback, Naked Raygun, Blonde Redhead, Henry Rollins, Yeah Yeah Yeahs, Girls Against Boys, and more.

✪ TRANSDREAMER RECORDS

P.O. Box 1955, New York NY 10113. (212)741-8861. Website: www.transdreamer.com.
Contact: Greg Caputo, marketing savant. President: Robert John. Record company. Estab. 2002. Staff size: 5. Released 4 CDs/year. Pays negotiable rate to artists on contract; ¾ statutory rate to publisher per song on record.
   • Also see the listing for Megaforce in this section of the book.
Distributed By Red/Sony.
How to Contact *Contact first and obtain permission to submit.*
Music Mostly **alternative/rock**. Artists include The Delgados, Arab Strap, Dressy Bessy, Bill Richini, and Wellwater Conspiracy.

▢ UAR RECORDS

P.O. Box 1264, 6020 W. Pottstown Rd., Peoria IL 61654-1264. (309)673-5755. Fax: (309)673-7636. E-mail: uarltd@A5.com. Website: www.unitedcyber.com. Contact: Jerry Hanlon, A&R director. Record company and music publisher (Jerjoy Music/BMI and Katysarah Music/ASCAP). Estab. 1978. Staff size: 2. Releases 3 or more CDs/year.
   • Also see the listings for Kaysarah Music (ASCAP) and Jerjoy Music (BMI) in the Music Publishers section of this book.
How to Contact "If you are an artist seeking a record deal, please send a sample of your vocal and/or songwriting work-guitar and vocal is fine, no more than 4 songs. Fully produced demos are NOT necessary. Also send brief information on your background in the business, your goals, etc. If you are NOT a songwriter, please send 4 songs maximum of cover tunes that we can use to evaluate your vocal ability. If you wish a reply, please send a SASE, otherwise, you will not receive an answer. If you want a critique of your vocal abilities, please so state as we do not routinely offer critiques. Unsolicited submissions are OK. If you wish all of your material returned to you, be sure to include mailing materials and postage. WE DO NOT RETURN PHONE CALLS."
Music Mostly **American** and **Irish country**. Released "When Jackie Sang The Walking Talking Dolly," "Far Side Banks of Jordan," "There's You," all recorded by Jerry Hanlon. "Lisa Dance With Me," "Philomena From Ireland," "Rainbow," "I'd Better Stand Up," all recorded by the Heggarty Twins from Northern Ireland and Jerry Hanlon. "An Ordinary Woman," "All Your Little Secrets," recorded by Anne More.
Tips "We are a small independent company, but our belief is that every good voice deserves a chance to be heard and our door is always open to new and aspiring artists."

⊘ UNIVERSAL RECORDS

1755 Broadway, 7th Floor, New York NY 10019. (212)841-8000. Fax: (212)331-2580. Website: www.universalrecords.com. **Universal City office:** 70 Universal City Plaza, 3rd Floor, Universal City CA 91608. (818)777-1000. Vice Presidents A&R: Bruce Carbone, Tse Williams. Labels include Uptown Records, Mojo Records, Republic Records, Bystorm Records and Gut Reaction Records. Record company.

- Universal Records is a subsidiary of Universal Music Group, one of the "Big 4" major labels.

How to Contact *Universal Records in California does not accept unsolicited submissions. The New York office only allows you to call first and obtain permission to submit.*

Music Artists include India Arie, Erykah Bad, Godsmack, Kaiser Chiefs, and Lindsey Lohan.

VAGRANT RECORDS

2118 Wilshire Blvd. #361, Santa Monica CA 90403. E-mail: publicity@vagrant.com. Website: www.vagrant.com. United Kingdom: 3rd Floor, 1a Adpar St., London W2 1DE. E-mail: vagrantuk@vagrant.com.

How to Contact Send demos to: Demos c/o Vagrant Records at US mailing address.

Music Rock, alternative. Artists include Black Rebel Motorcycle Club, Electric Owls, Far, J Roddy Walston and The Business, Murder by Death, Protest the Hero, School of Seven Bells, Senses Fail, Stars, The Hold Steady, Thrice, and more.

⚇ ⊘ THE VERVE MUSIC GROUP

1755 Broadway, 3rd Floor, New York NY 10019. (212)331-2000. Fax: (212)331-2064. E-mail: contact@vervemusicgroup.com. Website: www.vervemusicgroup.com. A&R Director: Dahlia Ambach. A&R Coordinator: Heather Buchanan. Los Angeles: 100 N. First St., Burbank CA 91502. (818)729-4804 Fax: (818)845-2564. Vice President A&R: Bud Harner. A&R Assistant: Heather Buchanan. Record company. Labels include Verve, GRP, Blue Thumb and Impulse! Records.

- Verve Music Group is a subsidiary of Universal Music Group, one of the "Big 4" major labels.

How to Contact *The Verve Music Group does not accept unsolicited submissions.*

Music Artists include Roy Hargrove, Diana Krall, George Benson, Al Jarreau, John Scofield, Natalie Cole, and David Sanborn.

VICTORY RECORDS

346 N. Justine St., 5th Floor, Chicago IL 60607. (312)666-8661. Fax: (312)666-8665. Website: www.victoryrecords.com.

How to Contact Send press kit by mail.

Music Alternative, metal, rock. Artists include The Audition, Bayside, Catch 22, Funeral For A Friend, Otep, Hawthorne Heights, Ringworm, Secret Lives of the Freemasons,

Silverstein, The Tossers, Voodoo Glow Skulls, William Control, Streetlight Manifesto, and more.

⊘ VIRGIN RECORDS

1750 Vine St., Los Angeles CA 90028. (323)692-1100. Fax: (310)278-6231. Website: www.virginrecords.com. New York office: 150 5th Ave., 3rd Floor, New York NY 10016. (212)786-8200 Fax:(212)786-8343. Labels include Rap-A-Lot Records, Pointblank Records, SoulPower Records, AWOL Records, Astralwerks Records, Cheeba Sounds and Noo Trybe Records. Record company.

• Virgin Records is a subsidiary of the EMI Group, one of the "Big 4" major labels.

Distributed By EMD.

How to Contact *Virgin Records does not accept recorded material or lyrics unless submitted by a reputable industry source.* "If your act has received positive press or airplay on prior independent releases, we welcome your written query. Send a letter of introduction accompanied by all pertinent artist information. Do not send a tape until requested. All unsolicited materials will be returned unopened."

Music Mostly **rock** and **pop**. Artists include Lenny Kravitz, Placebo, The Rolling Stones, Joss Stone, Ben Harper, Iggy Pop, and Boz Scaggs.

🏆 ⊘ WARNER BROS. RECORDS

3300 Warner Blvd., 3rd Floor, Burbank CA 91505. (818)846-9090. Fax: (818)953-3423. Website: www.wbr.com. **New York:** 75 Rockefeller Plaza, New York NY 10019. (212)275-4500 Fax:(212)275-4596. A&R: James Dowdall, Karl Rybacki. **Nashville:** 20 Music Square E., Nashville TN 37203. (615)748-8000 Fax:(615)214-1567. Labels include American Recordings, Eternal Records, Imago Records, Mute Records, Giant Records, Malpaso Records and Maverick Records. Record company.

• Warner Bros. Records is a subsidiary of Warner Music Group, one of the "Big 4" major labels.

Distributed By WEA.

How to Contact *Warner Bros. Records does not accept unsolicited material.* "All unsolicited material will be returned unopened. Those interested in having their tapes heard should establish a relationship with a manager, publisher or attorney that has an ongoing relationship with Warner Bros. Records."

Music Released *Van Halen 3* (album), recorded by Van Halen; *Evita* (soundtrack); and *Dizzy Up the Girl* (album), recorded by Goo Goo Dolls, both on Warner Bros. Records. Other artists include Faith Hill, Tom Petty & the Heartbreakers, Jeff Foxworthy, Porno For Pyros, Travis Tritt, Yellowjackets, Bela Fleck and the Flecktones, Al Jarreau, Joshua Redmond, Little Texas, and Curtis Mayfield.

⊘ WATERDOG MUSIC

(a.k.a. Waterdog Records), 329 W. 18th St., #313, Chicago IL 60616-1120. (312)421-7499. Fax: (312)421-1848. E-mail: waterdog@waterdogmusic.com. Website: www.

waterdogmusic.com. **Contact:** Rob Gillis, label manager. Labels include Whitehouse Records. Record company. Estab. 1991. Staff size: 2. Releases 2 CDs/year. Pays negotiable royalty to artists on contract; statutory rate to publisher per song on record.

Distributed By Big Daddy Music.

How to Contact *"Not accepting unsolicited materials, demos at this time.* If submission policy changes, it will be posted on our website."

Music Mostly **rock** and **pop**. Released *Good Examples of Bad Examples: The Best of Ralph Covert & The Bad Examples, Vol. 2* (album), released 2005. Other artists have included Middle 8, Al Rose & The Transcendos, Kat Parsons, Torben Floor (Carey Ott), MysteryDriver, Joel Frankel, Dean Goldstein & Coin, and Matt Tiegler.

Tips "Ralph Covert's children's music (Ralph's World) is released in Disney Sound. We are not looking for any other children's music performers or composers."

☑ WINCHESTER RECORDS

25 Troubadour Lane, Berkeley Springs WV 25411. (304)258-8314 or (304)258-9381. E-mail: mccoytroubadour@aol.com. Website: www.troubadourlounge.com. **Contact:** Jim or Bertha McCoy, owners. Labels include Master Records and Real McCoy Records. Record company, music publisher (Jim McCoy Music, Alear Music, New Edition Music/BMI), record producer (Jim McCoy Productions) and recording studio. Releases 20 singles and 10 LPs/year. Pays standard royalty to artists; statutory rate to publisher for each record sold.

How to Contact *Write first and obtain permission to submit.* Prefers CD with 5-10 songs and lead sheet. Include SASE. Responds in 1 month.

Music Mostly **bluegrass**, **church/religious**, **country**, **folk**, **gospel**, **progressive** and **rock**. Released "Runaway Girl" (single by Earl Howard/Jim McCoy) from *Earl Howard Sings His Heart Out* (album), recorded by Earl Howard (country), released 2002 on Winchester; *Jim McCoy and Friends Remember Ernest Tubb* (album), recorded by Jim McCoy (country), released January 2003 on Winchester; *The Best of Winchester Records* (album), recorded by RileeGray/J.B. Miller/Jim McCoy/Carroll County (country), released 2002 on Winchester.

☐ WORLD BEATNIK RECORDS

121 Walnut Ln., Rockwall TX 75032. Fax: (972)771-3797. E-mail: tropikalproductions@ gmail.com. Website: www.tropikalproductions.com/label.html. Producers: J. Towry (world beat, reggae, ethnic, jazz); Jimbe (reggae, world beat, ethnic); Arik Towry (ska, pop, ragga, rock). Labels include World Beatnik Records. Record company and record producer (Jimi Towry). Estab. 1983. Staff size: 4. Releases 6 singles, 6 LPs, 6 EPs and 6 CDs/year. Pays negotiable royalty to artists on contract; statutory rate to publisher per song on record.

Distributed By Midwest Records, Southwest Wholesale, Reggae OneLove, Ejaness Records, Ernie B's, CD Waterhouse and Borders.

How to Contact Submit demo tape by mail. Unsolicited submissions are OK. Prefers cassette, DAT, mini disk or VHS videocassette with lyric sheet. Include SASE. Responds in 2 weeks.

Music Mostly **world beat, reggae** and **ethnic**; also **jazz, hip-hop/dance** and **pop**. Released *I and I* (album by Abby I/Jimbe), recorded by Abby I (African pop); *Rastafrika* (album by Jimbe/Richard Ono), recorded by Rastafrika (African roots reggae); and *Vibes* (album by Jimbe/Bongo Cartheni), recorded by Wave (worldbeat/jazz), all released 2001/2002 on World Beatnik. Other artists include Ras Richi (Cameroon), Wisdom Ogbor (Nigeria), Joe Lateh (Ghana), Dee Dee Cooper, Ras Lyrix (St. Croix), Ras Kumba (St. Kitts), Gary Mon, Darbo (Gambia), Ricki Malik (Jamaica), Arik Miles, Narte's (Hawaii), Gavin Audagnotti (South Africa) and Bongo (Trinidad).

⬛ XEMU RECORDS

609 Kappock Street, Suite 1A, Bronx NY 10463. (212)807-0290. E-mail: xemu@xemu.com. Website: www.xemu.com. **Contact:** Sulphin Marx, A&R. Record company. Estab. 1992. Staff size: 4. Releases 4 CDs/year. Pays negotiable royalty to artists on contract; statutory rate to publisher per song on record.

Distributed By Redeye Distribution.

How to Contact *Write first and obtain permission to submit.* Prefers CD with 3 songs. Does not return material. Responds in 2 months.

Music Mostly **alternative**. Released *Happy Suicide, Jim!* (album) by The Love Kills Theory (alternative rock); *Howls From The Hills* (album) by Dead Meadow; *The Fall* (album), recorded by Mikki James (alternative rock); *A is for Alpha* (album), recorded by Alpha Bitch (alternative rock); *Hold the Mayo* (album), recorded by Death Sandwich (alternative rock); *Stockholm Syndrome* (album), recorded by Trigger Happy (alternative rock) all released on Xemu Records. Other artists include Malvert P. Redd, The Fifth Dementia, and the Neanderthal Spongecake.

🌐 XL RECORDINGS

Beggar's Group, One Codrington Mews, London W11 2EH. Website: www.xlrecordings.com. **US**: 304 Hudson Street, 7th Floor, New York NY 10013.

Music Alternative rock. Artists include Adele, Basement Jaxx, Be Your Own Pet, Beck, Dizzee Rascal, M.I.A, Peaches, Radiohead, Sigur Ros, The Horrors, The Raconteurs, The White Stripes, Thom Yorke, Vampire Weekend, and more.

ADDITIONAL RECORD COMPANIES

B

Bixio Music Group & Associates/IDM Music 102

Blues Alley Records 172

C

Celt Musical Services, Jan 173

D

DaVinci's Notebook Records 174

F

Fifth Avenue Media, Ltd. 109

Final Mix Inc. 176

First Time Music (Publishing) U.K. 109

Fresh Entertainment 110

G

Glad Music Co. 110

H

Hailing Frequency Music Productions 176

Hardison International Entertainment Corporation 194

Heart Consort Music 176

Heupferd Musikverlag GmbH 112

K

Kaysarah Music 115

Kuper Personal Management/Recovery Recordings 195

L

L.A. Entertainment, Inc. 177

Levy Management, Rick 196

M

McCoy Music, Jim 117

MusicJones Records 181

N

Neu Electro Productions 182

New Experience Records/Faze 4 Records 182

P

Pegasus Music 120

Pollybyrd Publications Limited 122

R

Ranco Music Publishing 123

S

Sabteca Music Co. 123

Silver Bow Management 202

T

Tas Music Co./Dave Tasse Entertainment 204

W

Warner Productions, Cheryl K. 205

World Records 184

Record Producers

The independent producer can best be described as a creative coordinator. He's often the one with the most creative control over a recording project and is ultimately responsible for the finished product. Some record companies have in-house producers who work with the acts on that label (although, in more recent years, such producer-label relationships are often non-exclusive). Today, most record companies contract out-of-house, independent record producers on a project-by-project basis.

WHAT RECORD PRODUCERS DO

Producers play a large role in deciding what songs will be recorded for a particular project and are always on the lookout for new songs for their clients. They can be valuable contacts for songwriters because they work so closely with the artists whose records they produce. They usually have a lot more freedom than others in executive positions and are known for having a good ear for potential hit songs. Many producers are songwriters and musicians themselves. Since they wield a great deal of influence, a good song in the hands of the right producer at the right time stands a good chance of being cut. And even if a producer is not working on a specific project, he is well-acquainted with record company executives and artists and can often get material through doors not open to you.

SUBMITTING MATERIAL TO PRODUCERS

It can be difficult to get your tapes to the right producer at the right time. Many producers write their own songs and even if they don't write, they may be involved in their own publishing companies so they have instant access to all the songs in their catalogs. Also, some genres are more dependent on finding outside songs than others. A producer working with a rock group or a singer-songwriter will rarely take outside songs.

It's important to understand the intricacies of the producer/publisher situation. If you pitch your song directly to a producer first, before another publishing company publishes the song, the producer may ask you for the publishing rights (or a percentage thereof) to your song. You must decide whether the producer is really an active publisher who will try to get the song recorded again and again or whether he merely wants the publishing because it means extra income for him from the current recording project. You may be

Icons

For more instructional information on the listings in this book, including explanations of symbols ( ), read the article *How To Use Songwriter's Market* on page 1.

For More Info

able to work out a co-publishing deal, where you and the producer split the publishing of the song. That means he will still receive his percentage of the publishing income, even if you secure a cover recording of the song by other artists in the future. Even though you would be giving up a little bit initially, you may benefit in the future.

Some producers will offer to sign artists and songwriters to "development deals." These can range from a situation where a producer auditions singers and musicians with the intention of building a group from the ground up, to development deals where a producer signs a band or singer-songwriter to his production company with the intention of developing the act and producing an album to shop to labels (sometimes referred to as a "baby record deal").

You must carefully consider whether such a deal is right for you. In some cases, such a deal can open doors and propel an act to the next level. In other worst-case scenarios, such a deal can result in loss of artistic and career control, with some acts held in contractual bondage for years at a time. Before you consider any such deal, be clear about your goals, the producer's reputation, and the sort of compromises you are willing to make to reach those goals. If you have any reservations whatsoever, don't do it.

The listings that follow outline which aspects of the music industry each producer is involved in, what type of music he is looking for, and what records and artists he's recently produced. Study the listings carefully, noting the artists each producer works with, and consider if any of your songs might fit a particular artist's or producer's style. Then determine whether they are open to your level of experience (see the A Sample Listing Decoded on page 7).

Consult the Category Index on page 333 to find producers who work with the type of music you write, and the Geographic Index at the back of the book to locate producers in your area.

ADDITIONAL RECORD PRODUCERS

There are **more record producers** located in other sections of the book! On page 185 use the list of Additional Record Producers to find listings within other sections who are also record producers.

⚡ ☑ "A" MAJOR SOUND CORPORATION

RR #1, Kensington PE COB 1MO Canada. (902)836-4571. E-mail: info@amajorsound.com. Website: www.amajorsound.com. **Contact:** Paul C. Milner, producer. Record producer and music publisher. Estab. 1989. Produces 8 CDs/year. Fee derived in part from sales royalty when song or artist is recorded, and/or outright fee from recording artist or record company, or investors.

How to Contact Submit demo package by mail. Unsolicited submissions are OK. Prefers CD with 5 songs and lyric sheet (lead sheet if available). Does not return material. Responds only if interested in 3 months.

Music Mostly **rock**, **A/C**, **alternative** and **pop**; also **Christian** and **R&B**. Produced *COLOUR* (album written by J. MacPhee/R. MacPhee/C. Buchanan/D. MacDonald), recorded by The Chucky Danger Band (pop/rock), released 2006; Winner of ECMA award; *Something In Between* (album, written by Matt Andersen), recorded by Matt Andersen and Friends (Blues), released 2008 on Weatherbox / Andersen; *In A Fever In A Dream* (album, written by Pat Deighan), recorded by Pat Deighan and The Orb Weavers (Rock), released in 2008 on Sandbar Music; *Saddle River String Band* (album, written by Saddle River Stringband), recorded by Saddle River Stringband (Blue Grass) released 2007 on Save As Music; Winner of ECMA award.

ALLRS MUSIC PUBLISHING CO. (ASCAP)

P.O. Box 1545, Smithtown NY 11787. (718)767-8995. E-mail: allrsmusic@aol.com. Website: www.geocities.com/allrsmusic. **Contact:** Renee Silvestri-Bushey, president. F.John Silvestri, founder Leslie Migliorelli, director of operations. Music publisher, record company (MIDI Track Records), music consultant, artist management, record producer. Voting member of NARAS (The Grammy Awards), Voting member of the Country Music Association (The CMA Awards), SGMA, Songwriters Guild of America (Diamond Member). Estab. 1994. Staff size: 5. Publishes 3 songs/year; publishes 2 new songwriters/year. Pays standard royalty.Affiliate(s) Midi-Track Publishing Co. (BMI).

How to Contact "Write or e-mail first to obtain permission to submit. *We do not accept unsolicited submissions.*" Prefers CD with 3 songs, lyric sheet and cover letter. Responds via e-mail in 6 months only if interested.

Music Mostly **country**, **gospel**, **top 40**, **R&B**, **MOR** and **pop**. Does not want showtunes, jazz, classical or rap. Published "Why Can't You Hear My Prayer" (single by F. John Silvestri/Leslie Silvestri), recorded by eight-time Grammy nominee Huey Dunbar of the group DLG (Dark Latin Groove) released on Midi Track Records including other multiple releases); "Chasing Rainbows" (single by F. John Silvestri/Leslie Silvestri), recorded by Tommy Cash (country), released on MMT Records (including other multiple releases); "Because of You" (single by F. John Silvestri/Leslie Silvestri), recorded by Iliana Medina, released 2002 on MIDI Track Records, also recorded by Grammy nominee Terri Williams, Of Always, Patsy Cline, released on KMA Records; also recorded by Grand Ole Opry member Ernie Ashworth, and other multiple releases.

Tips "Attend workshops, seminars, and visit our blog on our website for advise and info on the music industry."

▦ BIG BEAR

Box 944, Edgbaston, Birmingham B16 8UT United Kingdom. 44-121-454-7020. E-mail: admin@bigbearmusic.com. Website: www.bigbearmusic.com. Managing Director: Jim Simpson. Record producer, music publisher (Bearsongs) and record company (Big Bear Records). Produces 10 LPs/year. Fee derived from sales royalty.

- Also see the listings for Bearsongs in the Music Publishers section of this book and Big Bear Records in the Record Companies section of this book.

How to Contact *Write first about your interest, then submit demo tape and lyric sheet.* Does not return material. Responds in 2 weeks.

Music Blues, swing, and jazz.

◻ BLUES ALLEY RECORDS

Rt. 1, Box 288, Clarksburg WV 26301. (304)598-2583. E-mail: info@bluesalleymusic. com. Website: www.bluesalleymusic.com. **Contact:** Joshua Swiger, producer. Record producer, record company and music publisher (Blues Alley Publishing/BMI). Produces 4-6 LPs and 2 EPs/year. Fee derived from sales royalty when song or artist is recorded.

How to Contact Submit demo package by mail. Unsolicited submissions are OK. Will only accept CDs with lead sheets and typed lyrics. Does not return material. Responds in 6 weeks.

Music Mostly **country, pop, Christian,** and **rock**. Produced *Monongalia*, recorded by The New Relics (country), 2009; *Chasing Venus*, recorded by The New Relics (acoustic rock), 2006; *Sons of Sirens*, recorded by Amity (rock), 2004; and *It's No Secret*, recorded by Samantha Caley (pop country), 2004.

ⓝ ⊘ CABIN-ON-THE-LAKE MUSIC

4120 Dale Road, Ste. J-8, #180, Modesto CA 95356. (608)239-4121. Fax: (209)409-8343. E-mail: catlmusic@aim.com. Website: www.cabin-on-the-lake.com. **Contact:** James Miksche, producer. Estab. 2002. Produces 12-20 singles; 2 albums per year. Fees derived from sales royalty when song or artist is recorded.

How to Contact Submit demo by mail. Unsolicited submissions are OK. Send CD with 3 songs, lyric sheet, and cover letter. Does not return submissions. Responds only if interested.

Music Mostly interested in singer/songwriters, folk; also country/crossover, blues rock. Does not want rap, hard rock, hip-hop, or jazz. Produced "The Legend of Coby Gill" (single by Chris Lawrence) from *The Legend of Coby Gill* (album), recorded by Coby Gill (folk/country), 2010; "Give Me a Call" (single by Chris Lawrence), from *The Legend of Coby Gill* (album), recorded by Coby Gill (folk/country), 2010; "I Could Swear" written and recorded by Tom Davis, 2009.

⬚ JAN CELT MUSICAL SERVICES

4015 NE 12th Ave., Portland OR 97212. E-mail: flyheart@teleport.com. Website: http://home.teleport.com/ ~ flyheart. **Contact:** Jan Celt, owner. Record producer, music producer and publisher (Wiosna Nasza Music/BMI) and record company (Flying Heart Records). Estab. 1982. Produces 3-5 CDs/year.

• Also see the listing for Flying Heart Records in the Record Companies section of this book.

How to Contact Submit demo tape by mail. Unsolicited submissions are OK. Prefers high-quality cassette with 1-10 songs and lyric sheet. "SASE required for any response." Does not return materials. Responds in 4 months.

Music Mostly **R&B**, **rock** and **blues**; also **jazz**. Produced "Vexatious Progressions" (single), written and recorded by Eddie Harris (jazz); "Bong Hit" (single by Chris Newman), recorded by Snow Bud & the Flower People (rock); and "She Moved Away" (single by Chris Newman), recorded by Napalm Beach, all on Flying Heart Records. Other artists include The Esquires and Janice Scroggins.

⬚ COACHOUSE MUSIC

P.O. Box 1308, Barrington IL 60011. (847)382-7631. Fax: (847)382-7651. E-mail: coachouse1@aol.com. Website: coachousemusic.com. **Contact**: Michael Freeman, president. Record producer. Estab. 1984. Produces 6-8 CDs/year. Fee derived from flat fee and/or sales royalty when song or artist is recorded.

How to Contact *Write or e-mail first and obtain permission to submit.* Prefers CD with 3-5 songs and lyric sheet. Include SASE. Responds in 6 weeks.

Music Mostly **rock**, **pop** and **blues**; also **alternative rock** and **country/Americana/roots**. Produced *Casque Nu* (album), written and recorded by Charlelie Couture on Chrysalis EMI France (contemporary pop); *Time Will Tell* (album), recorded by Studebaker John on Blind Pig Records (blues); *Where Blue Begins* (album by various/D. Coleman), recorded by Deborah Coleman on Blind Pig Records (contemporary blues); *A Man Amongst Men* (album), recorded by Bo Diddley (blues); *and Voodoo Menz (album), recorded by Corey Harris and Henry Butler. Two WC Handy nominations;* produced *Pinetop Perkins & Friends* on Telarc recorded by Pinetop Perkins—Grammy nominated. Other artists include Paul Chastain, Candi Station, Eleventh Dream Day, Magic Slim, The Tantrums, The Pranks, The Bad Examples, Mississippi Heat and Sherri Williams.

Tips "Be honest, be committed, strive for excellence."

⬚ CREATIVE SOUL

Nashville TN 37179. (615)400-3910. Website: www.creativesoulonline.com. **Contact:** Eric Copeland, producer/writer. Record producer. Produces 5-10 singles and 8-15 albums/year. Fee derived from outright fee from recording artist or company. Other services include consulting/critique/review services.

How to Contact *Contact first by e-mail to obtain permission to submit demo.* Prefers CD with 2-3 songs and lyric sheet and cover sheet. Does not return submissions. Responds only if interested.

Music **contemporary**, **Christian**, **jazz**, and **instrumental**; also **R&B** and **pop/rock**. "If you are a Christian jazz or instrumentalist, then all the better!" Produced *Cedars Gray*, recorded by Cedars Gray (contemporary Christian); *It Is Of You*, recorded by Matt Pitzl (contemporary Christian); *Fairytale Life*, recorded by Stephanie Newton (contemporary Christian); all released on Creative Soul Records. Other artists include Brett Rush, Frances Drost, Kristyn Leigh, Tom Dolan, and Canopy Red

Tips "Contact us first by e-mail, we are here in Nashville for you. We offer monthly information and special consults in Nashville for artists and writers. We want to meet you and talk with you about your dreams. E-mail us and let's start talking about your music and ministry!"

⚏ ☑ DAVINCI'S NOTEBOOK RECORDS

69 Rockwood Ave., St. Catharines Ontario L2P 1E8 Canada. E-mail: admin@davincismusic. com. Website: www.davincismusic.com. **Owner:** Kevin Richard. Producer, record company, music publisher, distributor and recording studio (The Sound Kitchen). Estab. 1992. Produces 1 CD/year. Fee derived from outright fee from artist or commission on sales. "Distribution is on consignment basis. Artist is responsible for all shipping, taxes, and import/export duties."

How to Contact *"E-mail first for for permission to submit demo."* Prefers CD and bio. Does not return material. Responds in 6 weeks.

Music Mostly **rock**, **instrumental rock**, **New Age** and **progressive-alternative**; also **R&B**, **pop** and **jazz**. Produced *Windows* (album by Kevin Hotte/Andy Smith), recorded by Musicom on DaVinci's Notebook Records (power New Age); *Inventing Fire, Illumination, A Different Drum* (albums) written and recorded by Kevin Richard on DNR/Independent (instrumental rock); and *The Cunninghams* (album), written and recorded by The Cunninghams on Independent (gospel).

Tips "DNR is an artist-run label. Local bands and performers will receive priority. You should be more interested in getting a-foot-in-the-door exposure as opposed to making a fortune. Be satisfied with conquering the world using 'baby steps.' Indie labels don't have large corporate budgets for artist development. For non-local artists, we are more about online distribution than artist development. Being a local act means that you can perform live to promote your releases. For indie artist, selling from the stage is probably going to bring you the biggest volume of sales."

⚏ ☑ AL DELORY AND MUSIC MAKERS

E-mail: aldelory@mn.rr.com. Website: www.aldelory.com. **Contact:** Al DeLory, president. Record producer and career consultant (MUSIC MAKERS/ASCAP). Estab. 1987. Fee derived from outright fee from recording artist.

• Al DeLory has won two Grammy Awards and has been nominated five times.

How to Contact E-mail first and obtain permission to submit. Prefers CD. Include SASE. Responds in 2-3 months only if interested.

Music Mostly **pop** and **Latin**. Produced "Gentle On My Mind" (single), "By the Time I Get to Phoenix" (single) and "Wichita Lineman" (single), all recorded by Glen Campbell. Other artists include Lettermen, Wayne Newton, Bobbie Gentry, and Anne Murray.

Tips "Seek advice and council only with professionals with a track record and get the money up front."

THE EDWARD DE MILES MUSIC COMPANY

10573 W. Pico Blvd., #352, Los Angeles CA 90064-2348. Phone: (310)948-9652. Fax: (310)474-7705. E-mail: info@edmsahara.com. Website: www.edmsahara.com. **Contact:** Edward De Miles, president. Record producer, music publisher (Edward De Miles Music Co./BMI) and record company (Sahara Records and Filmworks Entertainment). Estab. 1981. Produces 5-10 CDs/year. Fee derived from sales royalty when song or artist is recorded.

• Also see the listing for Edward De Miles in the Music Publishers and Managers & Booking Agents sections, as well as Sahara Records and Filmworks Entertainment in the Record Companies section of this book.

How to Contact Does not accept unsolicited submissions.

Music Mostly **R&B/dance**, **top 40 pop/rock** and **contemporary jazz**; also **country**, **TV and film themes—songs and jingles**. **Produced** "Moments" and "Dance Wit Me" (singles) (dance), both written and recorded by Steve Lynn; and "Games" (single), written and recorded by D'von Edwards (jazz), all on Sahara Records. Other artists include Multiple Choice.

Tips "Copyright all material before submitting. Equipment and showmanship a must."

JOEL DIAMOND ENTERTAINMENT

Dept. SM, 3940 Laurel Canyon Blvd., Suite 441, Studio City CA 91604. (818)980-9588. Fax: (818)980-9422. E-mail: jdiamond20@aol.com. Website: www.joeldiamond.com. **Contact:** Joel Diamond. Record producer, music publisher and manager. Fee derived from sales royalty when song is recorded or outright fee from recording artist or record company.

• Also see the listing for Silver Blue Music/Oceans Blue Music in the Music Publishers section of this book.

How to Contact Does not return material. Responds only if interested.

Music Mostly **dance**, **R&B**, **soul** and **top 40/pop**. The 5 Browns—3 number 1 CDs for Sony/BMG, David Hasselhoff; produced "One Night In Bangkok" (single by Robey); "I Think I Love You," recorded by Katie Cassidy (daughter of David Cassidy) on Artemis Records; "After the Loving" (single), recorded by E. Humperdinck; "Forever Friends," recorded by Vaneza (featured on Nickelodeon's *The Brothers Garcia*); and "Paradise" (single), recorded by Kaci.

✪ FINAL MIX INC.

(formerly Final Mix Music), 2219 W. Olive Ave., Suite 102, Burbank CA 91506. E-mail: rob@finalmix.com. Website: www.finalmix.com. **Contact:** Theresa Frank, A&R. Record producer/remixer/mix engineer, independent label (3.6 Music, Inc.) and music publisher (Ximlanif Music Publishing). Estab. 1989. Releases 12 singles and 3-5 LPs and CDs/year. Fee derived from sales royalty when song or artist is recorded.

How to Contact *Does not accept unsolicited submissions.*

Music Mostly **pop**, **rock**, **dance**, **R&B** and **rap**. Produced and/or mixer/remixer for Mary Mary, LeAnn Rimes, Charice, Train, Aaliyah, Hilary Duff, Jesse McCartney, Christina Aguilera, American Idol, Ray Charles, Quincy Jones, Michael Bolton, K-Ci and Jo Jo (of Jodeci), Will Smith, and/or mixer/remixer for Janet Jackson, Ice Cube, Queen Latifah, Jennifer Paige, and The Corrs.

✪ HAILING FREQUENCY MUSIC PRODUCTIONS

7438 Shoshone Ave., Van Nuys CA 91406. (818)881-9888. Fax: (818)881-0555. E-mail: blowinsmokeband@ktb.net. Website: www.blowinsmokeband.com. President: Lawrence Weisberg. Vice President: Larry Knight. Record producer, record company (Blowin' Smoke Records), management firm (Blowin' Smoke Productions) and music publisher (Hailing Frequency Publishing). Estab. 1992. Produces 3 LPs and 3 CDs/year. Fee derived from sales royalty when song or artist is recorded or outright fee from artist.

- Also see the listing for Blowin' Smoke Productions/Records in the Managers & Booking Agents section of this book.

How to Contact *Write or call first and obtain permission to submit.* Prefers CD or DVD. "Write or print legibly with complete contact instructions." Include SASE. Responds in 1 month.

Music Mostly **contemporary R&B**, **blues** and **blues-rock**; also **songs for film**, **jingles for commercials** and **gospel (contemporary)**. Produced Sky King's "Tales from the Left Coast" (2010). Other artists include the Fabulous Smokettes. New division creates songs and music tracks for both the mainstream and adult film industries.

✪ HEART CONSORT MUSIC

410 First St. SW., Mt. Vernon IA 52314. E-mail: mail@heartconsortmusic.com. Website: www.heartconsortmusic.com. **Contact:** Catherine Lawson, manager. Record producer, record company and music publisher. Estab. 1980. Produces 2-3 CDs/year. Fee derived from sales royalty when song or artist is recorded.

How to Contact Submit demo package by mail. Unsolicited submissions are OK. Prefers CD or cassette with 3 songs and 3 lyric sheets. Include SASE. Responds in 3 months.

Music Mostly **jazz**, **New Age** and **contemporary**. Produced *New Faces* (album), written and recorded by James Kennedy on Heart Consort Music (world/jazz).

Tips "We are interested in jazz/New Age artists with quality demos and original ideas. We aim for an international audience."

☑ INTEGRATED ENTERTAINMENT

1815 JFK Blvd., #1612, Philadelphia PA 19103. (215)563-7147. E-mail: gelboni@aol.com. **Contact:** Gelboni, president. Record producer. Estab. 1991. Produces up to 6 projects/ year. Compensation is derived from outright fee from recording artist or record company and sales royalties.

How to Contact Submit demo package by mail. Solicited submissions only. CD only with 3 songs. "Draw a guitar on the outside of envelope so we'll know it's from a songwriter." Will respond if interested.

Music Mostly **rock** and **pop**. Produced *Gold Record* (album), written and recorded by Dash Rip Rock (rock) on Ichiban Records and many others.

☑ KAREN KANE PRODUCER/ENGINEER

(910)681-0220. E-mail: karenkane@mixmama.com. Website: www.mixmama.com. **Contact:** Karen Kane, producer/ recording and live sound engineer/audio instructor. Record producer and recording engineer. Estab. 1978. Produces 3-5 CDs/year. Fee derived from sales royalty when song or artist is recorded or outright fee from recording artist or record company.

How to Contact *E-mail first and obtain permission to submit. Unsolicited submissions are not OK.* "Please note: I am not a song publisher. My expertise is in album production." Does not return material. Responds in 1 week.

Music Mostly **acoustic music of any kind**, **rock**, **blues**, **pop**, **alternative**, **R&B/reggae**, **country**, and **bluegrass**. Produced *Independence Meal* (album), recorded by Alix Olson (blues), released on Subtle Sister Records; Topless (Juno-nominated album), recorded by Big Daddy G, released on Reggie's Records; *Mixed Wise and Otherwise* (Juno-nominated album), recorded by Harry Manx (blues). Other artists include Tracy Chapman (her first demo), Chad Mitchell, Ember Swift, Laura Bird, Wishing Chair, Blue Mule, Barenaked Ladies (live recording for a TV special), and Ron Wiseman.

Tips "Get proper funding to be able to make a competitive, marketable product."

◯ L.A. ENTERTAINMENT, INC.

7095 Hollywood Blvd., #826, Hollywood CA 90028. 1-800-579-9157. Fax: (323)924-1095. E-mail: info@warriorrecords.com. Website: www.WarriorRecords.com. **Contact:** Jim Ervin, A&R. Record producer, record company (Warrior Records) and music publisher (New Entity Music/ASCAP, New Copyright Music/BMI, New Euphonic Music/SESAC). Estab. 1988. Fee derived from sales royalty when song or artist is recorded.

How to Contact Submit demo package by mail. Unsolicited submissions are OK. Prefers CD and/or videocassette with original songs, lyric and lead sheet if available. "We do not review Internet sites. Do not send MP3s, unless requested. All written submitted materials (e.g., lyric sheets, letter, etc.) should be typed." Does not return material unless SASE is included. Responds in 2 months only via e-mail or SASE.

Music All styles. "All genres are utilized with our music supervision company for Film & TV, but our original focus is on **alternative rock** and **urban genres** (e.g., **R&B**, **rap**, **gospel**).

☐ LARK TALENT & ADVERTISING

P.O. Box 35726, Tulsa OK 74153. (918)786-8896. Fax: (918)786-8897. E-mail: janajae@ janajae.com. Website: www.janajae.com. **Contact:** Kathleen Pixley, vice president. Owner: Jana Jae. Record producer, music publisher (Jana Jae Music/BMI) and record company (Lark Record Productions, Inc.). Estab. 1980. Fee derived from sales royalty when song or artist is recorded.

- Also see the listings for Jana Jae Music in the Music Publishers section, Lark Record Productions in the Record Companies section, and Jana Jae Enterprises in the Managers & Booking Agents section of this book.

How to Contact Submit demo by mail. Unsolicited submissions are OK. Prefers CD or DVD with 3 songs and lead sheet. Does not return material. Responds in 1 month only if interested.

Music Mostly **country**, **bluegrass** and **classical**; also **instrumentals**. Produced "Bussin' Ditty" (single by Steve Upfold); "Mayonnaise" (single by Steve Upfold); and "Flyin' South" (single by Cindy Walker), all recorded by Jana Jae on Lark Records (country). Other artists include Sydni, Hotwire and Matt Greif.

☐ LINEAR CYCLE PRODUCTIONS

P.O. Box 2608, Sepulveda CA 91393-2608. E-mail: LCP@wgn.net. Website: www. linearcycleproductions.com. **Contact:** Manny Pandanceski, producer. Record producer. Estab. 1980. Produces 15-25 singles, 6-10 12" singles, 15-20 CDs/year. Fee derived from sales royalty when song or artist is recorded.

How to Contact Submit demo tape by mail. Unsolicited submissions are OK. Prefers cassette, 7 3/8 ips reel-to-reel or DVD. Only hard copies of recorded demos will be accepted. Demos submitted via mp3/AIFF must include an mp3 player in order for our firm to review the demos. Include SASE. Responds in 6 months.

Music Mostly **rock/pop**, **R&B/blues** and **country**; also **gospel** and **comedy**. Produced "Giving it All to Me" (single by Pandanceski/Katz/Purewhite), recorded by Monea Later (pop/dance), released 2010 on Tozic Googh Sounds. "P for the Bits" (G Glix) (single by Hyram Yip Pea) from his Last Sound Collection, recorded and released 2010 on "Swip" brand mp3s; and "Back into the Box Sho Nuff" (single by Blyma/Warmwater/Posh) recorded by Mister Quit, released 2010.

Tips "We only listen to songs and other material recorded on quality tapes and CDs. We will not accept any submissions via e-mail. If your demo is recorded on an mp3 or AIFF sound file, you must either burn the file onto a CD, or download the sound file into an mp3 player and send the player with the songs to our attention. Otherwise, anything sent via e-mail will be disposed of and will not be considered."

☐ MAC-ATTACK PRODUCTIONS

868 NE 81 St., Miami FL 33138. (305)757-4750. E-mail: GoMacster@aol.com. **Contact:** Michael McNamee, engineer/producer. Record producer and music publisher (Mac-Attack Publishing/ASCAP). Estab. 1986. Fee derived from outright fee from recording artist or record company.

How to Contact Submit demo by mail. Unsolicited submissions are OK. Prefers CD or DVD with 3-5 songs, lyric sheet and bio. Does not return material. Responds in up to 3 months.

Music Mostly **pop**, **alternative rock** and **dance**. Engineered Compositions (album), written and recorded by Paul Martin (experimental), released 2006 on PMR Music. Produced and engineered *Tuscan Tongue* (album by Caution Automatic), recorded by Caution Automatic (rock), released 2005 on C.A. Records; Produced and engineered "Never Gonna Let You Go" (single by Bruce Jordan/John Link/Michael McNamee), recorded by Bruce Jordan (pop), released 2002 on H.M.S. Records. Other artists include Acidosis, Kaseeno, Blowfly, Tally Tal, Nina Llopis, The Lead, Girl Talk, Tyranny of Shaw, and Jacobs Ladder.

☑ COOKIE MARENCO

P.O. Box 874, Belmont CA 94002. E-mail: info@bluecoastrecords.com. (650)595-8475. Music producer/engineer, founder Blue Coast Records, Downloads Now!, OTR Studios. "Over 20 years experience, 5 Grammy nominations, 2 gold records, proprietary surround recording technique, specialist in analog tape and high resolution audio for the internet. Estab. 1981. Produces 10 CDs/year. $2,000 per day payable in advance.

How to Contact *"No speculative projects." Does not accept unsolicited material.* Must have budget.

Music Mostly acoustic, high resolution, live-performance oriented **alternative modern rock**, **country**, **folk**, **rap**, **ethnic** and **avante-garde**; also **classical**, **pop** and **jazz**. Produced *Winter Solstice II* (album), written and recorded by various artists for Windham Hill Records (instrumental). Artists include Tony Furtado, Brain, Buckethead, Alex Degrassi, Turtle Island String Quartet, Praxis, Oregon, Mary Chapin Carpenter, Max Roach and Charle Haden & Quartet West.

Tips "Specialist in high quality ANALOG recording. Mixing to ½" or DSD digital. Full service mastering and dynamic website development."

☑ PETE MARTIN/VAAM MUSIC PRODUCTIONS

P.O. Box 29550, Hollywood CA 90029-0550. (323)664-7765. E-mail: pmarti3636@aol. com. Website: www.VaamMusic.com. **Contact:** Pete Martin, president. Record producer, music publisher (Vaam Music/BMI and Pete Martin Music/ASCAP) and record company (Blue Gem Records). Estab. 1982.

- Also see the listings for Vaam Music Group in the Music Publishers section of this book and Blue Gem Records in the Record Companies section of this book.

How to Contact Send CD or cassette with 2 songs and a lyric sheet. Send small packages only. Include SASE. Responds in 1 month.

Music Mostly **top 40/pop**, **country** and **R&B**.

Tips "Study the market in the style that you write. Songs must be capable of reaching top 5 on charts."

☑ ◻ SCOTT MATHEWS, D/B/A HIT OR MYTH PRODUCTIONS INC.

246 Almonte Blvd., Mill Valley CA 94941. E-mail: scott@scottmathews.com. Website: www.ScottMathews.com. Contact: Mary Ezzell, A&R Director. President: Scott Mathews. Assistant: Tom Luekens. Record producer, song doctor, studio owner and music publisher (Hang On to Your Publishing/BMI). Estab. 1990. Produces 6-9 CDs/year. Fee derived from recording artist or record company (with royalty points).

- Scott Mathews has several gold and platinum awards for sales of more than 15 million records. He has worked with more than 60 Rock & Roll Hall of Fame inductees and on several Grammy and Oscar-winning releases. He is currently working primarily with emerging artists while still making music with his legendary established artists.

How to Contact "No phone calls or publishing submissions, please." Submit demo CD by mail or an mp3 by email. "Unsolicited submissions are often the best ones and readily accepted. Include SASE if e-mail is not an option. Also include your e-mail address on your demo CD." Responds in 2 months.

Music Mostly rock/pop, alternative and singer/songwriters of all styles. In 2009 and 2010 Mathews has made music with Jimmy Buffett, Bonnie Raitt, Brian Wilson, Zac Brown, Chris Issak, and a long list of emerging artists. Produced 4 tracks on Anthology (Best of),recorded by John Hiatt (rock/pop), released 2001 on Hip-O. Has produced Elvis Costello, Roy Orbison, Rosanne Cash, Jerry Garcia, Huey Lewis, and many more. Has recorded classics with everyone from Barbra Streisand to John LeeHooker, including Keith Richards, George Harrison, Mick Jagger, Van Morrison, Bonnie Raitt, and Eric Clapton to namebut a few.

Tips "These days if you are not independent, you are dependent. The new artists that are coming up and achieving success in the music industry are the ones that prove they have a vision and can make incredible records without the huge financial commitment of a major label. When an emerging artist makes great product for the genre they are in, they are in the driver's seat to be able to make a fair and equitable deal for distribution, be it with a major or independent label. My philosophy is to go where you are loved. The truth is, a smaller label that is completely dedicated to you and shares your vision may help your career far more than a huge label that will not keep you around if you don't sell millions of units. Perhaps no label is needed at all, if you are up for the challenge of wearing a lot of hats. I feel too much pressure is put on the emerging artist when they have to pay huge sums back to the label in order to see their first royalty check. We all know those records can be made for a fraction of that cost without compromising quality or commercial appeal. I still believe in potential and our company is in business to back up that belief. It is up to us as record makers/visionaries to take that potential into the studio and come out with music that can compete with anything else on the market. Discovering, developing and producing artists that can sustain long careers is our main focus at Hit or Myth Productions. We are proud to be associated with so many legendary and timeless artists and our track record speaks for itself. If you love making music, don't let anyone dim that light. We look forward to hearing from you. (Please check out www. ScottMathews.com for more info, and also www.allmusic.com-keyword; Scott Mathews.) Accept no substitutes!"

☐ MUSICJONES RECORDS

(formerly SOUND WORKS ENTERTAINMENT PRODUCTIONS INC.) 990 Somerset Ct., Charlottesville VA 22906. (434)632-7860. E-mail: mike@musicjones.com. Website: www. musicjones.com. **Contact:** Michael E. Jones, president. Record producer, record company (MusicJones Records) and music publisher (MusicJones Music). Estab. 1989. Produces 16 singles, 2 LPs and 20 CDs/year. Fee derived from sales royalty when song or artist is recorded or outright fee from recording artist or record company.

How to Contact Submit demo package by mail. Unsolicited submissions are OK. Prefers cassette with 3-6 songs and lyric sheet. "Please include short bio and statement of goals and objectives." Does not return material. Responds in 6 weeks.

Music Mostly **country**, **folk** and **pop**; also **rock**. Recent album releases: *The Highway* featuring Mike Jones and "Oops My Bad" Featuring Ginger Granger. Also produced "Lonelyville," and "Alabama Slammer" (singles), both written and recorded by Wake Eastman; and "Good Looking Loser" (single), written and recorded by Renee Rubach, all on Sound Works Records (country). Other artists include Matt Dorman, Steve Gilmore, The Tackroom Boys, The Las Vegas Philharmonic, and J.C. Clark.

Tips "Put your ego on hold. Don't take criticism personally. Advice is meant to help you grow and improve your skills as an artist/songwriter. Be professional and business-like in all your dealings."

☑ MUSTROCK PRODUCTIONZ WORLDWIDE

E-mail: recordmode@hotmail.com. President: Ivan "Doc" Rodriguez. Record producer and recording/mixing/mastering engineer. Estab. 1987. Produces various singles and CDs/year. Fee derived from sales royalty and advance payment when song or artist is recorded. " We are not a record company. We provide services for a fee—we do not sign or represent artists. We are a work-for-hire company."

How to Contact *E-mail first and obtain permission to submit.* Prefers mp3, CD, DVD and lyric sheet. Does not return material. Responds in 2 months. "Unless booking our services, only opinion will be given—we do not shop deals."

Music Mostly **hip-hop**, **R&B** and **pop**; also **soul**, **ballads** and **soundtracks**. Produced "Poor Georgie" (by MC Lyte/DJ DOC), recorded by MC Lyte on Atlantic Records (rap). Other artists include Caron Wheeler, The Hit Squad, The Awesome II, Black Steel Music, Underated Productions, EPMD, Redman, Dr. Dre & Ed-Lover, Das-EFX, Biz Markie, BDP,

Eric B & Rakim, The Fugees, The Bushwackass, Shai and Pudgee, Alisha Keys, 50 cent, Tiro de Garcia, etc.

Tips "Services provided include ProTools production (pre/post/co), digital tracking, mixing, remixing, live show tapes, jingles, etc. For additinal credits, go to www.allmusic. com, type 'Ivan Doc Rodriguez' under 'artist' and enter, or send e-mail."

☐ NEU ELECTRO PRODUCTIONS

P.O. Box 1582, Bridgeview IL 60455. (630)257-6289. E-mail: neuelectro@email.com. Website: www.neuelectro.com. **Contact:** Bob Neumann, owner. Record producer and record company. Estab. 1984. Produces 16 singles, 16 12" singles, 20 LPs and 4 CDs/year. Fee derived from outright fee from record company or recording artist.

How to Contact Submit demo package by mail. Unsolicited submissions are OK. Prefers CD with 3 songs and lyric sheet or lead sheet. "Provide accurate contact phone numbers and addresses, promo packages and photos." Include SASE for reply. Responds in 2 weeks. "A production fee estimate will be returned to artist."

Music Mostly **dance**, **house**, **techno**, **rap** and **rock**; also **experimental**, **New Age** and **top 40**. Produced "Juicy" (single), written and recorded by Juicy Black on Dark Planet International Records (house); "Make Me Smile" (single), written and recorded by Roz Baker (house); *Reactovate-6* (album by Bob Neumann), recorded by Beatbox-D on N.E.P. Records (dance); and *Sands of Time* (album), recorded by Bob Neumann (New Age). Other artists include Skid Marx and The Deviants.

☑ NEW EXPERIENCE RECORDS/FAZE 4 RECORDS

P.O. Box 683, Lima OH 45802. E-mail: just_chilling_2002@yahoo.com. Website: www. faze4records.com. **Contact:** A&R Department. Music Publisher: James L. Milligan Jr. Record producer, music publisher (A New Rap Jam Publishing/ASCAP), management firm (Creative Star Management) and record company (New Experience Records, Grand-Slam Records and Pump It Up Records). Estab. 1989. Produces 15-20 12" singles, 2 LPs, 3 EPs and 2-5 CDs/year. Fee derived from sales royalty when song or artist is recorded or outright fee from record company, "depending on services required." Distributed by IODA, Distribution/Doodlebug Media.

- Also see the listings for A New Rap Jam Publishing in the Music Publishers section of this book.

How to Contact Write first to arrange personal interview. Address material to A&R Dept. or Talent Coordinator. Prefers CD with a minimum of 3 songs and lyric or lead sheet (if available). "If tapes are to be returned, proper postage should be enclosed and all tapes and letters should have SASE for faster reply." Responds in 6-8 weeks.

Music Mostly **pop**, **R&B** and **rap**; also **gospel**, **soul**, **contemporary gospel** and **rock**. Produced "The Son of God" (single by James Milligan/Anthony Milligan/Melvin Milligan) from *The Final Chapter* (album), recorded by T.M.C. Milligan Conection (R&B, Gospel), released 2002 on New Experience/Pump It Up Records. Other artists include Dion Mikel, Paulette Mikel, Melvin Milligan and Venesta Compton.

Tips "Do your homework on the music business. Be aware of all the new sampling laws. There are too many sound alikes. Be yourself. I look for what is different, vocal ability, voice range and sound stage presence, etc. Be on the look out for our new blues label Rough Edge Records/Rough Edge Entertainment. Blues material is now being reviewed. Send your best studio recorded material. Also be aware of the new digital downloading laws. People are being jailed and fined for recording music that has not been paid for. Do your homework. We have also signed Diamond Sound Productions, located in Fresno, CA and Ground Breakers Records. Now we can better serve our customers on the East and West Coast. You can also visit our website at www.faze4records.com for further information on our services. We are reviewing hip-hop and rap material that is positive, clean, and commercial; please no Gangsta rap if you want a deal with us as well as airplay. Also reviewing gospel music, gospel rap and anything with commercial appeal."

☑ WESTWIRES RECORDING USA

(formerly Westwires Digital USA), 1042 Club Ave., Allentown PA 18109. (610)435-1924. E-mail: info@westwires.com. Website: www.westwires.com. **Contact:** Wayne Becker, owner/producer. Record producer and production company. Fee derived from outright fee from record company or artist retainer.

How to Contact *Contact via e-mail for permission to submit.* "No phone calls, please." Submit demo by mail or mp3 by e-mail. Unsolicited submissions are OK. Prefers mp3 with lyrics in MS Word or Adobe PDF file format, or CD, DVD, or VHS videocassette with 3 songs and lyric sheet. Does not return material. Responds in 1 month.

Music Mostly **rock**, **R&B**, **dance**, **alternative**, **folk** and **eclectic**. Produced Ye Ren (Dimala Records), Weston (Universal/Mojo), Zakk Wylde (Spitfire Records). Other artists include Ryan Asher, Paul Rogers, Anne Le Baron, and Gary Hassay

Tips "We are interested in singer/songwriters and alternative artists living in the mid-Atlantic area. Must have steady gig schedule and established fan base."

☑ WLM MUSIC/RECORDING

2808 Cammie St., Durham NC 27705-2020. (919)471-3086. Fax: (919)471-4326. E-mail: wlm-musicrecording@nc.rr.com or wlm-band@nc.rr.com. **Contact:** Watts Lee Mangum, owner. Record producer. Estab. 1980. Fee derived from outright fee from recording artist. "In some cases, an advance payment requested for demo production."

How to Contact Submit demo by mail. Unsolicited submissions are OK. Prefers CD with 2-4 songs and lyric or lead sheet (if possible). Include SASE. Responds in 6 months.

Music Mostly **country**, **country/rock** and **blues/rock**; also **pop**, **rock**, **blues**, **gospel** and **bluegrass**. Produced "911," and "Petals of an Orchid" (singles), both written and recorded by Johnny Scoggins (country); and "Renew the Love" (single by Judy Evans), recorded by Bernie Evans (country), all on Independent. Other artists include Southern Breeze Band and Heart Breakers Band.

☑ WORLD RECORDS

5798 Deer Trail Dr., Traverse City MI 49684. E-mail: jack@worldrec.org. Website: www.worldrec.org. **Contact:** Jack Conners, producer. Record producer, engineer/technician and record company (World Records). Estab. 1984. Produces 1 CD/year. Fee derived from outright fee from recording artist.

How to Contact *Write first and obtain permission to submit.* Prefers CD with 1 or 2 songs. Include SASE. Responds in 6 weeks.

Music Mostly **classical**, **folk**, and **jazz**. Produced *Mahler, Orff, Collins* (album), recorded by Traverse Symphony Orchestra (classical), released 2006; *Reflections on Schubert* (album) recorded by Michael Coonrod (classical), released 2007. Other artists include Jeff Haas and The Camerata Singers.

☑ ZIG PRODUCTIONS

P.O. Box 120931, Arlington TN 76012. (214)354-8401. E-mail: billyherzig@hotmail.com. Website: www.zigproductions.com. **Contact:** Billy Herzig or Wendy Mazur. Record producer. Music publisher (Thistle Hill/BMI). Estab. 1998. "Occasionally I produce a single that is recorded separate from a full CD project." Produces 6-10 albums. Fee derived from sales royalty when song or artist is recorded and/or outright fee from recording artist. "Sometimes there are investors."

How to Contact Submit a demo by mail. Unsolicited submissions are OK. We do not return submissions.Responds only if interested.

Music Mostly **country**, **Americana**, and **rock**; also **pop**, **r&b**, and **alternative**. Produced "Ask Me to Stay" (single by King Cone/Josh McDaniel) from *Gallery*, recorded by King Cone (Texas country/Americana). released 2007 on King Cone; "A Cure for Awkward Silence" (single), recorded by Tyler Stock (acoustic rock), released 2007 on Payday Records; "Take Me Back" (single) from *Peace, Love & Crabs*, written and recorded by Deanna Dove (folk-rock), released 2007 on Island Girl. Also produced Robbins & Jones (country), Jordan Mycoskie (country), Carla Rhodes (comedy), Four Higher (alternative), Charis Thorsell (country), Shane Mallory (country), Rachel Rodriguez (blues-rock), Jessy Daumen (country), Frankie Moreno (rock/r&b), Shawna Russell (country), and many others.

ADDITIONAL RECORD PRODUCERS

A

Ariana Records 136

Atlan-Dec/Grooveline Records 137

Avita Records 137

B

Blue Gem Records 138

C

Collector Records 140

Cornelius Companies/Gateway
  Entertainment, Inc., The 105

Cosmotone Records 140

F

First Time Music (Publishing) U.K. 109

G

Glad Music Co. 110

H

Hammel Associates, Inc., R L 112

Hardison International Entertainment
  Corporation 194

K

Kaysarah Music 115

L

Lark Record Productions, Inc. 148

Loggins Promotion 196

M

Martin Productions, Rick 197

Maui Arts & Music Association/Survivo
  Records/Ten of Diamonds Music 116

McCoy Music, Jim 117

P

Panama Music Group of Companies, The
  152

Perla Music 120

Q

QUARK, Inc. 122

R

Ranco Records 154

S

Sahara Records and Filmworks
  Entertainment 158

Sinus Musik Produktion, Ulli Weigel 124

T

Ton Records 162

Topcat Records 162

V

Vaam Music Group 127

W

Warner Productions, Cheryl K. 205

World Beatnik Records 166

Record Producers

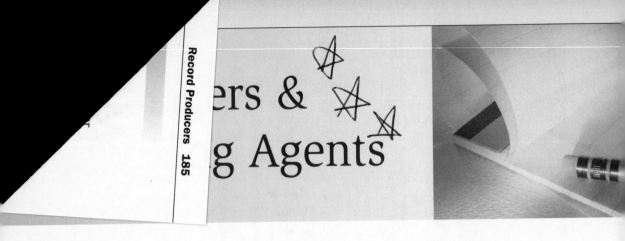

Before submitting to a manager or booking agent, be sure you know exactly what you need. If you're looking for someone to help you with performance opportunities, the booking agency is the one to contact. They can help you book shows either in your local area or throughout the country. If you're looking for someone to help guide your career, you need to contact a management firm. Some management firms may also handle booking; however, it may be in your best interest to look for a separate booking agency. A manager should be your manager—not your agent, publisher, lawyer or accountant.

MANAGERS

Of all the music industry players surrounding successful artists, managers are usually the people closest to the artists themselves. The artist manager can be a valuable contact, both for the songwriter trying to get songs to a particular artist and for the songwriter/performer. A manager and his connections can be invaluable in securing the right publishing deal or recording contract if the writer is also an artist. Getting songs to an artist's manager is yet another way to get your songs recorded, since the manager may play a large part in deciding what material his client uses. For the performer seeking management, a successful manager should be thought of as the foundation for a successful career.

The relationship between a manager and his client relies on mutual trust. A manager works as the liaison between you and the rest of the music industry, and he must know exactly what you want out of your career in order to help you achieve your goals. His handling of publicity, promotion and finances, as well as the contacts he has within the industry, can make or break your career. You should never be afraid to ask questions about any aspect of the relationship between you and a prospective manager.

Always remember that a manager works *for the artist*. A good manager is able to communicate his opinions to you without reservation, and should be willing to explain any confusing terminology or discuss plans with you before taking action. A manager needs to be able to communicate successfully with all segments of the music industry in order to get his client the best deals possible. He needs to be able to work with booking agents, publishers, lawyers and record companies.

Keep in mind that you are both working together toward a common goal: success for you and your songs. Talent, originality, professionalism and a drive to succeed are qualities that will attract a manager to an artist—and a songwriter.

BOOKING AGENTS

The function of the booking agent is to find performance venues for their clients. They usually represent many more acts than a manager does, and have less contact with their acts. A booking agent charges a commission for his services, as does a manager. Managers usually ask for a 15-20% commission on an act's earnings; booking agents usually charge around 10%. In the area of managers and booking agents, more successful acts can negotiate lower percentage deals than the ones set forth above.

SUBMITTING MATERIAL TO MANAGERS & BOOKING AGENTS

The firms listed in this section have provided information about the types of music they work with and the types of acts they represent. You'll want to refer to the Category Index on page 333 to find out which companies deal with the type of music you write, and the Geographic Index at the back of the book to help you locate companies near where you live. Then determine whether they are open to your level of experience (see A Sample Listing Decoded on page 7). Each listing also contains submission requirements and information about what items to include in a press kit and will also specify whether the company is a management firm or a booking agency. Remember that your submission represents you as an artist, and should be as organized and professional as possible.

ADDITIONAL MANAGERS & BOOKING AGENTS

There are more managers & booking agents located in other sections of the book! On page 208 use the list of Additional Managers & Booking Agents to find listings within other sections who are also managers/booking agents.

◪ BILL ANGELINI ENTERPRISES/BOOKYOUREVENT.COM

(formerly Management Plus), P.O. Box 132, Seguin TX 78155. (830)401-0061. Fax: (830)401-0069. E-mail: bill@bookyourevent.com. Website: www.bookyourevent.com. **Contact:** Bill Angelini, owner. Management firm and booking agency. Estab. 1980. Represents individual artists and groups from anywhere; currently handles 6 acts. Receives 10-15% commission. Reviews material for acts.

How to Contact Submit demo package by mail or EPK. Unsolicited submissions are OK. Press kit should include pictures, bio, and discography. Does not return material. Responds in 1 month.

Music Mostly **Latin American**, **Tejano** and **international**; also **Norteno** and **country**. Current acts include Jay Perez (Tejano), Ram Herrera (Tejano), Michael Salgado (Tejano), Flaco Jimenez (Tex-Mex), Electric Cowboys (tex-mex), Los Palominos (Tejano), Grupo Vida (Tejano), and Texmaniacs (Tex-Mex).

◪ ARTIST REPRESENTATION AND MANAGEMENT

1257 Arcade St., St. Paul MN 55106. (651)483-8754. Fax: (651)776-6338. E-mail: ra@armentertainment.com. Website: www.armentertainment.com. **Contact:** Roger Anderson, agent/manager. Management firm and booking agency. Estab. 1983. Represents artists from USA/Canada; currently handles 15 acts. Receives 15% commission. Reviews material for acts.

How to Contact Submit CD and DVD (preferable) by mail. Unsolicited submissions are OK. Please include minimum 3 songs. If seeking management, current schedule, bio, photo, press clippings should also be included. "Priority is placed on original artists with product who are currently touring." Does not return material. Responds only if interested within 30 days.

Music Mostly **melodic rock**. Current acts include Warrant, Firehouse, Winger, Skid Row, Scarlet Haze, Head East, Frank Hannon of Tesla, LA Guns featuring Phil Lewis, Dokken, Adler's Apetite, and Bret Michaels of Poison.

◪ BARNARD MANAGEMENT SERVICES (BMS)

2916 Main Street, Suite 200, Santa Monica CA 90405 (310)392-2916. E-mail: bms@barnardus.com. **Contact:** Russell Barnard, president. Management firm. Estab. 1979. Represents artists, groups and songwriters; currently handles 2 acts. Receives 10-20% commission. Reviews material for acts.

How to Contact *Write first and obtain permission to submit.* Prefers CD with 3-10 songs and lead sheet. Artists may submit DVD (15-30 minutes) by permission only. If seeking management, press kit should include cover letter, bio, photo, demo DVD/CD, lyric sheets, press clippings, video and résumé. Does not return material. Responds in 2 months.

Music Mostly **country crossover**, **blues**, **country**, **R&B**, **rock** and **soul**. Current acts include Mark Shipper (songwriter/author) and Bob Baker (singer/songwriter).

◙ BLANK & BLANK

One Belmont Ave., Suite 602, Bala Cynwyd PA 19004. (610)667-9900. Fax: (610)667-9901.
Contact: E. Robert Blank, manager. Management firm. Represents individual artists and groups. Reviews material for acts.

How to Contact *Contact first and obtain permission to submit.* Prefers CD, DVD, or videocassette. If seeking management, press kit should include cover letter, demo tape/CD and video. Does not return material.

◙ BLOWIN' SMOKE PRODUCTIONS/RECORDS

7438 Shoshone Ave., Van Nuys CA 91406-2340. (818)881-9888. Fax: (818)881-0555.
E-mail: blowinsmokeband@ktb.net. Website: www.blowinsmokeband.com. **Contact:**
Larry Knight, president. Management firm and record producer. Estab. 1990. Represents local and West Coast individual artists and groups; currently handles 6 acts. Receives 15-20% commission. Reviews material for acts.

- Also see the listing for Hailing Frequency Music Productions in the Record Producers section of this book.

How to Contact *Write or call first and obtain permission to submit.* Prefers cassette or CD. If seeking management, press kit should include cover letter, demo tape/CD, lyric sheets, press clippings, video if available, photo, bios, contact telephone numbers and any info on legal commitments already in place. Include SASE. Responds in 1 month.

Music Mostly **R&B**, **blues** and **blues-rock**. Works primarily with single and group vocalists and a few R&B/blues bands. Current acts include Larry "Fuzzy" Knight (blues singer/songwriter), King Floyd (R&B artist), The Blowin' Smoke Rhythm & Blues Band, The Fabulous Smokettes, Joyce Lawson, Sky King (rock/blues), and Guardians of the Clouds (alternative rock).

◙ THE BLUE CAT AGENCY

E-mail: bluecat_agency@yahoo.com. **Contact:** Karen Kindig, owner/agent. Management firm and booking agency. Estab. 1989. Represents established individual artists and/or groups from anywhere; currently handles 5 acts. Receives 10-15% commission. Reviews material for acts.

How to Contact *E-mail only for permission to submit.* Prefers cassette or CD. If seeking management, press kit should include, CD or tape, bio, press clippings and photo. SASE. Responds in 2 months.

Music Mostly **rock/pop "en espanol "** and **jazz/latin jazz**. Works primarily with bands (established performers only). Current acts include Ylonda Nickell, Kai Eckhardt, Alejandro Santos, Ania Paz, Gabriel Rosati.

◻ BREAD & BUTTER PRODUCTIONS

P.O. Box 1539, Wimberley TX 78676. (512)301-7117. E-mail: sgladson@gmail.com.
Contact: Steve Gladson, managing partner. Management firm and booking agency. Estab.

1969. Represents individual artists, songwriters and groups from anywhere; currently handles 6 acts. Receives 10-20% commission. Reviews material for acts.

How to Contact Submit demo package by mail. Unsolicited submissions OK. Prefers DVD or CD and lyric sheet. If seeking management, press kit should include cover letter, demo tape/CD, lyric sheets, press clippings, video, résumé, picture and bio or a list of your social networking sites. Does not return material. Responds in 1 month.

Music Mostly **alternative rock**, **country** and **R&B**; also **classic rock**, **folk** and **Americana**. Works primarily with singer/songwriters and original bands. Current acts include Lou Cabaza (songwriter/producer/manager), Duck Soup (band) and Gaylan Ladd (songwriter/singer/producer).

Tips "Remember why you are in this biz. The art comes first."

BROTHERS MANAGEMENT ASSOCIATES

141 Dunbar Ave., Fords NJ 08863. (732)738-0880. Fax: (732)738-0970. E-mail: bmaent@ yahoo.com. Website: www.bmaent.com. **Contact:** Allen A. Faucera, president. Management firm and booking agency. Estab. 1972. Represents artists, groups and songwriters; currently handles 25 acts. Receives 15-20% commission. Reviews material for acts.

How to Contact *Write first and obtain permission to submit.* Prefers CD or DVD with 3-6 songs and lyric sheets. Include photographs and résumé. If seeking management, include photo, bio, tape and return envelope in press kit. Include SASE. Responds in 2 months.

Music Mostly **pop**, **rock**, **MOR** and **R&B**. Works primarily with vocalists and established groups. Current acts include Nils Lofgren.

Tips "Submit very commercial material—make demo of high quality."

CLASS ACT PRODUCTIONS/MANAGEMENT/PETER KIMMEL'S MUSIC CATALOG

P.O. Box 55252, Sherman Oaks CA 91413. (818)980-1039. E-mail: peter.kimmel@ sbcglobal.net. **Contact:** Peter Kimmel, president. Management firm. Estab. 1985. Currently represents songwriters and music artists. Receives percentage of commission.

How to Contact Submit material via mail or e-mail. Unsolicited submissions are OK. For mail, include CD, cover letter, lyric sheets (essential) or submit electronic press kit by e-mail. Responds in 1 month.

Music All styles. Represents select first rate music material to music supervisors of films, television, commercials, etc.

Tips. "We are also affiliated with Sound Image Entertainment recording studios and video production. See website at www.soundimage.us and www.soundimagevideo.com."

CLOUSHER PRODUCTIONS

P.O. Box 1191, Mechanicsburg PA 17055. (717)766-7644. Fax: (717)766-1490. E-mail: cpinfo@msn.com. Website: www.clousher.com. **Contact:** Fred Clousher, owner. Booking agency and production company. Estab. 1972. Represents groups from anywhere; currently handles over 100 acts.

How to Contact Submit demo package by mail. Please, no electronic press kits. Unsolicited submissions are OK. Prefers CDs or DVD. Press kit should include bio, credits, pictures, song list, references, and your contact information. Does not return material. "Performer should check back with us!"

Music Mostly **country, oldies rock & roll,** and **ethnic** (German, Hawaiian, etc.); also **dance bands** (regional), **Dixieland**, and **classical musicians**. "We work mostly with country, old time R&R, regional variety dance bands, tribute acts, and all types of variety acts." Current acts include Jasmine Morgan (country/pop vocalist), Robin Right (country vocalist and Tammy Wynette tribute artist) and Stanky & The Coalminers (polka band).

Tips "The songwriters we work with are entertainers themselves, which is the aspect we deal with. They usually have bands or do some sort of show, either with tracks or live music. We engage them for stage shows, concerts, etc. We DO NOT review songs you've written. We do not publish music, or submit performers to recording companies for contracts. We strictly set up live performances for them."

☑ CONCEPT 2000 INC.

P.O. Box 2950, Columbus OH 43216-2950. (614)276-2000. Fax: (614)275-0163. E-mail: info2k@concept2k.com. Website: www.concept2k.com. **Florida office:** P.O. Box 2070, Largo FL 33779-2070. (727)585-2922. Fax: (727)585-3835. **Contact:** Brian Wallace, president. Management firm and booking agency. Estab. 1981. Represents international individual artists, groups and songwriters; currently handles 4 acts. Receives 20% commission. Reviews material for acts.

How to Contact Submit demo by mail. Unsolicited submissions are OK. Prefers CD with 4 songs. If seeking management, include demo tape, press clips, photo and bio. Does not return material. Responds in 2 weeks.

Music Mostly **rock, country, pop**, and **contemporary gospel**. Current acts include Satellites Down (rock); Gene Walker (jazz); Endless Summer (show group); Thomas Wynn and the Believers (country).

Tips "Send quality songs with lyric sheets. Production quality is not necessary."

☑ THE EDWARD DE MILES MUSIC COMPANY

10573 W. Pico Blvd., #352, Los Angeles CA 90064-2348. Phone: (310)948-9652. Fax: (310)474-7705. E-mail: info@edmsahara.com. Website: www.edmsahara.com. **Contact:** Edward de Miles, president. Management firm, booking agency, entertainment/sports promoter and TV/radio broadcast producer. Estab. 1984. Represents film, television, radio and musical artists; currently handles 15 acts. Receives 10-20% commission. Reviews material for acts. Regional operations in Chicago, Dallas, Houston and Nashville through marketing representatives. Licensed A.F. of M. booking agent.

- Also see listings for Edward De Miles in the Music Publishers and Record Producers sections, and Sahara Records and Filmworks Entertainment in the Record Companies section of this book.

How to Contact *Does not accept unsolicited materials.* Prefers CD with 3-5 songs, 8 × 10 b&w photo, bio and lyric sheet. "Copyright all material before submitting." If seeking management, include cover letter, bio, demo CD with 3-5 songs, 8 × 10 b&w photo, lyric sheet, press clippings and video if available in press kit. Include SASE. Does not return material. Responds in 1 month.

Music Mostly **country**, **dance**, **R&B/soul**, **rock**, **top 40/pop** and **urban contemporary**; also looking for material for **television, radio and film** productions. Works primarily with dance bands and vocalists. Current acts include Steve Lynn (R&B/dance), Multiple Choice (rap) and Devon Edwards (jazz).

Tips "Performers need to be well prepared with their presentations (equipment, showmanship a must)."

JOHN ECKERT ENTERTAINMENT CONSULTANTS

(formerly Pro Talent Consultants), 7723 Cora Dr., Lucerne CA 95458. (707)349-1809, (323)325-6662 (Los Angeles, CA). E-mail: talentconsultants@gmail.com. **Contact:** John Eckert, coordinator or Rich Clark. MarVista/Santa Monica management firm and booking agency. Estab. 1979. Represents individual artists and groups; currently handles 12 acts. Receives 15% commission. Reviews material for acts.

How to Contact Submit demo package by mail. Unsolicited submissions are OK. "We prefer CD (4 songs). Submit videocassette with live performance only." If seeking management, press kit should include an 8 × 10 photo, a cassette or CD of at least 4-6 songs, a bio on group/artist, references, cover letter, press clippings, video and business card, or a phone number with address. Does not return material. Responds in 5 weeks.

Music Mostly **country**, **country/pop** and **rock**. Works primarily with vocalists, show bands, dance bands, and bar bands. Current acts include The Rose Garden (pop/rock/country band); The Royal Guardsmen (pop/rock/top 40); The Hullaballoos (top 40/pop band); and Don Grady, (singer/songwriter, actor).

SCOTT EVANS PRODUCTIONS

P.O. Box 814028, Hollywood FL 33081-4028. (954)963-4449. E-mail: evansprod@aol.com. Website: www.theentertainmentmall.com. **Contact:** Ted Jones, new artists, or Jeanne K., Internet marketing and sales. Management firm and booking agency. Estab. 1979. Represents local, regional or international individual artists, groups, songwriters, comedians, novelty acts and dancers; currently handles over 200 acts. Receives 10-50% commission. Reviews material for acts.

How to Contact New artists can make submissions through the 'auditions' link located on the website. Unsolicited submissions are OK. "Please be sure that all submissions are copyrighted and not your original copy as we do not return material."

Music Mostly **pop**, **R&B** and **Broadway**. Deals with "all types of entertainers; no limitations." Current acts include Scott Evans and Company (variety song and dance), Dorit Zinger (female vocalist), Jeff Geist, Actors Repertory Theatre, Entertainment Express, Perfect Parties, Joy Deco (dance act), Flashback 2000 Revue (musical song and dance), Everybody Salsa (Latin song and dance) and Around the World (international song and dance).

Tips "Submit a neat, well put together, organized press kit."

☐ EXCLESISA BOOKING AGENCY

716 Windward Rd., Jackson MS 39206. (601)366-0220. E-mail: exclesis@bellsouth. net. Website: www.exclesisa-booking.com. **Contact:** Roy and Esther Wooten, booking managers/owners. Booking agency. Estab. 1989. Represents groups from anywhere; currently handles 9 acts. Receives 15% commission. Reviews material for acts.

How to Contact *Call first and obtain permission to submit.* Submit demo package by mail. Unsolicited submissions are OK. Prefers CD or videocassette. If seeking management, press kit should include CD or cassette, videocassette, pictures, address and telephone contact,and bio. Does not return material. Responds in 2 months.

Music Gospel only. Current acts include The Canton Spirituals, Darrell McFadden & The Disciples, The Jackson Southernaires, The Pilgrim Jubilees, Spencer Taylor & the Highway Q'cs, The Annointed Jackson Singers, Rev. Andrew Cheairs and the Songbirds, and Keith "The Wonderboy" Johnson.

Tips "Make sure your demo is clear with a good sound so the agent can make a good judgement."

⊞ ☑ FIRST TIME MANAGEMENT

Sovereign House, 12 Trewartha Rd., Praa Sands-Penzance, Cornwall TR20 9ST England (01736)762826. Fax: (01736)763328. E-mail: panamus@aol.com. Website: www. songwriters-guild.co.uk and www.myspace.com/guildofsongwriters. **Contact:** Roderick G. Jones, managing director. Management firm, record company (Digimix Records Ltd www.digimixrecords.com, Rainy Day Records, Mohock Records, Pure Gold Records) and music publisher (Panama Music Library, Melody First Music Library, Eventide Music Library, Musik' Image Music Library, Promo Sonor International Music Library, Caribbean Music Library, ADN Creation Music Library, Piano Bar Music Library, Corelia Music Library, PSI Music Library,Scamp Music Publishing, First Time Music (Publishing) U.K. (www.panamamusic.co.uk and www.myspace.com/scampmusicpublishing) —registered members of The Mechanical Copyright Protection Society (MCPS) and The Performing Right Society (PRS)). Estab. 1986. Represents local, regional and international individual artists, groups, composers, DJs and songwriters. Receives 15-25% commission. Reviews material for acts.

- Also see the listings for First Time Music (Publishing) in the Music Publishers section of this book.

How to Contact Submit demo package by mail. Unsolicited submissions are OK. Prefers CD with 3 songs, lyric sheets and also complete album projects where writer/performer has finished masters. If seeking management, press kit should include cover letter, bio, photo, demo tape/CD, press clippings and anything relevant to make an impression. Does not return material. Responds in 1 month only if interested.

Music All styles. Works primarily with songwriters, composers, DJs, rappers, vocalists, bands, groups and choirs. Current acts include Willow (pop), Bram Stoker (prog rock/gothic rock group), Kevin Kendle (New Age, holistic) Peter Arnold (folk/roots), David Jones (urban/R&B), Shanelle (R&B/dance), AudioJunkie & Stylus (dance/hardcore/funky house/electro house) Ray Guntrip (jazz); DJ Gammer (hardcore/hardhouse/dance).

Tips "Become a member of the Guild of International Songwriters and Composers (www.songwriters-guild.co.uk). Keep everything as professional as possible. Be patient and dedicated to your aims and objectives."

◻ HARDISON INTERNATIONAL ENTERTAINMENT CORPORATION

P.O. Box 1732, Knoxville TN 37901-1732. (865)688-8680. E-mail: dennishardinson@bellsouth.net. Website: www.myspace.com/hardison_music07 and http://www.hardisoninternational.netfirms.com. **Contact:** Dennis K. Hardison, CEO/founder. Dennis K. Hardison II, president; Travis J. Hardison, president, Denlatrin Record, a division of Hardison International Entertainment Corp. Contact: Management firm, booking agency, music publisher (Denlatrin Music) BMI, record label (Denlatrin Records) and record producer. Estab. 1984. Represents individual artists from anywhere; currently handles 3 acts. Receives 20% commission. Reviews material for acts. "We are seeking level-minded and patient individuals. Our primary interests are established recording acts with prior major deals."

- This company has promoted many acts in show business for over 30 years, including New Edition, Freddie Jackson, M.C. Lyte, Kool Moe Dee, Biz Markie, and Surface, to name a few.

How to Contact Submit demo package by mail. Unsolicited submissions are OK. Prefers CD with 3 songs only. If seeking management, press kit should include bio, promo picture and CD. Does not return materials. Responds in 6 weeks to the best material. Critiques available through MySpace, so enclose your MySpace address.

Music Mostly **R&B, hip-hop** and **rap**. Current acts include Dynamo (hip-hop), The Nafro Queens of Lagos, Nigeria, and Triniti (record producer, Public Enemy, Dynamo, among others, current studio and sound engineer for Chuck D).

Tips "We respond to the hottest material, so make it hot!"

☑ M. HARRELL & ASSOCIATES

5444 Carolina, Merrillville IN 46410. (219)887-8814. Fax: (480)345-2255. E-mail: mharrell@promos@gmail.com. **Contact:** Mary Harrell, owner. Booking agency. Estab. 1984. Represents individual artists, groups, songwriters, all talents—fashion, dancers, etc.; currently handles 30-40 acts. Receives 10-20% commission. Reviews material for acts.

How to Contact *Call first and obtain permission to submit.* Submit demo by mail. Prefers CD or DVD with 2-3 songs. Send résumé, bio, photo, CD and press clippings. "Keep it brief and current." Does not return material. Responds in 1 month.

Music country, **R&B**, **jazz**, **gospel**, **Big Band**, **light rock** and **reggae**. Current acts include Manny B (showact), Michael Essany (celebrity talk show host), Bill Shelton & 11th Avenue ('50s rock & roll), Bang (R&B/jazz), Julian Michaels (singer-songwriter/pop), and David Bacon, musician, theater director.

Tips "The bands listed can and do tour in the U.S. and Europe (variety, mostly R&B, jazz and top 40) as well as the Chicagoland area. They get steady work and repeat business, because they are good and beat their competition."

◙ INTERNATIONAL ENTERTAINMENT BUREAU

3612 N. Washington Blvd., Indianapolis IN 46205-3592. (317)926-7566. E-mail: ieb@prodigy.net. Booking agency. Estab. 1972. Represents individual artists and groups from anywhere; currently handles 145 acts. Receives 20% commission.

How to Contact *No unsolicited submissions.*

Music Mostly **rock**, **country**, and **A/C**; also **jazz**, **nostalgia**, and **ethnic**. Works primarily with bands, comedians and speakers. Current acts include Five Easy Pieces (A/C), Scott Greeson (country), and Cool City Swing Band (variety).

◙ JANA JAE ENTERPRISES

P.O. Box 35726, Tulsa OK 74153. (918)786-8896. Fax: (918)786-8897. E-mail: janajae@janajae.com. Website: www.janajae.com. **Contact:** Kathleen Pixley, agent. Booking agency, music publisher (Jana Jae Publishing/BMI) and record company (Lark Record Productions, Inc.). Estab. 1979. Represents individual artists and songwriters; currently handles 12 acts. Receives 15% commission. Reviews material for acts.

- Also see the listings for Jana Jae Music in the Music Publishers section, Lark Record Productions in the Record Companies section and Lark Talent & Advertising in the Record Producers section of this book.

How to Contact Submit demo by mail. Unsolicited submissions are OK. Prefers CD or DVD of performance. If seeking management, press kit should include cover letter, bio, photo, demo tape/CD, lyric sheets and press clippings. Does not return material.

Music Mostly **country**, **classical** and **jazz instrumentals**; also **pop**. Works with vocalists, show and concert bands, solo instrumentalists. Represents Jana Jae (country singer/fiddle player), Matt Greif (classical guitarist), Sydni (solo singer) and Hotwire (country show band).

◻ KUPER PERSONAL MANAGEMENT/RECOVERY RECORDINGS

515 Bomar, Houston TX 77006. (713)520-5791. Fax: (713)527-0202. E-mail: info@recoveryrecordings.com. Website: www.recoveryrecordings.com. **Contact:** Koop Kuper,

owner. Management firm, music publisher (Kuper-Lam Music/BMI, Uvula Music/ BMI, and Meauxtown Music/ASCAP) and record label (Recovery Recordings). Estab. 1979/2002. Represents individual artists, groups and songwriters from Texas; currently handles 5 acts. Receives 20% commission. Reviews material for acts.

How to Contact Submit demo package by mail. Unsolicited submissions are OK. Prefers CD. If seeking management, press kit should include cover letter, press clippings, photo, bio (1 page) tearsheets (reviews, etc.) and demo CD. Does not return material. Responds in 2 months.

Music Mostly **singer/songwriters**, **triple AAA**, **roots rock**, and **Americana**. Works primarily with self-contained and self-produced artists. Current acts include Philip Rodriguez (singer/songwriter), David Rodriguez (singer/songwriter), Def Squad Texas (hip-hop). U.S. Representative for the following Dutch groups: The Watchman (Dutch singer/songwriter), and The Very Girls (Dutch vocal duo).

Tips "Create a market value for yourself, produce your own master tapes, and create a cost-effective situation."

◙ RICK LEVY MANAGEMENT

4250 A1AS, D-11, St. Augustine FL 32080. (904)806-0817. Fax: (904)460-1226. E-mail: rick@ricklevy.com. Website: www.ricklevy.com. **Contact:** Rick Levy, president. Management firm, music publisher (Flying Governor Music/BMI) and record company (Luxury Records). Estab. 1985. Represents local, regional or international individual artists and groups; currently handles 5 acts. Receives 15-20% commission. Reviews material for acts.

How to Contact *Write or call first and obtain permission to submit.* Prefers CD or DVD with 3 songs and lyric sheet. If seeking management, press kit should include cover letter, bio, demo tape/CD, DVD demo, photo and press clippings. Include SASE. Responds in 2 weeks.

Music Mostly **R&B** (no rap), **pop**, **country** and **oldies**; also **children's** and **educational videos** for schools. Current acts include Jay & the Techniques ('60s hit group), The Original Box Tops ('60s), The Limits (pop), Freddy Cannon ('60s), The Fallin Bones (Blues/rock), Tommy Roe ('60s), The Bushwhackers (country).

Tips "If you don't have 200% passion and committment, don't bother. Be sure to contact only companies that deal with your type of music."

◖ LOGGINS PROMOTION

5018 Franklin Pike, Nashville TN 37220. (310)325-2800. Fax: (615)323-2200. E-mail: staff@ LogginsPromotion.com. Website: www.logginspromotion.com. **Contact:** Paul Loggins, CEO. Management firm and radio promotion. Represents individual artists, groups and songwriters from anywhere; currently handles 6 acts. Receives 20% commission. Reviews material for acts.

How to Contact If seeking management, press kit should include picture, short bio, cover letter, press clippings and CD (preferred). "Mark on CD which cut you, as the artist, feel is the strongest." Does not return material. Responds in 2 weeks.

Music Mostly **adult**, **top 40** and **AAA**; also **urban**, **rap**, **alternative**, **college**, **smooth jazz** and **Americana**. Works primarily with bands and solo artists.

☑ ⬙ MANAGEMENT BY JAFFE

68 Ridgewood Ave., Glen Ridge, NJ 07028. (973)743-1075. Fax: (973)743-1075. E-mail: jerjaf@aol.com. President: Jerry Jaffe. Management firm. Estab. 1987. Represents individual artists and groups from anywhere; currently handles 2 acts. Receives 20% commission. Reviews material for acts "rarely." Reviews for representation "sometimes."

How to Contact *Write or call first to arrange personal interview.* Prefers CD or DVD with 3-4 songs and lyric sheet. Does not return material. Responds in 2 months.

Music Mostly **rock/alternative**, **pop** and **Hot AC**. Works primarily with groups and singers/songwriters.

Tips "If you are influenced by Jesus & Mary Chain, please e-mail. Create some kind of 'buzz' first."

⬙ ☑ THE MANAGEMENT TRUST LTD.

411 Queen St. W, 3rd Floor, Toronto ON M5V 2A5 Canada. (416)979-7070. Fax: (416)979-0505. E-mail: mail@mgmtrust.ca. Website: www.mgmtrust.ca. Manager: Jake Gold. Manager: R.J. Guha. General Manager: Shelley Stertz. Management firm. Estab. 1986. Represents individual artists and/or groups; currently handles 8 acts.

How to Contact Submit demo package by mail (Attn: A&R Dept.). Unsolicited submissions are OK. If seeking management, press kit should include CD, bio, cover letter, photo and press clippings. Does not return material. Responds in 2 months.

Music All types.

☐ RICK MARTIN PRODUCTIONS

125 Fieldpoint Road, Greenwich CT 06830. E-mail: rick@easywaysystems.com. Website: www.rickmartinproductions.com and www.myspace.com/rickmartinproductions. **Contact:** Rick Martin, president. Personal manager and independent producer. Held the Office of Secretary of the National Conference of Personal Managers for 22 years. Represents vocalists; currently produces pop and country crossover music artists in private project studio and looking for a female vocalist in the general area of Greenwich, CT for production project. Receives 15% commission as a personal manager and/or customary production and publishing distributions.

How to Contact Please e-mail for initial contact. Do not submit unless permission received to do so.

Music Top 40 and **country crossover**. No hip-hop or rap.

Tips "Your demo does not have to be professionally produced to submit to producers, publishers, or managers. In other words, save your money. It's really not important what you've done. It's what you can do now that counts."

◙ PHIL MAYO & COMPANY

P.O. Box 304, Bomoseen VT 05732. (802)468-2554. Fax: (802)468-2554. E-mail: pmcamgphil@aol.com. **Contact:** Phil Mayo, President. Management firm and record company (AMG Records). Estab. 1981. Represents individual artists, groups and songwriters from anywhere; currently handles 4 acts. Receives 15-20% commission. Reviews material for acts.

How to Contact *Contact first and obtain permission to submit.* Prefers CD with 3 songs (professionally recorded) and lyric or lead sheet. If seeking management, include bio, photo and lyric sheet in press kit. Does not return material. Responds in 2 months.

Music Mostly **contemporary Christian pop**. Current and past acts have included John Hall, Guy Burlage, Jonell Mosser, Pam Buckland, Orleans, Gary Nicholson, and Jon Pousette-Dart.

◙ NOTEWORTHY PRODUCTIONS

124½ Archwood Ave., Annapolis MD 21401. (410)268-8232. Fax: (410)268-2167. E-mail: mcshane@mcnote.com. Website: www.mcnote.com. **Contact:** McShane Glover, president. Management firm and booking agency. Estab. 1985. Represents individual artists, groups and songwriters from everywhere; currently handles 6 acts. Receives 15-20% commission. Reviews material for acts.

How to Contact *Write first and obtain permission to submit.* Prefers CD/CDR with lyric sheet. If seeking management, press kit should include CD, photo, bio, venues played and press clippings (preferably reviews). "Follow up with a phone call 3-5 weeks after submission." Does not return material. Responds in 2 months.

Music Mostly **Americana**, **folk**, and **Celtic**. Works primarily with performing singer/songwriters. Current acts include toby Walker (blues) and Pat Wictor (roots).

◻ ON THE LEVEL MUSIC!

P.O. Box 508, Owego NY 13827. (607)222-4151. E-mail: fredny2020@yahoo.com. Contact: Fred Gage, CEO/president. Management firm, booking agency and music publisher (On The Level Music! Publishing). Estab. 1970. Represents individual artists, groups and songwriters from anywhere; currently handles 30 acts. Receives 15% commission. Reviews material for acts.

How to Contact Submit demo tape by mail. Unsolicited submissions are OK. Prefers CDs, DAT or VHS videocassette with 4 songs and lyric or lead sheet. If seeking management, press kit should include cover letter, bio, demo tape/CD, lyric sheets, press clippings, 8 × 10 photo and video. Does not return material. Responds in 1 month.

Music Mostly **rock**, **alternative** and **jazz**; also **blues**. Current acts include Ice River Blues and Summer Jam 2004.

◙ PRIME TIME ENTERTAINMENT

2430 Research Dr., Livermore CA 94550. (925)449-1724. Fax: (925)905-3813. E-mail: info@primetimeentertainment.com. Website: www.primetimeentertainment.com. Owner: Jim Douglas. Management firm and booking agency. Estab. 1988. Represents individual artists, groups and songwriters from anywhere. Receives 10-20% commission. Reviews material for acts.

How to Contact Submit demo package by mail. Unsolicited submissions are OK. Prefers CD with 3-5 songs. If seeking management, press kit should include 8 × 10 photo, reviews and CDs/tapes. Include SASE. Responds in 1 month.

Music Mostly **jazz**, **country** and **alternative**; also **ethnic**. Artists include Grant Geissman (fusion/jazz), Jody Watley (R&B), Ray Parker, Jr. (jazz/R&B), and Craig Chaquico (jazz).

Tips "It's all about the song."

◙ RAINBOW TALENT AGENCY

146 Round Pond Lane, Rochester NY 14626. (585)723-3334. Fax: (585)720-6172. E-mail: rtalent@frontiernet.net. Website: www.rainbowtalentagency.com. **Contact:** Carl Labate, President. Management firm and booking agency. Represents artists and groups; currently handles 4 acts. Receives 15-25% commission.

How to Contact Submit demo package by mail. Unsolicited submissions are OK. Prefers CD with minimum 3 songs. May send DVD if available; "a still photo and bio of the act; if you are a performer, it would be advantageous to show yourself or the group performing live. Theme
 are not helpful." If seeking management, include photos, bio, markets established, CD/DVD. Does not return material. Responds in 1 month.

Music Mostly **blues**, **rock**, and **R&B**. Works primarily with touring bands and recording artists. Current acts include Kristen Maxfield (R&B); Classic Albums Live (classic rock symphony); Nevergreen (pop reggae), and Spanky Haschmann Swing Orchestra (high energy swing).

Tips "My main interest is with groups or performers that are currently touring and have some product. And are at least 50% percent original. Strictly songwriters should apply elsewhere."

◻ RASPBERRY JAM MUSIC

(formerly Endangered Species Artist Management), 4 Berachah Ave., South Nyack NY 10960-4202. (845)353-4001. Fax: (845)353-4332. E-mail: muzik@verizon.net. Website: www.musicandamerica.com or www.anyamusic.com President: Fred Porter. Vice President: Suzanne Buckley. Management firm. Estab. 1979. Represents individual artists, groups and songwriters from anywhere; currently handles 3 acts. Receives 20% commission. Reviews material for acts.

How to Contact *Call first and obtain permission to submit.* Prefers CD with 3 or more songs and lyric sheet. "Please include a demo of your music, a clear, recent photograph as well as any current press, if any. A cover letter indicating at what stage in your career you are and expectations for your future. Please label the cassette and/or CD with your name and address as well as the song titles." If seeking management, press kit should include cover letter, bio, photo, demo/CD, lyric sheet and press clippings. Include SASE. Responds in 6 weeks.

Music Mostly **pop**, **rock** and **world**; also **Latin/heavy metal**, **R&B**, **jazz** and **instrumental**. Current acts include Jason Wilson & Tabarruk (pop/reggae, nominated for Juno award 2001), and Anya (teen singer).

Tips "Listen to everything, classical to country, old to contemporary, to develop an understanding of many writing styles. Write with many other partners to keep the creativity fresh. Don't feel your style will be ruined by taking a class or a writing seminar. We all process moods and images differently. This leads to uniqueness in the music."

REIGN MUSIC AND MEDIA, LLC

(formerly Bassline Entertainment, Inc.), P.O. Box 2394, New York NY 10185. E-mail: talent@reignmm.com. Website: www.reignmm.com. **Contact:** Talent Relations Dept. Multi-media/Artist Development firm. Estab. 1993 as Bassline Entertainment. Promotes/develops primarily local and regional vocalists, producers, and songwriters. Receives 20-25% commission. Reviews material for artists.

How to Contact Submit demo package by mail or e-mail. Unsolicited submissions are OK. Prefers CD, mp3, or video. Standard hard copy press kit or EPK should include cover letter, press clippings and/or reviews, bio, demo (in appropriate format), picture and accurate contact telephone number. Include SASE. Usually responds in 3 weeks.

Music Mostly **pop**, **R&B**, **club/dance** and **hip-hop/rap**; some **Latin**. Works primarily with singer/songwriters, producers, rappers and bands. Current acts include Sinceere (hip hop/R&B); R.Notes (pop/R&B) and Iceman (hip hop).

RIOHCAT MUSIC

P.O. Box 764, Hendersonville TN 37077-0764. (615)824-9313. Fax: (615)824-0797. E-mail: tachoir@bellsouth.net. Website: www.tachoir.com. **Contact:** Robert Kayne, manager. Management firm, booking agency, record company (Avita Records) and music publisher. Estab. 1975. Represents individual artists and groups; currently handles 4 acts. Receives 15-20% commission.

• Also see the listing for Avita Records in the Record Companies section of this book.

How to Contact *Contact first and obtain permission to submit.* Prefers CD and lead sheet. If seeking management, press kit should include cover letter, bio, photo, demo tape/CD and press clippings. Does not return material. Responds in 6 weeks.

Music Mostly **contemporary jazz** and **fusion**. Works primarily with jazz ensembles. Current acts include Group Tachoir (jazz), Tachoir/Manakas Duo (jazz) and Jerry Tachoir (jazz vibraphone artist).

⊕ ◻ ROBERTSON ENTERTAINMENT

106 Harding Road Kendenup 6323, Western Australia. (618)9851-4311. Fax: (618)9851-4225. E-mail: mmp@bluemaxx.com.au. Website: www.robertsonentertainment.com. **Contact:** Eddie Robertson. Booking agency. Estab. 1991. Represents individual artists and/or groups; currently handles 50 acts. Receives 20% commission. Reviews material for acts.

How to Contact *Write first and obtain permission to submit.* Unsolicited submissions are OK. Prefers cassette or videocassette with photo, information on style and bio. If seeking management, press kit should include photos, bio, cover letter, press clippings, video, demo, lyric sheets and any other useful information. Does not return material. Responds in 1 month.

Music Mostly **top 40/pop**, **jazz** and **'60s-'90s**; also **reggae** and **blues**. Works primarily with show bands and solo performers. Current acts include Faces (dance band), Peace Love & All That Stuff (retro band), and Soul Corporation (soul).

Tips "Send as much information as possible. If you do not receive a call after four to five weeks, follow up with letter or phone call."

◪ SA'MALL MANAGEMENT

P.O. Box 261488, Encino CA 91426. (818)506-8533. Fax: (818)506-8534. E-mail: samusa@ aol.com. Website: www.pplentertainmentgroup.com. **Contact:** Ted Steele, vice president of talent. Management firm, music publisher (Pollybyrd Publications) and record company (PPL Entertainment Group). Estab. 1990. Represents individual artists, groups and songwriters worldwide; currently handles 10 acts. Receives 10-25% commission. Reviews material for acts.

- Also see the listings for Pollybyrd Publications Limited and Zettitalia Music International in the Music Publishers section and PPL Entertainment Group in the Record Companies section of this book.

How to Contact *E-mail first and obtain permission to submit.* "Only professional full-time artists who tour and have a fan base need apply. No weekend warriors, please." Prefers CD or cassette. If seeking management, press kit should include picture, bio and tape. Include SASE. Responds in 2 months.

Music All types. Current acts include Riki Hendrix (rock), Buddy Wright (blues), Fhyne, Suzette Cuseo, The Band AKA, LeJenz, B.D. Fuoco, Juz-cuz, Donato, MoBeatz, and Kapital P.

◻ SANDALPHON MANAGEMENT

P.O. Box 542407, Grand Prairie TX 75054. (972)333-0876. E-mail: rotey01@gmail.com. **Contact:** Ruth Otey, president. Management firm, music publisher (Sandalphon Music Publishing/BMI), and record company (Sandalphon Records). Estab. 2005. Represents individual artists, groups, songwriters; works with individual artists and groups from anywhere. Currently handles 0 acts. Receives negotiable commission. Reviews material for acts.

How to Contact Submit demo by mail. Unsolicited submissions are fine. Prefers CD with 1-5 songs and lyric sheet, cover letter. "Include name, address, and contact information." Include SASE or SAE and IRC for outside the United States. Responds in 6-8 weeks.

Music Mostly **rock**, **country**, and **alternative**; also **pop**, **gospel**, and **blues**. "We are looking for singers, bands, and singer/songwriters who are original but would be current in today's music markets. We help singers, bands, and singer-songwriters achieve their personal career goals."

Tips "Submit material you feel best represents you, your voice, your songs, or your band. Fresh and original songs and style are a plus. We are a West Coast management company looking for singers, bands, and singer-songwriters who are ready for the next level. We are looking for those with talent who are capable of being national and international contenders."

⚏ ◐ SIEGEL ENTERTAINMENT LTD.

1736 W. 2nd Ave., Vancouver BC V6J 1H6 Canada. (604)736-3896. Fax: (604)736-3464. E-mail: siegelent@telus.net. Website: www.siegelent.com. **Contact:** Robert Siegel, president. Management firm and booking agency. Estab. 1975. Represents individual artists, groups and songwriters from anywhere; currently handles more than 100 acts (for bookings). Receives 15-20% commission. Reviews material for acts.

How to Contact *Does not accept unsolicited submissions. E-mail or write for permission to submit.* Does not return material. Responds in 1 month.

Music Mostly **rock**, **pop**, and **country**; also **specialty** and **children's**. Current acts include Johnny Ferreira & The Swing Machine, Lee Aaron, Kenny Blues Boss Wayne (boogie) and Tim Brecht (pop/children's).

⚏ ◻ SILVER BOW MANAGEMENT

Box 5, 720 6th St., New Westminster BC V3L 3C5 Canada. (604)523-9309. Fax: (604)395-6316. E-mail: saddlestone@shaw.ca. Website: www.saddlestone.net. President: Grant Lucas. CEO: Candice James. Management firm, music publisher (Saddlestone Publishing, Silver Bow Publishing), record company (Saddlestone Records) and record producer (Silver Bow Productions, Krazy Cat Productions). Estab. 1988. Represents individual artists, groups, songwriters internationally; currently handles 3 acts. Receives standard commission. Reviews material for acts.d

- Also see the listings for Saddlestone Publishing in the Music Publishers section and Silver Bow Productions in the Record Producers section of this book.

How to Contact Submit demo package by mail. Unsolicited submissions are OK. Prefers CDs with lyric sheets. If seeking management, press kit should include 8 × 10 photo, bio, cover letter, CD with lyric sheets, press clippings, video, résumé and current itinerary. "Visuals are everything—submit accordingly." Does not return material. Responds in 2 months.

Music Mostly **jazz**, **country**, **pop** and **rock**; also **R&B**, **Christian** and **alternative**. Works primarily with bands, vocalists and singer/songwriters. Current acts include The

Soulmates (pop/euro dance), Rick Valiant (jazz), Lane Swan (MOR), Kootenay Jack (rockabilly/country).

☑ T. SKORMAN PRODUCTIONS, INC.

5156 S. Orange Ave., Orlando FL 32809. (407)895-3000. Fax: (407)895-1422. E-mail: ted@tskorman.com. Website: www.tskorman.com. **Contact:** Ted Skorman, president. Management firm and booking agency. Estab. 1983. Represents groups; currently handles 40 acts. Receives 10-25% commission. Reviews material for acts.

How to Contact *E-mail first for permission to submit.* Prefers CD with 2 songs, or videocassette of no more than 6 minutes. "Live performance—no trick shots or editing tricks. We want to be able to view act as if we were there for a live show." If seeking management, press kit should include cover letter, bio, photo and demo CD or video. Does not return material. Responds only if interested.

Music Mostly **top 40**, **dance**, **pop**, and **country**. Works primarily with high-energy dance acts, recording acts, and top 40 bands. Current acts include Steph Carse (pop).

☑ SOUTHEASTERN ATTRACTIONS

1025 23rd St. South, Suite 302, Birmingham AL 35205. (205)307-6790. Fax: (205)307-6798. E-mail: staff@seattractions.com. Website: www.seattractions.com. **Contact:** Agent. Booking agency. Estab. 1967. Represents groups from anywhere; currently handles 200 acts. Receives 20% commission.

How to Contact Submit demo package by mail. Unsolicited submissions are OK. Prefers CD or DVD. Does not return material. Responds in 2 months.

Music Mostley **rock**, **alternative**, **oldies**, **country** and **dance**. Works primarily with bands. Current acts include Leaderdog (rock), Undergrounders (variety to contemporary), Style Band (Motown/dance), The Connection (Motown/dance), Rollin' in the Hay(bluegrass).

☑ STARKRAVIN' MANAGEMENT

11135 Weddington St., #424, N. Hollywood, CA 91601. (818)587-6801. Fax: (818)587-6802. E-mail: bcmclane@aol.com. Website: www.benmclane.com. **Contact:** B.C. McLane, Esq. Management and law firm. Estab. 1994. Represents individual artists, groups and songwriters. Receives 20% commission (management); $300/hour as attorney.

How to Contact Submit demo package by mail. Unsolicited submissions are OK. Prefers cassette. Does not return material. Responds in 1 month if interested.

Music Mostly **rock**, **pop** and **R&B**. Works primarily with bands.

☐ ST. JOHN ARTISTS

P.O. Box 619, Neenah WI 54957-0619. (920)722-2222. Fax: (920)725-2405. E-mail: jon@stjohn-artists.com. Website: www.stjohn-artists.com/. **Contact:** Jon St. John and Gary Coquoz, agents. Booking agency. Estab. 1968. Represents local and regional individual artists and groups; currently handles 20 acts. Receives 15-20% commission. Reviews material for acts.

How to Contact *Call first and obtain permission to submit.* Prefers CD or DVD. If seeking management, press kit should include cover letter, bio, photo, demo tape/CD, video and résumé. Include SASE.

Music Mostly **rock** and **MOR**. Current acts include Tribute (variety/pop/country), Boogie & the Yo-Yo's ('60s to 2000s), Vic Ferrari (Top 40 80's-2000's), Little Vito and the Torpedoes(variety 50's-2000's), Center Stage Variety Show Band (variety 60's-2000's) and Da Yoopers (musical comedy/novelty).

☑ TAS MUSIC CO./DAVE TASSE ENTERTAINMENT

N2467 Knollwood Dr., Lake Geneva WI 53147-9731. E-mail: david@baybreezerecords. com. Website: www.baybreezerecords.com. **Contact:** David Tasse. Booking agency, record company and music publisher. Represents artists, groups and songwriters; currently handles 21 acts. Receives 10-20% commission. Reviews material for acts.

How to Contact Submit demo tape by mail. Unsolicited submissions are OK. Prefers cassette with 2-4 songs and lyric sheet. Include performance videocassette if available. If seeking management, press kit should include tape, bio and photo. Does not return material. Responds in 3 weeks.

Music Mostly **pop** and **jazz**; also **dance, MOR, rock, soul** and **top 40**. Works primarily with show and dance bands. Current acts include Max Kelly (philosophic rock) and L.J. Young (rap).

☑ T.L.C. BOOKING AGENCY

37311 N. Valley Rd., Chattaroy WA 99003. (509)292-2201. Fax: (509)292-2205. E-mail: tlcagent@ix.netcom.com. Website: www.tlcagency.com. **Contact:** Tom or Carrie Lapsansky, agent/owners. Booking agency. Estab. 1970. Represents individual artists and groups from anywhere; currently handles 17 acts. Receives 10-15% commission. Reviews material for acts.

How to Contact *Call first and obtain permission to submit.* Prefers CD with 3-4 songs. Does not return material. Responds in 3 weeks.

Music Mostly **rock**, **country** and **variety**; also **comedians** and **magicians**. Works primarily with bands, singles and duos. Current acts include Nobody Famous (variety/ classic rock), Mr. Happy (rock), Mad Rush (rock), Dixie Dandies (dixieland), and The Charm (variety/top 40).

☑ UMBRELLA ARTISTS MANAGEMENT, INC.

2612 Erie Ave., P.O. Box 8369, Cincinnati OH 45208. (513)871-1500. Fax: (513)878-2240. E-mail: shertzman@cinci.rr.com. Website: www.stanhertzman.com. **Contact:** Stan Hertzman, president. Management consultation firm. Professional consultation and advice for artists and groups for specific circumstances on a pre-paid hourly basis.

How to Contact E-mail.

☐ UNIVERSAL MUSIC MARKETING

P.O. Box 2297, Universal City TX 78148. (210)653-3989. E-mail: earleowens@bellsouth. net. Website: www.bsw-records.com. **Contact:** Frank Willson, president. Management firm, record company (BSW Records), booking agency, music publisher and record producer (Frank Wilson). Estab. 1987. Represents individual artists and groups from anywhere; currently handles 12 acts. Receives 15% commission. Reviews material for acts.

• Also see the listings for BSW Records in the Music Publishers and Record Companies sections and Frank Wilson in the Record Producers section of this book.

How to Contact Submit demo package by mail. Unsolicited submissions are OK. Prefers CD or DVD with 3 songs and lyric sheet. If seeking management, include tape/CD, bio, photo and current activities. Include SASE. Responds in 6 weeks.

Music Mostly **country** and **light rock**; also **blues** and **jazz**. Works primarily with vocalists, singer/songwriters and bands. Current acts include Candee Land, Darlene Austin, Larry Butler, John Wayne, Sonny Marshall, Bobby Mountain, Crea Beal and Butch Martin (country). "Visit our website for an up-to-date listing of current acts."

☑ CHERYL K. WARNER PRODUCTIONS

P.O. Box 179, Hermitage TN 37076. Phone: (615)429-7849. E-mail: cherylkwarner@ comcast.net. Website: www.cherylkwarner.com. **Contact:** Cheryl K. Warner. Recording and stage production, music consulting, music publisher, record label, A&R. Currently works with 2 acts with expansion in the works. Reviews material for acts.

How to Contact Submit demo package by mail or e-mail. Unsolicited submissions are OK. Prefers CD or DVD, but will accept CD with 3 best songs, lyric or lead sheet, bio and picture. Press kit should include CD, DVD with up-to-date bio, cover letter, lyric sheets, press clippings, and picture. Does not return material. Responds in 6 weeks if interested.

Music Mostly **country/traditional and contemporary**, **Christian/gospel** and **A/C/pop/ rock**. Works primarily with singer/songwriters and bands with original and versatile style. Current acts include Cheryl K. Warner (recording artist/entertainer) and Cheryl K. Warner Band (support/studio).

☑ WEMUS ENTERTAINMENT

2006 Seaboard, Suite 400, Midland TX 79705. (432)689-3687. E-mail: wemus@aol. com. Website: www.wemus.com. **Contact:** Dennis Grubb, president. Management firm, booking agency and music publisher (Wemus Music, Inc.). Estab. 1983. Represents local and regional individual artists and groups; currently handles 4 acts. Receives 15-25% commission. Reviews material for acts.

How to Contact Submit via CD or DVD only with 3-5 songs per submission, along with lyric sheets. Unsolicited submissions are OK. "Make sure address, phone number and possible fax number is included in the packet, or a business card." Does not return material. Responds in 1 month if interested.

Music Mostly **country**. Current acts include The Image (variety), The Big Time (variety), The Pictures (variety) and Pryce Conner.

Tips "We preview and try to place good songs with national artists who are in need of good materials. We have a very tough qualification process and are very selective in forwarding materials to artists and their management."

⚄ ◯ WINTERLAND ENTERTAINMENT MANAGEMENT & PUBLISHING

(formerly T.J. Booker Ltd.), P.O. Box 969, Rossland BC VOG 1YO Canada. (250)362-7795. E-mail: winterland@netidea.com. **Contact:** Tom Jones, owner. Management firm, booking agency and music publisher. Estab. 1976. Represents individual artists, groups and songwriters from anywhere; currently handles 6 acts. Receives 15% commission. Reviews material for acts.

How to Contact Submit demo package by mail. Unsolicited submissions are OK. Prefers CD, cassette or videocassette with 3 songs. If seeking management, include demo tape or CD, picture, cover letter and bio in press kit. Does not return material. Responds in 1 month.

Music Mostly **MOR**, **crossover**, **rock**, **pop**, and **country**. "Only book on an occasional basis. If you wish to submit, you are welcome. If I can I will review and critique your material. It is a changing world musically, but if it works, it works. There is no replacement for excellence."

⚃ WORLDSOUND, LLC

17837 1st Ave. South Suite #3, Seattle WA 98148. (206)444-0300. Fax: (206)244-0066. E-mail: music@worldsound.com. Website: www.worldsound.com. **Contact:** Warren Wyatt, A&R manager. Management firm. Estab. 1976. Represents individual artists, groups and songwriters from anywhere; currently handles 8 acts. Receives 20% commission. Reviews material for acts.

How to Contact "Online, send us an e-mail containing a link to your website where your songs can be heard and the lyrics are available—PLEASE DO NOT E-MAIL SONG FILES! By regular mail, unsolicited submissions are OK." Prefers CD with 2-10 songs and lyric sheet. "If seeking management, please send an e-mail with a link to your website—your site should contain song samples, band biography, photos, video (if available), press and demo reviews. By mail, please send the materials listed above and include SASE." Responds in 1 month.

Music Mostly **rock**, **pop**, and **world**; also **heavy metal**, **hard rock**, and **top 40**. Works primarily with pop/rock/world artists. Current acts include Makana (world music), Treble (pop), La Neo (contemporary/Hawaiian), and Keith Olsen (music producer).

Tips "Always submit new songs/material, even if you have sent material that was previously rejected; the music biz is always changing."

⚃ ZANE MANAGEMENT, INC.

1650 Market St., One Liberty Place, 56th Floor, Philadelphia PA 19103. (215)575-3803. Fax: (215)575-3801. E-mail: lzr@braverlaw.com. Website: www.zanemanagement.

com. **Contact:** Lloyd Z. Remick, Esq., president. Entertainment/sports consultants and managers. Represents artists, songwriters, producers and athletes; currently handles 7 acts. Receives 10-15% commission.

How to Contact Submit demo tape by mail. Unsolicited submissions are OK. Prefers CD and lyric sheet. If seeking management, press kit should include cover letter, bio, photo, demo tape and video. Does not return material. Responds in 3 weeks.

Music Mostly **dance**, **easy listening**, **folk**, **jazz (fusion)**, **MOR**, **rock (hard and country)**, **soul** and **top 40/pop**. Current acts include Bunny Sigler (disco/funk), Peter Nero and Philly Pops (conductor), Cast in Bronze (rock group), Pieces of a Dream (jazz/crossover), Don't Look Down (rock/pop), Christian Josi (pop-swing), Bishop David Evans (gospel), Kevin Roth (children's music), and Rosie Carlino (standards/pop).

ADDITIONAL MANAGERS & BOOKING AGENTS

D

Deep South Entertainment 141

Diamond Entertainment, Joel 175

L

Lark Record Productions, Inc. 148

M

Modal Music, Inc. 150

P

Panama Music Group of Companies, The 152

Pollybyrd Publications Limited 122

Music Firms

Advertising, Audiovisual & Commercial

I t's happened a million times—you hear a jingle on the radio or television and can't get it out of your head. That's the work of a successful jingle writer, writing songs to catch your attention and make you aware of the product being advertised. But the field of commercial music consists of more than just memorable jingles. It also includes background music that many companies use in videos for corporate and educational presentations, as well as films and TV shows.

SUBMITTING MATERIAL

More than any other market listed in this book, the commercial music market expects composers to have made an investment in the recording of their material before submitting. A sparse, piano/vocal demo won't work here; when dealing with commercial music firms, especially audiovisual firms and music libraries, high quality production is important. Your demo may be kept on file at one of these companies until a need for it arises, and it may be used or sold as you sent it. Therefore, your demo tape or reel must be as fully produced as possible.

The presentation package that goes along with your demo must be just as professional. A list of your credits should be a part of your submission, to give the company an idea of your experience in this field. If you have no experience, look to local television and radio stations to get your start. Don't expect to be paid for many of your first jobs in the commercial music field; it's more important to get the credits and exposure that can lead to higher-paying jobs.

Commercial music and jingle writing can be a lucrative field for the composer/songwriter with a gift for writing catchy melodies and the ability to write in many different music styles. It's a very competitive field, so it pays to have a professional presentation package that makes your work stand out.

Three different segments of the commercial music world are listed here: advertising agencies, audiovisual firms and commercial music houses/music libraries. Each looks for a different type of music, so read these descriptions carefully to see where the music you write fits in.

ADVERTISING AGENCIES

Ad agencies work on assignment as their clients' needs arise. Through consultation and input from the creative staff, ad agencies seek jingles and music to stimulate the consumer to identify with a product or service.

When contacting ad agencies, keep in mind they are searching for music that can capture and then hold an audience's attention. Most jingles are short, with a strong, memorable hook. When an ad agency listens to a demo, it is not necessarily looking for a finished product so much as for an indication of creativity and diversity. Many composers put together a reel of excerpts of work from previous projects, or short pieces of music that show they can write in a variety of styles.

AUDIOVISUAL FIRMS

Audiovisual firms create a variety of products, from film and video shows for sales meetings, corporate gatherings and educational markets, to motion pictures and TV shows. With the increase of home video use, how-to videos are a big market for audiovisual firms, as are spoken word educational videos. All of these products need music to accompany them. For your quick reference, companies working to place music in movies and TV shows (excluding commercials) have a preceding their listing (also see the Film & TV Index on page 350 for a complete list of these companies).

Like ad agencies, audiovisual firms look for versatile, well-rounded songwriters. When submitting demos to these firms, you need to demonstrate your versatility in writing specialized background music and themes. Listings for companies will tell what facet(s) of the audiovisual field they are involved in and what types of clients they serve. Your demo tape should also be as professional and fully produced as possible; audiovisual firms often seek demo tapes that can be put on file for future use when the need arises.

COMMERCIAL MUSIC HOUSES & MUSIC LIBRARIES

Commercial music houses are companies contracted (either by an ad agency or the advertiser) to compose custom jingles. Since they are neither an ad agency nor an audiovisual firm, their main concern is music. They use a lot of it, too—some composed by inhouse songwriters and some contributed by outside, freelance writers.

Music libraries are different in that their music is not custom composed for a specific client. Their job is to provide a collection of instrumental music in many different styles that, for an annual fee or on a per-use basis, the customer can use however he chooses.

In the following listings, commercial music houses and music libraries, which are usually the most open to works by new composers, are identified as such by **bold** type.

The commercial music market is similar to most other businesses in one aspect: experience is important. Until you develop a list of credits, pay for your work may not be high. Don't pass up opportunities if a job is non- or low-paying. These assignments will add to your list of credits, make you contacts in the field, and improve your marketability.

Money & rights

Many of the companies listed in this section pay by the job, but there may be some situations where the company asks you to sign a contract that will specify royalty payments. If this happens, research the contract thoroughly, and know exactly what is expected of you and how much you'll be paid.

Depending on the particular job and the company, you may be asked to sell one-time rights or all rights. One-time rights involve using your material for one presentation only. All rights means the buyer can use your work any way he chooses, as many times as he likes. Be sure you know exactly what you're giving up, and how the company may use your music in the future.

In the commercial world, many of the big advertising agencies have their own publishing companies where writers assign their compositions. In these situations, writers sign contracts whereby they do receive performance and mechanical royalties when applicable.

ADDITIONAL LISTINGS

For additional names and addresses of ad agencies that may use jingles and/or commercial music, refer to the *Standard Directory of Advertising Agencies* (National Register Publishing). For a list of audiovisual firms, check out the latest edition of *AV Marketplace* (R.R. Bowker). Both these books may be found at your local library. To contact companies in your area, see the Geographic Index at the back of this book.

ADVERTEL, INC.

P.O. Box 18053, Pittsburgh PA 15236-0053. (412)344-4700. Fax: (412)344-4712. E-mail: pberan@advertel.com. Website: www.advertel.com. **Contact:** Paul Beran, president/CEO. **Telephonic/Internet production company.** Clients include small and multi-national companies. Estab. 1983. Uses the services of music houses and independent songwriters/composers for scoring of instrumentals (all varieties) and telephonic production. Commissions 3-4 composers/year. Pay varies. Buys all rights and phone exclusive rights.

How to Contact Submit demo of previous work. Prefers CD. "Most compositions are 2 minutes strung together in 6, 12, 18 minute length productions." Does not return material; prefers to keep on file. Responds "right away if submission fills an immediate need."

Music Uses all varieties, including unusual; mostly subdued music beds. Radio-type production used exclusively in telephone and Internet applications.

Tips "Go for volume. We have continuous need for all varieties of music in 2 minute lengths. Advertel now produces a religious radio program called 'Prayer-in-the-Air.' Feel free to submit songs with lyrics taken from scripture. We also look for catchy, memorable melodies. For those pro bono submissions, no compensation is offered—only national recognition."

☒ ALLEGRO MUSIC

3990 Sunsetridge, Suite 203, Moorpark CA 93021-3756. E-mail: dannymuse@adelphia. net. Website: www.danielobrien.com. **Owner:** Daniel O'Brien. Scoring service, jingle/commercial music production house. Clients include film-makers, advertisers, network promotions and aerobics. Estab. 1991. Uses the services of independent songwriters/composers and lyricists for scoring of films, TV and broadcast commercials, jingles for ad agencies and promotions, and commercials for radio and TV. Commissions 3 composers and 1 lyricist/year. Pays 50% royalty. Buys one-time rights.

How to Contact Query with résumé of credits or submit demo tape of previous work. Prefers CD, cassette and lyric sheet. Include SASE. Responds in 1 month (if interested).

Music Varied: Contemporary to orchestral.

CEDAR CREST STUDIO

#17 CR 830, Henderson AR 72544. Website: www.cedarcreststudio.com. **Contact:** Bob Ketchum, owner. **Audiovisual firm and jingle/commercial music production house.** Clients include corporate, industrial, sales, music publishing, training, educational, legal, medical, music and Internet. Estab. 1973. Sometimes uses the services of independent songwriters/composers for background music for video productions, jingles for TV spots and commercials for radio and TV. Pays by the job or by royalties. Buys all rights or one-time rights.

How to Contact Query with résumé of credits or submit demo tape of previous work. Prefers CD, cassette, or DVD. Does not return material. "We keep it on file for future reference." Responds in 2 months.

Music Uses up-tempo pop (not too "rocky"), unobtrusive—no solos for commercials and background music for video presentations.

Tips "Hang, hang, hang. Be open to suggestions. Improvise, adapt, overcome."

COMMUNICATIONS FOR LEARNING

395 Massachusetts Ave., Arlington MA 02474. (781)641-2350. E-mail: comlearn@thecia. net. Website: www.communicationsforlearning.com. **Contact:** Jonathan L. Barkan, executive producer/director. Video, multimedia, exhibit and graphic design firm. Clients include multi-nationals, industry, government, institutions, local, national and international nonprofits. Uses services of music houses and independent songwriters/ composers as theme and background music for videos and multimedia. Commissions 1-2 composers/year. Pays $2,000-5,000/job and one-time use fees. Rights purchased vary.

How to Contact Submit demo and work available for library use. Prefers CD to Web links. Does not return material; prefers to keep on file. "For each job we consider our entire collection." Responds in 3 months.

Music Uses all styles of music for all sorts of assignments.

Tips "Please don't call. Just send your best material available for library use on CD. We'll be in touch if a piece works and negotiate a price. Make certain your name and contact information are on the CD itself, not only on the cover letter."

◪ ◯ DISK PRODUCTIONS

1100 Perkins Rd., Baton Rouge LA 70802. Fax: (225)343-0210. E-mail: disk_productions@ yahoo.com. **Contact:** Joey Decker, director. **Jingle/production house.** Clients include advertising agencies and film companies. Estab. 1982. Uses the services of music houses, independent songwriters/composers and lyricists for scoring and background music for TV spots, films and jingles for radio and TV. Commissions 7 songwriters/composers and 7 lyricists/year. Pays by the job. Buys all rights.

How to Contact Submit demo of previous work. Prefers DVD, CD, cassette or DAT. Does not return material. Responds in 2 weeks.

Music Needs all types of music for jingles, music beds or background music for TV and radio, etc.

Tips "Advertising techniques change with time. Don't be locked in a certain style of writing. Give me music that I can't get from pay needle-drop."

◪ FINE ART PRODUCTIONS/RICHIE SURACI PICTURES, MULTIMEDIA, INTERACTIVE

67 Maple St., Newburgh NY 12550-4034. (914)527-9740. Fax: (845)561-5866. E-mail: rs7fap@bestweb.net. Website: www.idsi.net/~rs7fap/tentsales.htm. **Contact:** Richard Suraci, owner. Advertising agency, audiovisual firm, scoring service, **jingle/commercial**

music production house, motion picture production company (Richie Suraci Pictures) and **music sound effect library**. Clients include corporate, industrial, motion picture and broadcast firms. Estab. 1987. Uses services of independent songwriters/composers for scoring, background music and jingles for various projects and commercials for radio and TV. Commissions 1-2 songwriters or composers and 1-2 lyricists/year. Pays by the job, royalty or by the hours. Buys all rights.

How to Contact Submit demo tape of previous work or tape demonstrating composition skills, query with résumé of credits or write or call first to arrange personal interview. Prefers CD, DVD, cassette (or ½", ¾", or 1" videocassette) with as many songs as possible and lyric or lead sheets. Include SASE, but prefers to keep material on file. Responds in 1 year.

Music Uses all types of music for all types of assignments.

NOVUS

121 E. 24th St., 12 Floor, New York NY 10010. (212)487-1377. Fax: (212)505-3300. E-mail: novuscom@aol.com. Website: novuscommunications.com. **Contact:** Robert Antonik, managing director. Cross media marketing and communications company. Clients include corporations and interactive media. Estab. 1986. Uses the services of music houses, independent songwriters/composers and lyricists for scoring, background music for documentaries, commercials, multimedia applications, website, film shorts, and commercials for radio and TV. Commissions 2 composers and 4 lyricists/year. Pay varies per job. Buys one-time rights.

How to Contact *Request a submission of demo.* Query with résumé. Submit demo of work. Prefers CD with 2-3 songs. "We prefer to keep submitted material on file, but will return material if SASE is enclosed. Responds in 6 weeks.

Music Uses **all styles** for a variety of different assignments.

Tips "Always present your best and don't add quantity to your demo. Novus is a creative marketing and communications company. We work with various public relations, artists managements and legal advisors. We consult on multimedia events."

OMNI COMMUNICATIONS

Dept. SM, P.O. Box 302, Carmel IN 46082-0302. (317)846-2345. E-mail: omni@omniproductions.com. Website: www.omniproductions.com. President: W. H. Long. Creative Director: S.M. Long. Production Manager: Jim Mullet. Television, digital media production and audiovisual firm. Estab. 1978. Serves industrial, commercial and educational clients. Uses the services of music houses and songwriters for scoring of films and television productions, DVD's, CD-ROMs and internet streams; background music for voice overs; lyricists for original music and themes. Pays by the job. Buys all rights.

How to Contact Submit demo tape of previous work. Prefers CD or DVD. Does not return material. Responds in 2 weeks.

Music Varies with each and every project; from classical, contemporary to commercial industrial.

Tips "Submit good demo tape with examples of your range to command the attention of our producers."

Play Producers & Publishers

Finding a theater company willing to invest in a new production can be frustrating for an unknown playwright. But whether you write the plays, compose the music or pen the lyrics, it is important to remember not only where to start but how to start. Theater in the U.S. is a hierarchy, with Broadway, Off Broadway and Off Off Broadway being pretty much off limits to all but the Stephen Sondheims of the world.

Aspiring theater writers would do best to train their sights on nonprofit regional and community theaters to get started. The encouraging news is there are a great number of local theater companies throughout the U.S. with experimental artistic directors who are looking for new works to produce, and many are included in this section. This section covers two segments of the industry: theater companies and dinner theaters are listed under Play Producers (beginning on page 218), and publishers of musical theater works are listed under the Play Publishers heading (beginning on page 226). All these markets are actively seeking new works of all types for their stages or publications.

BREAKING IN

Starting locally will allow you to research each company carefully and learn about their past performances, the type of musicals they present, and the kinds of material they're looking for. When you find theaters you think may be interested in your work, attend as many performances as possible, so you know exactly what type of material each theater presents. Or volunteer to work at a theater, whether it be moving sets or selling tickets. This will give you valuable insight into the day-to-day workings of a theater and the creation of a new show. On a national level, you will find prestigious organizations offering workshops and apprenticeships covering every subject from arts administration to directing to costuming. But it could be more helpful to look into professional internships at theaters and attend theater workshops in your area. The more knowledgeable you are about the workings of a particular company or theater, the easier it will be to tailor your work to fit its style and the more responsive they will be to you and your work. (See the Workshops & Conferences section on page 288 for more information.) As a composer for the stage, you need to know as much as possible about a theater and how it works, its history and the different roles played by the people involved in it. Flexibility is the key to successful productions, and knowing how a theater works will only help you in cooperating and collaborating with the director, producer, technical people and actors.

If you're a playwright looking to have his play published in book form or in theater publications, see the listings under the Play Publishers section (page 226). To find play producers and publishers in your area, consult the Geographic Index at the back of this book.

PLAY PRODUCERS

ARKANSAS REPERTORY THEATRE

601 Main, P.O. Box 110, Little Rock AR 72201. (501)378-0445. Website: www.therep.org. **Contact:** Brad Mooy. Play producer. Estab. 1976. Produces 6-10 plays and musicals/year. "We perform in a 354-seat house and also have a 99-seat 2nd stage." Pays 5-10% royalty or $75-150 per performance.

How to Contact Query with synopsis, character breakdown and set description. Include SASE. Responds in 6 months.

Musical Theater "Small casts are preferred, comedy or drama and prefer shows to run 1:45 to 2 hours maximum. Simple is better; small is better, but we do produce complex shows. We aren't interested in children's pieces, puppet shows or mime. We always like to receive a tape of the music with the book."

Productions *Disney's Beauty & the Beast*, by Woolverton/Ashman/Rice/Menken (musical retelling of the myth); *Crowns*, by Taylor/Cunningham/Marberry (on the significance of African-American women's hats); and *A Chorus Line*, by Kirkwood/Hamlisch/Kleban (auditions).

Tips "Include a good cassette of your music, sung well, with the script."

BARTER THEATRE

P.O. Box 867, Abingdon VA 24212. (276)628-3991. Fax: (276)619-3335. E-mail: barterinfo@ bartertheatre.com. Website: www.bartertheatre.com. **Contact**: Richard Rose, Producing Artistic Director. Play/musical producer. Estab. 1933. Produces app. 10-12 plays and 6-8 musicals (at least 1 new musical)/year. Audience: tourist and local mix, mid-American/ Southern, diverse, all ages. Two spaces: 507-seat proscenium stage, 167-seat thrust stage.

How to Contact Query with synopsis, character breakdown, set description, and CD of the songs. Be sure CDs will play back properly. Include SASE. Responds in 1 year.

Musical Theater "We investigate all types. We are not looking for any particular standard. Prefer sellable titles with unique use of music. Prefer small cast musicals, although have done large-scale projects with marketable titles or subject matter. We do not accept one-act or juke-box musicals. We use original music in many of our plays. Does not wish to see very urban material, or material with very strong language.

Productions 2010 season includes: *Chaps!; Always Patsy Cline; Annie; Violet; Shake, Rattle and Roll: A Tribute to the King; The Full Monty*, and several children's musicals.

Tips "Be patient. Be talented. Be original and make sure subject matter fits our audience. And, please, make sure your CD will play before you send it in."

WILLIAM CAREY UNIVERSITY DINNER THEATRE

William Carey University, Hattiesburg MS 39401-5499. (601)318-6218. E-mail: thecom@ wmcarey.edu. **Contact:** O.L. Quave, managing director. Play producer. Produces 2 musicals/year. "Our dinner theater operates only in summer and plays to family audiences." Payment negotiable.

How to Contact Query with synopsis, character breakdown and set description. Does not return material. Responds in 1 month.

Musical Theater "Plays should be simply-staged, have small casts (8-10 maximum), and be suitable for family viewing; two hours maximum length. Score should require piano only, or piano, synthesizer."

Productions *Ring of Fire: The Johnny Cash Musical*; *Smoke on the Mountain*; *Spitfire Grill*; and *Pump Boys and Dinettes*.

CIRCA '21 DINNER PLAYHOUSE

1828 3rd Ave., Rock Island IL 61201. (309)786-7733 ext 2. Fax: (309)786-4119. E-mail: dpjh@circa21.com. Website: www.circa21.com. **Contact:** Dennis Hitchcock, producer. Play producer. Estab. 1977. Produces 1-2 plays and 4-5 musicals (1 new musical)/year. Plays produced for a general audience. Three children's works/year, concurrent with major productions. Payment is negotiable.

How to Contact Query with synopsis, character breakdown and set description or submit complete manuscript, score and tape of songs. Include SASE. Responds in 3 months.

Musical Theater "We produce both full length and one act children's musicals. Folk or fairy tale themes. Works that do not condescend to a young audience yet are appropriate for entire family. We're also seeking full-length, small cast musicals suitable for a broad audience." Would also consider original music for use in a play being developed.

Productions *A Closer Walk with Patsy Cline*, *Swingtime Canteen*, *Forever Plaid* and *Lost Highway*.

Tips "Small, upbeat, tourable musicals (like *Pump Boys*) and bright musically-sharp children's productions (like those produced by Prince Street Players) work best. Keep an open mind. Stretch to encompass a musical variety—different keys, rhythms, musical ideas and textures."

ENSEMBLE THEATRE OF CINCINNATI

1127 Vine St., Cincinnati OH 45202. (513)421-3555. Fax: (513)562-4104. E-mail: administration@cincyetc.com. Website: www.cincyetc.com. **Contact:** D. Lynn Meyers, producing artistic director. Play producer. Estab. 1986. Produces 6 plays and at least 1 new musical/year. Audience is multi-generational and multi-cultural. 191 seats, proscenium stage. Pays 5-8% royalty (negotiable).

How to Contact Please call or write to inquire if ETC is accepting new scripts.

Musical Theater "All types of musicals are acceptable. Cast not over ten; minimum set, please."

Productions *Hedwig & the Angry Inch*, by John Cameron Mitchel (rock star/transgender/ love story); *Alice in Wonderland*, by David Kisor and Joe McDonough (update of the classic tale); and *The Frog Princess*, by Joe McDonough and David Kisor (family retelling of classic tale).

Tips Looking for "creative, inventive, contemporary subjects or classic tales. If we ask you to send your script, please send materials as complete as possible, including a SASE."

LA JOLLA PLAYHOUSE

P.O. Box 12039, La Jolla CA 92039. (858)550-1070. Fax: (858)550-1075. E-mail: information@ljp.org. Website: www.lajollaplayhouse.org. **Contact**: Gabriel Greene, literary manager. Play producer. Estab. 1947. Produces 6-show season including 1-2 new musicals/year. Audience is University of California students to senior citizens. Performance spaces include a large proscenium theatre with 492 seats, a 3/4 thrust (384 seats), and a black box with up to 400 seats.

How to Contact Query with synopsis, character breakdown, 10-page dialogue sample, demo CD. Include SASE. Responds in 1-2 months.

Musical Theater "We prefer contemporary music but not necessarily a story set in contemporary times. Retellings of classic stories can enlighten us about the times we live in. For budgetary reasons, we'd prefer a smaller cast size."

Productions *Cry-Baby*, book and lyrics by Thomas Meehan and Mark O'Donnell, music by David Javerbaum and Adam Schlesinger; *Dracula, The Musical*, book and lyrics by Don Black and Christopher Hampton, music by Frank Wildhorn (adaptation of Bram Stoker's novel); *Thoroughly Modern Millie*, book by Richard Morris and Dick Scanlan, new music by Jeanine Tesori, new lyrics by Dick Scanlan (based on the 1967 movie); and *Jane Eyre*, book and additional lyrics by John Cairo, music and lyrics by Paul Gordon (adaptation of Charlotte Bronte's novel).

LOS ANGELES DESIGNERS' THEATRE

P.O. Box 1883, Studio City CA 91614-0883. (323)650-9600. Fax: (323)654-3210. E-mail: ladesigners@gmail.com. **Contact:** Richard Niederberg, artistic director. Play producer. Estab. 1970. Produces 20-25 plays and 8-10 new musicals/year. Audience includes Hollywood production executives in film, TV, records and multimedia. Plays are produced at several locations, primarily Studio City, California. Pay is negotiable.

How to Contact Query first. Does not return material. Responds only if interested. *Send proposals only*.

Musical Theater "We seek out controversial material. Street language OK, nudity is fine, religious themes, social themes, political themes are encouraged. Our audience is very 'jaded' as it consists of TV, motion picture and music publishing executives who have 'seen it all'." Does not wish to see bland, 'safe' material. We like first productions. In the cover letter state in great detail the proposed involvement of the songwriter, other than as a writer (i.e., director, actor, singer, publicist, designer, etc.). Also, state if there are any liens on the material or if anything has been promised."

Productions *St. Tim*, by Fred Grab (historical '60s musical); *Slipper and the Rose* (gang musical); and *1593—The Devils Due* (historical musical).

Tips "Make it very 'commercial' and inexpensive to produce. Allow for non-traditional casting. Be prepared with ideas as to how to transform your work to film or videotaped entertainment."

NEW YORK STATE THEATRE INSTITUTE

37 First St., Troy NY 12180. (518)274-3200. E-mail: nysti@capital.net. Website: www. nysti.org. **Contact:** Patricia Di Benedetto Snyder, producing artistic director. Play producer. Produces 5 plays (1 new musical)/year. Plays performed for student audiences grades K-12, family audiences and adult audiences. Theater seats 900 with full stage. Pay negotiable.

How to Contact Query with synopsis, character breakdown, set description and tape of songs. Include SASE. *Do not send ms unless invited.* Responds in 6 weeks for synopsis, 4 months for ms.

Musical Theater Looking for "intelligent and well-written book with substance, a score that enhances and supplements the book and is musically well-crafted and theatrical." Length: up to 2 hours. Could be play with music, musical comedy, musical drama. Excellence and substance in material is essential. Cast could be up to 20; orchestra size up to 8.

Productions *A Tale of Cinderella*, by W.A. Frankonis/Will Severin/George David Weiss (adaptation of fairy tale); *The Silver Skates*, by Lanie Robertson/Byron Janis/George David Weiss (adaptation of book); *The Snow Queen*, by Adrian Mitchell/Richard Peaslee (adaptation of fairy tale); and *Magna Carta*, by Ed Lange/Will Severin/George David Weiss (new musical drama).

Tips "There is a great need for musicals that are well-written with intelligence and substance which are suitable for family audiences."

NORTH SHORE MUSIC THEATRE

P.O. Box 62, Beverly MA 01915. (978)232-7200. Fax: (978)232-9999. E-mail: NorthShoreMusicTheatre@nsmt.org. Website: www.nsmt.org. **Contact:** Bill Hanney. Estab. 1955. Produces 1 Shakespearian play and 7 musicals (1 new musical)/year. General audiences. Performance space is an 1,500-seat arena theatre, 120-seat workshop. Pays royalty (all done via individual commission agreements).

How to Contact Submit synopsis and CD of songs. Include SASE. Responds within 6 months.

Musical Theater Prefers full-length adult pieces not necessarily arena-theatre oriented. Cast sizes from 1-30; orchestra's from 1-16.

Productions *Tom Jones*, by Paul Leigh, George Stiles; *I Sent A Letter to My Love*, by Melissa Manchester and Jeffrey Sweet; *Just So*, by Anthony Drewe & George Stiles (musical based on Rudyard Kipling's fables); *Letters from 'Nam*, by Paris Barclay (Vietnam War experience as told through letters from GI's); and *Friendship of the Sea*, by Michael Wartofsky & Kathleen Cahill (New England maritime adventure musical).

Tips "Keep at it!"

THE OPEN EYE THEATER

P.O. Box 959, 960 Main St., Margaretville NY 12455. Phone/Fax: (845)586-1660. E-mail: openeye@catskill.net. Website: www.theopeneye.org. **Contact:** Amie Brockway, producing artistic director. Play producer. Estab. 1972. Produces approximately 3 full length or 3 new plays for multi-generational audiences. Pays on a fee basis.

How to Contact Query first. "A manuscript will be accepted and read only if it is a play for all ages and is: 1) Submitted by a recognized literary agent; 2) Requested or recommended by a staff or company member; or 3) Recommended by a professional colleague with whose work we are familiar. Playwrights may submit a one-page letter of inquiry including a very brief plot synopsis. Please enclose a self-addressed (but not stamped) envelope. We will reply only if we want you to submit the script (within several months)."

Musical Theater "The Open Eye Theater is a not-for-profit professional company working in a community context. Through the development, production and performance of plays for all ages, artists and audiences are challenged and given the opportunity to grow in the arts. In residence, on tour, and in the classroom, The Open Eye Theater strives to stimulate, educate, entertain, inspire and serve as a creative resource."

Productions *Freddy, the King of Detectives*, by Sandra Fenichel Asher, music by Robert Cucinotta; *Twelfth Night or What You Will*, by William Shakespeare, music by Michael Anthony Worden; *The Wide Awake Princess*, adapted by David Paterson from the novel by Katherine Paterson, with music and lyrics by Steve Liebman; and *Pixies, Kings and Magical Things*, by Hans Christian Anderson, adapted by Ric Aver (four children's tales).

PLAYWRIGHTS HORIZONS

416 W. 42nd St., New York NY 10036. (212)564-1235. Fax: (212)594-0296. E-mail: literary@playwrightshorizons.org. Website: www.playwrightshorizons.org. **Contact:** Kent Nicholson, Director of Musical Theater. Estab. 1971. Produces about 5 plays and 1 new musical/year. "Adventurous New York City theater-going audience." Pays general Off-Broadway contract.

How to Contact Submit complete manuscript and tape or CD of songs. Attn: Kent Nicholson. Include SASE. Responds in 8 months.

Musical Theater American writers. "No revivals, one-acts or children's shows; otherwise we're flexible. We have a particular interest in scores with a distinctively contemporary and American flavor. We generally develop work from scratch; we're open to proposals for shows and scripts in early stages of development."

Productions *Me, Myself and I; After the Revolution; A Small Fire, Kin*

PRIMARY STAGES

307 West 38th St., Suite 1510, New York NY 10018. (212)840-9705. Fax: (212)840-9725. E-mail: info@primarystages.com. Website: www.primarystages.com. **Contact:** Michelle Bossy, associate artistic director. Play producer. Estab. 1984. Produces 4-5 plays/year. "New York theater-going audience representing a broad cross-section, in terms of age, ethnicity, and economic backgrounds. 199-seat, Off-Broadway theater."

How to Contact *"No unsolicited scripts accepted. Submissions by agents only."* Include SASE. Responds in up to 8 months.

Musical Theater "We are looking for work of heightened theatricality, that challenges realism—musical plays that go beyond film and televisions standard fare. We are looking for small cast shows under 6 characters total, with limited sets. We are interested in original works, that have not been produced in New York."

Productions *I Sent a Letter to My Love*, by Melissa Manchester/Jeffrey Sweet; *Nightmare Alley*, by Jonathan Brielle; *Call the Children Home*, by Mildred Kayden and Thomas Babe; *Adrift in Macao*, by Christopher Durang and Peter Melnick.

PRINCE MUSIC THEATER

100 S. Broad St., Suite 650, Philadelphia PA 19110. (215)972-1000. Fax: (215)972-1020. E-mail: info@princemusictheater.org. Website: www.princemusictheater.org. **Contact:** Marjorie Samoff, president and producing director. Play producer. Estab. 1984. Produces 4-5 musicals/year. "Our average audience member is in their mid-40s. We perform to ethnically diverse houses."

How to Contact Submit two-page synopsis with tape or CD of 4 songs. Include SASE. "May include complete script, but be aware that response is at least 10 months."

Tips "We only produce pieces that are music/lyric driven, not merely plays with music."

THE REPERTORY THEATRE OF ST. LOUIS

P.O. Box 191730, 130 Edgar Road, St. Louis MO 63119. (314)968-7340. E-mail: mail@repstl.org. Website: www.repstl.org/. **Contact:** Susan Gregg, associate artistic director. Play producer. Estab. 1966. Produces 9 plays and 1 or 2 musicals/year. "Conservative regional theater audience. We produce all our work at the Loretto Hilton Theatre." Pays by royalty.

How to Contact Query with synopsis, character breakdown and set description. Does not return material. Responds in 2 years.

Musical Theater "We want plays with a small cast and simple setting. No children's shows or foul language. After a letter of inquiry we would prefer script and demo tape."

Productions *Almost September* and *Esmeralda*, by David Schechter and Steve Lutvak; *Jack*, by Barbara Field and Hiram Titus; and *Young Rube*, by John Pielmeier and Nattie Selman, *Ace* by Robert Taylor and Richard Oberacker.

SECOND STAGE THEATRE

305 W. 43rd St., New York NY 10036. (212)787-8302. Fax: (212)397-7066. E-mail: info@2st.com. Website: 2st.com. **Contact:** Christopher Burney, associate artistic director. Play producer. Estab. 1979. Produces 4 plays and 1 musical (1 new musical)/year. Plays are performed in a small, 108-seat Off Broadway House. Pays per performance.

How to Contact Query with synopsis, character breakdown, set description, tape of 5 songs (no more). No unsolicited manuscripts. Include SASE. Responds in 6 months.

Musical Theater "We are looking for innovative, unconventional musicals that deal with sociopolitical themes."

Productions *Bachelorette*, by Leslye Headland; *Trust*, by Paul Weitz; *By the Way, Meet Vera Stark*, by Lynn Nottage

Tips "Submit through agent; have strong references; always submit the best of your material in small quantities: 5 outstanding songs are better than 10 mediocre ones."

SHAKESPEARE SANTA CRUZ

Theater Arts Center, U.C.S.C., 1156 High Street, Santa Cruz CA 95064. (831)459-2121. E-mail: iago@ucsc.edu. Website: www.shakespearesantacruz.org. **Contact:** Marco Barricelli, artistic director. Play producer. Estab. 1982. Produces 4 plays/year. Performance spaces are an outdoor redwood grove; and an indoor 540-seat thrust. Pay is negotiable.

How to Contact Query first. Include SASE. Responds in 2 months.

Musical Theater "Shakespeare Santa Cruz produces musicals in its Winter Holiday Season (Oct-Dec). We are also interested in composers' original music for pre-existing plays—including songs, for example, for Shakespeare's plays."

Productions *Cinderella*, by Kate Hawley (book and lyrics) and Gregg Coffin (composer); and *Gretel and Hansel*, by Kate Hawley (book and lyrics) and composer Craig Bohmler; *The Princess and the Pea*, by Kate Hawley (book and lyrics) and composer Adam Wernick; *Sleeping Beauty*, by Kate Hawley (book and lyrics) and composer Adam Wernick.

Tips "Always contact us before sending material."

THE TEN-MINUTE MUSICALS PROJECT

P.O. Box 461194, West Hollywood CA 90046. E-mail: info@TenMinuteMusicals.org. Website: www.TenMinuteMusicals.org. **Contact:** Michael Koppy, producer. Play producer. Estab. 1987. All pieces are new musicals. Pays $250 advance.

How to Contact Submit complete manuscript, score and CD or DVD of songs. Include SASE. Responds in 3 months.Musical Theater Seeks complete short stage musicals of 8-15 minutes in length. Maximum cast: 9. "No parodies—original music only."

Productions *Away to Pago Pago*, by Jack Feldman/Barry Manilow/John PiRoman/Bruce Sussman; *The Bottle Imp*, by Kenneth Vega (from the story of the same title by Robert Louis Stevenson); and *The Furnished Room*, by Saragail Katzman (from the story of the same title by O. Henry), and many others.

Tips "Start with a solid story—either an adaptation or an original idea—but with a solid beginning, middle and end (probably with a plot twist at the climax). We caution that it will surely take much time and effort to create a quality work. (Occasionally a clearly talented and capable writer and composer seem to have almost 'dashed' something off, under the misperception that inspiration can carry the day in this format. Works selected in previous rounds all clearly evince that considerable deliberation and craft were invested.) We're seeking short contemporary musical theater material, in the style of what might be found on Broadway, Off-Broadway or the West End. Think of shows like *Candide* or *Little Shop of Horrors*, pop operas like *Sweeney Todd* or *Chess*, or chamber musicals like *Once on this Island* or *Falsettos*. (Even small accessible operas like *The Telephone* or *Trouble in Tahiti* are possible models.) All have solid plots, and all rely on sung material to advance them. Of primary importance is to start with a strong story, even if it means postponing work on music and lyrics until the dramatic foundation is complete."

THUNDER BAY THEATRE

400 N. Second Ave., Alpena MI 49707. (989)354-2267. Website: www.thunderbaytheatre. com. Artistic Director: Mark S. Butterfuss. Play producer. Estab. 1967. Produces 12 productions/year including 5 musicals and 7 plays. Performance space is thrust stage. Pays variable royalty or per performance.

How to Contact Submit complete manuscript, score and tape of songs. Include SASE.

Musical Theater Small cast. Not equipped for large sets. Considers original background music for use in a play being developed or for use in a pre-existing play.

Productions 2009 Musicals *Brigadoon, The Producers, The Rat Pack Lounge, White Christmas, Beauty and the Beast.*

WEST END ARTISTS

c/o St. Luke's Theatre, 308 West 46th St., New York NY 10036. (212)947-3499. Fax: (212)265-4074. **West Coast:** 18034 Ventura Blvd. #291, Encino CA 91316. (818)623-0040. Fax: (818)623-0202. E-mail: egaynes@aol.com. **Contact:** Pamela Hall, associate artistic director. Artistic Director: Edmund Gaynes. Play producer. Estab. 1983. "We operate St. Luke's Theatre, Actors Temple Theatre, and Theatres at 45 Bleecker St. in New York City, and Whitmore-Lindley Theatre Center in Los Angeles." Produces 5 plays and 3 new musicals/year. Audience "covers a broad spectrum, from general public to heavy theater/ film/TV industry crowds. Pays 6% royalty.

How to Contact Submit complete manuscript, score and tape of songs. Include SASE. Responds in 3 months.

Musical Theater "Prefer small-cast musicals and revues. Full length preferred. Interested in children's shows also." Cast size: "Maximum 12; exceptional material with larger casts will be considered."

Productions Off-Broadway: *Picon Pie* - Lambs Theatre (2004-05); *Trolls* - Actors Playhouse, (2005); *The Big Voice: God or Merman?* - Actors Temple Theatre (2006-07); *Danny and Sylvia: The Danny Kaye Musical* — St. Luke's Theatre (2009-10); Dietrich and Chevalier: The Musical—St. Luke's Theatre (2010).

Tips "If you feel every word or note you have written is sacred and chiseled in stone and are unwilling to work collaboratively with a professional director, don't bother to submit."

WINGS THEATRE CO.

154 Christopher St., New York NY 10014. (212)627-2960. Fax: (212)462-0024. E-mail: jcorrick@wingstheatre.com. Website: www.wingstheatre.com. **Contact:** Laura Kleeman, literary manager. Artistic Director: Jeffrey Corrick. Play producer. Estab. 1987. Produces 3-5 plays and 3-5 musicals/year. Performance space is a 74-seat O.O.B. proscenium; repertoire includes a New Musicals Series, a gay-play series—we produce musicals in both series. Pays $100 for limited rights to produce against 6% of gross box office receipts.

How to Contact Submit complete manuscript, CD or tape of songs (score is not essential). Include SASE. Responds in 1 year. Musical Theater "Eclectic. Entertaining. Enlightening. This is an O.O.B. theater. Funds are limited." Does not wish to see "movies posing as plays. Television theater."

Productions *Scott & Zelda*, by Dave Bates (The Fitzgeralds); *Cowboys*, by Clint Jefferies (gay western spoof); and *The Three Musketeers*, by Clint Jefferies (musical adaptation).

Tips "Book needs to have a well-developed plot line and interesting, fully-realized characters. We place emphasis on well-written scripts, as opposed to shows which rely exclusively on the quality of the music to carry the show. Also be patient—we often hold onto plays for a full year before making a final decision."

PLAY PUBLISHERS

BAKER'S PLAYS

45 W. 25th St., New York, NY 10010. (212)206-8990. Fax: (212)206-1429. E-mail: info@ bakersplays.com. Website: www.bakersplays.com. **Contact:** Roxane Heinze-Bradshaw, Managing Editor. Play publisher. Estab. 1845. Publishes 25-30 plays and 5-10 new musicals/year. Plays are used by children's theaters, junior and senior high schools, colleges and community theaters. Pays negotiated book and production royalty. • See the listing for Baker's Plays High School Playwriting Contest in the Contests & Awards section.

How to Contact Submit complete manuscript and CD. Include SASE. Also accepts online submission—see website for more information. Responds in 4 months.

Musical Theater "Seeking musicals for teen production and children's theater production. We prefer large cast, contemporary musicals which are easy to stage and produce. Plot your shows strongly, keep your scenery and staging simple, your musical numbers and choreography easily explained and blocked out. Music must be camera-ready."

Productions *Stone Soup,* by Anne Glasner & Betty Hollinger (children's musical); *A Walk in the Sky,* book and lyrics by Dale Wasserman, music by Allan Jay Friedman (family musical); *Beanstalk! The Musical!* book by Ross Mihalko and Donna Swift, music by Linda Berg, lyrics by Ross Mihalko (children's musical).

CONTEMPORARY DRAMA SERVICE

885 Elkton Dr., Colorado Springs CO 80907. (719)594-4422. E-mail: editor@meriwether. com. Website: www.contemporarydrama.com. **Contact:** Arthur Zapel, associate editor. Play publisher. Estab. 1979. Publishes 40-50 plays and 4-6 new musicals/year. "We publish for young children and teens in mainstream Christian churches and for teens and college level in the secular market. Our musicals are performed in churches, schools and colleges." Pays 10-50% book and performance royalty.

How to Contact *Query first* then submit complete manuscript, score and tape of songs. Include SASE. Responds in 1 month.

Musical Theater "For churches we publish musical programs for children and teens to perform at Easter, Christmas or some special occasion. Our school musicals are for teens to perform as class plays or special entertainments. Cast size may vary from 15-25 depending on use. We prefer more parts for girls than boys. Music must be written in the vocal range of teens. Staging should be relatively simple but may vary as needed. We are not interested in elementary school material. Elementary level is OK for church music but not public school elementary. Music must have full piano accompaniment and be professionally scored for camera-ready publication."

Publications *Lucky, Lucky Hudson and the 12th Street Gang*, by Tim Kelly, book, and Bill Francoeur, music and lyrics (spoof of old time gangster movies); *Is There A Doctor in the House?*, by Tim Kelly, book, and Bill Francoeur, music and lyrics (adapted from Moliere comedy); and *Jitterbug Juliet* , by Mark Dissette, book, and Bill Francoeur, music and lyrics (spoof of *Romeo and Juliet*).

Tips "Familiarize yourself with our market. Send $1 postage for catalog. Try to determine what would fit in, yet still be unique."

THE DRAMATIC PUBLISHING COMPANY

311 Washington St., Woodstock IL 60098. (800)448-7469. Fax: (800)334-5302. E-mail: plays@dramaticpublishing.com. Website: www.dramaticpublishing.com. **Contact:** Linda Habjan, submissions editor. Play publisher. Publishes 35 plays and 3-5 musicals/year. Estab. 1885. Plays used by professional and community theaters, schools and colleges. Pays negotiable royalty.

How to Contact Submit complete manuscript, score and tape of songs. Include SASE. Responds in 3 months.

Musical Theater Seeking "children's musicals not over 1¼ hours, and adult musicals with 2 act format. No adaptations for which the rights to use the original work have not been cleared. If directed toward high school market, large casts with many female roles are preferred. For professional, stock and community theater small casts are better. Cost of producing a play is always a factor to consider in regard to costumes, scenery and special effects." Would also consider original music for use in a pre-existing play, "if we or the composer hold the rights to the non-musical work."

Publications *The Little Prince*, by Rick Cummins/John Scoullar; *Hans Brinker*, by Gayle Hudson/Bobbe Bramson; and *Bubbe Meises, Bubbe Stories,* by Ellen Gould/Holly Gewandter (all are full-length family musicals).

Tips "A complete score, ready to go is highly recommended. Tuneful songs which stand on their own are a must. Good subject matter which has wide appeal is always best but not required."

ELDRIDGE PUBLISHING CO., INC.

P.O. Box 14367, Tallahassee FL 32317. Phone/Fax: (850)385-2463. E-mail: info@histage. com. Website: www.histage.com. **Contact:** Susan Shore, musical editor. Play publisher. Estab. 1906. Publishes 50 plays and 1-2 musicals/year. Seeking "large cast musicals which appeal to students. We like variety and originality in the music, easy staging and costuming. Also looking for children's theater musicals which have smaller casts and are easy to tour. We serve the school market (6th grade through 12th); and church market (Christmas musicals)." Pays 50% royalty and 10% copy sales in school market.

How to Contact Submit manuscript, score or lead sheets and CD of songs. Include SASE. Responds in 1 month.

Publications *The Bard is Back*, by Stephen Murray ("a high school's production of Romeo & Juliet is a disaster!"); and *Boogie-Woogie Bugle Girls*, book by Craig Sodaro, music and lyrics by Stephen Murray (WWII themed musical).

Tips "We're always looking for talented composers but not through individual songs. We're only interested in complete school or church musicals. Lead sheets, CDs, and script are best way to submit. Let us see your work!"

ELDRIDGE PLAYS AND MUSICALS

P.O. Box 14367, Tallahassee FL 32317.(850)385-2463. Website: www.hiStage.com and www.95church.com. **Contact**: Meredith Edwards, senior editor. Drama publisher. "We publish complete musicals, not single songs." Estab. 1978. Publishes 1-2 musicals/year. Pays standard royalty.

How to Contact See website for submission guidelines. Materials should include complete musical including libretto, lyrics, lead sheets, and demo CD. Responds in 2 months.

Musical Theater "We are especially interested in musicals for schools (from grade school through high school)."

Publications *Elephans*, music by Larrance Fingerhut, books and lyrics by Jeff Goode; *Anne With An "e": The Green Gables Musical*, books and lyrics by Neil K. Newell and C. Michael Perry.

THE FREELANCE PRESS

670 Centre St., Suite 8, Jamaica Plain MA 02130. (617)524-7045. E-mail: info@ freelancepress.org. Website: www.freelancepress.org. Managing Editor: Narcissa Campion. Play publisher. Estab. 1979. Publishes up to 3 new musicals/year. "Pieces are primarily to be acted by elementary/middle school to high school students (9th and 10th grades); large casts (approximately 30); plays are produced by schools and children's theaters." Pays 10% of purchase price of script or score, 50% of collected royalty.

How to Contact Query first. Include SASE. Responds in 6 months.

Musical Theater "We publish previously produced musicals and plays to be acted by children in the primary grades through high school. Plays are for large casts (approximately 30 actors and speaking parts) and run between 45 minutes to 1 hour and 15 minutes. Subject matter should be contemporary issues (sibling rivalry, friendship, etc.) or adaptations of classic literature for children (*Syrano de Bergerac*, *Rip Van Winkle*, *Pied Piper*, *Treasure Island*, etc.). We do not accept any plays written for adults to perform for children."

Publications *Tortoise vs. Hare*, by Stephen Murray (modern version of classic); *Tumbleweed*, by Sebastian Stuart (sleepy time western town turned upside down); and *Mything Links*, by Sam Abel (interweaving of Greek myths with a great pop score).

Tips "We enjoy receiving material that does not condescend to children. They are capable of understanding many current issues, playing complex characters, handling unconventional material, and singing difficult music."

SAMUEL FRENCH, INC.

45 W. 25th St., New York NY 10010. (212)206-8990. Fax: (212)206-1429. Website: www. samuelfrench.com. Hollywood office: 7623 Sunset Blvd., Hollywood CA 90046. (323)876-

0570. Fax: (323)876-6822. President: Leon Embry. **Contact:** Roxane Heinze-Bradshaw, managing editor. Play publisher. Estab. 1830. Publishes approximately 100 plays and 10-20 new musicals/year. Amateur and professional theaters.

How to Contact *Query first.* Include SASE. Onlline query form is available. Responds in 10 weeks.

Musical Theater "We publish primarily successful musicals from the NYC, London and regional stage."

Publications *Evil Dead: The Musical,* by George Reinblatt—lyrics/book, and Frank Cipolla, Christopher Bond, Melissa Morris, George Reinblatt - music (Horror Movie parody); *Hats! The Musical,* book by Marcia Milgrom Dodge & Anthony Dodge, additional material by Rob Bartlett, Lynne Taylor-Corbett & Sharon Vaughn. Songs by Grammy, Golden Globe, and Tony winning songwriters (musical celebration of turning 50); *Adding Machine: A Musical,* composed by Joshua Schmidt, Libretto by Jason Loewith and Joshua Schmidt (dark comic of *The Adding Machine* by Elmer Rice).

HEUER PUBLISHING CO.

P.O. Box 248, Cedar Rapids IA 52406. Main Office: 211 First Ave., SE Suite 200, Cedar Rapids IA 52401. 1-800-950-7529. E-mail: editor@hitplays.com. Website: www.hitplays. com. Publisher: C. Emmett McMullen. Play publisher. Estab. 1928. Publishes plays, musicals, operas/operettas and guides (choreography, costume, production/staging) for amateur and professional markets, including junior and senior high schools, college/university and community theatres. Focus includes comedy, drama, fantasy, mystery and holiday. Pays by percentage royalty or outright purchase. Pays by outright purchase or percentage royalty.

How to Contact Query with musical CD/tape or submit complete manuscript and score. Include SASE. Responds in 2 months.

Musical Theater "We prefer one, two or three act comedies or mystery-comedies with a large number of characters."

Publications *Happily Ever After,* by Allen Koepke (musical fairytale); *Brave Buckaroo,* by Renee J. Clark (musical melodrama); and *Pirate Island,* by Martin Follose (musical comedy).

Tips "We are willing to review single-song submissions as cornerstone piece for commissioned works. Special interest focus in multicultural, historic, classic literature, teen issues, and biographies."

PIONEER DRAMA SERVICE

P.O. Box 4267, Englewood CO 80155. 1-800-333-7262. Fax: (303)779-4315. Website: www. pioneerdrama.com. **Contact:** Lori Conary, assistant editor. Play publisher. Estab. 1963. "Plays are performed by junior high and high school drama departments, church youth groups, college and university theaters, semi-professional and professional children's theaters, parks and recreation departments." Playwrights paid 50% royalty (10% sales) split when there are multiple authors/composers.

How to Contact Query with character breakdown, synopsis and set description or submit full manuscript and CD of music. Include SASE. Responds in 6 months.

Musical Theater "We seek full length children's musicals, high school musicals and one act children's musicals to be performed by children, secondary school students, and/or adults. We want musicals easy to perform, simple sets, many female roles and very few solos. Must be appropriate for educational market. We are not interested in profanity, themes with exclusively adult interest, sex, drinking, smoking, etc. Several of our full-length plays are being converted to musicals. We edit them, then contract with someone to write the music and lyrics."

Publications *The Big Bad Musical,* by Alec Strum, music and lyrics by Bill Francoeur; *Nottingham: a Totally Teen Musical Book,* by Flip Kobler and Cincy Marcus, music by Dennis Poore, lyrics by Flip Kobler; *The Elves and the Shoemaker— the musical,* by Katen Boettcher-Tate, music and lyrics by Bill Francoeur.

Tips "Research and learn about our company. Our website and catalog provide an incredible amount of information."

Classical Performing Arts

Finding an audience is critical to the composer of orchestral music. Fortunately, baby boomers are swelling the ranks of classical music audiences and bringing with them a taste for fresh, innovative music. So the climate is fair for composers seeking their first performance.

Finding a performance venue is particularly important because once a composer has his work performed for an audience and establishes himself as a talented newcomer, it can lead to more performances and commissions for new works.

BEFORE YOU SUBMIT

Be aware that most classical music organizations are nonprofit groups, and don't have a large budget for acquiring new works. It takes a lot of time and money to put together an orchestral performance of a new composition, therefore these groups are quite selective when choosing new works to perform. Don't be disappointed if the payment offered by these groups is small or even non-existent. What you gain is the chance to have your music performed for an appreciative audience. Also realize that many classical groups are understaffed, so it may take longer than expected to hear back on your submission. It pays to be patient, and employ diplomacy, tact and timing in your follow-up.

In this section you will find listings for classical performing arts organizations throughout the U.S. But if you have no prior performances to your credit, it's a good idea to begin with a small chamber orchestra, for example. Smaller symphony and chamber orchestras are usually more inclined to experiment with new works. A local university or conservatory of music, where you may already have contacts, is a great place to start.

All of the groups listed in this section are interested in hearing new works from contemporary classical composers. Pay close attention to the music needs of each group, and when you find one you feel might be interested in your music, follow submission guidelines carefully. To locate classical performing arts groups in your area, consult the Geographic Index at the back of this book.

ACADIANA SYMPHONY ORCHESTRA

412 Travis St., Lafayette, LA 70503. (337)232-4277. Fax: (337)237-4712. E-mail: SmolijMariusz@acadianasymphony.org.   Website: www.acadianasymphony.org. **Contact**: Jenny Krueger, executive director. Music Director: Mariusz Smolij. Symphony orchestra. Estab. 1984. Members are amateurs and professionals. Performs 20 concerts/year, including 1 new work. Commissions 1 new work/year. Performs in 2,230-seat hall with "wonderful acoustics." Pays "according to the type of composition."

How to Contact Call first. Does not return material. Responds in 2 months.

Music Full orchestra: 10 minutes at most. Reduced orchestra, educational pieces: short, up to 5 minutes.

Performances Quincy Hilliard's *Universal Covenant* (orchestral suite); James Hanna's *In Memoriam* (strings/elegy); and Gregory Danner's *A New Beginning* (full orchestra fanfare).

THE AMERICAN BOYCHOIR

19 Lambert Dr., Princeton NJ 08540. (609)924-5858. Fax: (609)924-5812. E-mail: admissions@americanboychoir.org.   Website: www.americanboychoir.org.   General Manager: Janet B. Kaltenbach. Music Director: Fernando Malvar-Ruiz. Professional boychoir. Estab. 1937. Members are musically talented boys in grades 4-8. Performs 150 concerts/year. Commissions 1 new work approximately every 3 years. Actively seeks high quality arrangements. Performs national and international tours, orchestral engagements, church services, workshops, school programs, local concerts, and at corporate and social functions.

How to Contact Submit complete score. Include SASE. Responds in 1 year.

Music Choral works in unison, SA, SSA, SSAA or SATB division; unaccompanied and with piano or organ; occasional chamber orchestra or brass ensemble. Works are usually sung by 28 to 60 boys. Composers must know boychoir sonority.

Performances *Four Seasons*, by Michael Torke (orchestral-choral); *Garden of Light*, by Aaron Kernis (orchestral-choral); *Reasons for Loving the Harmonica*, by Libby Larsen (piano); and *Songs Eternity*, by Steven Paulus (piano).

AMERICAN OPERA MUSICAL THEATRE CO.

400 W. 43rd St. #19D, New York NY 10036. (212)594-1839. Fax: (646)290-8471. **Contact:** Diana Corto, artistic director. Opera and musical theatre producing/presenting organization. Estab. 1995. Members are professionals with varying degrees of experience. Performs 2 operas, many concerts/year and 1 musical theatre production each year. Audience is sophisticated and knowledgeable about music and theatre. "We rent performance spaces in New York, and are either sponsored by a presenter, or are paid performance fees for opera and concerts."

How to Contact "We are only accepting photos and resumes at this time—no CDs or DVDs."

Music "Must be vocal (for opera or for music theatre). Cast should not exceed 10. Orchestration should not exceed 30, smaller groups preferred. No rock 'n' roll, brassy pop."

Performances Nationally and internationally: Puccini's *La Boheme*; Verdi's *Rigoletto*; *The Jewel Box*; *Iolanta*; *La Molinara* and *The World Goes Round*.

ANDERSON SYMPHONY ORCHESTRA

1124 Meridian Plaza, Anderson IN 46016. (765)644-2111. Fax: (765)644-7703. E-mail: aso@andersonsymphony.org. Website: www.andersonsymphony.org. **Contact:** Dr. Richard Sowers, conductor. Symphony orchestra. Estab. 1967. Members are professionals. Performs 7 concerts/year. Performs for typical mid-western audience in a 1,500-seat restored Paramount Theatre. Pay negotiable.

How to Contact Query first. Include SASE. Responds in several months.

Music "Shorter lengths better; concerti OK; difficulty level: mod high; limited by typically 3 full service rehearsals."

THE ATLANTA YOUNG SINGERS OF CALLANWOLDE

980 Briarcliff Rd. N.E., Atlanta GA 30306. (404)873-3365. Fax: (404)873-0756. E-mail: info@aysc.org. Website: www.aysc.org. **Contact:** Paige F. Mathis, music director. Children's chorus. Estab. 1975. Performs 3 major concerts/year as well as invitational performances and co-productions with other Atlanta arts organizations. Audience consists of community members, families, alumni, and supporters. Performs most often at churches. Pay is negotiable.

How to Contact Submit complete score and tape of piece(s). Include SASE. Responds in accordance with request.

Music "Subjects and styles appealing to 3rd-12th grade boys and girls. Contemporary concerns of the world of interest. Unusual sacred, folk, classic style. Internationally and ethnically bonding. Medium difficulty preferred, with or without keyboard accompaniment."

Tips "Our mission is to promote service and growth through singing."

AUGSBURG CHOIR

Augsburg College, 2211 Riverside Avenue S., Minneapolis MN 55454. (612)330-1265. E-mail: brauer@augsburg.edu. Website: www.augsburg.edu. **Contact:** Tina Brauer, coordinator. **Director of Choral Activities**: Peter A. Hendrickson. Vocal ensemble (SATB choir). Members are amateurs. Performs 25 concerts/year, including 1-6 new works. Commissions 0-2 composers or new works/year. Audience is all ages, "sophisticated and unsophisticated." Concerts are performed in churches, concert halls and schools. Pays for outright purchase.

How to Contact Query first. Include SASE. Responds in 1 month.

Music Seeking "sacred choral pieces, no more than 5-7 minutes long, to be sung a cappella or with obbligato instrument. Can contain vocal solos. We have 50-60 members in our choir."

Performances Carol Barnett's *Spiritual Journey*; Steven Heitzeg's *Litanies for the Living* (choral/orchestral); and Morton Lanriclsen's *O Magnum Mysteries* (a cappella choral).

BILLINGS SYMPHONY

2721 2nd Ave N., Suite 350, Billings MT 59101-1936. (406)252-3610. Fax: (406)252-3353. E-mail: symphony@billingssymphony.org. Website: www.billingssymphony.org. **Contact:** Anne Harrigan, music director. Symphony orchestra, orchestra and chorale. Estab. 1950. Members are professionals and amateurs. Performs 12-15 concerts/year, including 6-7 new works. Traditional audience. Performs at Alberta Bair Theater (capacity 1,416). Pays by outright purchase (or rental).

How to Contact Query first. Include SASE. Responds in 2 weeks.

Music Any style. Traditional notation preferred.

Performances 2010 Symphony in the Park includes: "Michael Jackson Spectacular"; "Glee" inspired versions of "Jump" by Van Halen and "Don't Stop Believing" by Journey. Highlights from our upcoming 60th Anniversary Season: Jenkins' "Palladio"; Mussorgsky's "Night on Bald Mountain"; A Tribute to the 50s Jukebox, and finale from Dvorak's "New World" Symphony.

Tips "Write what you feel (be honest) and sharpen your compositional and craftsmanship skills."

THE BOSTON PHILHARMONIC

295 Huntington Ave., #210, Boston MA 02115. (617)236-0999. Fax: (617)236-8613. E-mail: info@bostonphil.org. Website: www.bostonphil.org. **Music Director:** Benjamin Zander. Symphony orchestra. Estab. 1979. Members are professionals, amateurs and students. Performs 2 concerts/year. Audience is ages 30-70. Performs at New England Conservatory's Jordan Hall, Boston's Symphony Hall and Sanders Theatre in Cambridge. Both Jordan Hall and Sanders Theatre are small (approximately 1,100 seats) and very intimate.

How to Contact *Does not accept new music at this time.*

Music Full orchestra only.

Performances Dutilleuxs' *Tout un monde lointain* for cello and orchestra (symphonic); Bernstein's *Fancy Free* (symphonic/jazzy); Copland's *El Salon Mexico* (symphonic); Gershwin's *Rhapsody in Blue*; Shostakovitch's *Symphony No. 10*; Harbison's *Concerto for Oboe*; Holst's *The Planet Suite*; Schwantner's *New Morning for the World*; Berg's *Seven Early Songs*; and Ive's *The Unanswered Question*.

BRAVO! L.A.

16823 Liggett St., North Hills CA 91343. (818)892-8737. Fax: (818)892-1227. E-mail: info@bravo-la.com. Website: www.bravo-la.com. **Contact:** Cellist Dr. Janice Foy, director.

An umbrella organization of recording/touring musicians, formed in 1994. Includes the following musical ensembles: the New American Quartet (string quartet); The Ascending Wave (harp/cello duo); Celllissimo! L.A. (cello ensemble); Sierra Chamber Players (includes piano with strings or other combos); Trio Fantastico (piano, clarinet and 'cello); the Happy Band and the World Peace Orchestra (jazz groups playing all styles). The latest combo is solo cello with flamenco dancer, Jani Quintero.

How to Contact Submit scores/tape of pieces. Include SASE. Responds in a few months. "We also record DEMOS for those needing entry into various situations and we use a DEMO rate through the Musicians Union Local 47 as our contract for that. If you want to do a Limited Pressing recording, that also goes through the Union with an appropriate contract."

Music "We do all styles from classical to jazz. You can hear examples of most of the above ensembles on the site. You may also read about the latest musical antics of these musicians at the site."

Tips "Let Bravo! L.A. know about your latest or upcoming performances and if you have a tape/CD of it, please forward or send an audio clip! If you have trouble getting through the spam blocker, let me know! We do not provide funding but there are many different grants out there for different situations. Good luck!"

CALGARY BOYS CHOIR

Grace Lutheran Church, 3610 Sarcee Road SW, Calgary Alberta, Canada. (403)217-7790. Fax: (403)217-7796. E-mail: manager@calgaryboyschoir.ab.ca. Website: www.calgaryboyschoir.ab.ca. **Contact:** Gail Majeski, general manager. Artistic director: Lana Lysogor. Boys choir. Estab. 1973. Members are amateurs age 6 and up. Performs 5-10 concerts/year including 1-2 new works. Pay negotiable.

How to Contact Query first. Submit complete score and tape of piece(s). Include SASE. Responds in 6 weeks. Does not return material.

Music "Style fitting for boys choir. Lengths depending on project. Orchestration preferable a cappella/for piano/sometimes orchestra."

Performances Dr. William Jordan's *City of Peace*(world premiere Wednesday September 11, 2002); Lydia Adam's arrangement of *Mi'kmaq Honour Song*(May 26, 2002); *A Child's Evening Prayer*, Dr. Allan Bevan (May 10, 2008).

CANADIAN OPERA COMPANY

227 Front St. E., Toronto ON M5A 1E8 Canada. (416)363-6671. Fax: (416)363-5584. E-mail: sandrag@coc.ca. Website: www.coc.ca. **Contact:** Sandra J. Gavinchuk, music administrator. Opera company. Estab. 1950. Members are professionals. 68-72 performances, including a minimum of 1 new work/year. Pays by contract.

How to Contact Submit complete CDs or DVDs of vocal and/or operatic works. "Vocal works please." Include SASE. Responds in 5 weeks.

Music Vocal works, operatic in nature. "Do not submit works which are not for voice. Ask for requirements for the Composers-In-Residence program."

Performances Dean Burry's *Brothers Grimm* (children's opera, 50 minutes long); Dean Burry's Isis and the Seven Scorpions (45-minute opera for children); James Rolfe's *Swoon;* James Rolfe's *Donna* (work title for forthcoming work); Nixon in China by John Adams; L'Amour Do Loin by Saariaho.

Tips "We have a Composers-In-Residence program which is open to Canadian composers or landed immigrants."

CANTATA ACADEMY

CHORALEP.O. Box 1958, Royal Oak MI 48068-1958. (248)358-9868. **Contact:** Phillip O'Jibway, business manager. Music Director: Maurice Draughn, music director. Vocal ensemble. Estab. 1961. Members are professionals. Performs 10-12 concerts/year including 1-3 new works. "We perform in churches and small auditoriums throughout the Metro Detroit area for audiences of about 500 people." Pays variable rate for outright purchase.

How to Contact Submit complete score. Include SASE. Responds in 3 months.

Music Four-part a cappella and keyboard accompanied works, two and three-part works for men's or women's voices. Some small instrumental ensemble accompaniments acceptable. Work must be suitable for forty voice choir. No works requiring orchestra or large ensemble accompaniment. No pop.

Performances Libby Larsen's *Missa Gaia: Mass for the Earth* (SATB, string quartet, oboe, percussion, 4-hand piano); Dede Duson's *To Those Who See* (SATB, SSA); and Sarah Hopkins' *Past Life Melodies* (SATB with Harmonic Overtone Singing); Eric Whiteacre *Five Hebrew Love Songs*; Robert Convery's *Songs of the Children*.

Tips "Be patient. Would prefer to look at several different samples of work at one time."

CARMEL SYMPHONY ORCHESTRA

P.O. Box 761, Carmel IN 46082-0761. (317)844-9717. Fax: (317)844-9916. E-mail: info@ carmelsymphony.org. Website: www.carmelsymphony.org. **Contact**: Allen Davis, executive director. Symphony orchestra. Estab. 1976. Members are paid and non-paid professionals. Performs 15 concerts/year, including 1-2 new works. Audience is "37% senior citizens, 85% white." Performs in a 1,600-seat Palladium at the Center for the Performing Arts.

How to Contact *Query first*. Include SASE. Responds in 3 months.

Music "Full orchestra works, 5-60 minutes in length. Parents are encouraged to bring a child. 85-piece orchestra, medium difficult to difficult.

Performances Brahms' *Concerto in D Major for Violin and Orchestra*, Op. 77; Debussy's "La Mer"; Ravel's Second Suite from "Daphnis and Chloe"; Dvorak's *Carnival Overture*, Op. 92; and Sibelius' *Symphony No. 5* in E-flat Major, Op. 82. Outstanding guest artists include Michael Feinstein, Sylvia McNair, Cameron Carpenter, Dale Clevenger, and Angela Brown.

CHATTANOOGA GIRLS CHOIR

1831 Hickory Valley Rd., Chattanooga TN 37401. (423)296-1006. E-mail: office@ chattanoogagirlschoir.com. Website: chattanoogagirlschoir.com. **Contact**: LuAnne Holden, artistic director. Vocal ensemble. Estab. 1986. Members are amateurs. Performs 2 concerts/year including at least 1 new work. Audience consists of cultural and civic organizations and national and international tours. Performance space includes concert halls and churches. Pays for outright purchase or per performance.

How to Contact Query first. Include SASE. Responds in 6 weeks.

Music Seeks renaissance, baroque, classical, romantic, twentieth century, folk and musical theatre for young voices of up to 8 minutes. Performers include 5 treble choices: 4th grade (2 pts.); 5th grade (2 pts.) (SA); grades 6-9 (3 pts.) (SSA); grades 10-12 (3-4 pts.) (SSAA); and a combined choir: grades 6-12 (3-4 pts.) (SSAA). Medium level of difficulty. "Avoid extremely high Tessitura Sop I and extremely low Tessitura Alto II."

Performances Jan Swafford's *Iphigenia Book: Meagher* (choral drama); Penny Tullock's *How Can I Keep from Singing* (Shaker hymn).

CHEYENNE SYMPHONY ORCHESTRA

P.O. Box 851, Cheyenne WY 82003. (307)778-8561. Fax: (307)634-7512. E-mail: director@ cheyennesymphony.org. Website: www.cheyennesymphony.org. **Contact:** Chloe Illoway, executive director. Symphony orchestra. Estab. 1955. Members are professionals. Performs 5-6 concerts/year. "Orchestra performs for a conservative, mid-to-upper income audience of 1,200 season members."

How to Contact Query first to music director William Intriligator. Does not return material.

CIMARRON CIRCUIT OPERA COMPANY

P.O. Box 1085, Norman OK 73070. (405)364-8962. E-mail: info@ccocopera.org. Website: www.ccocopera.org. **Contact:** Kevin Smith, music director. Opera company. Estab. 1975. Members are semi professional. Performs 75 concerts/year including 1-2 new works. Commissions 1 or less new work/year. "CCOC performs for children across the state of Oklahoma and for a dedicated audience in central Oklahoma. As a touring company, we adapt to the performance space provided, ranging from a classroom to a full raised stage." Pay is negotiable.

How to Contact Query first. Does not return material. Responds in 6 months.

Music "We are seeking operas or operettas in English only. We would like to begin including new, American works in our repertoire. Children's operas should be no longer than 45 minutes and require no more than a synthesizer for accompaniment. Adult operas should be appropriate for families, and may require either full orchestration or synthesizer. CCOC is a professional company whose members have varying degrees of experience, so any difficulty level is appropriate. There should be a small to moderate number of principals. Children's work should have no more than four principals. Our slogan is 'Opera is a family thing to do.' If we cannot market a work to families, we do not want to see it."

Performances Menotti's *Amahl & the Night Visitors*; and Barab's *La Pizza Con Funghi*.

Tips "45-minute fairy tale-type children's operas with possibly a 'moral' work well for our market. Looking for works appealing to K-8 grade students. No more than four principles."

CONNECTICUT CHORAL ARTISTS/CONCORA

52 Main St., New Britain CT 06051. (860)224-7500. Fax: (860) 827-8890. E-mail: contact@concora.org. Website: www.concora.org. **Contact:** Laura Oliver, executive director. Richard Coffey, artistic director. Professional concert choir, also an 18-voice ensemble dedicated to contemporary a cappella works. Estab. 1974. Members are professionals. Performs 15 concerts/year, including 3-5 new works. "Mixed audience in terms of age and background; performs in various halls and churches in the region." Payment "depends upon underwriting we can obtain for the project."

How to Contact Query first. "No unsolicited submissions accepted." Include SASE. Responds in 1 year.

Music Seeking "works for mixed chorus of 36 singers; unaccompanied or with keyboard and/or small instrumental ensemble; text sacred or secular/any language; prefers suites or cyclical works, total time not exceeding 15 minutes. Performance spaces and budgets prohibit large instrumental ensembles. Works suited for 750-seat halls are preferable. Substantial organ or piano parts acceptable. Scores should be very legible in every way."

Performances Don McCullough's *Holocaust Contata* (choral with narration); Robert Cohen's *Sprig of Lilac: Peter Quince at the Clavier* (choral); Greg Bartholomew's *The 21st Century: A Girl Born in Afghanistan* (choral).

Tips "Use conventional notation and be sure manuscript is legible in every way. Recognize and respect the vocal range of each vocal part. Work should have an identifiable rhythmic structure."

DUO CLASICO

4 Essex St., Clifton NJ 07014. (973)655-4379. E-mail: wittend@mail.montclair.edu. Website: www.davidwitten.com. **Contact:** David Witten. Chamber music ensemble. Estab. 1986. Members are professionals. Performs 16 concerts/year including 4 new works. Commissions 1 composer or new work/year. Performs in small recital halls. Pays 10% royalty.

How to Contact Query first. Include SASE. Responds in 6 weeks.

Music "We welcome scores for flute solo, piano solo or duo. Particular interest in Latin American composers."

Performances Diego Luzuriaga's *La Muchica* (modern, with extended techniques); Robert Starer's *Yizkor & Anima Aeterna* (rhythmic); and Piazzolla's *Etudes Tanguistiques* (solo flute).

Tips "Extended techniques, or with tape, are fine!"

🌐 EUROPEAN UNION CHAMBER ORCHESTRA

Hollick, Yarnscombe EX31 3LQ United Kingdom. (44)1271 858249. Fax: (44)1271 858375. E-mail: eucorchl@aol.com. Website: www.etd.gb.com. **Contact:** Ambrose Miller, general manager. Chamber orchestra. Members are professionals. Performs 70 concerts/year, including 6 new works. Commissions 2 composers or new works/year. Performs regular tours of Europe, Americas and Asia, including major venues. Pays per performance or for outright purchase, depending on work.

How to Contact Query first. Does not return material. Responds in 6 weeks.

Music Seeking compositions for strings, 2 oboes and 2 horns with a duration of about 8 minutes.

Performances Peeter Vahi "Prayer Wheel"; James MacMillan "Kiss on Wood", arr Karkof.

Tips "Keep the work to less than 15 minutes in duration, it should be sufficiently 'modern' to be interesting but not too difficult as this could take up rehearsal time. It should be possible to perform without a conductor."

FONTANA CONCERT SOCIETY

359 S. Kalamazoo Mall, Suite 200, Kalamazoo MI 49007. (269)382-7774. Fax: (269)382-0812. E-mail: ab@fontanachamberarts.org. Website: www.fontanachamberarts.org. **Contact:** Mr. Ab Sengupta, executive and artistic director. Chamber music ensemble presenter. Estab. 1980. Members are professionals. Fontana Chamber Arts presents over 45 events, including the 6-week Summer Festival of Music and Art, which runs from mid-July to the end of August. Regional and guest artists perform classical, contemporary, jazz and nontraditional music. Commissions and performs new works each year. Fontana Chamber Arts presents 7 classical and 2 jazz concerts during the Fall/Winter season. Audience consists of well-educated individuals who accept challenging new works, but like the traditional as well. Summer—180 seat hall; Fall/winter—various venues, from 400 to 1,500 seats.

How to Contact Submit complete score, resume and tapes of piece(s). Include SASE. Responds in approximately 1 month.Music Chamber music—any combination of strings, winds, piano. No "pop" music, new age type. Special interest in composers attending premiere and speaking to the audience.

Performances 2010—Juilliard String Quartet; Ben Allison and Man Size Safe; Esperanza Spalding; Cyro Baptista *Banquet of the Spirits*; Tord Gustavsen Trio; eighth blackbird; 2008— Imani Winds Josephine Baker: *A Life of Le Jazz Hot!;* Mitsuko Uchida & Friends; 2007— Billy Child's *The Path Among the Trees* (Billy Child's Jazz Chamber Ensemble with Ying Quartet)

Tips "Provide a résumé and clearly marked tape of a piece played by live performers."

FORT WORTH CHILDREN'S OPERA

1300 Gendy St., Fort Worth TX 76107. (817)731-0833, ext. 19. Fax: (817)731-0835. E-mail: clyde@fwopera.org. Website: www.fwopera.org. **Contact:** Clyde Berry. Opera company. Estab. 1946. Members are professionals. Performs over 180 in-school performances/year." Audience consists of elementary school children; performs in major venues for district-wide groups and individual school auditoriums, cafetoriums and gymnasiums. Pays $40/performance.

How to Contact Submit complete score and tape of piece(s). Include SASE. Responds in 6 months.

Music "Familiar fairy tales or stories adapted to music of opera composers, or newly-composed music of suitable quality. Ideal length: 40-45 minutes. Piano or keyboard accompaniment. Should include moral, safety or school issues. Can be ethnic in subject matter and must speak to pre-K and grade 1-6 children. Prefer pieces with good, memorable melodies. Performed by young, trained professionals on 9-month contract. Requires work for four performers, doubled roles OK, SATB plus accompanist/narrator. Special interest in biligual (Spanish/English) works."

GREATER GRAND FORKS SYMPHONY ORCHESTRA

3350 Campus Rd., Mail Stop 7084, Grand Forks ND 58202-7084. (701)777-3359. Fax: (701)777-3320. E-mail: ggfso@und.edu. Website: www.ggfso.org. **Contact:** James Hannon, music director. Symphony orchestra. Estab. 1908. Members are professionals and/or amateurs. Performs 6 concerts/year. "New works are presented in 2-4 of our programs." Audience is "a mix of ages and musical experience. In 1997-98 we moved into a renovated, 420-seat theater." Pay is negotiable, depending on licensing agreements.

How to Contact Submit complete score or complete score and tape of pieces. Include SASE. Responds in 6 months.

Music "Style is open, instrumentation the limiting factor. Music can be scored for an ensemble up to but not exceeding: 3,2,3,2/4,3,3,1/3 perc./strings. Rehearsal time limited to 3 hours for new works."

Performances Michael Harwood's *Amusement Park Suite* (orchestra); Randall Davidson's *Mexico Bolivar Tango* (chamber orchestra); and John Corigliano's *Voyage* (flute and orchestra); Linda Tutas Haugen's *Fable of Old Turtle* (saxophone concerto); Michael Wittgraf's *Landmarks*; Joan Tower's *Made in America*.

HEARTLAND MEN'S CHORUS

P.O. Box 32374, Kansas City MO 64171-5374. (816)931-3338. Fax: (816)531-1367. E-mail: hmc@hmckc.org. Website: www.hmckc.org. **Contact:** Joseph Nadeau, artistic director. Men's chorus. Estab. 1986. Members are professionals and amateurs. Performs 3 concerts/year; 9-10 are new works. Commissions 1 composer or new works/year. Performs for a diverse audience at the Folly Theater (1,100 seats). Pay is negotiable.

How to Contact Query first. Include SASE. Responds in 2 months.

Music "Interested in works for male chorus (ttbb). Must be suitable for performance by a gay male chorus. We will consider any orchestration, or a cappella."

Performances Mark Hayes' *Two Flutes Playing* (commissioned song cycle); Alan Shorter's *Country Angel Christmas* (commissioned chidren's musical); Kevin Robinson's *Life is a Cabaret: The Music of Kander and Ebb* (commissioned musical).Tips "Find a text that relates to the contemporary gay experience, something that will touch peoples' lives."

HELENA SYMPHONY

P.O. Box 1073, Helena MT 59624. (406)442-1860. E-mail: boxoffice@helenasymphony. org. Website: www.helenasymphony.org. **Contact:** Allan R. Scott, music director and conductor. Symphony orchestra. Estab. 1955. Members are professionals and amateurs. Performs 7-10 concerts/year including new works. Performance space is an 1,800 seat concert hall. Payment varies.

How to Contact Query first. Include SASE. Responds in 3 months.

Music "Imaginative, collaborative, not too atonal. We want to appeal to an audience of all ages. We don't have a huge string complement. Medium to difficult okay—at frontiers of professional ability we cannot do."

Performances Eric Funk's *A Christmas Overture* (orchestra); Donald O. Johnston's *A Christmas Processional* (orchestra/chorale); and Elizabeth Sellers' *Prairie* (orchestra/ short ballet piece).

Tips "Try to balance tension and repose in your works. New instrument combinations are appealing."

HENDERSONVILLE SYMPHONY ORCHESTRA

P.O. Box 1811, Hendersonville NC 28739. (828)697-5884. Fax: (828)697-5765. E-mail: hso1@bellsouth.net. Website: www.hendersonvillesymphony.org. **Contact:** Sandie Salvaggio-Walker, general manager. Symphony orchestra. Estab. 1971. Members are professionals and amateurs. Performs 6 concerts/year. "We would welcome a new work per year." Audience is a cross-section of retirees, professionals and some children. Performance space is a 857-seat high school audiorium.

How to Contact Query first. Include SASE. Responds in 1 month.

Music "We use a broad spectrum of music (classical concerts and pops)."

Performances Nelson's *Jubilee* (personal expression in a traditional method); Britten's "The Courtly Dances" from Glorina (time-tested); and Chip Davis' arrangement for Mannheim Steamroller's *Deck the Halls* (modern adaptation of traditional melody).

Tips "Submit your work even though we are a community orchestra. We like to be challenged. We have the most heavily patronized fine arts group in the county. Our emphasis is on education."

HERSHEY SYMPHONY ORCHESTRA

P.O. Box 93, Hershey PA 17033. (800)533-3088. E-mail: drdackow@aol.com. **Contact:** Dr. Sandra Dackow, music director. Symphony orchestra. Estab. 1969. Members are professionals and amateurs. Performs 8 concerts/year, including 1-3 new works. Commissions "possibly 1-2" composers or new works/year. Audience is family and friends of community theater. Performance space is a 1,900 seat grand old movie theater. Pays commission fee.

How to Contact Submit complete score and tape of piece(s). Include SASE. Responds in 3 months.

Music "Symphonic works of various lengths and types which can be performed by a non-professional orchestra. We are flexible but like to involve all our players."

Performances Paul W. Whear's *Celtic Christmas Carol* (orchestra/bell choir) and Linda Robbins Coleman's *In Good King Charlie's Golden Days* (overture).

Tips "Please lay out rehearsal numbers/letter and rests according to phrases and other logical musical divisions rather than in groups of ten measures, etc., which is very unmusical and wastes time and causes a surprising number of problems. Also, please do not send a score written in concert pitch; use the usual transpositions so that the conductor sees what the players see; rehearsal is much more effective this way. Cross cue all important solos; this helps in rehearsal where instruments may be missing."

HUDSON VALLEY PHILHARMONIC

35 Market St., Poughkeepise NY 12601. (845)473-2072. Fax: (845)473-4259. E-mail: slamarca@bardavon.org. Website: www.bardavon.org. **Contact:** Stephen LaMarca, production manager. Symphony orchestra. Estab. 1969. Members are professionals. Performs 20 concerts/year including 1 new work. "Classical subscription concerts for all ages; Pops concerts for all ages; New Wave concerts—crossover projects with a rock 'n' roll artist performing with an orchestra. HVP performs in three main theatres which are concert auditoriums with stages and professional lighting and sound." Pay is negotiable.

How to Contact Query first. Include SASE. Responds only if interested.

Music "HVP is open to serious classical music, pop music and rock 'n' roll crossover projects. Desired length of work between 10-20 minutes. Orchestrations can be varied by should always include strings. There is no limit to difficulty since our musicians are professional. The ideal number of musicians to write for would include up to a Brahms-size orchestra 2222, 4231, T, 2P, piano, harp, strings."

Performances Joan Tower's *Island Rhythms* (serious classical work); Bill Vanaver's *P'nai El* (symphony work with dance); and Joseph Bertolozzi's *Serenade* (light classical, pop work).

Tips "Don't get locked into doing very traditional orchestrations or styles. Our music director is interested in fresh, creative formats. He is an orchestrator as well and can offer good advice on what works well. Songwriters who are into crossover projects should definitely submit works. Over the past four years, HVP has done concerts featuring the works of Natalie Merchant, John Cale, Sterling Morrison, Richie Havens, and R. Carlos Naka (Native American flute player), all reorchestrated by our music director for small orchestra with the artist."

INDIANA UNIVERSITY NEW MUSIC ENSEMBLE

Indiana University Bloomington, School of Music, Bloomington IN 47405-2200. E-mail: ddzubay@indiana.edu. Website: www.indiana.edu/~nme. **Contact**: David Dzubay, director. Performs solo, chamber and large ensemble works. Estab.1974. Members are students. Presents 4 concerts/year.

Music Peter Lieberson's *Free and Easy Wanderer*; Sven-David Sandstrom's *Wind Pieces*; Atar Arad's *Sonata*; and David Dzubay's *Dancesing in a Green Bay*.

KENTUCKY OPERA

323 West Broadway, Suite 601, Louisville KY 40202. (502)584-4500. Fax: (502)584-7484. E-mail: info@kyopera.org. Website: www.kyopera.org. **Contact:** Alise Oliver, artistic administration. Opera. Estab. 1952. Members are professionals. Performs 3 main stage/year. Performs at Brown Theatre, 1,400. Pays by royalty, outright purchase or per performance.

How to Contact *Write or call first before submitting. No unsolicited submissions.* Submit complete score. Include SASE. Responds in 6 months.

Music Seeks opera—1 to 3 acts with orchestrations. No limitations.

Performances *Cavalleria Rusticana, The Elixir of Love, Madame Butterfly*

LEXINGTON PHILHARMONIC SOCIETY

161 N. Mill St., Arts Place, Lexington KY 40507. (859)233-4226. Fax: (859)233-7896. Website: www.lexphil.org. **Contact:** Dr. George Zack, music director. Symphony orchestra. Estab. 1961. Members are professionals. Series includes "8 serious, classical subscription concerts (hall seats 1,500); 3 concerts called Pops the Series; 3 Family Concerts; 10 outdoor pops concerts (from 1,500 to 5,000 tickets sold); 5-10 run-out concerts (½ serious/½ pops); and 10 children's concerts." Pays via ASCAP and BMI, rental purchase and private arrangements.

How to Contact Submit complete score and tape of piece(s). Include SASE.

Music Seeking "good current pops material and good serious classical works. No specific restrictions, but overly large orchestra requirements, unusual instruments and extra rentals help limit our interest."

Performances "Visit our website for complete concert season listing."

Tips "When working on large-format arrangement, use cross-cues so orchestra can be cut back if required. Submit good quality copy, scores and parts. Tape is helpful."

LIMA SYMPHONY ORCHESTRA

133 N. Elizabeth St., Lima OH 45801. (419)222-5701. Fax: (419)222-6587. Website: www.limasymphony.com. **Contact:** Crafton Beck, music conductor. Symphony orchestra. Estab. 1953. Members are professionals. Performs 17-18 concerts including at least 1 new work/year. Commissions at least 1 composer or new work/year. Middle to older audience; also Young People's Series. Mixture for stage and summer productions. Performs in Veterans' Memorial Civic & Convention Center, a beautiful hall seating 1,670; various temporary

shells for summer outdoors events; churches; museums and libraries. Pays $2,500 for outright purchase (Anniversary commission) or grants $1,500-5,000.

How to Contact Submit complete score if not performed; otherwise submit complete score and tape of piece(s). Include SASE. Responds in 3 months.

Music "Good balance of incisive rhythm, lyricism, dynamic contrast and pacing. Chamber orchestra to full (85-member) symphony orchestra." Does not wish to see "excessive odd meter changes."

Performances Frank Proto's *American Overture* (some original music and fantasy); Werner Tharichen's *Concerto for Timpani and Orchestra*; and James Oliverio's *Pilgrimage—Concerto for Brass* (interesting, dynamic writing for brass and the orchestra).

Tips "Know your instruments, be willing to experiment with unconventional textures, be available for in depth analysis with conductor, be at more than one rehearsal. Be sure that individual parts are correctly matching the score and done in good, neat calligraphy."

LYRIC OPERA OF CHICAGO

20 N. Wacker Dr., Chicago IL 60606. (312)332-2244 ext. 3500. Fax: (312)419-8345. E-mail: jgriffin@lyricopera.org. Website: www.lyricopera.org. **Contact:** Julie Griffin-Meadors, music administrator. Opera company. Estab. 1953. Members are professionals. Performs 80 operas/year including 1 new work in some years. Commissions 1 new work every 4 or 5 years. "Performances are held in a 3,563 seat house for a sophisticated opera audience, predominantly 30+ years old." Payment varies.

How to Contact Query first. Does not return material. Responds in 6 months.

Music "Full-length opera suitable for a large house with full orchestra. No musical comedy or Broadway musical style. We rarely perform one-act operas. We are only interested in works by composers and librettists with extensive theatrical experience. We have few openings for new works, so candidates must be of the highest quality. Do not send score or other materials without a prior contact."

Performances William Bolcom's *View from the Bridge*; John Corigliano's *Ghosts of Versailles*; and Leonard Bernstein's *Candide*.

Tips "Have extensive credentials and an international reputation."

☑ MILWAUKEE YOUTH SYMPHONY ORCHESTRA

325 West Walnut St., Milwaukee WI 53212. (414)267-2950. Fax: (414)267-2960. E-mail: general@myso.org. Website: www.myso.org. **Contact:** Frances Richman, executive director. Multiple youth orchestras and other instrumental ensembles. Estab. 1956. Members are students. Performs 12-15 concerts/year including 1-2 new works. "Our groups perform in Uihlein Hall at the Marcus Center for the Performing Arts in Milwaukee plus area sites. The audiences usually consist of parents, music teachers and other interested community members, with periodic reviews in the Milwaukee Journal Sentinel." Payment varies.

How to Contact Query first. Include SASE. Does not return material. Responds in 1 month.

Performances James Woodward's *Tuba Concerto*.

Tips "Be sure you realize you are working with *students* (albeit many of the best in southeastern Wisconsin) and not professional musicians. The music needs to be on a technical level students can handle. Our students are 8-18 years of age, in 2 full symphony orchestras, a wind ensemble and 2 string orchestras, plus two flute choirs, advanced chamber orchestra and 15-20 small chamber ensembles."

MOORES OPERA CENTER

University of Houston, 120 Moores School of Music Building, Houston TX 77204-4201. (713)743-3009. E-mail: bross@uh.edu. Website: www.uh.edu/music/Mooresopera/. **Director of Opera:** Buck Ross. Opera/music theater program. Members are professionals, amateurs and students. Performs 12-14 concerts/year including 1 new work. Performs in a proscenium theater which seats 800. Pit seats approximately up to 75 players. Audience covers wide spectrum, from first time opera-goers to very sophisticated. Pays per performance.

How to Contact Submit complete score and tapes of piece(s). Include SASE. Responds in 6 months.

Music "We seek music that is feasible for high graduate level student singers. Chamber orchestras are very useful. No more than two and a half hours. No children's operas."

Performances *The Grapes of Wrath*, *Florencia en el Amazonas*, *Elmer Gantry*, *A Wedding*.

OPERA MEMPHIS

6745 Wolf River Parkway, Memphis TN 38120. (901)257-3100. Fax: (901)257-3109. E-mail: info@operamemphis.org. Website: www.operamemphis.org. **Contact:** Michael Ching, artistic director. Opera company. Estab. 1955. Members are professionals. Performs 8-12 concerts/year including new works. Occasionally commissions composers. Audience consists of older, wealthier patrons, along with many students and young professionals. Pay is negotiable.

How to Contact Query first. Include SASE. Responds in 1 year or less.

Music Accessible practical pieces for educational or second stage programs. Educational pieces should not exceed 90 minutes or 4-6 performers. We encourage songwriters to contact us with proposals or work samples for theatrical works. We are very interested in crossover work.

Performances Mike Reid's *Different Fields* (one act opera); David Olney's *Light in August* (folk opera); and Sid Selvidge's *Riversongs* (one act blues opera).

Tips "Spend many hours thinking about the synopsis (plot outline)."

☑ ORCHESTRA SEATTLE/SEATTLE CHAMBER SINGERS

P.O. Box 15825, Seattle WA 98115. (206)682-5208. E-mail: osscs@osscs.org. Website: www. osscs.org. **Contact:** Andrew Danilchik, librarian. Symphony orchestra, chamber music ensemble and community chorus. Estab. 1969. Members are amateurs and professionals.

Performs 8 concerts/year including 2-3 new works. Commissions 1-2 composers or new works/year. "Our audience is made up of both experienced and novice classical music patrons. The median age is 45 with an equal number of males and females in the upper income range. Most concerts now held in Benaroya Hall."

How to Contact Query first. Include SASE. Responds in 1 year.

Performances Beyer's *The Turns of a Girl*; Bernstein's Choruses from *The Lark*; Edstrom's Concerto for Jazz Piano and Orchestra.

PALMETTO MASTERSINGERS

P.O. Box 7441, Columbia SC 29202. (803)765-0777. E-mail: info@palmettomastersingers. org. Website: www.palmettomastersingers.org. **Contact:** Walter Cuttino, music director. 80 voice male chorus. Estab. 1981 by the late Dr. Arpad Darasz. Members are professionals and amateurs. Performs 8-10 concerts/year. Commissions 1 composer of new works every other year (on average). Audience is generally older adults, "but it's a wide mix." Performance space for the season series is the Koger Center (approximately 2,000 seats) in Columbia, SC. More intimate venues also available. Fee is negotiable for outright purchase.

How to Contact Query first. Include SASE. Or e-mail to info@palmettomastersingers. org.

Music Seeking music of 10-15 minutes in length, "not too far out tonally. Orchestration is negotiable, but chamber size (10-15 players) is normal. We rehearse once a week and probably will not have more than 8-10 rehearsals. These rehearsals (2 hours each) are spent learning a 1½-hour program. Only 1-2 rehearsals (max) are with the orchestra. Piano accompaniments need not be simplified, as our accompanist is exceptional."

Performances Randal Alan Bass' *Te Deum* (12-minute, brass and percussion); Dick Goodwin's *Mark Twain Remarks* (40 minute, full symphony); and Randol Alan Bass' *A Simple Prayer* (a capella 6 minute).

Tips "Contact us as early as possible, given that programs are planned by July. Although this is an amateur chorus, we have performed concert tours of Europe, performed at Carnegie Hall, The National Cathedral and the White House in Washington, DC. We are skilled amateurs."

PICCOLO OPERA COMPANY INC.

24 Del Rio Blvd., Boca Raton FL 33432-4734. (800)282-3161. Fax: (561)394-0520. E-mail: leejon51@msn.com. **Contact:** Lee Merrill, executive assistant. Traveling opera company. Estab. 1962. Members are professionals. Performs 1-50 concerts/year including 1-2 new works. Commissions 0-1 composer or new work/year. Operas are performed for a mixed audience of children and adults. Pays by performance or outright purchase. Operas in English.

How to Contact *Query first.* Include SASE.

Music "Productions for either children or adults. Musical theater pieces, lasting about one hour, for adults to perform for adults and/or youngsters. Performers are mature singers with experience. The cast should have few performers (up to 10), no chorus or ballet, accompanied by piano or local orchestra. Skeletal scenery. All in English."

Performances Menotti's *The Telephone*; Mozart's *Cosi Fan Tutte*; and Puccini's *La Boheme* (repertoire of more than 22 productions).

PRINCETON SYMPHONY ORCHESTRA

P.O. Box 250, Princeton NJ 08542. (609)497-0020. Fax: (609)497-0904. E-mail: info@ princetonsymphony.org. Website: www.princetonsymphony.org. **Contact:** Mark Laycock, music director. Symphony orchestra. Estab. 1980. Members are professionals. Performs 6-10 concerts/year including some new works. Commissions 1 composer or new work/ year. Performs in a "beautiful, intimate 800-seat hall with amazing sound." Pays by arrangement.

Music "Orchestra usually numbers 40-60 individuals."

PRISM SAXOPHONE QUARTET

30 Seaman Av., #4M, New York NY 10034 or 257 Harvey St., Philadelphia PA 19144. (215)438-5282. E-mail: info@prismquartet.com. Website: www.prismquartet.com. President, New Sounds Music Inc. Prism Quartet: Matthew Levy. Chamber music ensemble. Estab. 1984. Members are professionals. Performs 80 concerts/year including 10-15 new works. Commissions 4 composers or new works/year. "Ours are primarily traditional chamber music audiences." Pays royalty per performance from BMI or ASCAP or commission range from $100 to $15,000.

How to Contact Submit complete score (with parts) and tape of piece(s). Does not return material. Responds in 3 months.

Music "Orchestration—sax quartet, SATB. Lengths—5-25 minutes. Styles—contemporary, classical, jazz, crossover, ethnic, gospel, avant-garde. No limitations on level of difficulty. No more than 4 performers (SATB sax quartet). No transcriptions. The Prism Quartet places special emphasis on crossover works which integrate a variety of musical styles."

Performances David Liebman's *The Gray Convoy* (jazz); Bradford Ellis's *Tooka-Ood Zasch* (ethnic-world music); and William Albright's *Fantasy Etudes* (contemporary classical).

SACRAMENTO MASTER SINGERS

P.O. Box 417997, Sacramento CA 95841. (916)971-3159. Fax: (916)788-7464. E-mail: smsbusiness@surewest.net. Website: www.mastersingers.org. **Contact:** Ralph Hughes, conductor/artistic director. Vocal ensemble. Estab. 1984. Members are professionals and amateurs. Performs 9 concerts/year including 5-6 new works. Commissions 2 new works/ year. Audience is made up of mainly college age and older patrons. Performs mostly in churches with 500-900 seating capacity. Pays $200 for outright purchase.

How to Contact Submit complete score and tape of piece(s). Include SASE. Responds in 5 weeks.

Music "A cappella works; works with small orchestras or few instruments; works based on classical styles with a 'modern' twist; multi-cultural music; shorter works probably preferable, but this is not a requirement. We usually have 38-45 singers capable of a high level of difficulty, but find that often simple works are very pleasing."

Performances Joe Jennings' *An Old Black Woman, Homeless and Indistinct* (SATB, oboe, strings, dramatic).

Tips "Keep in mind we are a chamber ensemble, not a 100-voice choir."

▤ SAN FRANCISCO GIRLS CHORUS

44 Page Street, Suite 200, San Francisco CA 94102. (415)863-1752. E-mail: info@ sfgirlschorus.org. Website: www.sfgirlschorus.org. **Contact:** Susan McMane, artistic director. Choral ensemble. Estab. 1978. Advanced choral ensemble of young women's voices. Performs 8-10 concerts/year including 3-4 new works. Commissions 2 composers or new works/year. Concerts are performed for "choral/classical music lovers, plus family audiences and audiences interested in international repertoire. Season concerts are performed in a 800-seat church with excellent acoustics and in San Francisco's Davies Symphony Hall, a 2,800-seat state-of-the-art auditorium." Pay negotiable for outright purchase.

• The San Francisco Girls Chorus has won three Grammy Awards as guest performers on the San Francisco Symphony's recordings.

How to Contact Submit complete score and CD recording, if possible. Does not return material. Responds in 6 months.

Music "Music for treble voices (SSAA); a cappella, piano accompaniment, or small orchestration; 3-10 minutes in length. Wide variety of styles; 45 singers; challenging music is encouraged."

Performances See website under "Music/Commissions" for a listing of SFGC commissions. Examples: Jake Heggie's *Patterns* (piano, mezzo-soprano soloist, chorus); and Chen Yi's *Chinese Poems* (a cappella).

Tips "Choose excellent texts and write challenging music. The San Francisco Girls Chorus has pioneered in establishing girls choral music as an art form in the United States. The Girls Chorus is praised for its 'stunning musical standard' (San Francisco Chronicle) in performances in the San Francisco Bay Area and on tour. SFGC's annual concert season showcases the organization's concert/touring ensemble, Chorissima, in performances of choral masterworks from around the world, commissioned works by contemporary composers, and 18th-century music from the Venetian Ospedali and Mexican Baroque which SFGC has brought out of the archives and onto the concert stage. Chorissima tours through California with partial support provided by the California Arts Council Touring Program and have represented the U.S. and the City of San Francisco nationally and abroad. The chorus provides ensemble and solo singers for performances and recordings with the San Francisco Symphony and San Francisco Opera, Women's Philharmonic, and many other music ensembles. The Chorus has produced six solo CD recordings including: Voices of Hope and Peace, a recording that includes "Anne Frank: A Living Voice" by an American composer Linda Tutas Haugen; Christmas, featuring diverse holiday selections; Crossroads, a collection of world folk music; and Music from the

Venetian Ospedali, a disc of Italian Baroque music of which the New Yorker described the Chorus as "tremendously accomplished." The Chorus can also be heard on several San Francisco Symphony recordings, including three GRAMMY Award -winners."

SINGING BOYS OF PENNSYLVANIA

P.O. Box 206, Wind Gap PA 18091. (610)759-6002. Fax: (610)759-6042. Website: www. singingboysofpennsylvania.org. **Contact:** K. Bernard Schade, Ed. D., director. Vocal ensemble. Estab. 1970. Members are professional children. Performs 100 concerts/year including 3-5 new works. "We attract general audiences: family, senior citizens, churches, concert associations, university concert series and schools." Pays $300-3,000 for outright purchase.

How to Contact *Query first.* Does not return material. Responds in 3 weeks.

Music "We want music for commercials, voices in the SSA or SSAA ranges, sacred works or arrangements of American folk music with accompaniment. Our range of voices are from G below middle C to A (13th above middle C). Reading ability of choir is good but works which require a lot of work with little possibility of more than one performance are of little value. We sing very few popular songs except for special events. We perform music by composers who are well-known and works by living composers who are writing in traditional choral forms. Works which have a full orchestral score are of interest. The orchestration should be fairly light, so as not to cover the voices. Works for Christmas have more value than some other, since we perform with orchestras on an annual basis."

Performances Don Locklair's *The Columbus Madrigals* (opera).

Tips "It must be appropriate music and words for children. We do not deal in pop music. Folk music, classics and sacred are acceptable."

ST. LOUIS CHAMBER CHORUS

P.O. Box 11558, Clayton MO 63105. (636)458-4343. E-mail: maltworm@inlink.com. Website: www.chamberchorus.org. **Contact:** Philip Barnes, artistic director. Vocal ensemble, chamber music ensemble. Estab. 1956. Members are professionals and amateurs. Performs 6 concerts/year including 5-10 new works. Commissions 3-4 new works/year. Audience is "diverse and interested in unaccompanied choral work and outstanding architectural/acoustic venues." Performances take place at various auditoria noted for their excellent acoustics—churches, synagogues, schools and university halls. Pays by arrangement.

How to Contact Query first. Does not return material. "Panel of 'readers' submit report to Artistic Director. Responds in 3 months. 'General Advice' leaflet available on request."Music *"Only a cappella writing!* No contemporary 'popular' works; historical editions welcomed. No improvisatory works. Our programs are tailored for specific acoustics—composers should indicate their preference."

Performances Sir Richard Rodney Bennett's *A Contemplation Upon Flowers* (a cappella madrigal); Ned Rorem's *Ode to Man* (a cappella chorus for mixed voices); and Sasha

Johnson Manning's *Requiem* (a cappella oratorio).

Tips "We only consider a cappella works which can be produced in five rehearsals. Therefore pieces of great complexity or duration are discouraged. Our seasons are planned 2-3 years ahead, so much lead time is required for programming a new work. We will accept hand-written manuscript, but we prefer typeset music."

SUSQUEHANNA SYMPHONY ORCHESTRA

P.O. Box 963, Abingdon, MD 21009. E-mail: sheldon.bair@ssorchestra.org. Website: www.ssorchestra.org. **Contact:** Sheldon Bair, music director. Symphony orchestra. Estab. 1978. Members are amateurs. Performs 6 concerts/year including 1-2 new works. Composers paid depending on the circumstances. "We perform in 1 hall, 600 seats with fine acoustics. Our audience encompasses all ages."

How to Contact Query first. Include SASE. Responds in 3 or more months.

Music "We desire works for large orchestra, any length, in a 'conservative 20th and 21st century' style. Seek fine music for large orchestra. We are a community orchestra, so the music must be within our grasp. Violin I to 7th position by step only; Violin II—stay within 5th position; English horn and harp are OK. Full orchestra pieces preferred."

Performances *Stabat Mater*, by Stanislaw Moryto; *Elegy*, Amanda Harberg; *I Choose the Mountain*, by Stacey Zyriek; *Little Gift*, by Benny Russell.

⬛ TORONTO MENDELSSOHN CHOIR

60 Simcoe St., Toronto ON M5J 2H5 Canada. (416)598-0422. Fax: (416)598-2992. E-mail: manager@tmchoir.org or admin@tmchoir.org. Website: www.tmchoir.org. **Contact:** Eileen Keown, executive director. Vocal ensemble. Members are professionals and amateurs. Performs 25 concerts/year including 1-3 new works. "Most performances take place in Roy Thomson Hall. The audience is reasonably sophisticated, musically knowledgeable but with moderately conservative tastes." Pays by commission and ASCAP/SOCAN.

How to Contact Query first or submit complete score and tapes of pieces. Include SASE. Responds in 6 months.

Music All works must suit a large choir (180 voices) and standard orchestral forces or with some other not-too-exotic accompaniment. Length should be restricted to no longer than ½ of a nocturnal concert. The choir sings at a very professional level and can sight-read almost anything. "Works should fit naturally with the repertoire of a large choir which performs the standard choral orchestral repertoire."

Performances Holman's *Jezebel*; Orff's *Catulli Carmina*; and Lambert's *Rio Grande*.

⬛ VANCOUVER CHAMBER CHOIR

1254 W. Seventh Ave., Vancouver BC V6H 1B6 Canada. E-mail: info@vancouver chamberchoir.com. Website: www.vancouverchamberchoir.com. **Contact:** Jon Washburn, artistic director. Vocal ensemble. Members are professionals. Performs 40 concerts/year including 5-8 new works. Commissions 2-4 composers or new works/year. Pays SOCAN royalty or negotiated fee for commissions.

How to Contact Submit complete score and tape of piece(s). Does not return material. Responds in 6 months if possible.

Music Seeks "choral works of all types for small chorus, with or without accompaniment and/or soloists. Concert music only. Choir made up of 20 singers. Large or unusual instrumental accompaniments are less likely to be appropriate. No pop music."

Performances The VCC has commissioned and premiered over 200 new works by Canadian and international composers, including Alice Parker's *That Sturdy Vine* (cantata for chorus, soloists and orchestra); R. Murray Schafer's *Magic Songs* (SATB a cappella); and Jon Washburn's *A Stephen Foster Medley* (SSAATTBB/piano).

Tips "We are looking for choral music that is performable yet innovative, and which has the potential to become 'standard repertoire.' Although we perform much new music, only a small portion of the many scores which are submitted can be utilized."

VANCOUVER YOUTH SYMPHONY ORCHESTRA SOCIETY

3214 West 10th Ave., Vancouver BC V6K 2L2 Canada. (604)737-0714. Fax: (604)737-0739. E-mail: vyso@telus.net. Website: www.vyso.com. **Music Directors:** Roger Cole (artistic director and senior orchestra conductor), Jin Zhang (intermediate orchestra conductor), and Margitta Krebs (debut and junior orchestra conductor). Youth orchestra. "Four divisions consisting of musicians ranging in age from 8-22 years old." Estab. 1930. Members are amateurs. Performs 10-15 concerts/year in various lower mainland venues. Concert admission by donation.

Music "Extensive and varied orchestral repertoire is performed by all divisions. Please contact the VYSO for more information."

VIRGINIA OPERA

P.O. Box 2580, Norfolk VA 23501. (757)627-9545. E-mail: info@vaopera.com. Website: www.vaopera.org. **Director of Education:** Jeff Corrirean. Artistic Director: Peter Mark. Opera company. Estab. 1974. Members are professionals. Performs more than 560 concerts/year. Commissions vary on number of composers or new works/year. Concerts are performed for school children throughout Virginia, grades K-5, 6-8 and 9-12 at the Harrison Opera House in Norfolk, and at public/private schools in Virginia. Pays on commission.

How to Contact Query first. Include SASE. Response time varies.

Music "Audience accessible style approximately 45 minutes in length. Limit cast list to three vocal artists of any combination. Accompanied by piano and/or keyboard. Works are performed before school children of all ages. Pieces must be age appropriate both aurally and dramatically. Musical styles are encouraged to be diverse, contemporary as well as traditional. Works are produced and presented with sets, costumes, etc." Limitations: "Three vocal performers (any combination). One keyboardist. Medium to difficult acceptable, but prefer easy to medium. Seeking only pieces which are suitable for presentation as part of an opera education program for Virginia Opera's education and outreach department. Subject matter must meet strict guidelines relative to Learning

Objectives, etc. Musical idiom must be representative of current trends in opera, musical theater. Extreme dissonance, row systems not applicable to this environment."

Performances Seymour Barab's *Cinderella*; John David Earnest's *The Legend of Sleepy Hollow*; and Seymour Barab's *The Pied Piper of Hamelin*.

Tips "Theatricality is very important. New works should stimulate interest in musical theater as a legitimate art form for school children with no prior exposure to live theatrical entertainment. Composer should be willing to create a product which will find success within the educational system."

WHEATON SYMPHONY ORCHESTRA

344 Spring Ave., Glen Ellyn IL 60137. (630)858-5552. Fax: (630)790-9703. E-mail: dmattob@aol.com. **Contact:** Don Mattison, manager. Symphony orchestra. Estab. 1959. Members are professionals and amateurs. Performs 6 concerts/year including a varying number of new works. "No pay for performance but can probably record your piece."

How to Contact Query first. Include SASE. Responds in 1 month.

Music "This is a good amateur orchestra that wants pieces to be performed in the mode of John Williams or Samuel Barber, Corliango, etc. Large scale works for orchestra only. No avant garde, 12-tone or atonal material. Pieces should be 20 minutes or less and must be prepared in 3 rehearsals. Instrumentation needed for woodwinds in 3s, full brass 4-3-3-1, 4 percussion and strings—full-instrumentation only. Selections for full orchestra only. No pay for reading your piece, but we will record it at our expense. We will rehearse and give a world premiere of your piece if it is in the stated orchestration, probably with keyboard added."

Performances Richard Williams's *Symphony in G Minor* (4 movement symphony); Dennis Johnson's *Must Jesus Bear the Cross Alone, Azon* (traditional); and Michael Diemer's *Skating* (traditional style).

Contests & Awards

Participating in contests is a great way to gain exposure for your music. Prizes vary from contest to contest, from cash to musical merchandise to studio time, and even publishing and recording deals. For musical theater and classical composers, the prize may be a performance of your work. Even if you don't win, valuable contacts can be made through contests. Many times, contests are judged by music publishers and other industry professionals, so your music may find its way into the hands of key industry people who can help further your career.

HOW TO SELECT A CONTEST

It's important to remember when entering any contest to do proper research before signing anything or sending any money. We have confidence in the contests listed in *Songwriter's Market,* but it pays to read the fine print. First, be sure you understand the contest rules and stipulations once you receive the entry forms and guidelines. Then you need to weigh what you will gain against what they're asking you to give up. If a publishing or recording contract is the only prize a contest is offering, you may want to think twice before entering. Basically, the company sponsoring the contest is asking you to pay a fee for them to listen to your song under the guise of a contest, something a legitimate publisher or record company would not do. For those contests offering studio time, musical equipment or cash prizes, you need to decide if the entry fee you're paying is worth the chance to win such prizes.

Be wary of exorbitant entry fees, and if you have any doubts whatsoever as to the legitimacy of a contest, it's best to stay away. Songwriters need to approach a contest, award or grant in the same manner as they would a record or publishing company. Make your submission as professional as possible; follow directions and submit material exactly as stated on the entry form.

Contests in this section encompass all types of music and levels of competition. Read each listing carefully and contact them if the contest interests you. Many contests now have Web sites that offer additional information and even entry forms you can print. Be sure to read the rules carefully and be sure you understand exactly what a contest is offering before entering.

AGO AWARD IN ORGAN COMPOSITION

American Guild of Organists, 475 Riverside Dr., Suite 1260, New York NY 10115. (212)870-2310. Fax: (212)870-2163. E-mail: info@agohq.org. Website: www.agohq.org. **Contact:** Harold Calhoun, competitions administrator. For composers and performing artists. Biennial award.

Requirements Organ solo, no longer than 8 minutes in duration. Specifics vary from year to year. Deadline: TBA, but usually early spring of odd-numbered year. Go to the website for application.

Awards $2,000; publication by Hinshaw Music Inc.; performance at the biennial National Convention of the American Guild of Organists.

AGO/ECS PUBLISHING AWARD IN CHORAL COMPOSITION

American Guild of Organists, 475 Riverside Dr., Suite 1260, New York NY 10115. (212)870-2310. Fax: (212)870-2163. E-mail: info@agohq.org. Website: www.agohq.org. **Contact:** Harold Calhoun, competitions administrator. Biannual award.

Requirements Composers are invited to submit a work for SATB choir and organ in which the organ plays a significant and independent role. Work submitted must be unpublished and are usually 3.5 to 5 minutes in length. There is no age restriction. Deadline: TBA, "but usually late fall in even numbered years." Application information on the website.

Awards $2,000 cash prize, publication by ECS Publishing and premier performance at the AGO National Convention. Further details are published in *The American Organist*.

ALEA III INTERNATIONAL COMPOSITION PRIZE

855 Commonwealth Ave., Boston MA 02215. (617)353-3340. E-mail: aleaiii@bu.edu. Website: www.aleaiii.com. For composers. Annual award.

Purpose To promote and encourage young composers in the composition of new music.

Requirements Composers born after January 1, 1981 may participate; 1 composition per composer. Works may be for solo voice or instrument or for chamber ensemble up to 15 members lasting between 6 and 15 minutes. Available instruments are: one flute (doubling piccolo or alto), one oboe (doubling English horn), one clarinet (doubling bass clarinet), one bassoon, one saxophone, one horn, one trumpet, one trombone, one tuba, two percussion players, one harp, one keyboard player, one guitar, two violins, one viola, one cello, one bass, tape and one voice. "One of the 15 performers could play an unusual, exotic or rare instrument, or be a specialized vocalist. For more info and guidelines, please refer to our website." All works must be unpublished and must not have been publicly performed or broadcast, in whole or in part or in any other version before the announcement of the prize in late September or early October of 2011. Works that have won other awards are not eligible. Deadline: March 15, 2011. Send for application. Submitted work required with application. "Real name should not appear on score; a nom de plume should be signed instead. Sealed envelope with entry form should be attached to each score."

Awards ALEA III International Composition Prize: $2,500. Awarded once annually. Between 6-8 finalists are chosen and their works are performed in a competition concert by the ALEA III contemporary music ensemble. At the end of the concert, one piece will be selected to receive the prize. One grand prize winner is selected by a panel of judges.

Tips "Emphasis placed on works written in 20th and 21st century compositional idioms."

AMERICAN SONGWRITER LYRIC CONTEST

1303 16th Avenue S., 2nd Floor, Nashville TN 37212. (615)321-6096. Fax: (615)321-6097. E-mail: info@americansongwriter.com. Website: www.americansongwriter.com. **Contact:** Matt Shearon. Estab. 1984. For songwriters and composers. Award for each bimonthly issue of American Songwriter magazine, plus grand prize winner at year-end.

Purpose To promote and encourage the craft of lyric writing.

Requirements Contest is open to any amateur songwriter. AS defines an amateur as one who has not earned more than $5,000 from songwriting related to royalties, advances, or works for hire. Lyrics must be typed and a check for $12 (per entry) must be enclosed. Deadlines: January, March, May, July, September, November. See website for exact dates. Submit online through American Songspace or Sonicbids.com. Lyrics only. "If you enter two or more lyrics, you automatically receive a 1-year subscription to *American Songwriter* magazine (Canada: 3 or more; Other Countries: 4 or more)."

Awards A DX1 Martin Koa acoustic guitar valued at over $700 to bi-monthly contest winner. The annual winner will be chosen from the six bimonthly contest winners. First place winners also receive one legendary Shure SM58 microphone and four sets of Elixir Strings, and one Elixir Guitar Cable. GRAND PRIZE: The annual winner, chosen from the six contest winners, will receive round trip airfare to Nashville and a dream co-writing session. The 2008 winner Abbie Gardner received a co-writing session with Chris Stapleton, hit writer and performer with The SteelDrivers.

Tips "You do not have to be a subscriber to enter or win. You may submit as many entries as you like. All genres of music accepted."

ANNUAL NSAI SONG CONTEST

1710 Roy Acuff Place, Nashville TN 37203. (615)256-3354. E-mail: songcontest@nashvillesongwriters.com. Website: www.nsai.cmt.com. **Contact:** David Petrelli, NSAI Event Director.

Purpose "A chance for aspiring songwriters to be heard by music industry decision makers."

Requirements Entry fee: $35 per song (NSAI member); $45 per song (non-member). Submissions accepted from August 1-Oct. 31. In order to be eligible contestants must not be receiving income from any work submitted—original material only. Mail-in submissions must be in CD form and include entry form, lyrics and melody. Online submissions available through nsai.cmt.com. Visit website for complete list of rules and regulations. Deadline is different each year; check website or send for application. Samples are required with application in the format of cassette or CD.

Awards Grand Prize winner receives a one-on-one mentoring session with music superstar, Darius Rucker. CMT Listener's Choice award gives fans a chance to vote for their favorite song entry. Visit website for complete list of rules and prizes.

ARTISTS' FELLOWSHIPS

New York Foundation for the Arts, 20 Jay St., 7th Floor, Brooklyn NY 11201. (212)366-6900. Fax: (212)366-1778. E-mail: nyfaafp@nyfa.org. Website: www.nyfa.org. To receive an application, or contact the fellowship's department, call: (212)366-6900, ext. 219. **Contact**: Margie Lempert, senior officer. For songwriters, composers and musical playwrights. Annual award, but each category funded biennially. Estab. 1984.

Purpose "Artists' Fellowships are $7,000 grants awarded by the New York Foundation for the Arts to individual originating artists living in New York State. The Foundation is committed to supporting artists from all over New York State at all stages of their professional careers. Fellows may use the grant according to their own needs; it should not be confused with project support."

Requirements Must be 18 years of age or older; resident of New York State for 2 years prior to application; and cannot be enrolled in any graduate or undergraduate degree program. Applications will be available in July. Deadline: October. Samples of work are required with application. 1 or 2 original compositions on separate audiotapes or audio CDs and at least 2 copies of corresponding scores or fully harmonized lead sheets.

Awards All Artists' Fellowships awards are for $7,000. Payment of $6,300 upon verification of NY State residency, and remainder upon completion of a mutually agreed upon public service activity. Nonrenewable. "Fellowships are awarded on the basis of the quality of work submitted. Applications are reviewed by a panel of 5 composers representing the aesthetic, ethnic, sexual and geographic diversity within New York State. The panelists change each year and review all allowable material submitted."

Tips "Please note that musical playwrights may submit only if they write the music for their plays—librettists must submit in our playwriting category."

▣ THE ASCAP DEEMS TAYLOR AWARDS

American Society of Composers, Authors & Publishers, One Lincoln Plaza, New York NY 10023. E-mail: esansaurus@ascap.com. **Contact:** Esther SanSaurus.

Purpose The ASCAP Deems Taylor Awards Competition offers $250-1,000 prize for books, articles, liner notes, broadcasts and websites on the subject of music.

Requirements Deadline: Submissions accepted June 15 to July 31, 2010. There is no fee or submission form required but must be submitted with a cover letter. Written works must be published in the United States in English, during the calendar year of 2009. The subject matter may be biographical or critical, reportorial or historical - almost any form of nonfiction prose about music and/or its creators. However, instructional textbooks, how-to-guides, or works of fiction will not be accepted.

Awards Prize: $250-1,000.

THE BLANK THEATRE COMPANY YOUNG PLAYWRIGHTS FESTIVAL

P.O. Box 38756, Los Angeles CA 90038. (323)871-8018. Fax: (323)661-3903. E-mail: submissions@youngplaywrights.com. Website: www.youngplaywrights.com. Estab. 1993. For both musical and non-musical playwrights. Annual award.

Purpose "To give young playwrights an opportunity to learn more about playwriting and to give them a chance to have their work mentored, developed, and presented by professional artists."

Requirements Playwrights must be 19 years old or younger on March 15, 2010. Send legible, original plays of any length and on any subject (co-written plays are acceptable provided all co-writers meet eligibility requirements). Submissions must be postmarked by March 15 and must include a cover sheet with the playwright's name, date of birth, school (if any), home address, home phone number, e-mail address and production history. Pages must be numbered and submitted unbound (unstapled). For musicals, a tape or CD of a selection from the score should be submitted with the script. Manuscripts will not be returned. Please do not send originals. Semi-finalists and winners will be contacted in May.

Awards Winning playwrights receive a workshop presentation of their work.

BUSH ARTIST FELLOWS PROGRAM

E-900 First National Bank Bldg., 332 Minnesota St., Suite E-900, St. Paul MN 55101. (651)227-0891. Fax: (651)297-6485. E-mail: artists@bushfoundation.org. Website: www. bushfoundation.org. Estab. 1976. For songwriters, composers and musical playwrights. Applications in music composition are accepted in even-numbered years.

Purpose "To provide artists with significant financial support that enables them to further their work and their contribution to their communities."

Requirements Applicant must be U.S. Citizens or Permanent Residents AND a Minnesota, North Dakota, South Dakota or western Wisconsin resident for 12 of preceeding 36 months, 25 years or older, not a student. Deadline: late October. Send for application. Audio work samples required with application. "Music composition applications will not be taken again until the fall of 2006. Applications will be taken in the fall of 2006 in the following areas: music composition, scriptworks (screenwriting and playwriting), literature (creative non-fiction, fiction, poetry) and film/video.

Awards Fellowships: $48,000 stipend for a period of 12-24 months. "Five years after completion of preceding fellowship, one may apply again." Applications are judged by peer review panels.

CRS NATIONAL COMPOSERS COMPETITION

For songwriters, composers and performing artists. College faculty and gifted artists. Each annual competition is limited to the first 300 applicants—ALL FEES BEYOND THIS LIMIT WILL BE RETURNED. Email: crsnews@verizon.net.

Requirements For composers, songwriters, performing artists and ensembles. Each category requires a separate application fee. The work submitted must be non-published (prior to acceptance) and not commercially recorded on any label. The work submitted must not exceed nine performers. Each composer/performer may submit one work for each application submitted. (Taped performances by composers are additionally encouraged.) Composition must not exceed sixteen minutes in length. CRS reserves the right not to accept a First Prize Winner. Write with SASE for application or visit website. Add $3.50 for postage and handling. Must send a detailed résumé with application form available on our Web page under "Events" category. Samples of work required with application. Send score and parts with optional CD or DAT. Application fee: $50.

Awards First prize will consist of a commercially distributed new compact disc recording grant featuring one composition along with other distinguished composers and performing artists. Second and Third Prizes will be awarded Honorable Mention toward future recordings with CRS and Honorary Life Membership to the Society. Applications are judged by panel of judges determined each year.

EUROPEAN INTERNATIONAL COMPETITION FOR COMPOSERS/IBLA FOUNDATION

226 East 2nd St., Loft 1B, New York NY 10009. (212)387-0111. E-mail: iblanyc@aol.com. Website: www.ibla.org. **Contact:** Mr. Michael Yasenak, executive director. Chairman: Dr. S. Moltisanti. Estab. 1995. For songwriters and composers. Annual award.

Purpose "To promote the winners' career through exposure, publicity, recordings with Athena Records and nationwide distribution with the Empire Group."

Requirements Deadline: April 30. Send for application. Music score and/or recording of one work are required with application. Application fee is refunded if not admitted into the program.

Awards Winners are presented in concerts in Europe-Japan, USA.

FULBRIGHT SCHOLAR PROGRAM, COUNCIL FOR INTERNATIONAL EXCHANGE OF SCHOLARS

3007 Tilden St. NW, Suite 5L, Washington DC 20008-3009. (202)686-4000. E-mail: scholars@cies.iie.org. Website: www.cies.org. Estab. 1946. For composers and academics. Annual award.

Purpose "Awards for university lecturing and advanced research abroad are offered annually in virtually all academic disciplines including musical composition."

Requirements "U.S. citizenship at time of application; M.F.A., Ph.D. or equivalent professional qualifications; for lecturing awards, university teaching experience (some awards are for professionals non-academic)." Applications become available in March each year, for grants to be taken up 1½ years later. Application deadlines: August 1, all world areas. Write or call for application. Samples of work are required with application.

Awards "Benefits vary by country, but generally include round-trip travel for the grantee and for most full academic-year awards, one dependent; stipend in U.S. dollars and/or local currency; in many countries, tuition allowance for school age children; and book and baggage allowance. Grant duration ranges from 3 months-1 academic year."

HARVEY GAUL COMPOSITION CONTEST

The Pittsburgh New Music Ensemble, Inc., 527 Coyne Ter., Pittsburgh PA 15207. (412)889-7231. E-mail: contactpnme@gmail.com. Website: www.pnme. org. **Contact:** Jeffrey Nytch, DMA, managing director. For composers. Biennial.

Purpose Objective is to encourage composition of new music.

Requirements "Must be citizen of the US. Please submit score and recording, if available (CDs only) of a representative instrumental score." Send SASE for application or download from www.pnme.org. Samples of work are required with application. Entry fee: $20. Deadline: January 1, 2011 (postmark).

Awards Harvey Gaul Composition Contest: $6,000. Winner will receive commission for new work to be premiered by the PNME.

GREAT AMERICAN SONG CONTEST

PMB 135, 6327-C SW Capitol Hill Hwy., Portland OR 97239-1937. E-mail: info@ GreatAmericanSong.com. Website: www.GreatAmericanSong.com. **Contact:** Carla Starrett, event coordinator. Estab. 1998. For songwriters, composers and lyricists. Annual award.

- Also see the listing for Songwriters Resource Network in the Organizations section of this book.

Purpose To help songwriters get their songs heard by music-industry professionals; to generate educational and networking opportunities for participating songwriters; to help songwriters open doors in the music business.

Requirements Entry fee: $25. "Annual deadline. Check our website for details or send SASE along with your mailed request for information."

Awards Winners receive a mix of cash awards and prizes. The focus of the contest is on networking and educational opportunities. (All participants receive detailed evaluations of their songs by industry professionals.) Songs are judged by knowledgeable music-industry professionals, including prominent hit songwriters, producers and publishers.

Tips "Focus should be on the song. The quality of the demo isn't important. Judges will be looking for good songwriting talent. They will base their evaluations on the song—not the quality of the recording or the voice performance."

IAMA (INTERNATIONAL ACOUSTIC MUSIC AWARDS)

2881 E. Oakland Park Blvd, Suite 414, Fort Lauderdale, FL 33306. (954)537-3127. **Contact:** Jessica Brandon, artist relations. Established 2004. E-mail: info@inacoustic.com. Website:

http://www.inacoustic.com. For singer-songwriters, musicians, performing musicians in the acoustic genre.

Purpose "The purpose is to promote the excellence in Acoustic music performance and songwriting." Genres include: Folk, Alternative, Bluegrass, etc.

Requirements Visit website for entry form and details. "All songs submitted must be original. There must be at least an acoustic instrument (voice) in any song. Electric and Electronic instruments, along with loops is allowed but acoustic instruments (or voice) must be clearly heard in all songs submitted. Contestants may enter as many songs in as many categories as desired but each entry requires a separate CD, entry form, lyric sheet and entry fee. CDs and lyrics will not be returned. Winners will be chosen by a Blue Ribbon Judging Committee comprised of music industry professionals including A&R managers from record labels, publishers and producers. Entries are judged equally on music performance, production, originality, lyrics, melody and composition. Songs may be in any language. Winners will be notified by e-mail and must sign and return an affidavit confirming that winner's song is original and he/she holds rights to the song. Entry fee: $35/entry.

Awards Prizes: Overall Grand Prize receives $11,000.00 worth of merchandise, First Prizes in all categories win $900.00 worth of merchandise and services, Runner-Up prizes in all categories receive $600.00 worth of merchandise and services. All first prizes and runner-up winners will receive a track on IAMA compilation CD which goes out to radio stations.

Tips "Judging is based on music performance, music production, songwriting and originality/artistry."

KATE NEAL KINLEY MEMORIAL FELLOWSHIP

University of Illinois, College of Fine and Applied Arts, 608 E. Lorado Taft Dr. #100, Champaign IL 61820. (217)333-1661. Website: www.faa.uiuc.edu. **Contact:** Dr. Kathleen F. Conlin, chair. Estab. 1931. For students of architecture, art or music. Annual award.

Purpose The advancement of study in the fine arts.

Requirements "The Fellowship will be awarded upon the basis of unusual promise in the fine arts. Open to college graduates whose principal or major studies have been in the fields of architecture, art or music." Write or call for fall deadline. Send for application or call. Samples of work are required with application.

Awards "One major Fellowship which yield the sum of $20,000 each which is to be used by the recipients toward defraying the expenses of advanced study of the fine arts in America or abroad." Two or three smaller fellowships may also be awarded upon committee recommendations. Good for 1 year. Grant is nonrenewable.

L.A. DESIGNERS' THEATRE MUSIC AWARDS

P.O. Box 1883, Studio City CA 91614-0883. (323)650-9600. Fax: (323)654-3210. E-mail: ladesigners@gmail.com. Artistic Director: Richard Niederberg. For songwriters, composers, performing artists, musical playwrights and rights holders of music.

Purpose To produce new musicals, operettas, opera-boufes and plays with music, as well as new dance pieces with new music scores.

Requirements Submit nonreturnable cassette, tape, CD or any other medium by first or 4th class mail. "We prefer proposals to scripts." Acceptance: continuous. Submit nonreturnable materials with cover letter. No application form or fee is necessary.

Awards Music is commissioned for a particular project. Amounts are negotiable. Applications judged by our artistic staff.

Tips "Make the material 'classic, yet commercial' and easy to record/re-record/edit. Make sure rights are totally free of all 'strings,' 'understandings,' 'promises,' etc. ASCAP/BMI/SESAC registration is OK, as long as 'grand' or 'performing rights' are available."

THE JOHN LENNON SONGWRITING CONTEST

180 Brighton Rd., Suite 801, Clifton NJ 07012. E-mail: info@jlsc.com. Website: www.jlsc. com. Contact: Brianne Melville. Estab. 1996. For songwriters. Open year-round.

Purpose "The purpose of the John Lennon Songwriting Contest is to promote the art of songwriting by assisting in the discovery of new talent as well as providing more established songwriters with an opportunity to advance their careers."

Requirements Each entry must consist of the following: completed and signed application; audio cassette, CD or mp3 containing one song only, 5 minutes or less in length; lyric sheet typed or printed legibly (English translation is required when applicable); $30 entry fee. Deadline: December 15, 2009. Applications can be found in various music-oriented magazines and on our website. Prospective entrants can send for an application or contact the contest via e-mail at info@jlsc.com.

Awards Entries are accepted in the following 12 categories: rock, country, jazz, pop, world, gospel/inspirational, R&B, hip-hop, Latin, electronic, folk and children's music. Winners will receive EMI Publishing Contracts, Studio Equipment from Brian Moore Guitars, Roland, Edirol and Audio Technica, 1,000 CDs in full color with premium 6-panel Digipaks courtesy of Discmakers, and gift certificates from Musiciansfriend.com. One entrant wil be chosen to TOUR and PERFORM for one week on Warped Tour '06. One Lennon Award winning song will be named "Maxell Song of the Year" and take home an additional $20,000 in cash courtesy of the Maxell Corporation.

MAXIM MAZUMDAR NEW PLAY COMPETITION

One Curtain Up Alley, Buffalo NY 14202-1911. (716)852-2600. Fax: (716)852-2266. E-mail: newplays@alleyway.com. Website: www.alleyway.com. **Contact:** Literary Manager. For musical playwrights. Annual award.

Purpose Alleyway Theatre is dedicated to the development and production of new works. Winners of the competition will receive production and royalties.

Requirements Unproduced full-length work not less than 90 minutes long with cast limit of 10 and unit or simple set, or unproduced one-act work less than 15 minutes long with cast limit of 6 and simple set; prefers work with unconventional setting that explores the boundaries of theatricality; limit of 1 submission in each category; guidelines available online, no entry form. $25 playwright entry fee. Script, resume, SASE optional. CD or cassette mandatory. Deadline: July 1.

Awards Production for full-length play or musical with royalty and production for one-act play or musical.

Tips "Entries may be of any style, but preference will be given to those scripts which take place in unconventional settings and explore the boundaries of theatricality. No more than ten performers is a definite, unchangeable requirement."

MID-ATLANTIC SONG CONTEST

Songwriters' Association of Washington, PMB 106-137, 4200 Wisconsin Ave., NW, Washington DC 20016. E-mail: masc@saw.org. Website: www.saw.org. For songwriters and composers. Estab. 1982. Annual award.

- Also see the listing for Songwriters Association of Washington in the Organizations section.

Purpose This is one of the longest-running contests in the nation; SAW has organized twenty-seven contests since 1982. The competition is designed to afford rising songwriters in a wide variety of genres the opportunity to receive awards and exposure in an environment of peer competition.

Requirements Amateur status is important. Applicants should request a brochure/application using the contact information above. Rules and procedures are clearly explained in that brochure. CD and 3 copies of the lyrics are to be submitted with an application form and fee for each entry, or submit mp3 entries by applying online or through Sonicbids. Reduced entry fees are offered to members of Songwriters' Association of Washington; membership can be arranged simultaneously with entering. Multiple-song discounts are also offered. Applications are mailed out and posted on their website around June 1; the submission deadline is September 15; awards are typically announced late in the fall.

Awards The two best songs in each of ten categories win prize packages donated by the contest's corporate sponsors: BMI, Oasis CD Manufacturing, Omega Recording Studios, Mary Cliff and Sonic Bids. Winning songwriters are invited to perform in Washington, DC at the Awards Ceremony Gala, and the winning songs are included on a compilation CD. The best song in each category is eligible for three grand cash prizes. Certificates are awarded to other entries meriting honorable mention.

Tips "Enter the song in the most appropriate category. Make the sound recording the best it can be (even though judges are asked to focus on melody and lyric and not on production.) Avoid clichés, extended introductions, and long instrumental solos."

THELONIOUS MONK INTERNATIONAL JAZZ COMPOSERS COMPETITION

(Sponsored by BMI) Thelonious Monk Institute of Jazz, 5225 Wisconsin Ave. NW, #605, Washington DC 20015. (202)364-7272. Fax: (202)364-0176. E-mail: info@monkinstitute. org. Website: www.monkinstitute.org. **Contact:** Leonard Brown, program director. Estab. 1993. For songwriters and composers. Annual award.

Purpose The award is given to an aspiring jazz composer who best demonstrates originality, creativity and excellence in jazz composition.

Requirements Deadline: August 6. Send for application. Submission must include application form, resume of musical experience, CD or cassette, entry, four copies of the full score, and a photo. The composition features a different instrument each year. Entry fee: $35.

Awards $10,000. Applications are judged by panel of jazz musicians. "The Institute will provide piano, bass, guitar, drum set, tenor saxophone, and trumpet for the final performance. The winner will be responsible for the costs of any different instrumentation included in the composition."

SAMMY NESTICO AWARD/USAF BAND AIRMEN OF NOTE

201 McChord St., Bolling AFB, Washington DC 20032-0202. (202)767-1756. Fax: (202)767-0686. E-mail: USAFBand.af.mil. **Contact:** Alan Baylock, master sergeant. Estab. 1995. For composers. Annual award.

Purpose To carry on the tradition of excellence of Sammy Nestico's writing through jazz composition. The winner will have their composition performed by the USAF Airmen of Note, have it professionally recorded and receive a $1,000 follow up commission for a second work.

Requirements Unpublished work for jazz ensemble instrumentation (5,4,4,4) style, form and length are unrestricted. Deadline: October 2, 2006. Send for application. Samples of work are required with full score and set of parts (or CD recording).

Awards Performance by the USAF Band Airmen of Note; expense paid travel to Washington, DC for the performance; professionally produced recording of the winning composition; and $1,000 follow up commission for second work. Applications are judged by panel of musicians.

PULITZER PRIZE IN MUSIC

709 Journalism Building, Columbia University, New York NY 10027. (212)854-3841. Fax: (212)854-3342. E-mail: pulitzer@www.pulitzer.org. Website: www.pulitzer.org. **Contact:** Music Secretary. For composers and musical playwrights. Annual award.

Requirements "For distinguished musical composition by an American that has had its first performance or recording in the United States during the year." Entries should reflect current creative activity. Works that receive their American premiere between January 16, 2009 and December 31, 2009 are eligible. A public performance or the public release of a recording shall constitute a premiere. Deadline: December 31. Samples of work are required with application, biography and photograph of composer, date and place of performance, score or manuscript and recording of the work, entry form and $50 entry fee.

Awards "One award: $10,000. Applications are judged first by a nominating jury, then by the Pulitzer Prize Board."

ROCKY MOUNTAIN FOLKS FESTIVAL SONGWRITER SHOWCASE

Planet Bluegrass, ATTN: Songwriter Showcase, P.O. Box 769, Lyons CO 80540. (800)624-2422 or (303)823-0848. Fax: (303)823-0849. E-mail: brian@bluegrass.com. Website: www.bluegrass.com. **Contact:** Steve Szymanski, director. Estab. 1993. For songwriters, composers and performers. Annual award.

Purpose Award based on having the best song and performance.

Requirements Deadline: June. Finalists notified by July 14. Rules available on website. Samples of work are required with application. Send CD with $10/song entry fee. Can now submit online: www.sonicbids.com/rockymountainfolk06. Contestants cannot be signed to a major label or publishing deal. No backup musicians allowed. Awards: 1st Place is a 2006 Festival Main Stage set, custom Hayes Guitar, $100, and a free one song drumoverdubs (http://www.drumoverdubs.com) certificate (valued at $300); 2nd Place is $500 and a Baby Taylor Guitar; 3rd Place is $400 and a Baby Taylor Guitar; 4th Place is $300; 5th Place is $200; 6th to 10th Place is $100 each. Each finalist will also receive a complimentary three-day Folks Festival pass that includes onsite camping, and a Songwriter In The Round slot during the Festival on our workshop stage.

ROME PRIZE COMPETITION FELLOWSHIP

American Academy in Rome, 7 E. 60th St., New York NY 10022-1001. (212)751-7200. Fax: (212)751-7220. E-mail: info@aarome.org. Website: www.aarome.org. **Contact:** Programs Department. For composers. Annual award.

Purpose "Through its annual Rome Prize Competition, the academy awards up to thirty fellowships in eleven disciplines, including musical composition. Winners of the Rome Prize pursue independent projects while residing at the Academy's eleven acre center in Rome."

Requirements "Applicants for 11-month fellowships must be US citizens and hold a bachelor's degree in music, musical composition or its equivalent." Deadline: November 1. Entry fee: $30. Application guidelines are available through the Academy's website.

Awards "Up to two fellowships are awarded annually in musical composition. Fellowship consists of room, board, and a studio at the Academy facilities in Rome as well as a stipend of $26,000. In all cases, excellence is the primary criterion for selection, based on the quality of the materials submitted. Winners are announced in mid-April and fellowships generally begin in early September."

TELLURIDE TROUBADOUR CONTEST

Planet Bluegrass, ATTN: Troubadour Competition, P.O. Box 769, Lyons CO 80540. (303)823-0848 or (800)624-2422. Fax: (303)823-0849. E-mail: brian@bluegrass.com. Website: www.bluegrass.com. **Contact:** Steve Szymanski, director. Estab. 1991. For songwriters, composers and performers. Annual award.

Purpose Award based on having best song and performance.

Requirements Deadline: must be postmarked by April 16; notified May 5, if selected. Rules available on website. Send CD and $10/song entry fee (limit of 2 songs). Can now submit music online at www.sonicbids.com/telluride2006. Contestants cannot be signed to a major label or publishing deal. No backup musicians allowed.

Awards 1st: custom Shanti Guitar, $300 and Festival Main Stage Set; 2nd: $500; 3rd: $400; 4th: $300; 5th: $200. Applications judged by panel of judges.

THE TEN-MINUTE MUSICALS PROJECT

P.O. Box 461194, West Hollywood CA 90046. Website: www.TenMinuteMusicals.org. **Contact:** Michael Koppy, producer. For songwriters, composers and musical playwrights. Annual award.

Purpose "We are building a full-length stage musical comprised of complete short musicals, each of which play for between 8-14 minutes. Award is $250 for each work chosen for development towards inclusion in the project, plus a share of royalties when produced."

Requirements Deadline: August 31. Responds by November 30. See website for guidelines. Final submission should include script, CD or DVD, and lead sheets.

Awards $250 for each work selected. "Works should have complete stories, with a definite beginning, middle and end."

U.S.A. SONGWRITING COMPETITION

2881 E. Oakland Park Blvd., Suite 414, Ft. Lauderdale FL 33306. (954)537-3127. Fax: (954)537-9690. E-mail: info@songwriting.net. Website: www.songwriting.net. **Contact:** Contest Manager. Estab. 1994. For songwriters, composers, performing artists and lyricists. Annual award.

Purpose "To honor good songwriters/composers all over the world, especially the unknown ones."

Requirements Open to professional and beginner songwriters. No limit on entries. Each entry must include an entry fee, a cassette tape of song(s) and lyric sheet(s). Judged by music industry representatives. Past judges have included record label representatives and publishers from Arista Records, EMI and Warner/Chappell. Deadline: To be announced. Entry fee: To be announced. Send SASE with request or e-mail for entry forms at any time. Samples of work are not required.

Awards Prizes include cash and merchandise in 15 different categories: pop, rock, country, Latin, R&B, gospel, folk, jazz, "lyrics only" category, instrumental and many others.

Tips "Judging is based on lyrics, originality, melody and overall composition. CD-quality production is great but not a consideration in judging."

Y.E.S. FESTIVAL OF NEW PLAYS

Northern Kentucky University Dept. of Theatre, FA-205, Highland Heights KY 41099-1007. (859)572-6303. Fax: (859)572-6057. E-mail: forman@nku.edu. **Contact:** Sandra Forman, project director. Estab. 1983. For musical playwrights. Biennial award (odd numbered years).

Purpose "The festival seeks to encourage new playwrights and develop new plays and musicals. Three plays or musicals are given full productions."

Requirements "No entry fee. Submit a script with a completed entry form. Musicals should be submitted with a piano/conductor's score and/or a vocal parts score. Scripts may be submitted May 1 through Sept. 30, 2010, for the New Play Festival occuring April 2011. Send SASE for application."

Awards Three awards of $500. "The winners are brought to NKU at our expense to view late rehearsals and opening night." Submissions are judged by a panel of readers.

Tips "Plays/musicals which have heavy demands for mature actors are not as likely to be selected as an equally good script with roles for 18-30 year olds."

Organizations

One of the first places a beginning songwriter should look for guidance and support is a songwriting organization. Offering encouragement, instruction, contacts and feedback, these groups of professional and amateur songwriters can help an aspiring songwriter hone the skills needed to compete in the ever-changing music industry.

The type of organization you choose to join depends on what you want to get out of it. Local groups can offer a friendly, supportive environment where you can work on your songs and have them critiqued in a constructive way by other songwriters. They're also great places to meet collaborators. Larger, national organizations can give you access to music business professionals and other songwriters across the country.

Most of the organizations listed in this book are non-profit groups with membership open to specific groups of people—songwriters, musicians, classical composers, etc. They can be local groups with a membership of less than 100 people, or large national organizations with thousands of members from all over the country. In addition to regular meetings, most organizations occasionally sponsor events such as seminars and workshops to which music industry personnel are invited to talk about the business, and perhaps listen to and critique demo tapes.

Check the following listings, bulletin boards at local music stores and your local newspapers for area organizations. If you are unable to locate an organization within an easy distance of your home, you may want to consider joining one of the national groups. These groups, based in New York, Los Angeles and Nashville, keep their members involved and informed through newsletters, regional workshops and large yearly conferences. They can help a writer who feels isolated in his hometown get his music heard by professionals in the major music centers.

In the following listings, organizations describe their purpose and activities, as well as how much it costs to join. Before joining any organization, consider what they have to offer and how becoming a member will benefit you. To locate organizations close to home, see the Geographic Index at the back of this book.

ACADEMY OF COUNTRY MUSIC

5500 Balboa Blvd., #200, Encino CA 91316. (818)788-8000. Fax: (818)788-0999. E-mail: info@acmcountry.com. Website: www.acmcountry.com. **Contact:** Bob Romeo, executive director. Estab. 1964. Serves country music industry professionals. Eligibility for professional members is limited to those individuals who derive some portion of their income directly from country music. Each member is classified by one of the following categories: artist/entertainer, club/venue operator, musician, on-air personality, manager, talent agent, composer, music publisher, public relations, publications, radio, TV/motion picture, record company, talent buyer or affiliated (general). The purpose of ACM is to promote and enhance the image of country music. The Academy is involved year-round in activities important to the country music community. Some of these activities include charity fund-raisers, participation in country music seminars, talent contests, artist showcases, assistance to producers in placing country music on television and in motion pictures and backing legislation that benefits the interests of the country music community. The ACM is governed by directors and run by officers elected annually. Applications are accepted throughout the year. Membership is $75/year.

AMERICAN MUSIC CENTER, INC.

322 8th Ave., Suite 1401, New York NY 10001. (212)366-5260 x10. Fax: (212)366-5265. E-mail: allison@amc.net. Website: www.amc.net. **Contact:** Membership Department. The American Music Center, founded by a consortium led by Aaron Copland in 1939, is the first-ever national service and information center for new classical music and jazz by American composers. The Center has a variety of innovative new programs and services, including a montly Internet magazine (www.newmusicbox.org) for new American music, online databases of contemporary ensembles and ongoing opportunities for composers, an online catalog of new music for educators specifically targeted to young audiences, a series of professional development workshops, and an online listening library (www.newmusicjukebox.org). Each month, AMC provides its over 2,500 members with a listing of opportunities including calls for scores, competitions, and other new music performance information. Each year, AMC's Information Services Department fields thousands of requests concerning composers, performers, data, funding, and support programs. The AMC Collection at the New York Public Library for the Performing Arts presently includes over 60,000 scores and recordings, many unavailable elsewhere. "AMC also continues to administer several grant programs: the Aaron Copland Fund for Music; the Henry Cowell Performance Incentive Fund; and its own programs Live Music for Dance and the Composer Assistance Program." Members also receive a link their Web sites on www.amc.net. The American Music Center is not-for-profit and has an annual membership fee.

AMERICAN SOCIETY OF COMPOSERS, AUTHORS AND PUBLISHERS (ASCAP)

One Lincoln Plaza, New York NY 10023. (212)621-6000 (administration); (212)621-6240 (membership). E-mail: info@ascap.com. Website: www.ascap.com. President and Chairman of the Board: Marilyn Bergman. CEO: John LoFrumento. Executive Vice President/Membership: Todd Brabec. **Contact:** Member Services at (800)95-ASCAP. **Regional offices—West Coast:** 7920 Sunset Blvd., 3rd Floor, Los Angeles CA 90046, (323)883-1000; **Nashville:** 2 Music Square W., Nashville TN 37203, (615)742-5000; **Chicago:** 1608 N. Milwaukee Ave., Suite 1007, Chicago IL 60647, (773)394-4286; **Atlanta:** PMB 400-541 10th St. NW, Atlanta GA 30318, (404)351-1224; **Florida:** 420 Lincoln Rd., Suite 385, Miami Beach FL 33139, (305)673-3446; **United Kingdom:** 8 Cork St., London W1S 3LJ England, 011-44-207-439-0909; **Puerto Rico:** 654 Ave. Munoz Rivera, IBM Plaza Suite 1101 B, Hato Rey, Puerto Rico 00918, (787)281-0782. ASCAP is a membership association of over 240,000 composers, lyricists, songwriters, and music publishers, whose function is to protect the rights of its members by licensing and collecting royalties for the nondramatic public performance of their copyrighted works. ASCAP licensees include radio, television, cable, live concert promoters, bars, restaurants, symphony orchestras, new media, and other users of music. ASCAP is the leading performing rights society in the world. All revenues, less operating expenses, are distributed to members (about 86 cents of each dollar). ASCAP was the first US performing rights organization to distribute royalties from the Internet. Founded in 1914, ASCAP is the only society created and owned by writers and publishers. The ASCAP Board of Directors consists of 12 writers and 12 publishers, elected by the membership. ASCAP's Member Card provides exclusive benefits geared towards working music professionals. Among the benefits are health, musical instrument and equipment, tour and studio liability, term life and long term care insurance, discounts on musical instruments, equipment and supplies, access to a credit union, and much more. ASCAP hosts a wide array of showcases and workshops throughout the year, and offers grants, special awards, and networking opportunities in a variety of genres. Visit their website listed above for more information.

ARIZONA SONGWRITERS ASSOCIATION

428 E. Thunderbird Rd., #737, Phoenix AZ 85022. E-mail: azsongwriters@cox.net. Website: www.azsongwriters.com. **Contact**: Jon Iger, president. Estab. 1977. Members are all ages; all styles of music, novice to pro; many make money placing their songs in film and TV. Most members are residents of Arizona. Purpose is to educate about the craft and business of songwriting and to facilitate networking with business professionals and other songwriters, musicians, singers and studios. Offers instruction, e-newsletter, workshops, performance, and song pitching opportunities. Applications accepted year-round. Membership fee: $25/year.

ASSOCIATION OF INDEPENDENT MUSIC PUBLISHERS

Los Angeles Chapter: P.O. Box 69473, Los Angeles CA 90069. (818)771-7301. New York line: (212)391-2532. E-mail: LAinfo@aimp.org or NYinfo@aimp.org. Website: www. aimp.org. Estab. 1977. Purpose is to educate members on new developments in the music publishing industry and to provide networking opportunities. Offers monthly panels and networking events. Applications accepted year-round. Membership fee: NY: $75/year; LA: $76/year.

AUSTIN SONGWRITERS GROUP

P.O. Box 2578, Austin TX 78768. (512)698-4237. E-mail: info@austinsongwritersgroup. com. Website: www.austinsongwritersgroup.com. **Contact:** Lee Duffy, president. Vice President: Brent Allen. Estab. 1986. Serves all ages and all levels, from just beginning to advanced. "Prospective members should have an interest in the field of songwriting, whether it be for profit or hobby. The main purpose of this organization is to educate members in the craft and business of songwriting; to provide resources for growth and advancement in the area of songwriting; and to provide opportunities for performance and contact with the music industry." The primary benefit of membership to a songwriter is exposed to music industry professionals, which increases contacts and furthers the songwriter's education in both craft and business aspects. Offers competitions, instruction, lectures, library, newsletter, performance opportunities, evaluation services, workshops and contact with musi c industry professionals through special guest speakers at meetings, plus our yearly 'Austin Songwriters Symposium,' which includes instruction, song evaluations, and song pitching direct to those pros currently seeking material for their artists, publishing companies, etc." Applications accepted year-round. Membership fee: $100/year.

Tips Our newsletter is top-quality-packed with helpful information on all aspects of songwriting-craft, business, recording and producing tips, and industry networking opportunities. Go to our website and sign up for emails to keep you informed about on going and up coming events!"d

BALTIMORE SONGWRITERS ASSOCIATION

P.O. Box 22496, Baltimore MD 21203. (410)669-1075. E-mail: info@baltimoresongwriters. org. Website: www.baltimoresongwriters.org. **Contact:** Ken Gutberlet, president. Estab. 1997. "The BSA is an inclusive organization with all ages, skill levels and genres of music welcome." Offers instruction, newsletter, lectures, workshops, performance opportunities. Applications accepted year-round; membership not limited to location or musical status. Membership fee: $25.

Tips "We are trying to build a musical community that is more supportive and less competitive. We are dedicated to helping songwriters grow and become better in their craft."

THE BOSTON SONGWRITERS WORKSHOP

Voicemail: (888)886-6507 press 4. E-mail: slyness@verizon.net. Website: www. bostonsongwriters.org. Estab. 1988. "The Boston Songwriters Workshop is made up of a very diverse group of people, ranging in age from late teens to people in their sixties, and even older. The interest areas are also diverse, running the gamut from folk, pop and rock to musical theater, jazz, R&B, dance, rap and classical. Skill levels within the group range from relative newcomers to established veterans that have had cuts and/ or songs published. By virtue of group consensus, there are no eligibility requirements other than a serious desire to pursue one's songwriting ventures, and availability and interest in volunteering for the various activities required to run the organization. The purpose of the BSW is to establish a community of songwriters and composers within the greater Boston area, so that its members may better help each other to make further gains in their respective musical careers." Offers performance opportunities, instruction, newsletter, workshops and bi-weekly critique sessions. Applications accepted year-round. Membership: $35/year; newsletter subscription only: $10/year; guest (nonmember) fees: free, limited to two meetings.

BROADCAST MUSIC, INC. (BMI)

7 World Trade Center, 250 Greenwich St., New York NY 10007-0030. (212)220-3000. E-mail: newyork@bmi.com. Website: www.bmi.com. **Los Angeles:** 8730 Sunset Blvd., 3rd Floor West, Los Angeles CA 90069-2211. (310)659-9109. E-mail: losangeles@bmi.com. **Nashville:** 10 Music Square East, Nashville TN 37203. (615)401-2000. E-mail: nashville@bmi.com. **Miami:** 1691 Michigan Av., Miami FL 33139. (305)673-5148. E-mail: miami@bmi.com. **Atlanta:** 3340 Peachtree Rd., NE, Suite 570, Atlanta GA 30326. (404)261-5151. E-mail: atlanta@bmi.com. **Puerto Rico:** 1250 Av. Ponce de Leon, San Jose Building Santurce PR 00907. (787)754-6490. **United Kingdom:** 84 Harley House, Marylebone Rd., London NW1 5HN United Kingdom. 011-44-207-486-2036. E-mail: london@bmi.com. President and CEO: Del R. Bryant. Senior Vice Presidents, New York: Phillip Graham, Writer/Publisher Relations; Alison Smith, Performing Rights. Vice Presidents: New York: Charlie Feldman; Los Angeles: Barbara Cane and Doreen Ringer Ross; Nashville: Paul Corbin; Miami: Diane J. Almodovar; Atlanta: Catherine Brewton. Senior Executive, London: Brandon Bakshi. BMI is a performing rights organization representing approximately 300,000 songwriters, composers and music publishers in all genres of music, including pop, rock, country, R&B, rap, jazz, Latin, gospel and contemporary classical. "Applicants must have written a musical composition, alone or in collaboration with other writers, which is commercially published, recorded or otherwise likely to be performed." Purpose: BMI acts on behalf of its songwriters, composers and music publishers by insuring payment for performance of their works through the collection of licensing fees from radio stations, Internet outlets, broadcast and cable TV stations, hotels, nightclubs, aerobics centers and other users of music. This income is distributed to the writers and publishers in the form of royalty payments, based on how the music is used. BMI also undertakes intensive lobbying efforts in Washington D.C. on behalf of its affiliates, seeking to protect their performing rights through the enactment of new legislation and enforcement of current copyright law. In addition, BMI helps aspiring songwriters develop their skills through various workshops, seminars and competitions it sponsors throughout the country. Applications accepted year-round. There is no membership fee for songwriters; a one-time fee of $150 is required to affiliate an individually-owned publishing company; $250 for partnerships,

corporations and limited-liability companies. "Visit our website for specific contacts, e-mail addresses and additional membership information."

⚑ CANADA COUNCIL FOR THE ARTS/CONSEIL DES ARTS DU CANADA

350 Albert St., P.O. Box 1047, Ottawa ON K1P 5V8 Canada. (613)566-4414, ext. 5060. E-mail: info@canadacouncil.ca. Website: www.canadacouncil.ca. **Contact:** Christian Mondor, information officer. Estab. 1957. An independent agency that fosters and promotes the arts in Canada by providing grants and services to professional artists including songwriters and musicians. "Individual artists must be Canadian citizens or permanent residents of Canada, and must have completed basic training and/or have the recognition as professionals within their fields. The Canada Council offers grants to professional musicians to pursue their individual artistic development and creation. There are specific deadline dates for the various programs of assistance. Visit our website at www.canadacouncil.ca/music for more details."

⚑ CANADIAN COUNTRY MUSIC ASSOCIATION

30-B Commercial Road, Toronto ON M4G 1Z4 Canada. (416)947-1331. Fax: (416)947-5924. E-mail: country@ccma.org. Website: www.ccma.org. **Contact:** Brandi Mills, communications & marketing. Estab. 1976. Members are artists, songwriters, musicians, producers, radio station personnel, managers, booking agents and others. Offers newsletter, workshops, performance opportunities and the CCMA awards every September. "Through our newsletters and conventions we offer a means of meeting and associating with artists and others in the industry. The CCMA is a federally chartered, nonprofit organization, dedicated to the promotion and development of Canadian country music throughout Canada and the world and to providing a unity of purpose for the Canadian country music industry." See website for membership information and benefits.

CENTRAL CAROLINA SONGWRITERS ASSOCIATION (CCSA)

131 Henry Baker Road, Zebulon, NC 27597. (919) 269-6240. Website: www.ccsa-raleigh. com. **Contact:** Tony Dickens, president, or vice president Diana Dimsdale. Established in 1997, CCSA welcomes songwriters of all experience levels from beginner to professional within the local RDU/Triad/Eastern area of North Carolina to join our group. Our members' musical background varies, covering a wide array of musical genres. CCSA meets monthly in Raleigh, NC. We are unable to accept applications from incarcerated persons or those who do not reside in the local area as our group's primary focus is on songwriters who are able to attend the monthly meetings-to ensure members get the best value for their yearly dues. CCSA strives to provide each songwriter and musician a resourceful organization where members grow musically by networking and sharing with one another. Offers annual songwriters forum, periodic workshops, critiques at the monthly meetings, opportunities to perform and network with fellow members. Applications are accepted year round. Dues are $24/year (pro-rated for new members at $2/month by date of application) with annual renewal each January.

CENTRAL OREGON SONGWRITERS ASSOCIATION

782 SW Rimrock Way, Redmond OR 97756. (541)548-6306. E-mail: administrator@ centraloregonmusic.com. Website: www.centraloregonmusic.com. President: Claudia Valiquet. Estab. 1993. "Our members range in age from their 20s into their 80s. Membership includes aspiring beginners, accomplished singer/songwriter performing artists and all in between. Anyone with an interest in songwriting (any style) is invited to and welcome at COSA. COSA is a nonprofit organization to promote, educate and motivate members in the skills of writing, marketing and improving their craft." Offers competitions, instruction, newsletter, lectures, library, workshops, performance opportunities, songwriters round, awards, evaluation services and collaboration. Applications accepted year-round. Membership fee is $25.

THE COLLEGE MUSIC SOCIETY

312 E. Pine St., Missoula MT 59802. (406)721-9616. Fax: (406)721-9419. E-mail: cms@ music.org. Website: www.music.org. Estab. 1959. Serves college, university and conservatory professors, as well as independent musicians. "The College Music Society promotes music teaching and learning, musical creativity and expression, research and dialogue, and diversity and interdisciplinary interaction. A consortium of college, conservatory, university, and independent musicians and scholars interested in all disciplines of music, the Society provides leadership and serves as an agent of change by addressing concerns facing music in higher education." Offers journal, newsletter, lectures, workshops, performance opportunities, job listing service, databases of organizations and institutions, music faculty and mailing lists. Applications accepted year-round. Membership fee: $70 (regular dues), $35 (student dues), $35 (retiree dues).

CONNECTICUT SONGWRITERS ASSOCIATION

P.O. Box 511, Mystic CT 06355. E-mail: info@ctsongs.com. Website: www.ctsongs. com. **Contact:** Bill Pere, Executive Director. Associate Director: Kay Pere. "We are an educational, nonprofit organization dedicated to improving the art and craft of original music. Founded in 1979, CSA has had almost 2,000 active members and has become one of the best known and respected songwriters' associations in the country. Membership in the CSA admits you to 12-18 seminars/workshops/song critique sessions per year throughout Connecticut and surrounding region. Out-of-state members may mail in songs for free critiques at our meetings. Noted professionals deal with all aspects of the craft and business of music including lyric writing, music theory, music technology, arrangement and production, legal and business aspects, performance techniques, song analysis and recording techniques. CSA offers song screening sessions for members and songs that pass become eligible for inclusion on the CSA sampler anthology through various retail and online outlets and are brought to national music conferences. CSA is well connected in both the independent music scene and the traditional music industry. CSA also offers showcases and concerts which are open to the public and designed to give artists a venue for performing their original material for an attentive, listening audience.

CSA benefits help local soup kitchens, group homes, hospice, world hunger, libraries, nature centers, community centers and more. CSA encompasses ballads to bluegrass and Bach to rock. Our monthly newsletter, Connecticut Songsmith, offers free classified advertising for members, and has been edited and published continuously by Bill Pere since 1980. Annual dues: $40; senior citizen and full time students $30; organizations $80. Join online or by mail. Memberships are tax-deductible as business expenses or as charitable contributions to the extent allowed by law."

DALLAS SONGWRITERS ASSOCIATION

Sammons Center for the Arts, 3630 Harry Hines, Box 20, Dallas TX 75219. (214)750-0916. E-mail: info@dallassongwriters.org. Website: www.dallassongwriters.org. **Contact:** Roger Russell, membership director. President: Buck Morgan. Founding President Emeritis: Barbara McMillen. Estab. 1986. Serves songwriters and lyricists of Dallas/Ft. Worth metroplex. Members are adults ages 18-75, Dallas/Ft. Worth area songwriters/lyricists who are or aspire to be professionals. Purpose is to provide songwriters an opportunity to meet other songwriters, share information, find co-writers and support each other through group discussions at monthly meetings; to provide songwriters an opportunity to have their songs heard and critiqued by peers and professionals by playing cassettes and providing an open mike at monthly meetings and open mics, showcases, and festival stages, and by offering contests judged by publishers; to provide songwriters opportunities to meet other music business professionals by inviting guest speakers to monthly meetings and workshops; and to provide songwriters opportunities to learn more about the craft of songwriting and the business of music by presenting mini-workshops at each monthly meeting. "We offer a chance for the songwriter to learn from peers and industry professionals and an opportunity to belong to a supportive group environment to encourage the individual to continue his/her songwriting endeavors." Offers competitions (including the Annual Song Contest with over $5,000 in prizes, and the Quarterly Lyric Contest), field trips, instruction, lectures, newsletter, performance opportunities, social outings, workshops and seminars. "Our members are eligible for discounts at several local music stores and seminars." Applications accepted year-round. Membership fee: $50. "When inquiring by phone, please leave complete mailing address and phone number or e-mail address where you can be reached day and night."

THE FIELD

161 Sixth Ave., 14th Floor, New York NY 10013. (212)691-6969. Fax: (212)255-2053. E-mail: pele@thefield.org. Website: www.thefield.org. **Contact:** any staff member. Estab. 1986. "Founded by artists for artists, The Field has been dedicated to providing impactful services to thousands of performing artists in New York City and beyond since 1986. From fostering creative exploration to stewarding innovative fundraising strategies, we are delighted to help artists reach their fullest potential. More than 1,900 performing artists come to The Field annually to build their businesses, 2,000+ new art works are developed under our stewardship each year, and our services are replicated in 11

cities across the US and in Europe. At the same time, we remain true to our grassroots origin and artist-centered mission: to strategically and comprehensively serve the myriad artistic and administrative needs of independent performing artists and companies who work in the fields of dance, theater, music, text, and performance art. Our core values of affordability, accessibility and rigorous delivery infuse all of our interactions. Field services include career-building workshops (grant writing, touring, internet strategies, etc.), fiscal sponsorship, creative residences in New York City and out of town, an "Artists' Kinkos" Resource Center, and Membership benefits." Offers fiscal sponsorship, arts management & creative workshops, residencies and performance opportunities. Applications accepted year-round. Membership fee: $100/year.

Tips "The Field offers the most affordable and accessible fiscal sponsorship program in New York City. The Sponsored Artist Program offered by The Field enables performing artists and groups to accumulate the funds they need to make their artistic and career goals a reality. Fiscal sponsorship provides independent performing artists and groups with: eligibility to apply for most government, foundation, and corporate grants which require a 501(c)(3), not-for-profit status; eligibility to receive tax-deductible donations of both money and goods from individuals; and other services where 501(c)(3) status is necessary."

🌐 THE GUILD OF INTERNATIONAL SONGWRITERS & COMPOSERS

Sovereign House, 12 Trewartha Road, Praa Sands, Penzance, Cornwall TR20 9ST England. (01736)762826. Fax: (01736)763328. email: songmag@aol.com. Website: www.songwriters-guild.com and www.myspace.com/guildofsongwriters. General Secretary: Carole Jones. The Guild of International Songwriters & Composers is an international music industry organisation based in England in the United Kingdom. Guild members are songwriters, composers, lyricists, poets, performing songwriters, musicians, music publishers, studio owners, managers, independent record companies, music industry personnel, etc., from many countries throughout the world. The Guild of International Songwriters & Composers has been publishing Songwriting and Composing Magazine since 1986, which is issued free to all Guild members throughout their membership. The Guild of International Songwriters and Composers offers advice, guidance, assistance, copyright protection service, information, encouragement, contact information, Intellectual property/copyright protection of members works through the Guild's Copyright Registration Centre along with other free services and more to Guild members with regard to helping members achieve their aims, ambitions, progression and advancement in respect to the many different aspects of the music industry. Information, advice and services available to Guild members throughout their membership includes assistance, advice and help on many matters and issues relating to the music industry in general. Annual membership fees: are £55. For further information please visit the Guild's website or MySpace page.

HAWAI'I SONGWRITERS ASSOCIATION

P.O. Box 231325, Las Vegas, NV, 89105. (702)897-9066. E-mail: stanrubens@aol.com. Website: www.stanrubens.com. **Contact:** Stan Rubens, secretary. Estab. 1972. "We have two classes of membership: Professional (must have had at least one song commercially published and for sale to general public) and Regular (any one who wants to join and share in our activities). Both classes can vote equally, but only Professional members can hold office. Must be 18 years old to join. Our members include musicians, entertainers and record producers. Membership is world-wide and open to all varieties of music, not just ethnic Hawaiian. President, Stan Rubens, has published 4 albums." Offers competitions, instruction, monthly newsletter, lectures, workshops, performance opportunities and evaluation services. Applications accepted year-round. Membership fee: $24. Stan Rubens teaches songwriting either privately or in group or school sessions.

⊕ ☑ INTERNATIONAL SONGWRITERS ASSOCIATION LTD.

P.O. Box 46, Limerick City, Ireland. E-mail: jliddane@songwriter.iol.ie. Website: www. songwriter.co.uk. Contact: Anna M. Sinden, membership department. Serves songwriters and music publishers. "The ISA headquarters is in Limerick City, Ireland, and from there it provides its members with assessment services, copyright services, legal and other advisory services and an investigations service, plus a magazine for one yearly fee. Our members are songwriters in more than 50 countries worldwide, of all ages. There are no qualifications, but applicants under 18 are not accepted. We provide information and assistance to professional or semi-professional songwriters. Our publication, Songwriter, which was founded in 1967, features detailed exclusive interviews with songwriters and music publishers, as well as directory information of value to writers." Offers competitions, instruction, library, newsletter and a weekly e-mail newsletter Songwriter Newswire. Applications accepted year-round. Membership fee for European writers is £19.95; for non-European writers, US $30.

KNOXVILLE SONGWRITERS ASSOCIATION

P.O. Box 603, Knoxville TN 37901. (865)573-1025. E-mail: deblair@mindspring.com. Website: www.knoxvillesongwritersassociation.org. **Contact:** Gene Blair. Estab. 1982. Serves songwriters of all ages. "Some have been members since 1982, others are beginners. Members must be interested in learning the craft of songwriting. Not only a learning organization but a support group of songwriters who wants to learn what to do with their song after it has been written. We open doors for aspiring writers. The primary benefit of membership is to supply information to the writer on how to write a song. Many members have received major cuts." Offers showcases, instruction, lectures, library, newsletter, performance opportunities, evaluation services and workshops. Applications accepted year-round. Membership fee: $30/year.

LOS ANGELES MUSIC NETWORK

P.O. Box 2446, Toluca Lake CA 91610-2446. (818)769-6095. E-mail: info@lamn.com. Website: www.lamn.com. **Contact:** Tess Taylor, president. Estab. 1988. "Connections. Pèrformance opportunities. Facts. Career advancement. All that is available with your membership in the Los Angeles Music Network (LAMN). Our emphasis is on sharing knowledge and information, giving you access to top professionals and promoting career development. LAMN is an association of music industry professionals, i.e., artists, singers, songwriters, and people who work in various aspects of the music industry with an emphasis on the creative. Members are ambitious and interested in advancing their careers. LAMN promotes career advancement, communication and education among artists and creatives. LAMN sponsors industry events and educational panels held at venues in the Los Angeles area and now in other major music hubs around the country (New York, Las Vegas, Phoenix, and San Francisco). LAMN Jams are popular among our members. Experience LAMN Jams in L.A. or N.Y. by performing your original music in front of industry experts who can advance your career by getting your music in the hands of hard-to-reach music supervisors. the 'anti-American Idol' singer-songwriter contest gives artists an opportunity to perform in front of industry experts and receive instant feedback to their music, lyrics and performance. As a result of the exposure, Tim Fagan won the John Mayer Songwriting Contest and was invited to tour with the Goo Goo Dolls, Lifehouse, and recently, the platinum recording artist Colbie Caillat. This paired him with multi-platinum songwriter and recording artist John Mayer, with whom Fagan co-wrote 'Deeper.' Publisher Robert Walls has pitched music from LAMN Jam performers to hit TV shows like The OC and Gray's Anatomy, and the upcoming flick The Devil Wears Prada. Other performers have received offers including publishing and production deals and studio gigs. Offers performance opportunities, instruction, newsletter, lectures, seminars, music industry job listings, career counseling, resume publishing, mentor network, and many professional networking opportunities. See our website for current job listings and a calendar of upcoming events. Applications accepted year-round. Annual membership fee is $115.

☒ MANITOBA MUSIC

1-376 Donald St., Winnipeg MB R3B 2J2 Canada. (204)942-8650. Fax: (204)942-6083. E-mail: info@manitobamusic.com. Website: www.manitobamusic.com. **Contact:** Sara Stasiuk, Executive Director. Estab. 1987. Organization consists of "songwriters, producers, agents, musicians, managers, retailers, publicists, radio, talent buyers, media, record labels, etc. (no age limit, no skill level minimum). Must have interest in the future of Manitoba's music industry." The main purpose of Manitoba Music is to foster growth in all areas of the Manitoba music industry primarily through education, promotion and lobbying. Offers newsletter, extensive website, directory of Manitoba's music industry, workshops and performance opportunities. Manitoba Music is also involved with the Western Canadian Music Awards festival, conference and awards show. Applications accepted year-round. Membership fee: $50 (Canadian funds).

Resources

MEET THE COMPOSER

90 John St., Suite 312, New York NY 10038. (212)645-6949. Fax: (212)645-9669. E-mail: mtc@meetthecomposer.org. Website: www.meetthecomposer.org. Estab. 1974. "Meet The Composer serves composers working in all styles of music, at every career stage, through a variety of grant programs and information resources. A nonprofit organization, Meet The Composer raises money from foundations, corporations, individual patrons and government sources and designs programs that support all genres of music—from folk, ethnic, jazz, electronic, symphonic, and chamber to choral, music theater, opera and dance. Meet The Composer awards grants for composer fees to non-profit organizations that perform, present, or commission original works. This is not a membership organization; all composers are eligible for support. Meet The Composer was founded in 1974 to increase artistic and financial opportunities for composers by fostering the creation, performance, dissemination, and appreciation of their music." Offers grant programs and information services. Deadlines vary for each grant program.

MEMPHIS SONGWRITERS' ASSOCIATION

4728 Spottswood, #191, Memphis TN 38117-4815. (901)626-4127 or (901)577-0906. E-mail: admin@memphissongwriters.org. Website: www.memphissongwriters.org and www.myspace.com/memphissongwriters. **Contact:** Phillip Beasley, MSA president. Estab. 1973. "MSA is a nonprofit songwriters organization serving songwriters nationally. Our mission is to dedicate our services to promote, advance, and help songwriters in the composition of music, lyrics and songs; to work for better conditions in our profession; and to secure and protect the rights of MSA songwriters. The Memphis Songwriters Association are organizational members of the Folk Alliance (FA.org). We also supply copyright forms. We offer critique sessions for writers at our monthly meetings. We also have monthly open mic songwriters night to encourage creativity, networking and co-writing. We host an annual songwriter's seminar and an annual songwriter's showcase, as well as a bi-monthly guest speaker series, which provide education, competition and entertainment for the songwriter. In addition, our members receive a bimonthly newsletter to keep them informed of MSA activities, demo services and opportunities in the songwriting field." Annual fee: $50; Student/Senior: $35.

MINNESOTA ASSOCIATION OF SONGWRITERS

P.O. Box 4262, Saint Paul MN 55104. E-mail: info@mnsongwriters.org. Website: www. mnsongwriters.org. "Includes a wide variety of members, ranging in age from 18 to 80; type of music is very diverse, ranging from alternative rock to contemporary Christian; skill levels range from beginning songwriters to writers with recorded and published material. Main requirement is an interest in songwriting. Although most members come from the Minneapolis-St. Paul area, others come in from surrounding cities, nearby Wisconsin, and other parts of the country. Some members are full-time musicians, but most represent a wide variety of occupations. MAS is a nonprofit community of songwriters which informs, educates, inspires and assists its members in the art and business of songwriting." Offers instruction, newsletter, lectures, workshops, performance opportunities and evaluation services. Applications accepted year-round. Membership fee: Individual: $25; Business: $65.

Tips "Members are kept current on resources and opportunities. Original works are played at meetings and are critiqued by involved members. Through this process, writers hone their skills and gain experience and confidence in submitting their works to others."

⊠ MUSIC BC INDUSTRY ASSOCIATION

#530-425 Carrall St., Vancouver BC V6B 6E3 Canada. (604)873-1914. 1-888-866-8570 (Toll Free in BC). Fax: (604)873-9686. E-mail: info@musicbc.org. Website: www.musicbc.org. Estab. 1990. Music BC(formerly PMIA) is a non-profit society that supports and promotes the spirit, development, and growth of the BC music community provincially, nationally, and internationally. Music BC provides education, resources, advocacy, opportunities for funding, and a forum for communication. Visit website for membership benefits.

NASHVILLE SONGWRITERS ASSOCIATION INTERNATIONAL (NSAI)

1710 Roy Acuff Place, Nashville TN 37203. (615)256-3354 or (800)321-6008. Fax: (615)256-0034. E-mail: nsai@nashvillesongwriters.com. Website: www.nashvillesongwriters.com. Executive Director: Barton Herbison. Purpose: a not-for-profit service organization for both aspiring and professional songwriters in all fields of music. Membership: Spans the United States and several foreign countries. Songwriters may apply in one of four annual categories: Active ($150 U.S currency for songwriters are actively working to improve in the craft of writing and/or actively pursing a career within the songwriting industry); Student ($100 U.S for full-time college, high school, or middle school students); Professional ($100 U.S. currency for songwriters who are staff writers for a publishing company or earn 51 percent of their annual income from songwriting, whether from advances, royalties, or performances, or are generally regarded as a professional songwriter within the music industry); Lifetime (please contact NSAI for details). Membership benefits: music industry information and advice, song evaluations, eNews, access to industry professionals through weekly Nashville workshops and several annual events, regional workshops, use of office facilities, discounts on books and discounts on NSAI's three annual events. There are also "branch" workshops of NSAI. Workshops must meet certain standards and are accountable to NSAI. Interested coordinators may apply to NSAI.d

- Also see the listing for NSAI Songwriters Symposium (formerly NSAI Spring Symposium) in the Workshops section of this book.

THE NATIONAL ASSOCIATION OF COMPOSERS/USA (NACUSA)

P.O. Box 49256, Barrington Station, Los Angeles CA 90049. E-mail: nacusa@music-usa.org. Website: www.music-usa.org/nacusa. **Contact**: Daniel Kessner, president. Estab. 1932. Serves songwriters, musicians and classical composers. "We are of most value to the concert hall composer. Members are serious music composers of all ages and from all parts of the country, who have a real interest in composing, performing, and listening to modern concert hall music. The main purpose of our organization is to perform, publish, broadcast and write news about composers of serious concert hall music—mostly chamber and solo pieces. Composers may achieve national notice of their work through our newsletter and concerts, and the fairly rare feeling of supporting a non-commercial music enterprise dedicated to raising the musical and social position of the serious composer." Offers competitions, lectures, performance opportunities, library and newsletter. Applications accepted year-round. Membership fee: National (regular): $25; National (students/seniors): $15.

- Also see the listing for NACUSA Young Composers' Competition in the Contests section of this book.

Tips "99% of the money earned in music is earned, or so it seems, by popular songwriters who might feel they owe the art of music something, and this is one way they might help support that art. It's a chance to foster fraternal solidarity with their less prosperous, but wonderfully interesting classical colleagues at a time when the very existence of serious art seems to be questioned by the general populace."

OPERA AMERICA

330 Seventh Ave., 16th Floor, New York NY 10001. (212)796-8620. Fax: (212)796-8631. E-mail: info@operaamerica.org. Website: www.operaamerica.org. **Contact:** Rebecca Ackerman, membership manager. Estab. 1970. Members are composers, librettists, musicians, singers, and opera/music theater producers. Offers conferences, workshops, and seminars for artists. Publishes online database of opera/music theater companies in the US and Canada, database of opportunities for performing and creative artists, online directory of opera and musical performances world-wide and US, and an online directory of new works created and being developed by current-day composers and librettists, to encourage the performance of new works. Applications accepted year-round. Publishes quarterly magazine and a variety of electronic newsletters. Membership fee is on a sliding scale by membership level.

PACIFIC NORTHWEST SONGWRITERS ASSOCIATION

P.O. Box 98564, Seattle WA 98198. (206)824-1568. E-mail: pnsapals@hotmail.com. "PNSA is a nonprofit organization, serving the songwriters of the Puget Sound area since 1977. Members have had songs recorded by national artists on singles, albums, videos and network television specials. Several have released their own albums and the group has done an album together. For only $45 per year, PNSA offers monthly workshops, a quarterly newsletter and direct contact with national artists, publishers, producers and record companies. New members are welcome and good times are guaranteed. And remember, the world always needs another great song!"

PITTSBURGH SONGWRITERS ASSOCIATION

222 Pennsylvania Ave., California PA 15419. E-mail: vstragand@aol.com, jferreri@ zoominternet.net. Website: (under construction). **Contact:** Van Stragand (412)418-8647 or Joe Ferreri (724)640-0671. Estab. 1983. "We are a non-profit organization dedicated to helping its members develop and market their songs. Writers of any age and experience level welcome. Current members are from all age brackets. All musical styles and interests are welcome. Our organization wants to serve as a source of quality material for publishers and other industry professionals. We assist members in developing their songs and their professional approach. We provide meetings, showcases, collaboration opportunities, instruction, industry guests, library and social outings. Annual dues: $40 with discounts available for students and seniors. We have no initiation fee. Prospective members are invited to attend two free meetings. Interested parties please call contacts above."

RHODE ISLAND SONGWRITERS' ASSOCIATION (RISA)

33 Greylawn Ave., Warwick RI 02889. E-mail: generalinfo@risongwriters.com; memberships@risongwriters.com. Website: www.risongwriters.com. **Co-Chairs:** John Fuzek and Bill Furney. Estab. 1993. "Membership consists of novice and professional songwriters. RISA provides opportunities to the aspiring writer or performer as well as the established regional artists who have recordings, are published and perform regularly. The only eligibility requirement is an interest in the group and the group's goals. Non-writers are welcome as well." The main purpose is to "encourage, foster and conduct the art and craft of original musical and/or lyrical composition through education, information, collaboration and performance." Offers instruction, newsletter, lectures, workshops, performance opportunities and evaluation services. Applications accepted year-round. Membership fees: $25/year (individual); $30/year (family/band). "The group holds twice monthly critique sessions; twice monthly performer showcases (one performer featured) at a local coffeehouse; songwriter showcases (usually 6-8 performers); weekly open mikes; and a yearly songwriter festival called 'Hear In Rhode Island,' featuring approximately 50 Rhode Island acts, over two days."

SAN DIEGO SONGWRITERS GUILD

3368 Governor Dr., Suite F-326, San Diego CA 92122. E-mail: sdsongwriters@hotmail. com. Website: www.sdsongwriters.org. **Contact:** Joseph Carmel, membership/ correspondence. Estab. 1982. "Members range from their early 20s to senior citizens with a variety of skill levels. Several members perform and work full time in music. Many are published and have songs recorded. Some are getting major artist record cuts. Most members are from San Diego county. New writers are encouraged to participate and meet others. All musical styles are represented." The purpose of this organization is to "serve the needs of songwriters and artists, especially helping them in the business and craft of songwriting through industry guest appearances." Offers competitions, newsletter, workshops, performance opportunities, discounts on services offered by fellow members, in-person song pitches and evaluations by publishers, producers and A&R executives. Applications accepted year-round. Membership dues: $25 annually. Meeting admission for non-members: $20 (may be applied toward membership if joining within 30 days). **Tips** "Members benefit most from participation in meetings and concerts. Generally, one major meeting held monthly. E-mail for meeting details. Can join at meetings."

SESAC INC.

55 Music Square East, Nashville, TN, 37203. (615)320-0055. Fax: (615) 329-9627. **New York**: 152 W. 57th St., 57th Floor, New York NY 10019. (212)586-3450. Fax: (212)489-5699. Website: www.sesac.com. **Los Angeles**: 501 Santa Monica Blvd., Suite 450, Santa Monica CA 90401. (310)393-9671. Fax: (310)393-6497; **Atlanta**: 981 Joseph E. Lowery Blvd NW, Ste 111, Atlanta, GA 30318. (404)867-1330. Fax: (404)897-1306; **Miami:** 420 Lincoln Rd, Ste 502, Miami FL 33139, (305)534-7500. Fax: (305)534-7578; **London:** 67 Upper Berkeley St., London WIH 7QX United Kingdom. (020)76169284. **Contact:** Trevor Gale, senior vice president writer/publisher relations. Chief Operating Officer: Pat Collins. "SESAC is a selective organization taking pride in having a repertory based on quality rather than quantity. Serves writers and publishers in all types of music who have their works performed by radio, television, nightclubs, cable TV, etc. Purpose of organization is to collect and distribute performance royalties to all active affiliates. As a SESAC affiliate, the individual may obtain equipment insurance at competitive rates. Music is reviewed upon invitation by the Writer/Publisher Relations dept."

⊠ SOCAN

(SOCIETY OF COMPOSERS, AUTHORS AND MUSIC PUBLISHERS OF CANADA) Head Office: 41 Valleybrook Dr., Toronto ON M3B 2S6 Canada. English Information Center: (866)(307)6226. French Information Center: (866) (800)55-SOCAN. Fax: (416)445-7108. Website: www.socan.ca. CEO: Andre LeBel. Vice President Member Relations & General Manager, West Coast Division: Kent Sturgeon. Vice President Member Services: Jeff King. Director, Member Relations: Lynne Foster. " SOCAN is the Canadian copyright collective for the communication and performance of musical works. We administer these rights on behalf of our members (composers, lyricists, songwriters, and their publishers) and those of affiliated international organizations by licensing this use of their music in Canada. The fees collected are distributed as royalties to our members and to affiliated organizations throughout the world. We also distribute royalties received from those organizations to our members for the use of their music worldwide. SOCAN has offices in Toronto, Montreal, Vancouver, Edmonton, and Dartmouth."

SOCIETY OF COMPOSERS & LYRICISTS

8447 Wilshire Blvd., Suite 401, Beverly Hills CA 90211. (310)281-2812. Fax: (310)284-4861. E-mail: execdir@thescl.com. Website: www.thescl.com. The professional nonprofit trade organization for members actively engaged in writing music/lyrics for films, TV, and/ or video games, or are students of film composition or songwriting for film. Primary mission is to advance the interests of the film and TV music community. Offers an award-winning quarterly publication, educational seminars, screenings, special member-only events, and other member benefits. Applications accepted year-round. Membership fee: $135 Full Membership (composers, lyricists, songwriters—film/TV music credits must be submitted); $85 Associate/Student Membership for composers, lyricists, songwriters without credits only; $135 Sponsor/Special Friend Membership (music editors, music supervisors, music attorneys, agents, etc.).

⬥ ⬜ SODRAC INC.

Tower B, Suite 1010, 1470 Peel Montreal Quebec H3A 1T1 Canada. (514)845-3268. Fax: (514)845-3401. E-mail: sodrac@sodrac.ca. Website: www.sodrac.ca **Contact:** Jean-Francois Marquis, membership department (author, composer and publisher) or Gilles Lessard, visual arts and crafts department (visual artist and rights owner). Estab. 1985. "SODRAC is a reproduction rights collective society facilitating the clearing of rights on musical and artistic works based on the Copyright Board of Canada tariffs or through collective agreements concluded with any users and is responsible for the distribution of royalties to its national and international members. The Society counts over 6,000 Canadian members and represents musical repertoire originating from nearly 100 foreign countries and manages the right of over 25,000 Canadian and foreign visual artists. SODRAC is the only reproduction rights society in Canada where both songwriters and music publishers are represented, equally and directly." Serves those with an interest in songwriting and music publishing no matter what their age or skill level is. " Members must have written or published at least one musical work that has been reproduced on an audio (CD, cassette, or LP) or audio-visual support (TV, DVD, video), or published five musical works that have been recorded and used for commercial purposes. The new member will benefit from a society working to secure his reproduction rights (mechanicals) and broadcast mechanicals." Applications accepted year-round.

SONGWRITERS ASSOCIATION OF WASHINGTON

PMB 106-137, 4200 Wisconsin Ave. NW, Washington DC 20016. (301)654-8434. E-mail: membership@SAW.org. Website: www.saw.org. Estab. 1979. "SAW is a nonprofit organization operated by a volunteer board of directors. It is committed to providing its members opportunities to learn more about the art of songwriting, learn more about the music business, perform in public, and connect with fellow songwriters. SAW sponsors various events to achieve these goals: workshops, open mics, songwriter exchanges, and showcases. In addition, SAW organizes the Mid-Atlantic Song Contest open to entrants nationwide each year; "the competition in 2008 will be the 25th contest SAW has adjudicated since 1982, making it one of the longest-running song contests in the nation." (Contest information masc@saw.org). As well as maintaining a website, SAW publishes a monthly e-newsletter for members containing information on upcoming local events, member news, contest information, and articles of interest, as well as a member directory, a valuable tool for networking. Joint membership with the Washington Area

Music Association as well as a two-year membership are available at a savings. Use the contact information above for membership inquiries.

THE SONGWRITERS GUILD OF AMERICA

Los Angeles Office: (323)462-1108. E-mail: la@songwritersguild.com. **Nashville Office**: 209 10th Ave. S., Suite 321, Nashville TN 37203. (615)742-9945. Fax: (615)742-9948. E-mail: nash@songwritersguild.com. **SGA Administration:** 209 10th Ave. S., Suite 321, Nashville TN 37203. (615)742-9945. Fax: (615)742-9948. E-mail: corporate@songwritersguild.com. President: Rick Carnes. SGAF Director of Operations: Mark Saxon. Estab. 1931. "The Songwriters Guild of America Foundation offers a series of workshops with discounts for some to SGA members, including online classes and song critique opportunities. There is a charge for some songwriting classes and seminars; however, online classes and some monthly events may be included with an SGA membership. Charges vary depending on the class or event. Current class offerings and workshops vary. Visit website to sign up for the newsletter and e-events, and for more information on current events and workshops. Some current events in Nashville are the Ask-a-Pro and ProCritique sessions that give SGA members the opportunity to present their songs and receive constructive feedback from industry professionals. Various performance opportunities are also available to members, including an SGA Showcase at the Bluebird. The New York office hosts a weekly Pro-Shop, which is coordinated by producer/musician/award winning singer Ann Johns Ruckert. For each of six sessions an active publisher, producer or A&R person is invited to personally screen material from SGA writers. Participation is limited to 10 writers and an audit of one session. Audition of material is required. Various performance opportunities and critique sessions are also available from time to time. SGAF Week is held periodically and is a week of scheduled events and seminars of interest to songwriters that includes workshops, seminars and showcases."

- Also see the Songwriters Guild of America listing in the Organizations section.

SONGWRITERS HALL OF FAME (SONGHALL)

330 W. 58th St., Suite 411, New York NY 10019-1827. (212)957-9230. Fax: (212)957-9227. E-mail: info@songhall.org. Website: www.songhall.org. **Contact**: Managing Director: April Anderson. Estab. 1969. "SongHall membership consists of songwriters of all levels, music publishers, producers, record company executives, music attorneys, and lovers of popular music of all ages. There are different levels of membership, all able to vote in the election for inductees, except Associates who pay only $25 in dues, but are unable to vote. SongHall's mission is to honor the popular songwriters who write the soundtrack for the world, as well as providing educational and networking opportunities to our members through our workshop and showcase programs." Offers: newsletter, workshops, performance opportunities, networking meetings with industry pros and scholarships for excellence in songwriting. Applications accepted year-round. Membership fees: $25 and up.

SONGWRITERS RESOURCE NETWORK

PMB 135, 6327-C SW Capitol Hill Hwy, Portland OR 97239-1937. E-mail: info@ SongwritersResourceNetwork.com. Website: www.SongwritersResourceNetwork.com. **Contact:** Steve Cahill, president. Estab. 1998. "For songwriters and lyricists of every kind, from beginners to advanced." No eligibility requirements. "Purpose is to provide free information to help songwriters develop their craft, market their songs, and learn about songwriting opportunities." Sponsors the annual Great American Song Contest, offers marketing tips and website access to music industry contacts. "We provide leads to publishers, producers and other music industry professionals." Visit website or send SASE for more information.

- Also see the listing for Great American Song Contest in the Contests and Awards section of this book.

SOUTHWEST VIRGINIA SONGWRITERS ASSOCIATION

P.O. Box 698, Salem VA 24153. Website: www.svsa.info. **Contact:** Greg Trafidlo. Estab. 1981. 80 members of all ages and skill all levels, mainly country, folk, gospel, contemporary and rock but other musical interests too. "The purpose of SVSA is to increase, broaden and expand the knowledge of each member and to support, better and further the progress and success of each member in songwriting and related fields of endeavor." Offers performance opportunities, evaluation services, instruction, newsletter, workshops, monthly meetings and monthly newsletter. Application accepted year-round. Membership fee: $20/year.

TEXAS ACCOUNTANTS & LAWYERS FOR THE ARTS

1540 Sul Ross, Houston TX 77006-4730. (713)526-4876. Fax: (713)526-1299. E-mail: info@ talarts.org. Website: www.talarts.org. **Contact:** Erin Rodgers, staff attorney, or Kristian Salinas, office manager. Estab. 1979. TALA's members include accountants, attorneys, museums, theatre groups, dance groups, actors, artists, musicians and filmmakers. Our members are of all age groups and represent all facets of their respective fields. TALA is a nonprofit organization that provides pro bono legal and accounting services to income-eligible artists from all disciplines and to nonprofit arts organizations. TALA also provides mediation services for resolving disputes as a low cost-nonadversarial alternative to litigation. Offers newsletter, lectures, library and workshops. Applications accepted year-round. Annual membership fee for students: $30; artists: $50; bands: $100; non-profit organizations: $200.

Tips TALA's speakers program presents low-cost seminars on topics such as The Music Business, Copyright and Trademark, and The Business of Writing. These seminars are held annually at a location in Houston. TALA's speaker's program also provides speakers for seminars by other organizations.

Resources

TORONTO MUSICIANS' ASSOCIATION

A.F. or M Local 149, 15 Gervais Dr., Suite 500, Toronto ON M3C 1Y8 Canada. (416)421-1020. Fax: (416)421-7011. E-mail: info@tma149.ca. Website: www.tma149.ca. Executive Director: Jim Biros. Estab. 1887. "Local 149 of the American Federation of Musicians of the United States and Canada is the Professional Association for musicians in the greater Toronto Area. A member driven association of 3,500 members, the TMA represents professional musicians in all facets of music in the greater Toronto area. Dedicated to the development of musical talent and skills the Toronto Musicians' Association has for the past 100 years fostered the opportunity through the collective efforts of our members for professional musicians to live and work in dignity while receiving fair compensation." Joining fee: $225 (Canadian); student fee: $100 (Canadian). Thereafter, members pay $61.25 per quarter. Student must have proof of school enrollment.

VOLUNTEER LAWYERS FOR THE ARTS

1 E. 53rd St., 6th Floor, New York NY 10022. (212)319-ARTS (2787), ext. 1 (Monday-Friday 10am-6pm). Fax: (212)752-6575. E-mail: epaul@vlany.org. Website: www.vlany. org. **Contact:** Elena M. Paul, esq., executive director. Estab. 1969. Serves songwriters, musicians and all performing, visual, literary and fine arts artists and groups. Offers legal assistance and representation to eligible individual artists and arts organizations who cannot afford private counsel and a mediation service. VLA sells publications on arts-related issues and offers educational conferences, lectures, seminars and workshops. In addition, there are affiliates nationwide who assist local arts organizations and artists. Call for information.

WEST COAST SONGWRITERS

(formerly Northern California Songwriters Association), 1724 Laurel St., Suite 120, San Carlos CA 94070. (650)654-3966. E-mail: ian@westcoastsongwriters.org. Website: www. westcoastsongwriters.org. **Contact:** Ian Crombie, executive director. Serves songwriters and musicians. Estab. 1979. "Our 1,200 members are lyricists and composers from ages 16-80, from beginners to professional songwriters. No eligibility requirements. Our purpose is to provide the education and opportunities that will support our writers in creating and marketing outstanding songs. WCS provides support and direction through local networking and input from Los Angeles and Nashville music industry leaders, as well as valuable marketing opportunities. Most songwriters need some form of collaboration, and by being a member they are exposed to other writers, ideas, critiquing, etc." Offers annual West Coast Songwriters Conference, "the largest event of its kind in northern California. This 2-day event held the second weekend in September features 16 seminars, 50 screening sessions (over 1,200 songs listened to by industry professionals) and a sunset concert with hit songwriters performing their songs." Also offers monthly visits from major publishers, songwriting classes, competitions, seminars conducted by hit songwriters ("we sell audio tapes of our seminars—list of tapes available on request"), mail-in song-screening service for members who cannot attend due to time or location, a monthly e-newsletter, monthly performance opportunities and workshops. Applications accepted year-round. Dues: $40/year for students; $75/year, regular membership; $99 band membership; $100 + contributing membership.

Tips "WCS's functions draw local talent and nationally recognized names together. This is of a tremendous value to writers outside a major music center. We are developing a strong songwriting community in Northern and Southern California. We serve the San Jose, Monterey Bay, East Bay, San Francisco, Los Angeles, Sacramento and Portland, WA areas and we have the support of some outstanding writers and publishers from both Los Angeles and Nashville. They provide us with invaluable direction and inspiration."

Workshops & Conferences

For a songwriter just starting out, conferences and workshops can provide valuable learning opportunities. At conferences, songwriters can have their songs evaluated, hear suggestions for further improvement and receive feedback from music business experts. They are also excellent places to make valuable industry contacts. Workshops can help a songwriter improve his craft and learn more about the business of songwriting. They may involve classes on songwriting and the business, as well as lectures and seminars by industry professionals.

Each year, hundreds of workshops and conferences take place all over the country. Songwriters can choose from small regional workshops held in someone's living room to large national conferences such as South by Southwest in Austin, Texas, which hosts more than 6,000 industry people, songwriters and performers. Many songwriting organizations—national and local—host workshops that offer instruction on just about every songwriting topic imaginable, from lyric writing and marketing strategy to contract negotiation. Conferences provide songwriters the chance to meet one on one with publishing and record company professionals and give performers the chance to showcase their work for a live audience (usually consisting of industry people) during the conference. There are conferences and workshops that address almost every type of music, offering programs for songwriters, performers, musical playwrights and much more.

This section includes national and local workshops and conferences with a brief description of what they offer, when they are held and how much they cost to attend. Write or call any that interest you for further information. To find out what workshops or conferences take place in specific parts of the country, see the Geographic Index at the end of this book.

APPEL FARM ARTS AND MUSIC FESTIVAL

P.O. Box 888, Elmer NJ 08318. (856)358-2472. Fax: (856)358-6513. E-mail: perform@ appelfarm.org. Website: www.appelfarm.org. **Contact:** Sean Timmons, artistic director. Estab Festival: 1989; Series: 1970. "Our annual open air festival is the highlight of our year-round Performing Arts Series which was established to showcase the finest contemporary songwriters. Festival includes a diversity of styles including rock, roots, folk, world music, blues, etc." Past performers have included The Avett Brothers, Rufus Wainwright, Fountains of Wayne, Indigo Girls, Ani DiFranco, They Might Be Giants, Randy Newman, Jackson Browne, David Gray and more. Programs for songwriters and musicians include performance opportunities as part of Festival and Performing Arts Series and an emerging artists series, First Fridays @ The Gallery. Programs for musical playwrights also include performance opportunities as part of Performing Arts Series. Festival is a one-day event held in June, and Performing Arts Series is held year-round. Both are held at the Appel Farm Arts and Music Center in Southern New Jersey. Up to 20 songwriters/musicians participate in each event. Participants are songwriters, individual vocalists, bands, ensembles, vocal groups, composers, individual instrumentalists and dance/mime/movement. Participants are selected by on line submissions. Applicants should forward links to their web sites, myspace pages etc. Application materials accepted year round. Faculty opportunities are available as part of residential Summer Arts Program for children, July/August.

ASCAP "I CREATE MUSIC" EXPO

Estab. 2006. (800)278-1287. Fax: (212)621-6387. E-mail: expo@ascap.com. Website: www.ascap.com. 3-day event held in April.

ASCAP MUSICAL THEATRE WORKSHOP

1 Lincoln Plaza, New York NY 10023. (212)621-6234. Fax: (212)621-6558. E-mail: mkerker@ascap.com. Website: www.ascap.com. **Contact:** Michael A. Kerker, director of musical theatre. Estab. 1981. Workshop is for musical theatre composers and lyricists only. Its purpose is to nurture and develop new musicals for the theatre. Offers programs for songwriters. Offers programs annually, usually April through May. Event took place in New York City. Four musical works are selected. Others are invited to audit the workshop. Participants are amateur and professional songwriters, composers and musical playwrights. Participants are selected by demo CD submission. Deadline: mid-March. Also available: the annual ASCAP/Disney Musical Theatre Workshop in Los Angeles. It takes place in January and February. Deadline is late November. Details similar to New York workshop as above.

ASCAP WEST COAST/LESTER SILL SONGWRITERS WORKSHOP

7920 Sunset Blvd., 3rd Floor, Los Angeles CA 90046. (323)883-1000. Fax: (323)883-1049. E-mail: info@ascap.com. Website: www.ascap.com. Annual workshop for advanced songwriters sponsored by the ASCAP Foundation. Re-named in 1995 to honor ASCAP's late Board member and industry pioneer Lester Sill, the workshop takes place over a four-week period and features prominent guest speakers from various facets of the music business. Workshop dates and deadlines vary from year to year; refer to www.ascap.com for updated info. 2010 Deadline was August 27. Applicants must submit two songs on a CD (cassette tapes not accepted), lyric sheets, brief bio and short explanation as to why they would like to participate, e-mail address, and telephone number. Limited number of participants are selected each year.

BMI-LEHMAN ENGEL MUSICAL THEATRE WORKSHOP

7 World Trade Center, 250 Greenwich St., New York NY 10007. (212)230-3000. E-mail: musicaltheatre@bmi.com. Website: www.bmi.com. **Contact:** Jean Banks, senior director of musical theatre. Estab. 1961. " BMI is a music licensing company which collects royalties for affiliated writers and publishers. We offer programs to musical theatre composers, lyricists and librettists. The BMI-Lehman Engel Musical Theatre Workshops were formed if an effort to refresh and stimulate professional writers, as well as to encourage and develop new creative talent for the musical theatre." Each workshop meets 1 afternoon a week for 2 hours at BMI, New York. Participants are professional songwriters, composers and playwrights. BMI-Lehman Musical Theatre Workshop Showcase presents the best of the workshop to producers, agents, record and publishing company execs, press and directors for possible option and production. Go to BMI.com - click on Musical Theatre - for application. Tape and lyrics of 3 compositions required with applications" BMI also sponsors a jazz composers workshop. For more information contact Raette Johnson at rjohnson@bmi.com.

BROADWAY TOMORROW PREVIEWS

c/o Science of Light, Inc., 191 Claremont Ave., Suite 53, New York NY 10027. E-mail: solministry@earthlink.net. Website: www.solministry.com/bway_tom.html. **Contact:** Elyse Curtis, PhD, artistic director. Estab. 1983. Purpose is the enrichment of American theater by nurturing new musicals. Offers series in which composers living in New York city area present self-contained scores of their new musicals in concert. Submission is by audio cassette or CD of music, synopsis, cast breakdown, résumé, reviews, if any, acknowledgement postcard and SASE. Participants selected by screening of submissions. Programs are presented in fall and spring with possibility of full production of works presented in concert.

CMJ MUSIC MARATHON, MUSICFEST & FILMFEST

100 Fifth Av., 11th Floor, New York NY 10011. (212)277-7120. Fax: (212)719-9396. Website: www.cmj.com/marathon/. **Contact:** Operations Manager. Estab. 1981. Premier annual alternative music gathering of more than 9,000 music business and film professionals. Fall, NYC. Features 4 days and nights of more than 50 panels and workshops focusing on every facet of the industry; exclusive film screenings; keynote speeches by the world's most intriguing and controversial voices; exhibition area featuring live performance

stage; over 1,000 of music's brightest and most visionary talents (from the unsigned to the legendary) performing over 4 evenings at more than 50 of NYC's most important music venues. Participants are selected by submitting demonstration tape. Go to website for application (through Sonicbids.com).

CUTTING EDGE MUSIC BUSINESS CONFERENCE

1524 N. Claiborne Ave., New Orleans LA 70116. (504)945-1800. Fax: (504)945-1873. E-mail: cut_edge@bellsouth.net. Website: www.jass.com/cuttingedge. Executive Producer: Eric L. Cager. Showcase Producer: Nathaniel Franklin. Estab. 1993. "The conference is a five-day international conference which covers the business and educational aspects of the music industry. As part of the conference, the New Works showcase features over 200 bands and artists from around the country and Canada in showcases of original music. All music genres are represented." Offers programs for songwriters and performers. "Bands and artists should submit material for consideration of entry into the New Works showcase." Event takes place during August in New Orleans. 1,000 songwriters/musicians participate in each event. Participants are songwriters, vocalists and bands. Send for application. Deadline: June 1. "The Music Business Institute offers a month-long series of free educational workshops for those involved in the music industry. The workshops take place each October. Further information is available via our website."

HOLLYWOOD REPORTER/BILLBOARD FILM & TV MUSIC CONFERENCE

Sofitel LA, 8555 Beverly Blvd., Los Angeles CA 90048. (646)654-4643. E-mail: lkastner@ billboard.com. Website: www.billboardevents.com/. **Contact**: Lisa Kastner. Estab. 1995. Promotes all music for film and television. Offers programs for songwriters and composers. Held at the Directors Guild of America in October. More than 350 songwriters/musicians participate in each event. Participants are professional songwriters, composers, plus producers, directors, etc. Conference panelists are selected by invitation. For registration information, call the Special Events Dept. at Hollywood Reporter. Fee: $349-499/person.

INDEPENDENT MUSIC CONFERENCE

InterMixx.com, Inc., 304 Main Ave., PMB 287, Norwalk CT 06851. (203)606-4649. E-mail: imc08@intermixx.com. Website: www.indiemusicon.com. Executive Director: Noel Ramos. Estab. 1992. "The purpose of the IMC is to bring together rock, hip hop and acoustic music for of panels and showcases. Offers programs for songwriters, composers and performers. 250 showcases at 20 clubs around the city. Also offer a DJ cutting contest." Held annually at the Sheraton Society Hill Hotel in Philadelphia in September. 3,000 amateur and professional songwriters, composers, individual vocalists, bands, individual instrumentalists, attorneys, managers, agents, publishers, A&R, promotions, club owners, etc. participate each year. Send for application.

KERRVILLE FOLK FESTIVAL

Kerrville Festivals, Inc., P.O. Box 291466, Kerrville TX 78029. (830)257-3600. Fax: (830)257-8680. E-mail: info@kerrville-music.com. Website: www.kerrvillefolkfestival. com. **Contact:** Dalis Allen, producer. Estab. 1972. Hosts 3-day songwriters' school, a 4-day music business school and New Folk concert competition sponsored by Performing Songwriter magazine. Festival produced in late spring and late summer. Spring festival lasts 18 days and is held outdoors at Quiet Valley Ranch. 110 or more songwriters participate. Performers are professional songwriters and bands. Participants selected by submitting demo, by invitation only. Send cassette, or CD, promotional material and list of upcoming appearances. "Songwriter and music schools include lunch, experienced professional instructors, camping on ranch and concerts. Rustic facilities. Food available at reasonable cost. Audition materials accepted at above address. These three-day and four-day seminars include noon meals, handouts and camping on the ranch. Usually held during Kerrville Folk Festival, first and second week in June. Write or check the website for contest rules, schools and seminars information, and festival schedules. Also establishing a Phoenix Fund to provide assistance to ill or injured singer/songwriters who find themselves in distress."

- Also see the listing for New Folk Concerts For Emerging Songwriters in the Contests & Awards section of this book.

LAMB'S RETREAT FOR SONGWRITERS

Presented by SPRINGFED ARTS, a nonprofit organization, P.O. Box 304, Royal Oak MI 48068-0304. (248)589-1594. Fax: (248)589-9981. E-mail: johndlamb@ameritech. net. Website: www.springfed.org. **Contact:** John D. Lamb, director. Estab. 1995. Offers programs for songwriters on annual basis. November 4-7, 2010 and November 11-14, 2009 at The Birchwood Inn, Harbor Springs, MI. 60 songwriters/musicians participate in each event. Participants are amateur and professional songwriters. Anyone can participate. Send for registration or e-mail. Deadline: two weeks before event begins. Fee: $275-495, includes all meals. Facilities are single/double occupancy lodging with private baths; 2 conference rooms and hospitality lodge. Offers song assignments, songwriting workshops, song swaps, open mic and one-on-one mentoring. Faculty are noted songwriters, such as Michael Smith, Jonathan Byrd, Anais Mitchell, Don Henry, Sally Barris, LJ Booth. Partial scholarships may be available by writing: Blissfest Music Organization, Jim Gillespie, P.O. Box 441, Harbor Springs, MI 49740. Deadline: 2 weeks before event.

MANCHESTER MUSIC FESTIVAL

P.O. Box 33, Manchester VT 05254. (802)362-1956 or (800)639-5868. Fax: (802)362-0711. E-mail: info@mmfvt.org. Website: www.manchestermusicfestival.org. **Contact:** Robyn Madison, managing director. Estab. 1974. Offers classical music education and performances. Summer program for young professional musicians offered in tandem with a professional concert series in the mountains of Manchester VT. Up to 23 young professionals, age 19 and up, are selected by audition for the Young Artists Program, which provides instruction, performance and teaching opportunities, with full scholarship for all participants. Commissioning opportunities for new music, and performance opportunities for professional chamber ensembles and soloists for both summer and fall/winter concert series. "Celebrating 34 years of fine music."

⬛ MUSIC & ADVERTISING CONFERENCE

(646)654-4660. E-mail: bbevents@billboard.com. Website: www.billboardevents. com. "Join Billboard and Adweek in Chicago to explore how the worlds of music and advertising are intertwined, and examine how big brands, artists and music supervisors are benefiting from working together during captivating keynotes interviews, informative case studies, and interactive panel discussions." Event takes place September 15-16, 2010 in Chicago at The Westin Michigan Avenue. Billboard offers attendees a special room rate to stay at venue. Cost: $259/night (plus tax); registration price: $249 EarlyBird rates; Pre-Registration $349; Full registration $449; walk-up $499.

MUSIC BUSINESS SOLUTIONS/CAREER BUILDING WORKSHOPS

P.O. Box 230266, Boston MA 02123-0266. (888)655-8335. E-mail: success@mbsolutions. com. Website: www.mbsolutions.com. **Contact:** Peter Spellman, director. Estab. 1991. Workshop titles include "Discovering Your Music Career Niche," "How to Release an Independent Record" and "Promoting and Marketing Music in the 21st Century." Offers programs for music entrepreneurs, songwriters, musical playwrights, composers and performers. Offers programs year-round, annually and bi-annually. Event takes place at various colleges, recording studios, hotels, conferences. 10-100 songwriters/musicians participate in each event. Participants are both amateur and professional songwriters, vocalists, music business professionals, composers, bands, musical playwrights and instrumentalists. Anyone can participate. Fee: varies. "Music Business Solutions offers a number of other services and programs for both songwriters and musicians including: private music career counseling, business plan development and internet marketing; publication of Music Biz Insight: Power Reading for Busy Music Professionals, a bimonthly e-zine chock full of music management and marketing tips and resources. Free subscription with e-mail address."

THE NEW HARMONY PROJECT

P.O. Box 441062, Indianapolis IN 46244-1062. (317)464-1103. E-mail: newharmony@ne-wharmonyproject.org. Website: www.newharmonyproject.org. **Contact:** Joel Grynheim, conference director. Estab. 1986. Selected scripts receive various levels of development with rehearsals and readings, both public and private. "Our mission is to nurture writers and their life-affirming scripts. This includes plays, screenplays, musicals and TV scripts." Offers programs for musical playwrights. Event takes place in May/June in southwest Indiana. Participants are amateur and professional writers and media professionals. Send for application.

▨ NEWPORT FOLK FESTIVAL

P.O. Box 3865, Newport, RI 02840. (401)848-5055. E-mail: info@newportfolkfest.net. Website: www.newportfolkfest.com. **Contact:** George Wein. July 30-August 1, 2010. Held at the International Tennis Hall of Fame and Fort Adams State Park.

▨ NEWPORT JAZZ FESTIVAL

Newport, RI. E-mail: jazz@newportjazzfest.net. Website: www.newportjazzfest.com. **Contact:** George Wein. Estab. 1954. "Hailed by the New York Times as 'the festival that put jazz festivals on the map,' the Newport Jazz Festival®, now the CareFusion Newport Jazz Festival, was founded by Jazz pianist George Wein in 1954 as the first outdoor music festival of its kind devoted entirely to Jazz, and is now universally acknowledged as the grandfather of all Jazz festivals. During the last half-century, the name Newport has become synonymous with the best in Jazz music. In its long illustrious history, the Newport Jazz Festival has presented a virtual pantheon of Jazz immortals alongside an array of rising young artists: Duke Ellington's 1956 rebirth framing Paul Gonzalves' epic solo; subject of the classic 1958 documentary "Jazz on a Summer's Day; origin of famous recordings by Thelonious Monk, John Coltrane and Miles Davis; showcase for emerging young masters including Wynton Marsalis, Diana Krall, Joshua Redman and Esperanza Spalding. Referred to as a Mecca of Jazz, the event draws thousands of people from all over the world to it's uniquely picturesque outdoor stages at the International Tennis Hall of Fame and Fort Adams State Park."

NORFOLK CHAMBER MUSIC FESTIVAL

September-May address: Woolsey Hall, 500 College St., Suite 301, New Haven CT 06520. (203)432-1966. Fax: (203)432-2136. E-mail: norfolk@yale.edu. Website: www.yale.edu/norfolk. June-August address: Ellen Battell, Stoeckel Estate, Routes 44 and 272, Norfolk CT 06058. (860)542-3000. Fax: (860)542-3004. **Contact:** Deanne E. Chin, operations manager. Estab. 1941. Festival season of chamber music. Offers programs for composers and performers. Offers programs summer only. Approximately 45 fellows participate. Participants are up-and-coming composers and instrumentalists. Participants are selected by following a screening round. Auditions are held in New Haven, CT. Send for application. Deadline: January 16. Fee: $50. Held at the Ellen Battell Stoeckel Estate, the Festival offers a magnificent Music Shed with seating for 1,000, practice facilities, music library, dining hall, laundry and art gallery. Nearby are hiking, bicycling and swimming.

▨ NORTH BY NORTHEAST MUSIC FESTIVAL AND CONFERENCE

189 Church St., Lower Level, Toronto ON M5B 1Y7 Canada. (416)863-6963. Fax: (416)863-0828. E-mail: info@nxne.com. Website: www.nxne.com. **Contact:** Andy McClean, managing director. Estab. 1995. "Our festival takes place mid-June at over 30 venues across downtown Toronto, drawing over 2,000 conference delegates, 500 bands and 50,000 music fans. Musical genres include everything from folk to funk, roots to rock, polka to punk and all points in between, bringing exceptional new talent, media front-runners,

music business heavies and music fans from all over the world to Toronto." Participants include emerging and established songwriters, vocalists, composers, bands and instrumentalists. Festival performers are selected by submitting a CD and accompanying press kit or applying through sonicbids.com. Application forms are available by website or by calling the office. Submission period each year is from November 1 to the third weekend in January. Submissions "early bird" fee: $25. Conference registration fee: $149-249. "Our conference is held at the deluxe Holiday Inn on King and the program includes mentor sessions—15-minute one-on-one opportunities for songwriters and composers to ask questions of industry experts, roundtables, panel discussions, keynote speakers, etc. North By Northeast 2008 will be held June 12-15."

NSAI SONG CAMPS

1710 Roy Acuff Place, Nashville TN 37023. 1-800-321-6008 or (615)256-3354. Fax: (615)256-0034. E-mail: songcamps@nashvillesongwriters.com. Website: www. nashvillesongwriters.com. **Contact:** Deanie Williams, NSAI Events Director. Estab. 1992. Offers programs strictly for songwriters. Event held 4 times/year in Nashville. "We provide most meals and lodging is available. We also present an amazing evening of music presented by the faculty." Camps are 3 days long, with 36-112 participants, depending on the camp. "There are different levels of camps, some having preferred prerequisites. Each camp varies. Please call, e-mail or refer to website. It really isn't about the genre of music, but the quality of the song itself. Song Camp strives to strengthen the writer's vision and skills, therefore producing the better song. Song Camp is known as 'boot camp' for songwriters. It is guaranteed to catapult you forward in your writing! Participants are all aspiring songwriters led by a pro faculty. We do accept lyricists only and composers only with the hopes of expanding their scope." Participants are selected through submission of 2 songs with lyric sheet. Song Camp is open to NSAI members, although anyone can apply and upon acceptance join the organization. There is no formal application form. See website for membership and event information.

- Also see the listing for Nashville Songwriters Association International (NSAI) in the Organizations section of this book.

NSAI SONGWRITERS SONGPOSIUM

1710 Roy Acuff Pl., Nashville TN 37203. (615)256-3354 OR 1-800-321-6008. Fax: (615)256-0034. E-mail: events@NashvilleSongwriters.com. Website: www.nashvillesongwriters.com. Covers "all types of music. Participants take part in publisher evaluations, as well as large group sessions with different guest speakers." Offers annual programs for songwriters. Event takes place in April in downtown Nashville. 300 amateur songwriters/musicians participate in each event. Send for application.

⚑ ORFORD FESTIVAL

Orford Arts Centre, 3165 Chemim DuParc, Orford QC J1X 7A2 Canada. (819)843-9871 or 1-800-567-6155. Fax: (819)843-7274. E-mail: centre@arts-orford.org. Website: www.

arts-orford.org. **Contact:** Anne-Marie Dubois, registrar/information manager. Artistic Coordinator: Nicolas Bélanger. Estab. 1951. "Each year, the Orford Arts Centre produces up to 35 concerts in the context of its Music Festival. It receives artists from all over the world in classical and chamber music." Offers master classes for music students, young professional classical musicians and chamber music ensembles. New offerings include master classes for all instruments,voice, and opera. Master classes last 2 months and take place at Orford Arts Centre from the end of June to the middle of August. 350 students participate each year. Participants are selected by demo tape submissions. Send for application. Closing date for application is mid to late March. Check our website for specific dates and deadlines. Scholarships for qualified students.

N ⊕ REGGAE SUMFEST

Shops 9 & 10 Parkway Plaza, Rose Hall, Montego Bay, Jamaica. Fax: 953-8295. E-mail: office@reggaesumfest.com. Website: reggaesumfest.com. **Contact:** Tina Mae Davis, administration manager and festival manager. "Reggae Sumfest is a musical event to which we welcome 30,000+ patrons each year. The festival showcases the best of Dancehall and Reggae music, as well as top R & B/Hip Hop performers. The festival also offers delicious Jamaican cuisine as well as arts and crafts from all over the island. The main events of the festival is held at Catherine Hall, Montego Bay, Jamaica over a three-day period which usually falls in the third week of July, from Sunday to Saturday." Reggae Sumfest is presented by Summerfest Productions and accepts press kit submissions for persons wishing to perform at the festival between November and January each year. Send to address above.

THE SONGWRITERS GUILD OF AMERICA FOUNDATION

1560 Broadway, Suite #408, New York NY 10036. (212)768-7902. E-mail: ny@ songwritersguild.com . Website: www.songwritersguild.com. Director of Operations: Mark Saxon. The Foundation is in charge of many events, including workshops in the NY, Nashville, and L.A. areas.

SONGWRITERS PLAYGROUND®

75-A Lake Rd., #366, Congers NY 10920. (845)267-0001. E-mail: heavyhitters@earthlink. net. **Contact:** Barbara Jordan, director. Estab. 1990. "To help songwriters, performers and composers develop creative and business skills through the critically acclaimed programs Songwriters Playground[[PIRg]], The 'Reel' Deal on Getting Songs Placed in Film and Television, and the Mind Your Own Business Seminars. We offer programs year-round. Workshops last anywhere from 2-15 hours. Workshops are held at various venues throughout the United States. Prices vary according to the length of the workshop." Participants are amateur and professionals. Anyone can participate. Send or call for application.

SOUTH BY SOUTHWEST MUSIC CONFERENCE

SXSW Headquarters, P.O. Box 4999, Austin TX 78765. (512)467-7979. Fax: (512)451-0754. E-mail: sxsw@sxsw.com. Website: www.sxsw.com. **Contact:** Conference Organizer. **UK and Ireland:** Cill Ruan, 7 Ard na Croise, Thurles, Co. Tipperary Ireland. Phone: 353-504-26488. Fax: 353-504-26787. E-mail: una@sxsw.com. **Contact:** Una Johnston. **Europe:** Einsiedlerweg 6, D-72074 Tuebingen-Pfrondorf 72074, Germany. (49-7071-885-604. E-mail: mirko@sxsw.com. **Contact:** Mirko Whitfield. **Asia:** Meijidori Bldg. 403, 2-3-21 Kabuki-cho Shinjuku-ku, Tokyo 160-0021 Japan. Phone: +82 3-5292-5551. Fax: +82 3-5292-5552. E-mail: info@sxsw-asia.com. **Contact:** Hiroshi Asada. **Australia/New Zealand/Hawaii:** 20 Hordern St., Newtown NSW 2042 Australia. Phone: 61-2-9557-7766. Fax: 61-2-9557-7788. E-mail: tripp@sxsw.om. **Contact:** Phil Tripp. Estab. 1987. South by Southwest (SXSW) is a private company based in Austin, Texas, with a year-round staff of professionals dedicated to building and delivering conference and festival events for entertainment and related media industry professionals. Since 1987, SXSW has produced the internationally-recognized music and media conference and festival (SXSW). As the entertainment business adjusted to issues of future growth and development, in 1994, SXSW added conferences and festivals for the film industry (SXSW Film) as well as for the blossoming interactive media (SXSW Interactive Festival). Now three industry events converge in Austin during a Texas-sized week, mirroring the ever increasing convergence of entertainment/media outlets. The next SXSW Music Conference and Festival will be held March 16-20, 2011 at the Austin Convention Center in Austin, TX. Offers panel discussions, "Crash Course" educational seminars and nighttime showcases. SXSW Music seeks out speakers who have developed unique ways to create and sell music. From Thursday through Saturday, the conference includes over fifty sessions including a panel of label heads discussing strategy, interviews with notable artists, topical discussions, demo listening sessions and the mentor program. And when the sun goes down, a multitude of performances by musicians and songwriters from across the country and around the world populate the SXSW Music Festival, held in venues in central Austin." Write, e-mail or visit website for dates and registration instructions.
Tips "Go to the website in August to apply for showcase consideraton. SXSW is also involved in North by Northeast (NXNE), held in Toronto, Canada in late Spring."

THE SWANNANOA GATHERING—CONTEMPORARY FOLK WEEK

Warren Wilson College, P.O. Box 9000, Asheville NC 28815-9000. E-mail: gathering@ warren-wilson.edu. Website: www.swangathering.com. Director: Jim Magill. "For anyone who ever wanted to make music for an audience, we offer a comprehensive week in artist development, including classes in Songwriting, Performance, and Vocal Coaching, 2010 staff included Christine Lavin, Peter Mulvey, Catie Curtis, Sara Hickman, Abbie Gardner, Vance Gilbert, Jack Williams, Jon Vezner, David Roth, Siobhan Quinn, and Ray Chesna." For a brochure or other info contact The Swannanoa Gathering at the phone number/ address above. Takes place last week in July. 2010 Tuition: $440. Housing (including all meals): $ 350. Annual program of The Swannanoa Gathering Folk Arts Workshops.

Resources

THE TEN-MINUTE MUSICALS PROJECT

P.O. Box 461194, West Hollywood CA 90046. E-mail: info@TenMinuteMusicals.org. Website: www.TenMinuteMusicals.org. **Contact:** Michael Koppy, producer. Estab. 1986. Promotes short complete stage musicals. Offers programs for songwriters, composers and musical playwrights. "Works selected are generally included in full-length 'anthology musical'—11 of the first 16 selected works are now in the show *Stories 1.0,* for instance." Awards a $250 royalty advance for each work selected. Participants are amateur and professional songwriters, composers and musical playwrights. Participants are selected by demonstration CD or DVD, script, lead sheets. Send website for submission guidelines. Deadline: August 31st annually.

TUNESMITH PRO—THE NEXT STEP

Tunesmith Entertainment, 1002 18th Ave. South, Nashville TN 37212. (812)608-0686. E-mail: info@tunesmith.net. Website: www.tunesmithpro.ning.com; www.tunesmith. net/forums. **Contact**: Nancy Cassidy. Based on beautiful music row in Nashville Tunesmith Entertainment offers songwriters and artists in all genres of music the NEXT STEP in their musical careers. If you have been to school long enough and want to get in the top level of the music business, visit our websites today for more information.

UNDERCURRENTS

P.O. Box 94040, Cleveland OH 44101-6040. (440)331-0700. E-mail: music@undercurrents. com. Website: www.undercurrents.com. **Contact:** John Latimer, executive director. Estab. 1989. A music, event and art marketing and promotion network with online and offline exposure featuring music showcases, seminars, trade shows, networking forums. Ongoing programs and performances for songwriters, composers, and performers. Participants are selected by EPK, demo, biography and photo. Register at www.undercurrents.com.

WEST COAST SONGWRITERS CONFERENCE

(formerly Northern California Songwriters Association Conference), 1724 Laurel St., Suite 120, San Carlos CA 94070. (650)654-3966. E-mail: info@westcoastsongwriters.org. Website: www.westcoastsongwriters.org. **Contact:** Ian Crombie, executive director. Estab. 1980. "Conference offers opportunity and education. 16 seminars, 50 song screening sessions (1,500 songs reviewed), performance showcases, one on one sessions and concerts." Offers programs for lyricists, songwriters, composers and performers. "During the year we have competitive live Songwriter competitions. Winners go into the playoffs. Winners of the playoffs perform at the sunset concert at the conference." Event takes place second weekend in September at Foothill College, Los Altos Hills CA. Over 500 songwriters/musicians participate in this event. Participants are songwriters, composers, musical playwrights, vocalists, bands, instrumentalists and those interested in a career in the music business. Send for application. Deadline: September 1. Fee: $150-275. "See our listing in the Organizations section."

WESTERN WIND WORKSHOP IN ENSEMBLE SINGING

263 W. 86th St., New York NY 10024. (212)873-2848 or (800)788-2187. Fax: (212)873-2849. E-mail: workshops@westernwind.org. Website: www.westernwind.org. **Contact**: William Zukoff, executive producer. Estab. 1981. Participants learn the art of ensemble singing—no conductor, one on-a-part. Workshop focuses on blend, diction, phrasing and production. Offers programs for performers. Limited talent-based scholarship available. Offers programs annually. Takes place June, July and August in the music department at Smith College, Northampton MA. 70-80 songwriters and/or musicians participate in each event. Participants are amateur and professional vocalists. Anyone can participate. Send for application or register at their website. Workshop takes place in the Smith College music department. Arrangers' works are frequently studied and performed. Also offers additional workshops President's Day weekend in Brattleboro VT and Columbus Day weekend in Woodstock VT.

WINTER MUSIC CONFERENCE INC.

3450 NE 12th Terrace, Ft. Lauderdale FL 33334. (954)563-4444. Fax: (954)563-1599. E-mail: info@wintermusicconference.com. Website: www.wintermusicconference.com. President: Margo Possenti. Estab. 1985. Features educational seminars and showcases for dance, hip hop, alternative and rap. Offers programs for songwriters and performers. Offers programs annually. Event takes place March of each year in Miami FL. 3,000 songwriters/musicians participate in each event. Participants are amateur and professional songwriters, composers, musical playwrights, vocalists, bands and instrumentalists. Participants are selected by submitting demo tape. Send SASE, visit website or call for application. Deadline: February. Event held at either nightclubs or hotel with complete staging, lights and sound.

Retreats & Colonies

This section provides information on retreats and artists' colonies. These are places for creatives, including songwriters, to find solitude and spend concentrated time focusing on their work. While a residency at a colony may offer participation in seminars, critiques or performances, the atmosphere of a colony or retreat is much more relaxed than that of a conference or workshop. Also, a songwriter's stay at a colony is typically anywhere from one to twelve weeks (sometimes longer), while time spent at a conference may only run from one to fourteen days.

Like conferences and workshops, however, artists' colonies and retreats span a wide range. Yaddo, perhaps the most well-known colony, limits its residencies to artists "working at a professional level in their field, as determined by a judging panel of professionals in the field." The Brevard Music Center offers residencies only to those involved in classical music. Despite different focuses, all artists' colonies and retreats have one thing in common: They are places where you may work undisturbed, usually in nature-oriented, secluded settings.

SELECTING A COLONY OR RETREAT

When selecting a colony or retreat, the primary consideration for many songwriters is cost, and you'll discover that arrangements vary greatly. Some colonies provide residencies as well as stipends for personal expenses. Some suggest donations of a certain amount. Still others offer residencies for substantial sums but have financial assistance available.

When investigating the various options, consider meal and housing arrangements and your family obligations. Some colonies provide meals for residents, while others require residents to pay for meals. Some colonies house artists in one main building; others provide separate cottages. A few have provisions for spouses and families. Others prohibit families altogether.

Overall, residencies at colonies and retreats are competitive. Since only a handful of spots are available at each place, you often must apply months in advance for the time period you desire. A number of locations are open year-round, and you may find planning to go during the "off-season" lessens your competition. Other colonies, however, are only available during certain months. In any case, be prepared to include a sample of your best work with your application. Also, know what project you'll work on while in residence and have alternative projects in mind in case the first one doesn't work out once you're there.

Each listing in this section details fee requirements, meal and housing arrangements, and space and time availability, as well as the retreat's surroundings, facilities and special activities. Of course, before making a final decision, send a SASE to the colonies or retreats that interest you to receive their most up-to-date details. Costs, application requirements and deadlines are particularly subject to change.

MUSICIAN'S RESOURCE

For other listings of songwriter-friendly colonies, see *Musician's Resource* (available from Watson-Guptill—www.watsonguptill.com), which not only provides information about conferences, workshops and academic programs but also residencies and retreats. Also check the Publications of Interest section in this book for newsletters and other periodicals providing this information.

BREVARD MUSIC CENTER

P.O. Box 312, 349 Andante Ln., Brevard NC 28712. (828)862-2100. Fax: (828)884-2036. E-mail: bmc@brevardmusic.org. Website: www.brevardmusic.org. **Contact:** Dorothy Knowles, admissions coordinator. Estab. 1936. Offers 6-week residencies from June through the first week of August. Open to professional and student composers, pianists, vocalists, collaborative pianists and instrumentalists of classical music. A 2-week jazz workshop is offered in June. Accommodates 400 at one time. Personal living quarters include cabins. Offers rehearsal, teaching and practice cabins.

Costs $4,100 for tuition, room and board. Scholarships are available.

Requirements Call for application forms and guidelines. $50 application fee. Participants are selected by audition or demonstration tape and then by invitation. There are 80 different audition sites throughout the US.

⊕ THE TYRONE GUTHRIE CENTRE

Annaghmakerrig, Newbliss, County Monaghan, Ireland. (353)(047)54003. Fax: (353) (047)54380. E-mail: info@tyroneguthrie.ie. Website: www.tyroneguthrie.ie. **Contact**: Resident Director. Estab. 1981. Offers year-round residencies. Artists may stay for anything from 1 week to 3 months in the Big House, or for up to 6 months at a time in one of the 5 self-catering houses in the old farmyard. Open to artists of all disciplines. Accommodates 13 in the big house and up to 7 in the farmyard cottages. Personal living quarters include bedroom with bathroom en suite. Offers a variety of workspaces. There is a music room for composers and musicians with a Yamaha C3M-PE conservative grand piano, a performance studio with a Yamaha upright, a photographic darkroom and a number of studios for visual artists, one of which is wheelchair accessible. At certain times of the year it is possible, by special arrangement, to accommodate groups of artists, symposiums, master classes, workshops and other collaborations.

Costs Irish and European artists: €300/week for the big house; 150 for self-catering cottages; others pay €650 per week, all found, for a residency in the Big House and 325 per week (plus gas and electricity costs) for one of the self-catering farmyard houses. To qualify for a residency, it is necessary to show evidence of a significant level of achievement in the relevant field.

Requirements Application forms and guidelines are available on the web. Accepts inquiries via telephone, fax or e-mail. Submit application form with CV to be reviewed by the selection committee of board members at quarterly meetings.

THE HAMBIDGE CENTER

Attn: Residency Director, P.O. Box 339, Rabun Gap GA 30568. (706)746-5718. Fax: (706)746-9933 E-mail: director@hambidge.org. Website: www.hambidge.org. **Contact**: Deb Sanders, residency chair. Estab. 1934 (Center); 1988 (residency). Offers 2-week to 2-month residencies year round. Open to all artists. Accommodates 8 at one time. Personal living quarters include a private cottage with kitchen, bath, and living/studio space. Offers

composer/musical studio equipped with piano. Activities include communal dinners February through December and nightly or periodic sharing of works-in-progress.
Costs $200/week
Requirements Send SASE for application forms and guidelines, or available on website. Accepts inquiries via fax and e-mail. Application fee: $30. Deadlines: January 15, April 15, and September 15.

ISLE ROYALE NATIONAL PARK ARTIST-IN-RESIDENCE PROGRAM
800 E. Lakeshore Dr., Houghton MI 49931. (906)482-0984. Fax: (906)482-8753. E-mail: ISRO_Parkinfo@nps.gov. Website: www.nps.gov/ISRO/. **Contact:** Greg Blust, coordinator. Estab. 1991. Offers 2-3 week residencies from mid-June to mid-September. Open to all art forms. Accommodates 1 artist with 1 companion at one time. Personal living quarters include cabin with shared outhouse. A canoe is provided for transportation. Offers a guest house at the site that can be used as a studio. The artist is asked to contribute a piece of work representative of their stay at Isle Royale, to be used by the park in an appropriate manner. During their residency, artists will be asked to share their experience (1 presentation per week of residency, about 1 hour/week) with the public by demonstration, talk, or other means.
Requirements Deadline: postmarked February 16, 2010. Send for application forms and guidelines. Accepts inquiries via fax or e-mail. A panel of professionals from various disciplines, and park representatives will choose the finalists. The selection is based on artistic integrity, ability to reside in a wilderness environment, a willingness to donate a finished piece of work inspired on the island, and the artist's ability to relate and interpret the park through their work.

KALANI OCEANSIDE RETREAT
VILLAGERR 2 Box 4500, Pahoa-Beach Road HI 96778-9724. (808)965-7828 or 800-800-6886. Fax: (808)965-0527. E-mail: kalani@kalani.com. Website: www.kalani.com. **Contact:** Richard Koob, director. Estab. 1980. Offers 2-week to 2-month residencies. Open to all artists who can verify professional accomplishments. Accommodates 120 at one time. Personal living quarters include private cottage or lodge room with private or shared bath. Full (3 meals/day) dining service. Offers shared studio/library spaces. Activities include opportunity to share works in progress, ongoing yoga, hula and other classes; beach, thermal springs, Volcanoes National Park nearby; olympic pool/spa on 120-acre facility.
Costs $84-240/night lodging with stipend, including 3 meals/day. Transportation by rental car from $45/day, Kalani service $65/trip, or taxi $90/trip.
Requirements Accepts inquiries via fax or e-mail.

THE MACDOWELL COLONY
100 High St., Peterborough NH 03458. (603)924-3886. Fax: (603)924-9142. E-mail: admissions@macdowellcolony.org. Website: www.macdowellcolony.org. **Contact:**

Resources

Admissions Director. Estab. 1907. Offers year-round residencies of up to 8 weeks. Open to writers and playwrights, composers, film/video makers, visual artists, architects and interdisciplinary artists. Personal living quarters include single rooms with shared baths. Offers private studios on 450-acre grounds. Travel assistance and artist grants awarded based on need.

Costs None (contributions accepted).

Requirements Visit website for application forms and guidelines (which include work sample requirements). Application deadline: January 15, April 15 and September 15.

SITKA CENTER FOR ART & ECOLOGY

P.O. Box 65, Otis OR 97368-0065. (541)994-5485. Fax: (541)994-8024. E-mail: info@ sitkacenter.org. Website: www.sitkacenter.org. **Contact:** Eric Vines, executive director. Estab. 1971. Offers 4-month residencies in October through January or February through May; shorter residencies are available upon arrangement. Open to emerging, mid-career, or professional artists and naturalists. Residences include 5 living quarters, each self-contained with a sleeping area, kitchen and bathroom. Offers 4 studios. Workshops or presentations are encouraged; an exhibition/presentation to share residents' works is held in January and May.

Costs Residency and housing provided. The resident is asked to provide some form of community service on behalf of Sitka.

Requirements *Applications due by April 21 for a Fall or Spring residency.* Send completed application with résumé, 2 letters of recommendation, work samples and SASE. For application details, see website.

VIRGINIA CENTER FOR THE CREATIVE ARTS

154 San Angelo Dr., Amherst VA 24521. (434)946-7236. Fax: (434)946-7239. E-mail: vcca@vcca.com. Website: www.vcca.com. **Contact:** Suny Monk, executive director. Estab. 1971. Offers residencies year-round, typical residency lasts 2 weeks to 2 months. Open to originating artists: composers, writers and visual artists. Accommodates 25 at one time. Personal living quarters include 22 single rooms, 2 double rooms, bathrooms shared with one other person. All meals are served. Kitchens for fellows' use available at studios and residence. The VCCA van goes into town twice a week. Fellows share their work regularly. Four studios have pianos.

Costs No transportation costs are covered. "Artists are accepted into the VCCA without regard for their ability to contribute financially to their residency. Daily cost is $180 per Fellow. We ask Fellows to contribute according to their ability."

Requirements Send SASE for application form or download from website. Applications are reviewed by panelists. Application fee: $30. Deadline: May 15 for October-January residency; September 15 for February-May residency; January 15 for June-September residency.

State & Provincial Grants

A rts councils in the United States and Canada provide assistance to artists (including poets) in the form of fellowships or grants. These grants can be substantial and confer prestige upon recipients; however, **only state or province residents are eligible**. Because deadlines and available support vary annually, query first (with a SASE) or check websites for guidelines.

UNITED STATES ARTS AGENCIES

Alabama State Council on the Arts, 201 Monroe St., Montgomery AL 36130-1800. (334)242-4076. E-mail: staff@arts.alabama.gov. Website: www.arts.state.al.us.

Alaska State Council on the Arts, 411 W. Fourth Ave., Suite 1-E, Anchorage AK 99501-2343. (907)269-6610 or (888)278-7424. E-mail: aksca_info@eed.state.ak.us. Website: www.eed. state.ak.us/aksca.

Arizona Commission on the Arts, 417 W. Roosevelt St., Phoenix AZ 85003-1326. (602)771-6501. E-mail: info@azarts.gov. Website: www.azarts.gov.

Arkansas Arts Council, 1500 Tower Bldg., 323 Center St., Little Rock AR 72201. (501)324-9766. E-mail: info@arkansasarts.com. Website: www.arkansasarts.com.

California Arts Council, 1300 I St., Suite 930, Sacramento CA 95814. (916)322-6555. E-mail: info@caartscouncil.com. Website: www.cac.ca.gov.

Colorado Council on the Arts, 1625 Broadway, Suite 2700, Denver CO 80202. (303)892-3802. E-mail: online form. Website: www.coloarts.state.co.us.

Connecticut Commission on Culture & Tourism, Arts Division, One Financial Plaza, 755 Main St., Hartford CT 06103. (860)256-2800. Website: www.cultureandtourism.org.

Delaware Division of the Arts, Carvel State Office Bldg., 4th Floor, 820 N. French St., Wilmington DE 19801. (302)577-8278 (New Castle Co.) or (302)739-5304 (Kent or Sussex Counties). E-mail: delarts@state.de.us. Website: www.artsdel.org.

District of Columbia Commission on the Arts & Humanities, 410 Eighth St. NW, 5th Floor, Washington DC 20004. (202)724-5613. E-mail: cah@dc.gov. Website: http://dcarts.dc.gov.

Florida Arts Council, Division of Cultural Affairs, R.A. Gray Building, Third Floor, 500 S. Bronough St., Tallahassee FL 32399-0250. (850)245-6470. E-mail: info@florida-arts.org. Website: http://dcarts.dc.gov.

Georgia Council for the Arts, 260 14th St., Suite 401, Atlanta GA 30318. (404)685-2787. E-mail: gaarts@gaarts.org. Website: www.gaarts.org.

Guam Council on the Arts & Humanities Agency, P.O. Box 2950, Hagatna GU 96932. (671)646-2781. Website: www.guam.net.

Hawai'i State Foundation on Culture & the Arts, 2500 S. Hotel St., 2nd Floor, Honolulu HI 96813. (808)586-0300. E-mail: ken.hamilton@hawaii.gov. Website: http.state.hi.us/sfca.

Idaho Commission on the Arts, 2410 N. Old Penitentiary Rd., Boise ID 83712. (208)334-2119 or (800)278-3863. E-mail: info@arts.idaho.gov. Website: www.arts.idaho.gov.

Illinois Arts Council, James R. Thompson Center, 100 W. Randolph, Suite 10-500, Chicago IL 60601. (312)814-6750. E-mail: iac.info@illinois.gov. Website: www.state.il.us/agency/iac.

Indiana Arts Commission, 150 W. Market St., Suite 618, Indianapolis IN 46204. (317)232-1268. E-mail: IndianaArtsCommission@iac.in.gov. Website: www.in.gov/arts.

Iowa Arts Council, 600 E. Locust, Des Moines IA 50319-0290. (515)281-6412. Website: www.iowaartscouncil.org.

Kansas Arts Commission, 700 SW Jackson, Suite 1004, Topeka KS 66603-3761. (785)296-3335. E-mail: KAC@arts.state.ks.us. Website: http://arts.state.ks.us.

Kentucky Arts Council, 21st Floor, Capital Plaza Tower, 500 Mero St., Frankfort KY 40601-1987. (502)564-3757 or (888)833-2787. E-mail: kyarts@ky.gov. Website: http://artscouncil.ky.gov.

Louisiana Division of the Arts, Capitol Annex Bldg., 1051 N. 3rd St., 4th Floor, Room #420, Baton Rouge LA 70804. (225)342-8180. Website: www.crt.state.la.us/arts.

Maine Arts Commission, 193 State St., 25 State House Station, Augusta ME 04333-0025. (207)287-2724. E-mail: MaineArts.info@maine.gov. Website: www.mainearts.com.

Maryland State Arts Council, 175 W. Ostend St., Suite E, Baltimore MD 21230. (410)767-6555. E-mail: msac@msac.org. Website: www.msac.org.

Massachusetts Cultural Council, 10 St. James Ave., 3rd Floor, Boston MA 02116-3803. (617)727-3668. E-mail: mcc@art.state.ma.us. Website: www.massculturalcouncil.org.

Michigan Council of History, Arts and Libraries, 702 W. Kalamazoo St., P.O. Box 30705, Lansing MI 48909-8205. (517)241-4011. E-mail: artsinfo@michigan.gov. Website: www.michigan.gov.

Minnesota State Arts Board, Park Square Court, 400 Sibley St., Suite 200, St. Paul MN 55101-1928. (651)215-1600 or (800)866-2787. E-mail: msab@arts.state.mn.us. Website: www.arts.state.mn.us.

Mississippi Arts Commission, 501 N. West St., Suite 701B, Woolfolk Bldg., Jackson MS 39201. (601)359-6030. Website: www.arts.state.ms.us.

Missouri Arts Council, 815 Olive St., Suite 16, St. Louis MO 63101-1503. (314)340-6845 or (866)407-4752. E-mail: moarts@ded.mo.gov. Website: www.missouriartscouncil.org.

Montana Arts Council, 316 N. Park Ave., Suite 252, Helena MT 59620-2201. (406)444-6430. E-mail: mac@mt.gov. Website: www.art.state.mt.us.

National Assembly of State Arts Agencies, 1029 Vermont Ave. NW, 2nd Floor, Washington DC 20005. (202)347-6352. E-mail: nasaa@nasaa-arts.org. Website: www.nasaa-arts.org.

Nebraska Arts Council, 1004 Farnam St., Plaza Level, Omaha NE 68102. (402)595-2122 or (800)341-4067. Website: www.nebraskaartscouncil.org.

Nevada Arts Council, 716 N. Carson St., Suite A, Carson City NV 89701. (775)687-6680. E-mail: online form. Website: http://dmla.clan.lib.nv.us/docs/arts.

New Hampshire State Council on the Arts, 2½ Beacon St., 2nd Floor, Concord NH 03301-4974. (603)271-2789. Website: www.nh.gov/nharts.

New Jersey State Council on the Arts, 225 W. State St., P.O. Box 306, Trenton NJ 08625. (609)292-6130. Website: www.njartscouncil.org.

New Mexico Arts, Dept. of Cultural Affairs, P.O. Box 1450, Santa Fe NM 87504-1450. (505)827-6490 or (800)879-4278. Website: www.nmarts.org.

New York State Council on the Arts, 175 Varick St., New York NY 10014. (212)627-4455. Website: www.nysca.org.

North Carolina Arts Council, 109 East Jones St., Cultural Resources Building, Raleigh NC 27601. (919)807-6500. E-mail: ncarts@ncmail.net. Website: www.ncarts.org.

North Dakota Council on the Arts, 1600 E. Century Ave., Suite 6, Bismarck ND 58503. (701)328-7590. E-mail: comserv@state.nd.us. Website: www.state.nd.us/arts.

Commonwealth Council for Arts and Culture (Northern Mariana Islands), P.O. Box 5553, CHRB, Saipan MP 96950. (670)322-9982 or (670)322-9983. E-mail: galaidi@vzpacifica.net. Website: www.geocities.com/ccacarts/ccacwebsite.html.

Ohio Arts Council, 727 E. Main St., Columbus OH 43205-1796. (614)466-2613. Website: www.oac.state.oh.us.

Oklahoma Arts Council, Jim Thorpe Building, 2101 N. Lincoln Blvd., Suite 640, Oklahoma City OK 73105. (405)521-2931. E-mail: okarts@arts.ok.gov. Website: www.arts.state.ok.us.

Oregon Arts Commission, 775 Summer St. NE, Suite 200, Salem OR 97301-1280. (503)986-0082. E-mail: oregon.artscomm@state.or.us. Website: www.oregonartscommission.org.

Pennsylvania Council on the Arts, 216 Finance Bldg., Harrisburg PA 17120. (717)787-6883. Website: www.pacouncilonthearts.org.

Institute of Puerto Rican Culture, P.O. Box 9024184, San Juan PR 00902-4184. (787)724-0700. E-mail: www@icp.gobierno.pr. Website: www.icp.gobierno.pr.

Rhode Island State Council on the Arts, One Capitol Hill, Third Floor, Providence RI 02908. (401)222-3880. E-mail: info@arts.ri.gov. Website: www.arts.ri.gov.

South Carolina Arts Commission, 1800 Gervais St., Columbia SC 29201. (803)734-8696. E-mail: info@arts.state.sc.us. Website: www.southcarolinaarts.com.

South Dakota Arts Council, 711 E. Wells Ave., Pierre SD 57501-3369. (605)773-3301. E-mail: sdac@state.sd.us. Website: www.artscouncil.sd.gov.

Tennessee Arts Commission, 401 Charlotte Ave., Nashville TN 37243-0780. (615)741-1701. Website: www.arts.state.tn.us.

Texas Commission on the Arts, E.O. Thompson Office Building, 920 Colorado, Suite 501, Austin TX 78701. (512)463-5535. E-mail: front.desk@arts.state.tx.us. Website: www.arts.state.tx.us.

Utah Arts Council, 617 E. South Temple, Salt Lake City UT 84102-1177. (801)236-7555. Website: http://arts.utah.gov.

Vermont Arts Council, 136 State St., Drawer 33, Montpelier VT 05633-6001. (802)828-3291. E-mail: online form. Website: www.vermontartscouncil.org.

Virgin Islands Council on the Arts, 5070 Norre Gade, St. Thomas VI 00802-6872. (340)774-5984. Website: http://vicouncilonarts.org.

Virginia Commission for the Arts, Lewis House, 223 Governor St., 2nd Floor, Richmond VA 23219. (804)225-3132. E-mail: arts@arts.virginia.gov. Website: www.arts.state.va.us.

Washington State Arts Commission, 711 Capitol Way S., Suite 600, P.O. Box 42675, Olympia WA 98504-2675. (360)753-3860. E-mail: info@arts.wa.gov. Website: www.arts.wa.gov.

West Virginia Commission on the Arts, The Cultural Center, Capitol Complex, 1900 Kanawha Blvd. E., Charleston WV 25305-0300. (304)558-0220. Website: www.wvculture.org/arts.

Wisconsin Arts Board, 101 E. Wilson St., 1st Floor, Madison WI 53702. (608)266-0190. E-mail: artsboard@arts.state.wi.us. Website: www.arts.state.wi.us.

Wyoming Arts Council, 2320 Capitol Ave., Cheyenne WY 82002. (307)777-7742. E-mail: ebratt@state.wy.us. Website: http://wyoarts.state.wy.us.

CANADIAN PROVINCES ARTS AGENCIES

Alberta Foundation for the Arts, 10708-105 Ave., Edmonton AB T5H 0A1. (780)427-9968. Website: www.affta.ab.ca/index.shtml.

British Columbia Arts Council, P.O. Box 9819, Stn. Prov. Govt., Victoria BC V8W 9W3. (250)356-1718. E-mail: BCArtsCouncil@gov.bc.ca. Website: www.bcartscouncil.ca.

The Canada Council for the Arts, 350 Albert St., P.O. Box 1047, Ottawa ON K1P 5V8. (613)566-4414 or (800)263-5588 (within Canada). Website: www.canadacouncil.ca.

Manitoba Arts Council, 525-93 Lombard Ave., Winnipeg MB R3B 3B1. (204)945-2237 or (866)994-2787 (in Manitoba). E-mail: info@artscouncil.mb.ca. Website: www. artscouncil.mb.ca.

New Brunswick Arts Board (NBAB), 634 Queen St., Suite 300, Fredericton NB E3B 1C2. (506)444-4444 or (866)460-2787. Website: www.artsnb.ca.

Newfoundland & Labrador Arts Council, P.O. Box 98, St. John's NL A1C 5H5. (709)726-2212 or (866)726-2212. E-mail: nlacmail@nfld.net. Website: www.nlac.nf.ca.

Nova Scotia Department of Tourism, Culture, and Heritage, Culture Division, 1800 Argyle St., Suite 601, P.O. Box 456, Halifax NS B3J 2R5. (902)424-4510. E-mail: cultaffs@gov. ns.ca. Website: www.gov.ns.ca/dtc/culture.

Ontario Arts Council, 151 Bloor St. W., 5th Floor, Toronto ON M5S 1T6. (416)961-1660 or (800)387-0058 (in Ontario). E-mail: info@arts.on.ca. Website: www.arts.on.ca.

Prince Edward Island Council of the Arts, 115 Richmond St., Charlottetown PE C1A 1H7. (902)368-4410 or (888)734-2784. E-mail: info@peiartscouncil.com. Website: www. peiartscouncil.com.

Québec Council for Arts & Literature, 79 boul. René-Lévesque Est, 3e étage, Québec QC G1R 5N5. (418)643-1707 or (800)897-1707. E-mail: info@calq.gouv.qc.ca. Website: www.calq. gouv.qc.ca.

The Saskatchewan Arts Board, 2135 Broad St., Regina SK S4P 1Y6. (306)787-4056 or (800)667-7526 (Saskatchewan only). E-mail: sab@artsboard.sk.ca. Website: www. artsboard.sk.ca.

Yukon Arts Funding Program, Cultural Services Branch, Dept. of Tourism & Culture, Government of Yukon, Box 2703 (L-3), Whitehorse YT Y1A 2C6. (867)667-8589 or (800)661-0408 (in Yukon). E-mail: arts@gov.yk.ca. Website: www.tc.gov.yk.ca/216. html.

Resources

Publications of Interest

Knowledge about the music industry is essential for both creative and business success. Staying informed requires keeping up with constantly changing information. Updates on the evolving trends in the music business are available to you in the form of music magazines, music trade papers and books. There is a publication aimed at almost every type of musician, songwriter and music fan, from the most technical knowledge of amplification systems to gossip about your favorite singer. These publications can enlighten and inspire you and provide information vital in helping you become a more well-rounded, educated, and, ultimately, successful musical artist.

This section lists all types of magazines and books you may find interesting. From songwriters' newsletters and glossy music magazines to tip sheets and how-to books, there should be something listed here that you'll enjoy and benefit from.

PERIODICALS

Allegheny Music Works, 1611 Menoher Blvd., Johnstown PA 15905. (814)255-4007. Website: www.alleghenymusicworks.com. *Monthly tip sheet.*

Alternative Press, 1305 West 80th Street, Suite 2F, Cleveland OH 44102-1996. (216)631-1510. Email: subscriptions@altpress.com. Website: http://altpress.com. *Reviews, news, and features for alternative and indie music fans.*

American Songwriter Magazine, 50 Music Square W., Suite 604, Nashville TN 37203-3227. (615)321-6096. E-mail: info@americansongwriter.com. Website: www.americansongwriter.com. *Bimonthly publication for and about songwriters.*

Back Stage East, 770 Broadway, 4th Floor, New York NY 10003. (646)654-5700.

Back Stage West, 5055 Wilshire Blvd., Los Angeles CA 90036. (323)525-2358 or (800)745-8922. Website: www.backstage.com. *Weekly East and West Coast performing artist trade papers.*

Bass Player, P.O. Box 57324, Boulder CO 80323-7324. (800)234-1831. E-mail: bassplayer@ neodata.com. Website: www.bassplayer.com. *Monthly magazine for bass players with lessons, interviews, articles, and transcriptions.*

Billboard, 1515 Broadway, New York NY 10036. (800)745-8922. E-mail: bbstore@ billboard.com. Website: www.billboard.com. *Weekly industry trade magazine.*

Canadian Musician, 23 Hannover Dr., Suite 7, St. Catharines ON L2W 1A3 Canada. (877)746-4692. Website: www.canadianmusician.com. *Bimonthly publication for amateur and professional Canadian musicians.*

Chart, 200-41 Britain St., Toronto ON M5A 1R7 Canada. (416)363-3101. E-mail: chart@ chartnet.com. Website: www.chartattack.com. *Monthly magazine covering the Canadian and international music scenes.*

CMJ New Music Report/CMJ New Music Monthly, 151 W. 25th St., 12 Floor, New York NY 10001. (917)606-1908. Website: www.cmj.com. *Weekly college radio and alternative music tip sheet.*

Country Line Magazine,16150 S. IH-35, Buda TX 78610. (512)295-8400. E-mail: editor@ countrylinemagazine.com. Website: www.countrylinemagazine.com. *Monthly Texas-only country music cowboy and lifestyle magazine.*

Daily Variety, 5700 Wilshire Blvd., Suite 120, Los Angeles CA 90036. (323)857-6600. Website: www.variety.com. *Daily entertainment trade newspaper.*

Entertainment Law & Finance, New York Law Publishing Co., 345 Park Ave. S., 8th Floor, New York NY 10010. (212)545-6174. *Monthly newsletter covering music industry contracts, lawsuit filings, court rulings and legislation.*

Exclaim!, 7-B Pleasant Blvd., Suite 966, Toronto ON M4T 1K2 Canada. (416)535-9735. E-mail: exclaim@exclaim.ca. Website: http://exclaim.ca. *Canadian music monthly covering all genres of non-mainstream music.*

Fast Forward, Disc Makers, 7905 N. Rt. 130, Pennsauken NJ 08110-1402. (800)468-9353. Website: www.discmakers.com/music/ffwd. *Quarterly newsletter featuring companies and products for performing and recording artists in the independent music industry.*

Guitar Player, 1601 W. 23rd St., Suite 200, Lawrence KS 60046-0127. (800)289-9839. Website: www.guitarplayer.com. *Monthly guitar magazine with transcriptions, columns, and interviews, including occasional articles on songwriting.*

Jazztimes, 8737 Colesville Rd., 9th Floor, Silver Spring MD 20910-3921. (301)588-4114. Website: www.jazztimes.com. *10 issues/year magazine covering the American jazz scene.*

Music Business International Magazine, 460 Park Ave., S. of 9th, New York NY 10116. (212)378-0406. *Bimonthly magazine for senior executives in the music industry.*

Music Connection Magazine, 16130 Ventura Blvd., Suite 540, Encino CA 91436. (818)795-0101. E-mail: contactMC@musicconnection.com. Website: www.musicconnection.com. *Biweekly music industry trade publication.*

Music Morsels, P.O. Box 2760, Acworth GA 30102. (678)445-0006. Fax: (678)494-9269. E-mail: SergeEnt@aol.com. Website: www.serge.org/musicmorsels.htm. *Monthly songwriting publication.*

Music Row Magazine, 1231 17th Ave. S, Nashville TN 37212. (615)321-3617. E-mail: info@musicrow.com. Website: www.musicrow.com. *Biweekly Nashville industry publication.*

Offbeat Magazine, OffBeat Publications, 421 Frenchman St., Suite 200, New Orleans LA 70116. (504)944-4300. E-mail: offbeat@offbeat.com. Website: www.offbeat.com. *Monthly magazine covering Louisiana music and artists.*

The Performing Songwriter, P.O. Box 40931, Nashville TN 37204. (800)883-7664. E-mail: order@performingsongwriter.com. Website: www.performingsongwriter.com *Bimonthly songwriters' magazine.*

Radio and Records, 2049 Century Park East, 41st Floor, Los Angeles CA 90067. (310)553-4330. Fax: (310)203-9763. E-mail: subscribe@radioandrecords.com. Website: www. radioandrecords.com. *Weekly newspaper covering the radio and record industries.*

Radir, Radio Mall, 2412 Unity Ave. N., Dept. WEB, Minneapolis MN 55422. (800)759-4561. E-mail: info@bbhsoftware.com. Website: www.bbhsoftware.com. *Quarterly radio station database on disk.*

Sing Out!, P.O. Box 5460, Bethlehem PA 18015. (888)SING-OUT. Fax: (610)865-5129. E-mail: info@singout.org. Website: www.singout.org. *Quarterly folk music magazine.*

Songcasting, 15445 Ventura Blvd. #260, Sherman Oaks CA 91403. (818)377-4084. *Monthly tip sheet.*

Songlink International, 23 Belsize Crescent, London NW3 5QY England. Website: www. songlink.com.*10 issues/year newsletter including details of recording artists looking for songs; contact details for industry sources; also news and features on the music business.*

Variety, 5700 Wilshire Blvd., Suite 120, Los Angeles CA 90036. (323)857-6600. Fax: (323)857-0494. Website: www.variety.com. *Weekly entertainment trade newspaper.*

Words and Music, 41 Valleybrook Dr., Don Mills ON M3B 2S6 Canada. (416)445-8700. Website: www.socan.ca. *Monthly songwriters' magazine.*

BOOKS & DIRECTORIES

101 Songwriting Wrongs & How to Right Them, by Pat & Pete Luboff, Writer's Digest Books, 4700 E. Galbraith Rd., Cincinnati OH 45236. (800)448-0915. Website: www. writersdigest.com.

The A&R Registry, by Ritch Esra, SRS Publishing, 7510 Sunset Blvd. #1041, Los Angeles CA 90046-3418. (800)377-7411 or (800)552-7411. E-mail: musicregistry@compuserve.com.

The Billboard Guide to Music Publicity, revised edition, by Jim Pettigrew, Jr., Billboard Books, 1695 Oak St., Lakewood NJ 08701. (800)344-7119.

Breakin' Into Nashville, by Jennifer Ember Pierce, Madison Books, University Press of America, 4501 Forbes Rd., Suite 200, Lanham MD 20706. (800)462-6420.

CMJ Directory, 151 W. 25th St., 12th Floor, New York NY 10001. (917)606-1908. Website: www.cmj.com.

The Craft and Business of Songwriting, by John Braheny, Writer's Digest Books, 4700 E. Galbraith Rd., Cincinnati OH 45236. (800)448-0915. Website: www.writersdigest.com.

The Craft of Lyric Writing, by Sheila Davis, Writer's Digest Books, 4700 E. Galbraith Rd., Cincinnati OH 45236. (800)448-0915. Website: www.writersdigest.com.

Disc Makers, by Jason Ojalvo, Disc Makers, 7905 N. Rt. 130, Pennsauken NJ 08110. (800)468-9353. E-mail: discman@discmakers.com. Website: www.discmakers.com.

Hollywood Creative Directory, 3000 W. Olympic Blvd. #2525, Santa Monica CA 90404. (800)815-0503. Website: www.hcdonline.com. *Lists producers in film and TV.*

The Hollywood Reporter, 5055 Wilshire Blvd., Los Angeles CA 90036. (323)525-2150. Website: www.hollywoodreporter.com.

How to Get Somewhere in the Music Business from Nowhere with Nothing, by Mary Dawson, CQK Books, fico CQK Music Group, 2221 Justin Rd., Suite 119-142, Flower Mound TX 75028. (972)317-2720. Fax: (972)317-4737. Website: www. FromNowhereWithNothing.com.

How to Promote Your Music Successfully on the Internet, by David Nevue, Midnight Rain Productions, P.O. Box 21831, Eugene OR 97402. Website: www.rainmusic.com.

How to Make It in the New Music Business: Lessons, Tips, and Inspirations from Music's Biggest and Best, by Robert Wolff, Billboard Books. Website: www.billboard.com.

How You Can Break Into the Music Business, by Marty Garrett, Lonesome Wind Corporation, P.O. Box 2143, Broken Arrow OK 74013-2143. (800)210-4416.

Louisiana Music Directory, OffBeat, Inc., 421 Frenchmen St., Suite 200, New Orleans LA 70116. (504)944-4300. Website: www.offbeat.com.

Lydian Chromatic Concept of Tonal Organization, Volume One: The Art and Science of Tonal Gravity, by George Russell, Concept Publishing Company, 258 Harvard St., #296, Brookline MA 02446-2904. E-mail: lydconcept@aol.com. Website: www. lydianchromaticconcept.com.

Melody in Songwriting, by Jack Perricone, Berklee Press, 1140 Boylston St., Boston MA 02215. (617)747-2146. E-mail: info@berkleepress.com. Website: www.berkleepress.com.

Music Attorney Legal & Business Affairs Registry, by Ritch Esra and Steve Trumbull, SRS Publishing, 7510 Sunset Blvd. #1041, Los Angeles CA 90046-3418. (800)552-7411. E-mail: musicregistry@compuserve.com or srspubl@aol.com.

Resources

The Music Business Registry, by Ritch Esra, SRS Publishing, 7510 Sunset Blvd. #1041, Los Angeles CA 90046-3418. (800)552-7411. E-mail: musicregistry@compuserve.com or srspu bl@aol.com. Website: www.musicregistry.com.

Music Directory Canada, seventh edition, Norris-Whitney Communications Inc., 23 Hannover Dr., Suite 7, St. Catherines ON L2W 1A3 Canada. (877)RING-NWC. E-mail: mail@nor.com. Website: http://nor.com.

Music Law: How to Run Your Band's Business, by Richard Stin, Nolo Press, 950 Parker St., Berkeley CA 94710-9867. (510)549-1976. Website: www.nolo.com.

Music, Money and Success: The Insider's Guide to the Music Industry, by Jeffrey Brabec and Todd Brabec, Schirmer Books, 1633 Broadway, New York NY 10019.

The Music Publisher Registry, by Ritch Esra, SRS Publishing, 7510 Sunset Blvd. #1041, Los Angeles CA 90046-3418. (800)552-7411. E-mail: musicregistry@compuserve.com or srspubl@aol.com.

Music Publishing: A Songwriter's Guide, revised edition, by Randy Poe, Writer's Digest Books, 4700 E. Galbraith Rd., Cincinnati OH 45236. (800)448-0915. Website: www.writersdigest.com.

The Musician's Guide to Making & Selling Your Own CDs & Cassettes, by Jana Stanfield, Writer's Digest Books, 4700 E. Galbraith Rd., Cincinnati OH 45236. (800)448-0915. Website: www.writersdigest.com.

Musicians' Phone Book, The Los Angeles Music Industry Directory, Get Yourself Some Publishing, 28336 Simsalido Ave., Canyon Country CA 91351. (805)299-2405. E-mail: mpb@earthlink.net. Website: www.musiciansphonebook.com.

Nashville Music Business Directory, by Mark Dreyer, NMBD Publishing, 9 Music Square S., Suite 210, Nashville TN 37203. (615)826-4141. E-mail: nmbd@nashvilleconnection.com. Website: www.nashvilleconnection.com.

Nashville's Unwritten Rules: Inside the Business of the Country Music Machine, by Dan Daley, Overlook Press, One Overlook Dr., Woodstock NY 12498. (845)679-6838. E-mail: overlook@netstep.net.

National Directory of Independent Record Distributors, P.O. Box 452063, Lake Mary FL 32795-2063. (407)834-8555. E-mail: info@songwriterproducts.com. Website: www.songwriterproducts.com.

The Official Country Music Directory, ICMA Music Directory, P.O. Box 271238, Nashville TN 37227.

Performance Magazine Guides, 1203 Lake St., Suite 200, Fort Worth TX 76102-4504. (817)338-9444. E-mail: sales@performancemagazine.com. Website: www.performancemagazine.com.

Radio Stations of America: A National Directory, P.O. Box 452063, Lake Mary FL 32795-2063. (407)834-8555. E-mail: info@songwriterproducts.com. Website: www. songwriterproducts.com.

The Real Deal—How to Get Signed to a Record Label from A to Z, by Daylle Deanna Schwartz, Billboard Books, 1695 Oak St., Lakewood NJ 08701. (800)344-7119.

Recording Industry Sourcebook, Music Books Plus, P.O. Box 670, 240 Portage Rd., Lewiston NY 14092. (800)265-8481. Website: www.musicbooksplus.com.

Reharmonization Techniques, by Randy Felts, Berklee Press, 1140 Boylston St., Boston MA 02215. (617)747-2146. E-mail: info@berkleepress.com. Website: www.berkleepress.com.

The Songwriters Idea Book, by Sheila Davis, Writer's Digest Books, 4700 E. Galbraith Rd., Cincinnati OH 45236. (800)448-0915. Website: www.writersdigest.com.

Songwriter's Market Guide to Song & Demo Submission Formats, Writer's Digest Books, 4700 E. Galbraith Rd., Cincinnati OH 45236. (800)448-0915. Website: www. writersdigest.com.

Songwriter's Playground—Innovative Exercises in Creative Songwriting, by Barbara L. Jordan, Creative Music Marketing, 1085 Commonwealth Ave., Suite 323, Boston MA 02215. (617)926-8766.

The Songwriter's Workshop: Harmony, by Jimmy Kachulis, Berklee Press, 1140 Boylston St., Boston MA 02215. (617)747-2146. E-mail: info@berkleepress.com. Website: www. berkleepress.com.

The Songwriter's Workshop: Melody, by Jimmy Kachulis, Berklee Press, 1140 Boylston St., Boston MA 02215. (617)747-2146. E-mail: info@berkleepress.com. Website: www. berkleepress.com.

Songwriting and the Creative Process, by Steve Gillette, Sing Out! Publications, P.O. Box 5640, Bethlehem PA 18015-0253. (888)SING-OUT. E-mail: singout@libertynet.org. Website: www.singout.org/sopubs.html.

Songwriting: Essential Guide to Lyric Form and Structure, by Pat Pattison, Berklee Press, 1140 Boylston St., Boston MA 02215. (617)747-2146. E-mail: info@berkleepress.com. Website: www.www.berkleepress.com.

Songwriting: Essential Guide to Rhyming, by Pat Pattison, Berklee Press, 1140 Boylston St., Boston MA 02215. (617)747-2146. E-mail: info@berkleepress.com. Website: www. berkleepress.com.

The Songwriting Sourcebook: How to Turn Chords Into Great Songs, by Rikky Rooksby, Backbeat Books, 600 Harrison St., San Francisco CA 94107. (415)947-6615. E-mail: books@musicplayer.com. Website: www.backbeatbooks.com.

The Soul of the Writer, by Susan Tucker with Linda Lee Strother, Journey Publishing, P.O. Box 92411, Nashville TN 37209. (615)952-4894. Website: www.journeypublishing.com.

Successful Lyric Writing, by Sheila Davis, Writer's Digest Books, 4700 E. Galbraith Rd., Cincinnati OH 45236. (800)448-0915. Website: www.writersdigest.com.

This Business of Music Marketing and Promotion, by Tad Lathrop and Jim Pettigrew, Jr., Billboard Books, Watson-Guptill Publications, 770 Broadway, New York NY 10003. E-mail: info@watsonguptill.com.

Tim Sweeney's Guide to Releasing Independent Records, by Tim Sweeney, TSA Books, 31805 Highway 79 S., Temecula CA 92592. (909)303-9506. E-mail: info@tsamusic. com. Website: www.tsamusic.com.

Tim Sweeney's Guide to Succeeding at Music Conventions, by Tim Sweeney, TSA Books, 31805 Highway 79 S., Temecula CA 92592. (909)303-9506. Website: www. tsamusic.com.

Texas Music Industry Directory, Texas Music Office, Office of the Governor, P.O. Box 13246, Austin TX 78711. (512)463-6666. E-mail: music@governor.state.tx.us. Website: www.governor.state.tx.us/music.

Tunesmith: Inside the Art of Songwriting, by Jimmy Webb, Hyperion, 77 W. 66th St., 11th Floor, New York NY 10023. (800)759-0190.

Volunteer Lawyers for the Arts Guide to Copyright for Musicians and Composers, One E. 53rd St., 6th Floor, New York NY 10022. (212)319-2787.

Writing Better Lyrics, by Pat Pattison, Writer's Digest Books, 4700 E. Galbraith Rd., Cincinnati OH 45236. (800)448-0915. Website: www.writersdigest.com.

Writing Music for Hit Songs, by Jai Josefs, Schirmer Trade Books, 257 Park Ave. S., New York NY 10010. (212)254-2100.

The Yellow Pages of Rock, The Album Network, 120 N. Victory Blvd., Burbank CA 91502. (800)222-4382. Fax: (818)955-9048. E-mail: ypinfo@yprock.com.

Resources

Websites of Interest

The Internet provides a wealth of information for songwriters and performers, and the number of sites devoted to music grows each day. Below is a list of websites that can offer you information, links to other music sites, contact with other songwriters, and places to showcase your songs. Due to the dynamic nature of the online world, this is certainly not a comprehensive list, but it gives you a place to start on your Internet journey to search for opportunities to get your music heard.

About.com Musicians' Exchange http://musicians.about.com/
> Site features headlines and articles of interest to independent musicians and songwriters, as well as links and label profiles.

Absolute Punk www.absolutepunk.net
> Searchable online community focusing on punk and rock music, including news, including reviews, articles and interviews; forums to discuss music and pop culture.

American Music Center www.amc.net
> Classical and jazz archives. Includes a list of organizations and contacts for composers.

American Society of Composers, Authors and Publishers (ASCAP) www.ascap.com
> Database of works in ASCAP's repertoire. Includes performer, songwriter, and publisher information as well as membership information and industry news.

American Songwriter Magazine Homepage www.americansongwriter.com
> This is the official homepage for *American Songwriter Magazine*. Features an online article archive, e-mail newsletter, and links.

Backstage Commerce www.backstagecommerce.com
> Provides secure online support for the sale of music goods for independent artists.

Bathtub Music www.bathtubmusic.com
> Online distributor of independent music; receives commission on any sales made.

rd Music Group Demos www.beairdmusicgroup.com
Nashville demo service which offers a variety of demo packages.

Billboard.com www.billboard.com
Industry news and searchable online database of music companies by subscription.

The Blues Foundation www.blues.org
Nonprofit organization located in Memphis, TN; website contains information on the foundation, membership, and events.

Broadcast Music, Inc. (BMI) www.bmi.com
Offers lists of song titles, writers, and publishers of the BMI repertoire. Includes membership information and general information on songwriting and licensing.

The Buzz Factor www.thebuzzfactor.com
Website offers free tips on the music marketing and self-promotion ideas.

Buzznet www.buzznet.com
Searchable networking and news site featuring music and pop culture; photos, videos, concert reviews, more.

CDBABY www.cdbaby.com
An online CD store dedicated to the sales of independent music.

CDFreedom www.cdfreedom.com
An online CD store for independent musicians.

Cadenza www.cadenza.org
Online resource for contemporary and classical music and musicians, including methods of contacting other musicians.

Center for the Promotion of Contemporary Composers (CPCC) www.under.org/cpcc
Website for CPCC, an internet-based service organization for composers.

Chorus America www.chorusamerica.org
The website for Chorus America, a national organization for professional and volunteer choruses. Includes job listings and professional development information.

Finetune www.finetune.com
Internet Radio/streaming audio. User can create personalized channels and playlists online.

Film Music Network www.filmmusicworld.com or www.filmmusic.net
Network of links, news, and job-listings within the film music world.

Fourfront Media and Music www.knab.com
Site offers information on product development, promotion, publicity, and performance.

Garageband www.garageband.com
Online music hosting site where independent musicians can post music and profiles which can be critiqued by listeners.

Get Signed www.getsigned.com

Interviews with musicians, songwriters, and industry veterans, how-to business information, and more.

Government Liaison Services www.trademarkinfo.com

An intellectual property research firm. Offers a variety of trademark searches.

Guitar Nine Records www.guitar9.com

Offers articles on songwriting, music theory, guitar techniques, etc.

Google www.google.com

Online search engine can be used to look up music, information, lyrics.

Harmony Central www.harmony-central.com

Online community for musicians with in-depth reviews and discussions.

Harry Fox Agency www.harryfox.com

Offers a comprehensive FAQ about licensing songs for use in recording, performance, and film.

iLike www.ilike.com

Music networking site. Signed and unsigned artists can sign up for free artists' page and upload songs and events. Works with other social networks such as www.facebook.com.

Independent Distribution Network www.idnmusic.com

Website of independent bands distributing their music with advice on everything from starting a band to finding labels.

Independent Songwriter Web Magazine www.independentsongwriter.com/

Independent music reviews, classifieds, message board and chat sessions.

Indie-Music.com http://indie-music.com/

Website of how-to articles, record label directory, links to musicians and venue listings.

Jazz Corner www.jazzcorner.com

Portal for the websites of jazz musicians and organizations. Includes the jazz video share, jukebox, and the "Speakeasy" bulletin board.

Just Plain Folks www.jpfolks.com or www.justplainfolks.org

Website for songwriting organization featuring messageboards, lyric feedback forums, member profiles and music, contact listings, chapter homepages, and more.

Last.fm www.last.fm/

Music tracking and social networking site.

Li'l Hank's Guide for Songwriters in L.A. www.halsguide.com

Website for songwriters with information on clubs, publishers, books, etc. Links to other songwriting sites.

Live365 www.live365.com/index.live

Internet radio/audio stream search engine.

Livejournal www.livejournal.com

Social networking community using open source technology; music communities provide news, interviews, and reviews.

Los Angeles Goes Underground http://lagu.somaweb.org/

Website dedicated to underground rock bands from Los Angeles and Hollywood.

Lyrical Line www.lyricalline.com

Offers places to upload original songs for critique or exposure, industry news and more.

Lyric Ideas www.lyricideas.com

Offers songwriting prompts, themes, and creative techniques for songwriting.

Lyricist www.lyricist.com/

Site offers advice, tips, and events in the music industry.

MI2N (the Music Industry News Network) www.mi2n.com

Offers news on happenings in the music industry and career postings.

The Muse's Muse www.musesmuse.com/

Classifieds, catalog of music samples, songwriting articles, newsletter, and chat room.

MOG http://mog.com/

Internet radio/streaming audio. Contains music news and concert reviews, personalized recommendations.

Music Books Plus www.musicbooksplus.com

Online bookstore dedicated to music books on every music-related topic, plus a free newsletter.

Music Publishers Association www.mpa.org/

Ofers directories for music publishers and imprints, copyright resource center and information on the organization.

Music Yellow Pages www.musicyellowpages.com/

Listings of music-related businesses.

MySpace www.myspace.com

Social networking site featuring music web pages for musicians and songwriters.

Nashville Songwriters Association International (NSAI) www.nashvillesongwriters. com

Official NSAI homepage. Offers news, links, online registration and message board for members.

National Association of Composers USA (NACUSA) www.music-usa.org/nacusa

A nonprofit organization devoted to the promotion and performance of American concert hall music.

National Music Publishers Association www.nmpa.org

Organization's online site filled with information about copyright, legislation, and other concerns of the music publishing world.

Online Rock www.onlinerock.com/

Range of membership options including a free option, offers webpage services, articles, chat rooms, links, and more.

Opera America www.operaamerica.org/

Website of Opera America features information on advocacy and awareness programs, publications, conference schedules, and more.

Outersound www.outersound.com

Information on educating yourself in the music industry and a list of music magazines to advertise in or get reviewed by.

Pandora www.pandora.com

A site created by the founders of the Music Genome Project; a searchable music radio/streaming audio site.

Performer Mag www.performermag.com

Offers articles, music industry news, classifieds and reviews.

Performing Songwriter Magazine Homepage www.performingsongwriter.com

Official homepage for the magazine features articles and links.

Pitchfork www.pitchforkmedia.com

Offers Indie news, reviews, media, and features.

Public Domain Music www.pdinfo.com/

Articles on public domain works and copyright including public domain song lists, research sources, tips and FAQs.

PUMP Audio www.pumpaudio.com/

License music for film and television on a non-exclusive basis. No submission fees, rights retained by songwriter.

Purevolume www.purevolume.com

Music hosting site with searchable database of songs by signed and unsigned artists. Musicians and songwriters can upload songs and events.

The Recording Project www.recordingproject.com/

Online community for musicians and recording artists, every level welcome.

Record Producer.com www.record-producer.com

Extensive site dedicated to audio engineering and record production. Offers a free newsletter, online instruction, and e-bookson various aspects of record production and audio engineering.

Rhythm Net www.rhythmnet.com

Online CD store for independent musicians.

Rock and Roll Hall of Fame + Museum www.rockhall.com/
Website for the Rock and Roll Hall of Fame and Museum, including events listings, visitor info, and more.

SESAC Inc. www.sesac.com
Website for performing rights organization with songwriter profiles, industry news updates, licensing information, and links to other sites.

SingerSongwriter www.singersongwriter.ws
Resources for singer-songwriters, including an extensive list, featured resources and lists of radio stations organized geographically.

Slacker www.slacker.com
Internet Radio/streaming audio. User can create personalized channels and playlists online.

Soma FM www.somafm.com
Internet underground/alternative radio with commercial-free broadcasting from San Francisco.

Song Catalog www.songcatalog.com
Online song catalog database for licensing.

Songlink www.songlink.com
Offers opportunities to pitch songs to music publishers for specific recording projects and industry news.

SongRamp www.songramp.com
Online songrwriting organization with message boards, blogs, news, and streaming music channels. Offers variety of membership packages.

SongsAlive! www.songsalive.org
Online songwriters organization and community.

Songwriter 101 www.songwriter101.com
Offers articles, industry news, and message boards.

Songwriter's Guild of America (SGA) www.songwritersguild.com
Industry news, member services information, newsletters, contract reviews, and more.

Songwriter's Resource Network www.songwritersresourcenetwork.com
News and education resource for songwriters, lyricists, and composers.

SongwriterUniverse www.songwriteruniverse.com
In-depth articles, business information, education and recommended reading.

SoundPedia http://soundpedia.com
Internet Radio/streaming audio. User can create personalized channels and playlists online.

The Songwriting Education Resource www.craftofsongwriting.com

An educational website for songwriters. Offers discussion boards, a
links.

Sonic Bids www.sonicbids.com

Features an online press kit with photos, bio, music samples, date calendar. Free
trial period first month for artists/bands to sign up, newsletter.

StarPolish www.starpolish.com

Features articles and interviews on the music industry.

SummerSongs Songwriting Camps www.summersongs.com

Information about songwriting camps, staff, and online registration.

TAXI www.taxi.com

Independent A&R vehicle that shops demos to A&R professionals.

United States Copyright Office www.copyright.gov

Homepage for the US Copyright office. Offers information on registering songs.

The Velvet Rope www.velvetrope.com

Famous/infamous online music industry message board.

Weirdo Music www.weirdomusic.com

Online music magazine with articles, reviews, downloads, and links to Internet
Radio shows.

Yahoo! http://new.music.yahoo.com/

Search engine with radio station guide, music industry news, and listings.

YouTube www.youtube.com

Social networking site which hosts audiovisual content. Searchable database
provides links to music videos, interviews and more.

ary

A cappella. Choral singing without accompaniment.

AAA form. A song form in which every verse has the same melody; often used for songs that tell a story.

AABA, ABAB. A commonly used song pattern consisting of two verses, a bridge and a verse, or a repeated pattern of verse and bridge, where the verses are musically the same.

A&R Director. Record company executive in charge of the Artists and Repertoire Department who is responsible for finding and developing new artists and matching songs with artists.

A/C. Adult contemporary music.

Advance. Money paid to the songwriter or recording artist, which is then recouped before regular royalty payment begins. Sometimes called "up front" money, advances are deducted from royalties.

AFIM. Association for Independent Music (formerly NAIRD). Organization for independent record companies, distributors, retailers, manufacturers, etc.

AFM. American Federation of Musicians. A union for musicians and arrangers.

AFTRA. American Federation of Television and Radio Artists. A union for performers.

AIMP. Association of Independent Music Publishers.

Airplay. The radio broadcast of a recording.

AOR. Album-Oriented Rock. A radio format that primarily plays selections from rock albums as opposed to hit singles.

Arrangement. An adaptation of a composition for a recording or performance, with consideration for the melody, harmony, instrumentation, tempo, style, etc.

ASCAP. American Society of Composers, Authors and Publishers. A performing rights society. (See the Organizations section.)

Assignment. Transfer of rights of a song from writer to publisher.

Audio Visual Index (AVI). A database containing title and production information for cue sheets which are available from a performing rights organization. Currently, BMI, ASCAP, SOCAN, PRS, APRA and SACEM contribute their cue sheet listings to the AVI.

Audiovisual. Refers to presentations that use audio backup for visual material.

Background music. Music used that creates mood and supports the spoken dialogue of a radio program or visual action of an audiovisual work. Not feature or theme music.

b&w. Black and white.

Bed. Prerecorded music used as background material in commercials. In rap music, often refers to the sampled and looped drums and music over which the rapper performs.

Black box. Theater without fixed stage or seating arrangements, capable of a variety of formations. Usually a small space, often attached to a major theater complex, used for workshops or experimental works calling for small casts and limited sets.

BMI. Broadcast Music, Inc. A performing rights society. (See the Organizations section.)

Booking agent. Person who schedules performances for entertainers.

Bootlegging. Unauthorized recording and selling of a song.

Business manager. Person who handles the financial aspects of artistic careers.

Buzz. Attention an act generates through the media and word of mouth.

b/w. Backed with. Usually refers to the B-side of a single.

C&W. Country and western.

Catalog. The collected songs of one writer, or all songs handled by one publisher.

CD. Compact Disc (see below).

CD-R. A recordable CD.

CD-ROM. Compact Disc-Read Only Memory. A computer information storage medium capable of holding enormous amounts of data. Information on a CD-ROM cannot be deleted. A computer user must have a CD-ROM drive to access a CD-ROM.

Chamber music. Any music suitable for performance in a small audience area or chamber.

Chamber orchestra. A miniature orchestra usually containing one instrument per part.

Chart. The written arrangement of a song.

Charts. The trade magazines' lists of the best-selling records.

CHR. Comtemporary Hit Radio. Top 40 pop music.

Collaboration. Two or more artists, writers, etc., working together on a single project; for instance, a playwright and a songwriter creating a musical together.

Compact disc. A small disc (about 4.7 inches in diameter) holding digitally encoded music that is read by a laser beam in a CD player.

Composers. The men and women who create musical compositions for motion pictures and other audio visual works, or the creators of classical music composition.

Co-publish. Two or more parties own publishing rights to the same song.

Copyright. The exclusive legal right giving the creator of a work the power to control the publishing, reproduction and selling of the work. Although a song is technically copyrighted at the time it is written, the best legal protection of that copyright comes through registering the copyright with the Library of Congress.

Copyright infringement. Unauthorized use of a copyrighted song or portions thereof.

Cover recording. A new version of a previously recorded song.

Crossover. A song that becomes popular in two or more musical categories (e.g., country and pop).

Cut. Any finished recording; a selection from a LP. Also to record.

DAT. Digital Audio Tape. A professional and consumer audio cassette format for recording and playing back digitally-encoded material. DAT cassettes are approximately one-third smaller than conventional audio cassettes.

DCC. Digital Compact Cassette. A consumer audio cassette format for recording and playing back digitally-encoded tape. DCC tapes are the same size as analog cassettes.

Demo. A recording of a song submitted as a demonstration of a writer's or artist's skills.

Derivative work. A work derived from another work, such as a translation, musical arrangement, sound recording, or motion picture version.

Distributor. Wholesale marketing agent responsible for getting records from manufacturers to retailers.

Donut. A jingle with singing at the beginning and end and instrumental background in the middle. Ad copy is recorded over the middle section.

E-mail. Electronic mail. Computer address where a company or individual can be reached via modem.

Engineer. A specially-trained individual who operates recording studio equipment.

Enhanced CD. General term for an audio CD that also contains multimedia computer information. It is playable in both standard CD players and CD-ROM drives.

EP. Extended play record or cassette containing more selections than a standard single, but fewer than a standard album.

EPK. Electronic press kit. Usually contains photos, sound files, bio information, reviews, tour dates, etc. posted online. Sonicbids.com is a popular EPK hosting website.

Final mix. The art of combining all the various sounds that take place during the recording session into a two-track stereo or mono tape. Reflects the total product and all of the energies and talents the artist, producer and engineer have put into the project.

Fly space. The area above a stage from which set pieces are lowered and raised during a performance.

Folio. A softcover collection of printed music prepared for sale.

Following. A fan base committed to going to gigs and buying albums.

Foreign rights societies. Performing rights societies other than domestic which have reciprocal agreements with ASCAP and BMI for the collection of royalties accrued by foreign radio and television airplay and other public performance of the writer members of the above groups.

Harry Fox Agency. Organization that collects mechanical royalties.

Grammy. Music industry awards presented by the National Academy of Recording Arts and Sciences.

Hip-hop. A dance oriented musical style derived from a combination of disco, rap and R&B.

Hit. A song or record that achieves top 40 status.

Hook. A memorable "catch" phrase or melody line that is repeated in a song.

House. Dance music created by remixing samples from other songs.

Hypertext. Words or groups of words in an electronic document that are linked to other text, such as a definition or a related document. Hypertext can also be linked to illustrations.

Indie. An independent record label, music publisher or producer.

Infringement. A violation of the exclusive rights granted by the copyright law to a copyright owner.

Internet. A worldwide network of computers that offers access to a wide variety of electronic resources.

ips. Inches per second; a speed designation for tape recording.

IRC. International reply coupon, necessary for the return of materials sent out of the country. Available at most post offices.

Jingle. Usually a short verse set to music designed as a commercial message.

Lead sheet. Written version (melody, chord symbols and lyric) of a song.

Leader. Plastic (non-recordable) tape at the beginning and between songs for ease in selection.

Libretto. The text of an opera or any long choral work. The booklet containing such text.

Listing. Block of information in this book about a specific company.

LP. Designation for long-playing record played at 331/3 rpm.

Lyric sheet. A typed or written copy of a song's lyrics.

Market. A potential song or music buyer; also a demographic division of the record-buying public.

Master. Edited and mixed tape used in the production of records; the best or original copy of a recording from which copies are made.

MD. MiniDisc. A 2.5 inch disk for recording and playing back digitally-encoded music.

Mechanical right. The right to profit from the physical reproduction of a song.

Mechanical royalty. Money earned from record, tape and CD sales.

MIDI. Musical instrument digital interface. Universal standard interface that allows musical instruments to communicate with each other and computers.

Mini Disc. (See *MD* above.)

Mix. To blend a multi-track recording into the desired balance of sound, usually to a 2-track stereo master.

Modem. MOdulator/DEModulator. A computer device used to send data from one computer to another via telephone line.

MOR. Middle of the road. Easy-listening popular music.

MP3. File format of a relatively small size that stores audio files on a computer. Music saved in a MP3 format can be played only with a MP3 player (which can be downloaded onto a computer).

Ms. Manuscript.

Multimedia. Computers and software capable of integrating text, sound, photographic-quality images, animation and video.

Music bed. (See *Bed* above.)

Music jobber. A wholesale distributor of printed music.

Music library. A business that purchases canned music, which can then be bought by producers of radio and TV commercials, films, videos and audiovisual productions to use however they wish.

Music publisher. A company that evaluates songs for commercial potential, finds artists to record them, finds other uses (such as TV or film) for the songs, collects income generated by the songs and protects copyrights from infringement.

Music Row. An area of Nashville, TN, encompassing Sixteenth, Seventeeth and Eighteenth avenues where most of the major publishing houses, recording studios, mastering labs, songwriters, singers, promoters, etc. practice their trade.

NARAS. National Academy of Recording Arts and Sciences.

The National Academy of Songwriters (NAS). The largest U.S. songwriters' association. (See the Organizations section.)

Needle-drop. Refers to a type of music library. A needledrop music library is a licensed library that allows producers to borrow music on a rate schedule. The price depends on how the music will be used.

Network. A group of computers electronically linked to share information and resources.

NMPA. National Music Publishers Association.

One-off. A deal between songwriter and publisher which includes only one song or project at a time. No future involvement is implicated. Many times a single song contract accompanies a one-off deal.

One-stop. A wholesale distributor of who sells small quantities of records to "mom and pop" record stores, retailers and jukebox operators.

Operetta. Light, humorous, satiric plot or poem, set to cheerful light music with occasional spoken dialogue.

Overdub. To record an additional part (vocal or instrumental) onto a basic multi-track recording.

Parody. A satirical imitation of a literary or musical work. Permission from the owner of the copyright is generally required before commercial exploitation of a parody.

Payola. Dishonest payment to broadcasters in exchange for airplay.

Performing rights. A specific right granted by U.S. copyright law protecting a composition from being publicly performed without the owner's permission.

Performing rights organization. An organization that collects income from the public performance of songs written by its members and then proportionally distributes this income to the individual copyright holder based on the number of performances of each song.

Personal manager. A person who represents artists to develop and enhance their careers. Personal managers may negotiate contracts, hire and dismiss other agencies and personnel relating to the artist's career, review material, help with artist promotions and perform many services. Piracy. The unauthorized reproduction and selling of printed or recorded music.

Pitch. To attempt to solicit interest for a song by audition.

Playlist. List of songs a radio station will play.

Points. A negotiable percentage paid to producers and artists for records sold.

Producer. Person who supervises every aspect of a recording project.

Production company. Company specializing in producing jingle packages for advertising agencies. May also refer to companies specializing in audiovisual programs.

Professional manager. Member of a music publisher's staff who screens submitted material and tries to get the company's catalog of songs recorded.

Proscenium. Permanent architectural arch in a theater that separates the stage from the audience.

Public domain. Any composition with an expired, lapsed or invalid copyright, and therefore belonging to everyone.

Purchase license. Fee paid for music used from a stock music library.

Query. A letter of inquiry to an industry professional soliciting his interest.

R&B. Rhythm and blues.

Rack Jobber. Distributors who lease floor space from department stores and put in racks of albums.

Rate. The percentage of royalty as specified by contract.

Release. Any record issued by a record company.

Residuals. In advertising or television, payments to singers and musicians for use of a performance.

RIAA. Recording Industry Association of America.

Royalty. Percentage of money earned from the sale of records or use of a song.

RPM. Revolutions per minute. Refers to phonograph turntable speed.

SAE. Self-addressed envelope (with no postage attached).

SASE. Self-addressed stamped envelope.

SATB. The abbreviation for parts in choral music, meaning Soprano, Alto, Tenor and Bass.

Score. A complete arrangement of all the notes and parts of a composition (vocal or instrumental) written out on staves. A full score, or orchestral score, depicts every orchestral part on a separate staff and is used by a conductor.

Self-contained. A band or recording act that writes all their own material.

SESAC. A performing rights organization, originally the Society of European Stage Authors and Composers. (See the Organizations section.)

SFX. Sound effects.

Shop. To pitch songs to a number of companies or publishers.

Single. 45 rpm record with only one song per side. A 12£ single refers to a long version of one song on a 12£ disc, usually used for dance music.

Ska. Fast tempo dance music influenced primarily by reggae and punk, usually featuring horns, saxophone and bass.

SOCAN. Society of Composers, Authors and Music Publishers of Canada. A Canadian performing rights organization. (See the Organizations section.)

Solicited. Songs or materials that have been requested.

Song plugger. A songwriter representative whose main responsibility is promoting uncut songs to music publishers, record companies, artists and producers.

Song shark. Person who deals with songwriters deceptively for his own profit.

SoundScan. A company that collates the register tapes of reporting stores to track the actual number of albums sold at the retail level.

Soundtrack. The audio, including music and narration, of a film, videotape or audiovisual program.

Space stage. Open stage that features lighting and, perhaps, projected scenery.

Split publishing. To divide publishing rights between two or more publishers.

Staff songwriter. A songwriter who has an exclusive agreement with a publisher.

Statutory royalty rate. The maximum payment for mechanical rights guaranteed by law that a record company may pay the songwriter and his publisher for each record or tape sold.

Subpublishing. Certain rights granted by a U.S. publisher to a foreign publisher in exchange for promoting the U.S. catalog in his territory.

Synchronization. Technique of timing a musical soundtrack to action on film or video.

Take. Either an attempt to record a vocal or instrument part, or an acceptable recording of a performance.

Tejano. A musical form begun in the late 1970s by regional bands in south Texas, its style reflects a blended Mexican-American culture. Incorporates elements of rock, country, R&B and jazz, and often features accordion and 12-string guitar.

Thrust stage. Stage with audience on three sides and a stagehouse or wall on the fourth side.

Top 40. The first 40 songs on the pop music charts at any given time. Also refers to a style of music which emulates that heard on the current top 40.

Track. Divisions of a recording tape (e.g., 24-track tape) that can be individually recorded in the studio, then mixed into a finished master.

Trades. Publications covering the music industry.

12-Single. A 12-inch record containing one or more remixes of a song, originally intended for dance club play.

Unsolicited. Songs or materials that were not requested and are not expected.

Vocal score. An arrangement of vocal music detailing all vocal parts, and condensing all accompanying instrumental music into one piano part.

Website. An address on the World Wide Web that can be accessed by computer modem. It may contain text, graphics and sound.

Wing space. The offstage area surrounding the playing stage in a theater, unseen by the audience, where sets and props are hidden, actors wait for cues, and stagehands prepare to chance sets.

World music. A general music category which includes most musical forms originating outside the U.S. and Europe, including reggae and calypso. World music finds its roots primarily in the Caribbean, Latin America, Africa and the south Pacific.

World Wide Web (WWW). An Internet resource that utilizes hypertext to access information. It also supports formatted text, illustrations and sounds, depending on the user's computer capabilities.

Category Indexes

The Category Indexes are a good place to begin searching for a market. They break down the listings by section (music publishers, record companies, etc.) and by the type of music they are interested in. For example, if you write country songs, and are looking for a publisher to pitch them, go to the Music Publishers heading and then check the companies listed under the Country subheading. The music categories cover a wide range of variations within each genre, so be sure to read each listing thoroughly to make sure your own unique take on that genre is a good match. Some listings do not appear in these indexes because they did not cite a specific preference. Listings that were very specific, or whose music descriptions don't quite fit into these categories also do not appear. (Category listings for **Music Publishers** begin on this page, **Record Companies** on page 336, **Record Producers** on page 340 and **Managers & Booking Agents** begin on page 342.)

MUSIC PUBLISHERS

Adult Contemporary (also easy listening, middle of the road, AAA, ballads, etc.)

Come Alive Communications, Inc. 104

Corelli Music Group 105

Emstone Music Publishing 108

Hammel Associates, Inc., R L 112

Ivory Pen Entertainment 114

MIDI Track Publishing 117

Must Have Music 118

New Rap Jam Publishing, A 119

Pegasus Music 120

Ranco Music Publishing 123

Tourmaline Music, Inc. 125

Your Best Songs Publishing 128

Alternative (also modern rock, punk, college rock, new wave, hardcore, new music, industrial, ska, indie rock, garage, etc.)

Cornelius Companies/Gateway Entertainment, Inc., The 105

Intoxygene Sarl 114

Sandalphon Music Publishing 124

Tourmaline Music, Inc. 125

Blues

Brandon Hills Music, LLC 103

Nervous Publishing 118

New Rap Jam Publishing, A 119

Sandalphon Music Publishing 124

Children's

Brandon Hills Music, LLC 103

Piano Press 121

Classical (also opera, chamber music, serious music, choral, etc.)

Jae Music, Jana 114

Country (also western, C&W, bluegrass, cowboy songs, western swing, honky-tonk, etc.)

Abear Publishing 102

All Rock Music 102

Brandon Hills Music, LLC 103

Come Alive Communications, Inc. 104

Copperfield Music Group 105

Cornelius Companies/Gateway Entertainment, Inc., The 105

De Miles Music Company, The Edward 106

Emstone Music Publishing 108

Glad Music Co. 110

G Major Publishing 111

Hammel Associates, Inc., R L 112

Jae Music, Jana 114

Kaysarah Music 115

Lita Music 115

Maui Arts & Music Association/Survivor Records/Ten of Diamonds Music 116

McClure & Trowbridge Publishing, Ltd. 116

McCoy Music, Jim 117

MIDI Track Publishing 117

M & T Waldoch Publishing, Inc. 116

Must Have Music 118

Nervous Publishing 118

Newbraugh Brothers Music 119

New Rap Jam Publishing, A 119

Pegasus Music 120

Peters Music, Justin 120

Platinum Planet Music, Inc. 121

Ranco Music Publishing 123

Red Sundown Music 123

Sabteca Music Co. 123

Sandalphon Music Publishing 124

Sony/ATV Music Publishing 125

Thistle Hill 125

Tourmaline Music, Inc. 125

Transamerika Musikverlag KG 126

Trio Productions, Inc./Songscape Music, LLC 126

Vaam Music Group 127

Wilcom Publishing 127

Your Best Songs Publishing 128

Dance

De Miles Music Company, The Edward 106

Fresh Entertainment 110

M & T Waldoch Publishing, Inc. 116

Platinum Planet Music, Inc. 121

QUARK, Inc. 122

Ranco Music Publishing 123

Folk (also acoustic, Celtic, etc.)

Heupferd Musikverlag GmbH 112

Kaysarah Music 115

Newbraugh Brothers Music 119

Piano Press 121

Instrumental (also background music, musical scores, etc.)

Alpha Music Inc. 102

De Miles Music Company, The Edward 106

Jae Music, Jana 114

Sinus Musik Produktion, Ulli Weigel 124

Jazz (also fusion, bebop, swing, etc.)

Heupferd Musikverlag GmbH 112

Ivory Pen Entertainment 114

Jae Music, Jana 114

Perla Music 120

Latin (also Spanish, salsa, Cuban, conga, Brazilian, cumbja, rancheras, Mexican, meringue, Tejano, Tex Mex, etc.)

McClure & Trowbridge Publishing, Ltd. 116

Metal (also thrash, grindcore, heavy metal, etc.)

Intoxygene Sarl 114

M & T Waldoch Publishing, Inc. 116

Your Best Songs Publishing 128

New Age (also ambient)

Heupferd Musikverlag GmbH 112

Intoxygene Sarl 114

Maui Arts & Music Association/Survivor Records/Ten of Diamonds Music 116

Sinus Musik Produktion, Ulli Weigel 124

Your Best Songs Publishing 128

Novelty (also comedy, humor, etc.)

Peters Music, Justin 120

Piano Press 121

Pop (also top 40, top 100, popular, chart hits, etc.)

Come Alive Communications, Inc. 104

Copperfield Music Group 105

Cornelius Companies/Gateway Entertainment, Inc., The 105

De Miles Music Company, The Edward 106

Emstone Music Publishing 108

Fresh Entertainment 110

G Major Publishing 111

Hammel Associates, Inc., R L 112

Ivory Pen Entertainment 114

Maui Arts & Music Association/Survivor Records/Ten of Diamonds Music 116

MIDI Track Publishing 117

M & T Waldoch Publishing, Inc. 116

Must Have Music 118

New Rap Jam Publishing, A 119

Pegasus Music 120

Peters Music, Justin 120

QUARK, Inc. 122

Red Sundown Music 123

Sabteca Music Co. 123

Sandalphon Music Publishing 124

Sinus Musik Produktion, Ulli Weigel 124

Thistle Hill 125

Transamerika Musikverlag KG 126

Vaam Music Group 127

Wilcom Publishing 127

Your Best Songs Publishing 128

Rap (also hip-hop, bass, etc.)

Fresh Entertainment 110

Ivory Pen Entertainment 114

McClure & Trowbridge Publishing, Ltd. 116

New Rap Jam Publishing, A 119

Religious (also gospel, sacred, Christian, church, hymns, praise, inspirational, worship, etc.)

Brandon Hills Music, LLC 103

Come Alive Communications, Inc. 104

Copperfield Music Group 105

Corelli Music Group 105

Cornelius Companies/Gateway
    Entertainment, Inc., The 105

G Major Publishing 111

Hammel Associates, Inc., R L 112

Ivory Pen Entertainment 114

Lita Music 115

McClure & Trowbridge Publishing, Ltd.
    116

McCoy Music, Jim 117

MIDI Track Publishing 117

Must Have Music 118

Newbraugh Brothers Music 119

New Rap Jam Publishing, A 119

Sandalphon Music Publishing 124

SME Publishing Group 124

Tourmaline Music, Inc. 125

Rock (also rockabilly, AOR, rock 'n' roll, etc.)

All Rock Music 102

De Miles Music Company, The Edward
    106

Hammel Associates, Inc., R L 112

Heupferd Musikverlag GmbH 112

Lita Music 115

McClure & Trowbridge Publishing, Ltd.
    116

McCoy Music, Jim 117

M & T Waldoch Publishing, Inc. 116

Must Have Music 118

Nervous Publishing 118

Newbraugh Brothers Music 119

New Rap Jam Publishing, A 119

Ranco Music Publishing 123

Red Sundown Music 123

Sandalphon Music Publishing 124

Sinus Musik Produktion, Ulli Weigel 124

Thistle Hill 125

Tourmaline Music, Inc. 125

Transamerika Musikverlag KG 126

Wilcom Publishing 127

Your Best Songs Publishing 128

World (also reggae, ethnic, calypso, international, world beat, etc.)

Heupferd Musikverlag GmbH 112

Kaysarah Music 115

Peters Music, Justin 120

Transamerika Musikverlag KG 126

RECORD COMPANIES
Adult Contemporary (also easy listening, middle of the road, AAA, ballads, etc.)

Ranco Records 154

Roll On Records 157

Alternative (also modern rock, punk, college rock, new wave, hardcore, new music, industrial, ska, indie rock, garage, etc.)

4AD 135

Astralwerks 136

Deep South Entertainment 141

Elektra Records 142

Eyeball Records 143

Fat Wreck Chords 144

Fearless Records 144

Fueled By Ramen 144

Gonzo! Records Inc. 145

Gotham Records 145

Hottrax Records 146

Idol Records 146

Matador Records 148

Metal Blade Records 149

Oglio Records 152

Paper + Plastick 153

RAVE Records, Inc. 154

Redemption Records 155

Rise Records 156

Rotten Records 157

Rough Trade Records 158

Sandalphon Records 159

Skeleton Crew 159

Smog Veil Records 160

Ton Records 162

Transdreamer Records 163

Vagrant Recprds 164

Victory Records 164

Xemu Records 167

XL Recordings 167

Blues

Heart Music, Inc. 145

Parliament Records 153

Sandalphon Records 159

Texas Rose Records 161

Ton Records 162

Topcat Records 162

Classical (also opera, chamber music, serious music, choral, etc.)

Cambria Records & Publishing 138

Lark Record Productions, Inc. 148

North Star Music 151

Tangent® Records 160

Country (also western, C&W, bluegrass, cowboy songs, western swing, honky-tonk, etc.)

Atlan-Dec/Grooveline Records 137

Blue Gem Records 138

Cherry Street Records 139

Collector Records 140

Deep South Entertainment 141

Hottrax Records 146

Lark Record Productions, Inc. 148

NBT Records 150

Outstanding Records 152

Roll On Records 157

Rustic Records 158

Sandalphon Records 159

Sony Music Nashville 160

Sugar Hill Records 160

Texas Rose Records 161

UAR Records 163

Vagrant Recprds 164

Winchester Records 166

Dance

Atlan-Dec/Grooveline Records 137

Gonzo! Records Inc. 145

Parliament Records 153

Quark Records 154

Ranco Records 154

RAVE Records, Inc. 154

Robbins Entertainment LLC 156

Sahara Records and Filmworks Entertainment 158

World Beatnik Records 166

Folk (also acoustic, Celtic, etc.)

Heart Music, Inc. 145

Kill Rock Stars 148

NBT Records 150

Waterdog Music 165

Winchester Records 166

Instrumental (also background music, musical scores, etc.)

Lark Record Productions, Inc. 148

North Star Music 151

Sahara Records and Filmworks
  Entertainment 158

Tangent® Records 160

Jazz (also fusion, bebop, swing, etc.)

Ariana Records 136

Atlan-Dec/Grooveline Records 137

Avita Records 137

Cherry Street Records 139

Fresh Entertainment 144

Heart Music, Inc. 145

Hottrax Records 146

Magna Carta Records 148

North Star Music 151

Outstanding Records 152

Sahara Records and Filmworks
  Entertainment 158

Tangent® Records 160

Topcat Records 162

World Beatnik Records 166

Latin (also Spanish, salsa, Cuban, conga, Brazilian, cumbja, rancheras, Mexican, meringue, Tejano, Tex Mex, etc.)

Outstanding Records 152

Metal (also thrash, grindcore, heavy metal, etc.)

Magna Carta Records 148

Metal Blade Records 149

Rise Records 156

Roadrunner Records 156

Rotten Records 157

Victory Records 164

New Age (also ambient)

North Star Music 151

Tangent® Records 160

Novelty (also comedy, humor, etc.)

Oglio Records 152

Rustic Records 158

Pop (also top 40, top 100, popular, chart hits, etc.)

Alternative Tentacles 135

Aware Records 138

Blue Gem Records 138

Deep South Entertainment 141

Dental Records 142

Fresh Entertainment 144

Fueled By Ramen 144

Gonzo! Records Inc. 145

Gotham Records 145

Heart Music, Inc. 145

Hottrax Records 146

Idol Records 146

Parliament Records 153

Quark Records 154

Red Admiral Records, LLP 155

Redemption Records 155

Robbins Entertainment LLC 156

Roll On Records 157

Sahara Records and Filmworks
  Entertainment 158

Sandalphon Records 159

Simply Grand Music Inc 159

Texas Rose Records 161

Waterdog Music 165

World Beatnik Records 166

Rap (also hip-hop, bass, etc.)

Atlan-Dec/Grooveline Records 137

Fresh Entertainment 144

Parliament Records 153

World Beatnik Records 166

Religious (also gospel, sacred, Christian, church, hymns, praise, inspirational, worship, etc.)

Atlan-Dec/Grooveline Records 137

Fresh Entertainment 144

NBT Records 150

Parliament Records 153

Roll On Records 157

Rustic Records 158

Sandalphon Records 159

Texas Rose Records 161

Winchester Records 166

Rock (also rockabilly, AOR, rock 'n' roll, etc.)

Alternative Tentacles 135

Ariana Records 136

Atlan-Dec/Grooveline Records 137

Aware Records 138

Blackheart Records 138

Blue Gem Records 138

Chattahoochee Records 139

Cherry Street Records 139

Collector Records 140

Deep South Entertainment 141

EARACHE RECORDS 142

Eyeball Records 143

Fat Wreck Chords 144

Fearless Records 144

Fresh Entertainment 144

Fueled By Ramen 144

Gotham Records 145

Heart Music, Inc. 145

Hottrax Records 146

Idol Records 146

Kill Rock Stars 148

Magna Carta Records 148

Megaforce Records 149

NBT Records 150

Nervous Records 151

Oglio Records 152

Outstanding Records 152

Paper + Plastick 153

Ranco Records 154

Rise Records 156

Roadrunner Records 156

Roll On Records 157

Rotten Records 157

Sandalphon Records 159

Skeleton Crew 159

Smog Veil Records 160

Tangent® Records 160

Texas Rose Records 161

Ton Records 162

Touch and Go/Quarterstick Records 162

Transdreamer Records 163

Vagrant Recprds 164

Victory Records 164

Waterdog Music 165

Winchester Records 166

XL Recordings 167

World (also reggae, ethnic, calypso, international, world beat, etc.)

Modal Music, Inc. 150

North Star Music 151

Tangent® Records 160

World Beatnik Records 166

RECORD PRODUCERS
Adult Contemporary (also easy listening, middle of the road, AAA, ballads, etc.)
Category 171

Integrated Entertainment 177

Mustrock Productionz Worldwide 181

Alternative (also modern rock, punk, college rock, new wave, hardcore, new music, industrial, ska, indie rock, garage, etc.)
Blues Alley Records 172

Coachouse Music 173

DaVinci's Notebook Records 174

Kane Producer/Engineer, Karen 177

L.A. Entertainment, Inc. 177

Mac-Attack Productions 179

Marenco, Cookie 179

Mathews, d/b/a Hit or Myth Productions Inc., Scott 180

Westwires Recording USA 183

Blues
Big Bear 172

Celt Musical Services, Jan 173

Coachouse Music 173

Hailing Frequency Music Productions 176

Kane Producer/Engineer, Karen 177

Linear Cycle Productions 178

WLM Music/Recording 183

Classical (also opera, chamber music, serious music, choral, etc.)
Lark Talent & Advertising 178

Marenco, Cookie 179

World Records 184

Country (also western, C&W, bluegrass, cowboy songs, western swing, honky-tonk, etc.)
Cabin-on-the-Lake Music 172

Coachouse Music 173

De Miles Music Company, The Edward 175

Kane Producer/Engineer, Karen 177

Lark Talent & Advertising 178

Linear Cycle Productions 178

Marenco, Cookie 179

Martin, Pete/Vaam Music Productions 179

MusicJones Records 181

WLM Music/Recording 183

Dance
Cabin-on-the-Lake Music 172

De Miles Music Company, The Edward 175

Diamond Entertainment, Joel 175

Final Mix Inc. 176

Mac-Attack Productions 179

Neu Electro Productions 182

Westwires Recording USA 183

Folk (also acoustic, Celtic, etc.)
Marenco, Cookie 179

MusicJones Records 181

Westwires Recording USA 183

World Records 184

Instrumental (also background music, musical scores, etc.)
Creative Soul 173

Lark Talent & Advertising 178

Jazz (also fusion, bebop, swing, etc.)

Big Bear 172

Cabin-on-the-Lake Music 172

Celt Musical Services, Jan 173

Creative Soul 173

DaVinci's Notebook Records 174

De Miles Music Company, The Edward 175

Heart Consort Music 176

Marenco, Cookie 179

World Records 184

Latin (also Spanish, salsa, Cuban, conga, Brazilian, cumbja, rancheras, Mexican, meringue, Tejano, Tex Mex, etc.)

DeLory and Music Makers, Al 174

New Age (also ambient)

DaVinci's Notebook Records 174

Heart Consort Music 176

Neu Electro Productions 182

Novelty (also comedy, humor, etc.)

Linear Cycle Productions 178

Pop (also top 40, top 100, popular, chart hits, etc.)

Blues Alley Records 172

Cabin-on-the-Lake Music 172

Coachouse Music 173

Creative Soul 173

DaVinci's Notebook Records 174

DeLory and Music Makers, Al 174

De Miles Music Company, The Edward 175

Diamond Entertainment, Joel 175

Final Mix Inc. 176

Kane Producer/Engineer, Karen 177

Linear Cycle Productions 178

Mac-Attack Productions 179

Marenco, Cookie 179

Martin, Pete/Vaam Music Productions 179

Mathews, d/b/a Hit or Myth Productions Inc., Scott 180

MusicJones Records 181

Mustrock Productionz Worldwide 181

Neu Electro Productions 182

New Experience Records/Faze 4 Records 182

WLM Music/Recording 183

Rap (also hip-hop, bass, etc.)

Final Mix Inc. 176

L.A. Entertainment, Inc. 177

Marenco, Cookie 179

Mustrock Productionz Worldwide 181

Neu Electro Productions 182

New Experience Records/Faze 4 Records 182

Religious (also gospel, sacred, Christian, church, hymns, praise, inspirational, worship, etc.)

Blues Alley Records 172

Creative Soul 173

Hailing Frequency Music Productions 176

L.A. Entertainment, Inc. 177

Linear Cycle Productions 178

New Experience Records/Faze 4 Records 182

WLM Music/Recording 183

Rock (also rockabilly, AOR, rock 'n' roll, etc.)

Celt Musical Services, Jan 173

Coachouse Music 173

Creative Soul 173

DaVinci's Notebook Records 174

Hailing Frequency Music Productions 176

Integrated Entertainment 177

Kane Producer/Engineer, Karen 177

Linear Cycle Productions 178

Mathews, d/b/a Hit or Myth Productions Inc., Scott 180

MusicJones Records 181

Neu Electro Productions 182

New Experience Records/Faze 4 Records 182

Westwires Recording USA 183

WLM Music/Recording 183

World (also reggae, ethnic, calypso, international, world beat, etc.)

Kane Producer/Engineer, Karen 177

MANAGERS & BOOKING AGENTS

Adult Contemporary (also easy listening, middle of the road, AAA, ballads, etc.)

Brothers Management Associates 190

First Time Management 193

International Entertainment Bureau 195

Kuper Personal Management/Recovery Recordings 195

Loggins Promotion 196

Management by Jaffe 197

Skorman Productions, Inc., T. 203

St. John Artists 203

Tas Music Co./Dave Tasse Entertainment 204

Warner Productions, Cheryl K. 205

Winterland Entertainment Management & Publishing 206

Zane Management, Inc. 206

Alternative (also modern rock, punk, college rock, new wave, hardcore, new music, industrial, ska, indie rock, garage, etc.)

Bread & Butter Productions 189

First Time Management 193

Kuper Personal Management/Recovery Recordings 195

Loggins Promotion 196

Management by Jaffe 197

On the Level Music! 198

Prime Time Entertainment 199

Sandalphon Management 201

Silver Bow Management 202

Southeastern Attractions 203

Umbrella Artists Management, Inc. 204

Blues

Barnard Management Services (BMS) 188

Blowin' Smoke Productions/Records 189

First Time Management 193

Noteworthy Productions 198

On the Level Music! 198

Robert Entertainment 201

Sandalphon Management 201

Universal Music Marketing 205

Children's

First Time Management 193

Levy Management, Rick 196

Siegel Entertainment Ltd. 202

Classical (also opera, chamber music, serious music, choral, etc.)

Clousher Productions 190

First Time Management 193

Jae Enterprises, Jana 195

Country (also western, C&W, bluegrass, cowboy songs, western swing, honky-tonk, etc.)

Angelini Enterprises, Bill/BookYourEvent.com 188

Barnard Management Services (BMS) 188

Bread & Butter Productions 189

Clousher Productions 190

Concept 2000 Inc. 191

De Miles Music Company, The Edward 191

Eckert Entertainment Consultants, John 192

First Time Management 193

Harrell & Associates, M. 194

International Entertainment Bureau 195

Jae Enterprises, Jana 195

Levy Management, Rick 196

Martin Productions, Rick 197

Noteworthy Productions 198

Prime Time Entertainment 199

Sandalphon Management 201

Siegel Entertainment Ltd. 202

Silver Bow Management 202

Skorman Productions, Inc., T. 203

Southeastern Attractions 203

T.L.C. Booking Agency 204

Universal Music Marketing 205

Warner Productions, Cheryl K. 205

Wemus Entertainment 205

Winterland Entertainment Management & Publishing 206

Dance

Clousher Productions 190

De Miles Music Company, The Edward 191

First Time Management 193

Martin Productions, Rick 197

Reign Music and Media, LLC 200

Southeastern Attractions 203

Tas Music Co./Dave Tasse Entertainment 204

Zane Management, Inc. 206

Folk (also acoustic, Celtic, etc.)

Bread & Butter Productions 189

First Time Management 193

Noteworthy Productions 198

Zane Management, Inc. 206

Instrumental (also background music, musical scores, etc.)

First Time Management 193

Jae Enterprises, Jana 195

Raspberry Jam Music 199

Jazz (also fusion, bebop, swing, etc.)

Blue Cat Agency, The 189

Concept 2000 Inc. 191

First Time Management 193

Harrell & Associates, M. 194

International Entertainment Bureau 195

Jae Enterprises, Jana 195

Loggins Promotion 196

On the Level Music! 198

Prime Time Entertainment 199

Raspberry Jam Music 199

Riohcat Music 200

Robert Entertainment 201

Tas Music Co./Dave Tasse Entertainment 204

Universal Music Marketing 205

Zane Management, Inc. 206

Latin (also Spanish, salsa, Cuban, conga, Brazilian, cumbja, rancheras, Mexican, meringue, Tejano, Tex Mex, etc.)

Angelini Enterprises, Bill/BookYourEvent.com 188

Blue Cat Agency, The 189

First Time Management 193

Raspberry Jam Music 199

Reign Music and Media, LLC 200

Metal (also thrash, grindcore, heavy metal, etc.)

Artist Representation and Management 188

First Time Management 193

Raspberry Jam Music 199

WorldSound, LLC 206

New Age (also ambient)

First Time Management 193

Novelty (also comedy, humor, etc.)

First Time Management 193

T.L.C. Booking Agency 204

Pop (also top 40, top 100, popular, chart hits, etc.)

Artist Representation and Management 188

Blue Cat Agency, The 189

Brothers Management Associates 190

Concept 2000 Inc. 191

De Miles Music Company, The Edward 191

Eckert Entertainment Consultants, John 192

Evans Productions, Scott 192

First Time Management 193

Jae Enterprises, Jana 195

Levy Management, Rick 196

Loggins Promotion 196

Management by Jaffe 197

Martin Productions, Rick 197

Mayo & Company, Phil 198

Raspberry Jam Music 199

Reign Music and Media, LLC 200

Robert Entertainment 201

Sandalphon Management 201

Siegel Entertainment Ltd. 202

Silver Bow Management 202

Skorman Productions, Inc., T. 203

Starkravin' Management 203

Tas Music Co./Dave Tasse Entertainment 204

Umbrella Artists Management, Inc. 204

Warner Productions, Cheryl K. 205

Winterland Entertainment Management & Publishing 206

WorldSound, LLC 206

Zane Management, Inc. 206

Rap (also hip-hop, bass, etc.)

First Time Management 193

Hardison International Entertainment Corporation 194

Loggins Promotion 196

Reign Music and Media, LLC 200

Religious (also gospel, sacred, Christian, church, hymns, praise, inspirational, worship, etc.)

Concept 2000 Inc. 191

Exclesisa Booking Agency 193

First Time Management 193

Harrell & Associates, M. 194

Mayo & Company, Phil 198

Sandalphon Management 201

Silver Bow Management 202

Warner Productions, Cheryl K. 205

Rock (also rockabilly, AOR, rock 'n' roll, etc.)

Artist Representation and Management 188

Barnard Management Services (BMS) 188

Blowin' Smoke Productions/Records 189

Blue Cat Agency, The 189

Bread & Butter Productions 189

Brothers Management Associates 190

Clousher Productions 190

De Miles Music Company, The Edward 191

Eckert Entertainment Consultants, John 192

Harrell & Associates, M. 194

International Entertainment Bureau 195

Loggins Promotion 196

Management by Jaffe 197

Martin Productions, Rick 197

On the Level Music! 198

Rainbow Talent Agency 199

Raspberry Jam Music 199

Sandalphon Management 201

Siegel Entertainment Ltd. 202

Silver Bow Management 202

Southeastern Attractions 203

Starkravin' Management 203

St. John Artists 203

Tas Music Co./Dave Tasse Entertainment 204

T.L.C. Booking Agency 204

Umbrella Artists Management, Inc. 204

Universal Music Marketing 205

Winterland Entertainment Management & Publishing 206

WorldSound, LLC 206

Zane Management, Inc. 206

World (also reggae, ethnic, calypso, international, world beat, etc.)

Angelini Enterprises, Bill/BookYourEvent. com 188

Clousher Productions 190

First Time Management 193

Harrell & Associates, M. 194

Noteworthy Productions 198

Prime Time Entertainment 199

Raspberry Jam Music 199

Robert Entertainment 201

WorldSound, LLC 206

Openness to Submissions Index

Use this index to find companies open to your level of experience. It is recommended to use this index in conjunction with the Category Indexes found on page 333. Once you have compiled a list of companies open to your experience and music, read the information in these listings, paying close attention to the **How to Contact** subhead. (Also see A Sample Listing Decoded on page 7.)

◖ OPEN TO BEGINNERS

Manager Booking Agents
Bread & Butter Productions 189
Eckert Entertainment Consultants, John 192
Evans Productions, Scott 192
Exclesisa Booking Agency 193
Hardison International Entertainment Corporation 194
Kuper Personal Management/Recovery Recordings 195
Loggins Promotion 196
Martin Productions, Rick 197
On the Level Music! 198
Raspberry Jam Music 199
Reign Music and Media, LLC 200
Robert Entertainment 201
Sandalphon Management 201
Silver Bow Management 202
St. John Artists 203

Universal Music Marketing 205
Winterland Entertainment Management & Publishing 206

Music Publisher
All Rock Music 102
Brandon Hills Music, LLC 103
Corelli Music Group 105
Fifth Avenue Media, Ltd. 109
Fresh Entertainment 110
Glad Music Co. 110
Hammel Associates, Inc., R L 112
Ivory Pen Entertainment 114
Kaysarah Music 115
McCoy Music, Jim 117
M & T Waldoch Publishing, Inc. 116
Nervous Publishing 118
Peters Music, Justin 120
QUARK, Inc. 122
Ranco Music Publishing 123
Red Sundown Music 123

Sabteca Music Co. 123

Sandalphon Music Publishing 124

Thistle Hill 125

Record Company

Atlan-Dec/Grooveline Records 137

Blue Gem Records 138

Chattahoochee Records 139

Collector Records 140

Deep South Entertainment 141

Dental Records 142

Fresh Entertainment 144

Gonzo! Records Inc. 145

Gotham Records 145

Hottrax Records 146

Megaforce Records 149

Modal Music, Inc. 150

NBT Records 150

Nervous Records 151

North Star Music 151

Ranco Records 154

Redemption Records 155

Roll On Records 157

Rotten Records 157

Sandalphon Records 159

Tangent® Records 160

Ton Records 162

UAR Records 163

World Beatnik Records 166

Record Producers

Blues Alley Records 172

Celt Musical Services, Jan 173

Coachouse Music 173

L.A. Entertainment, Inc. 177

Lark Talent & Advertising 178

Linear Cycle Productions 178

Mac-Attack Productions 179

Mathews, d/b/a Hit or Myth Productions Inc., Scott 180

MusicJones Records 181

Neu Electro Productions 182

◙ PREFERS EXPERIENCED, BUT OPEN TO BEGINNERS

Manager Booking Agents

Angelini Enterprises, Bill/BookYourEvent. com 188

Artist Representation and Management 188

Blank & Blank 189

Blowin' Smoke Productions/Records 189

Brothers Management Associates 190

Class Act Productions/Management/Peter Kimmel's Music Catalog 190

Clousher Productions 190

Concept 2000 Inc. 191

Jae Enterprises, Jana 195

Management Trust Ltd., The 197

Rainbow Talent Agency 199

Riohcat Music 200

Sa'Mall Management 201

Skorman Productions, Inc., T. 203

Southeastern Attractions 203

Starkravin' Management 203

Tas Music Co./Dave Tasse Entertainment 204

T.L.C. Booking Agency 204

Warner Productions, Cheryl K. 205

Wemus Entertainment 205

WorldSound, LLC 206

Zane Management, Inc. 206

Music Publisher

Abear Publishing 102

Alpha Music Inc. 102

Christmas & Holiday Music 103

Come Alive Communications, Inc. 104

Cornelius Companies/Gateway Entertainment, Inc., The 105

De Miles Music Company, The Edward 106

Emstone Music Publishing 108

First Time Music (Publishing) U.K. 109

G Major Publishing 111

Goodnight Kiss Music 111

Heupferd Musikverlag GmbH 112

Jae Music, Jana 114

Maui Arts & Music Association/Survivor Records/Ten of Diamonds Music 116

Must Have Music 118

Newbraugh Brothers Music 119

New Rap Jam Publishing, A 119

Piano Press 121

Pollybyrd Publications Limited 122

Sinus Musik Produktion, Ulli Weigel 124

SME Publishing Group 124

Transamerika Musikverlag KG 126

Vaam Music Group 127

Wilcom Publishing 127

Record Company

Alternative Tentacles 135

Blackheart Records 138

Cherry Street Records 139

Idol Records 146

Kill Rock Stars 148

Lark Record Productions, Inc. 148

Magna Carta Records 148

Metal Blade Records 149

Outstanding Records 152

Panama Music Group of Companies, The 152

Parliament Records 153

Quark Records 154

Rustic Records 158

Texas Rose Records 161

Topcat Records 162

Transdreamer Records 163

Winchester Records 166

Xemu Records 167

Record Producers

Creative Soul 173

DeLory and Music Makers, Al 174

Hailing Frequency Music Productions 176

Heart Consort Music 176

Integrated Entertainment 177

Kane Producer/Engineer, Karen 177

Martin, Pete/Vaam Music Productions 179

New Experience Records/Faze 4 Records 182

Westwires Recording USA 183

WLM Music/Recording 183

World Records 184

☑ ONLY OPEN TO PREVIOUSLY PUBLISHED SONGWRITERS/WELL-ESTABLISHED ACTS

Manager Booking Agents

Blue Cat Agency, The 189

De Miles Music Company, The Edward 191

Levy Management, Rick 196

Management by Jaffe 197

Noteworthy Productions 198

Siegel Entertainment Ltd. 202

Music Publisher

Pegasus Music 120

Openness Index

Record Company

American Recordings 135

Ariana Records 136

Astralwerks 136

Cambria Records & Publishing 138

Oglio Records 152

Robbins Entertainment LLC 156

Record Producers

Final Mix Inc. 176

⊘ DOES NOT ACCEPT UNSOLICITED MATERIAL/ ONLY ACCEPTS MATERIAL REFERRED BY AN INDUSTRY SOURCE

Manager Booking Agents

Barnard Management Services (BMS) 188

Harrell & Associates, M. 194

International Entertainment Bureau 195

Umbrella Artists Management, Inc. 204

Music Publisher

Bixio Music Group & Associates/IDM Music 102

Chrysalis Music Group 104

Copperfield Music Group 105

Disney Music Publishing 107

EMI Christian Music Publishing 107

EMI Music Publishing 108

Intoxygene Sarl 114

MIDI Track Publishing 117

Perla Music 120

Sony/ATV Music Publishing 125

Trio Productions, Inc./Songscape Music, LLC 126

Universal Music Publishing 127

Warner/Chappell Music, Inc. 127

Record Company

Angel Records 136

Atlantic Records 137

Avita Records 137

Aware Records 138

Capitol Records 139

Columbia Records 140

Cosmotone Records 140

Curb Records 141

Elektra Records 142

Epic Records 142

Heart Music, Inc. 145

Interscope/Geffen/A&M Records 147

Island/Def Jam Music Group 147

J Records 147

Matador Records 148

MCA Nashville 149

RAVE Records, Inc. 154

RCA Records 155

Reprise Records 156

Sahara Records and Filmworks Entertainment 158

Sony BMG 160

Sony Music Nashville 160

Sugar Hill Records 160

Tommy Boy Entertainment LLC 161

Universal Records 164

Verve Music Group, The 164

Virgin Records 165

Warner Bros. Records 165

Waterdog Music 165

Record Producers

Cabin-on-the-Lake Music 172

De Miles Music Company, The Edward 175

Diamond Entertainment, Joel 175

Marenco, Cookie 179

Film & TV Index

This index lists companies who place music in motion picture and TV shows (excluding commercials). To learn more about their film/TV experience, read the information under **Film & TV** in their Listings. It is recommended to use this index in conjunction with the Openness to Submissions Index beginning on page 346.

Music Publishers
Alpha Music Inc. 102
Bixio Music Group & Associates/IDM Music 102
Christmas & Holiday Music 103
De Miles Music Company, The Edward 106
First Time Music (Publishing) U.K. 109
Fresh Entertainment 110
Goodnight Kiss Music 111
Heupferd Musikverlag GmbH 112
Intoxygene Sarl 114
MIDI Track Publishing 117
QUARK, Inc. 122
Ranco Music Publishing 123
Sinus Musik Produktion, Ulli Weigel 124
Transamerika Musikverlag KG 126

Advertising, Audiovisual
Allegro Music 212
Disk Productions 213

Record Producers
Cabin-on-the-Lake Music 172
De Miles Music Company, The Edward 175
Mustrock Productionz Worldwide 181

Record Companies
Sahara Records and Filmworks Entertainment 158

Geographic Index

This Geographic Index will help you locate companies by state as well as those in countries outside the U.S. It is recommended to use this index in conjunction with the Openness to Submissions Index on page 346. Once you find the names of companies in this index you are interested in, check the listings within each section for addresses, phone numbers, contact names and submission details.

ARIZONA
Conferences & Workshops
Ariana Records 136

ARKANSAS
Publishers of Poetry
G Major Publishing 111

CALIFORNIA
Book/Chapbook Publishers
Diamond Entertainment, Joel 175

Final Mix Inc. 176

Hailing Frequency Music Productions 176

L.A. Entertainment, Inc. 177

Linear Cycle Productions 178

Marenco, Cookie 179

Martin, Pete/Vaam Music Productions 179

Mathews, d/b/a Hit or Myth Productions Inc., Scott 180

Publishers of Poetry
Christmas & Holiday Music 103

Chrysalis Music Group 104

Disney Music Publishing 107

EMI Music Publishing 108

Goodnight Kiss Music 111

Must Have Music 118

Piano Press 121

Pollybyrd Publications Limited 122

Sabteca Music Co. 123

Sony/ATV Music Publishing 125

Vaam Music Group 127

Warner/Chappell Music, Inc. 127

Wilcom Publishing 127

FLORDIA
Book/Chapbook Publishers
Mac-Attack Productions 179

FLORIDA
Publishers of Poetry
Emstone Music Publishing 108

GEORGIA
Conferences & Workshops
Atlan-Dec/Grooveline Records 137

Fresh Entertainment 144

Hottrax Records 146

Publishers of Poetry
Fresh Entertainment 110

HAWAII
Publishers of Poetry
Maui Arts & Music Association/Survivor
Records/Ten of Diamonds Music 116

ILLINOIS
Book/Chapbook Publishers
Cabin-on-the-Lake Music 172

Coachouse Music 173

De Miles Music Company, The Edward
175

Neu Electro Productions 182

Conferences & Workshops
Aware Records 138

Modal Music, Inc. 150

Sahara Records and Filmworks
Entertainment 158

UAR Records 163

Waterdog Music 165

Publishers of Poetry
De Miles Music Company, The Edward
106

Kaysarah Music 115

INDIANA
Conferences & Workshops
Indiana University New Music Ensemble
243

Publishers of Poetry
Hammel Associates, Inc., R L 112

IOWA
Book/Chapbook Publishers
Heart Consort Music 176

KENTUCKY
Book/Chapbook Publishers
Creative Soul 173

MARYLAND
Publishers of Poetry
Ivory Pen Entertainment 114

MICHIGAN
Book/Chapbook Publishers
World Records 184

Conferences & Workshops
RAVE Records, Inc. 154

NEVADA
Book/Chapbook Publishers
MusicJones Records 181

Publishers of Poetry
Pollybyrd Publications Limited 122

NEW JERSEY
Publishers of Poetry
Perla Music 120

NEW YORK
Book/Chapbook Publishers
Mustrock Productionz Worldwide 181

Conferences & Workshops
Angel Records 136
Astralwerks 136
Atlantic Records 137
Columbia Records 140
Dental Records 142
Elektra Records 142
Epic Records 142
Interscope/Geffen/A&M Records 147
Island/Def Jam Music Group 147
J Records 147
Quark Records 154
RCA Records 155
Robbins Entertainment LLC 156
Sony BMG 160
Tommy Boy Entertainment LLC 161
Transdreamer Records 163
Universal Records 164
Verve Music Group, The 164
Virgin Records 165
Warner Bros. Records 165
Xemu Records 167

Publishers of Poetry
Alpha Music Inc. 102
Bixio Music Group & Associates/IDM Music 102
EMI Music Publishing 108
Fifth Avenue Media, Ltd. 109
MIDI Track Publishing 117
QUARK, Inc. 122
Sony/ATV Music Publishing 125
Warner/Chappell Music, Inc. 127

NORTH CAROLINA
Book/Chapbook Publishers
WLM Music/Recording 183

Conferences & Workshops
Deep South Entertainment 141
Sugar Hill Records 160

OHIO
Book/Chapbook Publishers
New Experience Records/Faze 4 Records 182

Conferences & Workshops
Tangent® Records 160

Publishers of Poetry
New Rap Jam Publishing, A 119

OKLAHOMA
Book/Chapbook Publishers
Lark Talent & Advertising 178

Conferences & Workshops
Cherry Street Records 139
Lark Record Productions, Inc. 148

Publishers of Poetry
Jae Music, Jana 114
SME Publishing Group 124

OREGON
Book/Chapbook Publishers
Celt Musical Services, Jan 173

PENNSYLVANIA
Book/Chapbook Publishers
Integrated Entertainment 177
Westwires Recording USA 183

Conferences & Workshops

Megaforce Records 149

RHODE ISLAND
Conferences & Workshops

Newport Folk Festival 294

Newport Jazz Festival 294

North Star Music 151

TENNESSEE
Conferences & Workshops

Atlantic Records 137

Avita Records 137

Capitol Records 139

Columbia Records 140

Curb Records 141

Epic Records 142

Island/Def Jam Music Group 147

MCA Nashville 149

RCA Records 155

Sony Music Nashville 160

Warner Bros. Records 165

TEXAS
Conferences & Workshops

Cosmotone Records 140

Heart Music, Inc. 145

Idol Records 146

Texas Rose Records 161

Topcat Records 162

World Beatnik Records 166

Publishers of Poetry

Glad Music Co. 110

UNITED KINGDOM
Book/Chapbook Publishers

Big Bear 172

UNITED KINGDOM ENGLAND, WALES, SCOTLAND, N. IRELAND
Conferences & Workshops

Nervous Records 151

Panama Music Group of Companies, The 152

Publishers of Poetry

First Time Music (Publishing) U.K. 109

Nervous Publishing 118

WASHINGTON
Conferences & Workshops

Kill Rock Stars 148

Publishers of Poetry

Corelli Music Group 105

Your Best Songs Publishing 128

WEST VIRGINIA
Conferences & Workshops

NBT Records 150

Winchester Records 166

Publishers of Poetry

McCoy Music, Jim 117

Newbraugh Brothers Music 119

General Index

4AD 135

A

Abear Publishing 102

Academy of Country Music 268

Acadiana Symphony Orchestra 232

Advertel, Inc. 212

AGO Award in Organ Composition 254

AGO/ECS Publishing Award in Choral Composition 254

ALEA III International Composition Prize 254

Allegro Music 212

All Rock Music 102

ALLRS MUSIC PUBLISHING CO. (ASCAP) 171

Alpha Music Inc. 102

Alternative Tentacles 135

American Boychoir, The 232

American Music Center, Inc. 268

American Opera Musical Theatre Co. 232

American Recordings 135

American Society of Composers, Authors and Publishers (ASCAP) 268

American Songwriter Lyric Contest 255

Anderson Symphony Orchestra 233

Angelini Enterprises, Bill/BookYourEvent. com 188

Angel Records 136

Annual NSAI Song Contest 255

Appel Farm Arts and Music Festival 289

Ariana Records 136

Arizona Songwriters Association 269

Arkansas Repertory Theatre 218

Artist Representation and Management 188

Artists' Fellowships 256

ASCAP 289

ASCAP Deems Taylor Awards, The 256

ASCAP Musical Theatre Workshop 289

ASCAP West Coast/Lester Sill Songwriters Workshop 289

Association of Independent Music Publishers 269

Astralwerks 136

Atlan-Dec/Grooveline Records 137

Atlanta Young Singers of Callanwolde, The 233

Atlantic Records 137

Augsburg Choir 233

Austin Songwriters Group 270

Avita Records 137

Aware Records 138

B

Baker's Plays 226

Baltimore Songwriters Association 270

Barnard Management Services (BMS) 188

Barter Theatre 218

Big Bear 172

Billings Symphony 234

Bixio Music Group & Associates/IDM Music 102

Blackheart Records 138

Blank & Blank 189

Blank Theatre Company Young Playwrights Festival, The 257

Blowin' Smoke Productions/Records 189

Blue Cat Agency, The 189

Blue Gem Records 138

Blues Alley Records 172

BMI-Lehman Engel Musical Theatre Workshop 290

Boston Philharmonic, The 234

Boston Songwriters Workshop, The 270

Brandon Hills Music, LLC 103

BRAVO! L.A. 234

Bread & Butter Productions 189

Brevard Music Center 302

Broadcast Music, Inc. (BMI) 271

Broadway Tomorrow Previews 290

Brothers Management Associates 190

Bush Artist Fellows Program 257

C

Cabin-on-the-Lake Music 172

Calgary Boys Choir 235

Cambria Records & Publishing 138

Canada Council for the Arts/Conseil des Arts du Canada 272

Canadian Country Music Association 272

Canadian Opera Company 235

Cantata Academy 236

Capitol Records 139

Carey University Dinner Theatre, William 218

Carmel Symphony Orchestra 236

Cedar Crest Studio 212

Celt Musical Services, Jan 173

Central Carolina Songwriters Association (CCSA) 272

Central Oregon Songwriters Association 273

Chattahoochee Records 139

Chattanooga Girls Choir 237

Cherry Street Records 139

Cheyenne Symphony Orchestra 237

Christmas & Holiday Music 103

Chrysalis Music Group 104

Cimarron Circuit Opera Company 237

Circa '21 Dinner Playhouse 219

Class Act Productions/Management/Peter Kimmel's Music Catalog 190

Clousher Productions 190

CMJ Music Marathon, MusicFest & FilmFest 290

Coachouse Music 173

Collector Records 140

College Music Society, The 273

Columbia Records 140

Come Alive Communications, Inc. 104

Communications for Learning 213

Concept 2000 Inc. 191

Connecticut Choral Artists/Concora 238

Connecticut Songwriters Association 273

Contemporary Drama Service 226

Copperfield Music Group 105

Corelli Music Group 105

Cornelius Companies/Gateway Entertainment, Inc., The 105

Cosmotone Records 140

Creative Soul 173

General Index

Cringe Music (PRS, MCPS) 106

CRS National Composers Competition 258

Curb Records 141

Cutting Edge Music Business Conference 291

D

Dallas Songwriters Association 274

DaVinci's Notebook Records 174

Deep Elm Records 141

Deep South Entertainment 141

Define Something in Nothing Music 106

DeLory and Music Makers, Al 174

De Miles Music Company, The Edward 106, 175, 191

Dental Records 142

Diamond Entertainment, Joel 175

Disk Productions 213

Disney Music Publishing 107

Dramatic Publishing Company, The 227

Dunsdon Music Publishing 107

Duo Clasico 238

E

EARACHE RECORDS 142

Eckert Entertainment Consultants, John 192

Eldridge Plays and Musicals 228

Eldridge Publishing Co., Inc. 227

Elektra Records 142

EMI Christian Music Publishing 107

EMI Music Publishing 108

Emstone Music Publishing 108

Ensemble Theatre of Cincinnati 219

Epic Records 142

Epitaph Records 143

European International Competition for Composers/IBLA Music Foundation 258

European Union Chamber Orchestra 239

Evans Productions, Scott 192

Exclesisa Booking Agency 193

Eyeball Records 143

F

Fatt Chantz Music 108

Fatt Chantz Records 143

Fat Wreck Chords 144

Fearless Records 144

Field, The 274

Fifth Avenue Media, Ltd. 109

Final Mix Inc. 176

Fine Art Productions/Richie Suraci Pictures, Multimedia, Interactive 213

First Time Management 193

First Time Music (Publishing) U.K. 109

Fontana Concert Society 239

Fort Worth Children's Opera 240

Freelance Press, The 228

French, Inc., Samuel 228

Fresh Entertainment 110, 144

Fueled By Ramen 144

Fulbright Scholar Program, Council for International Exchange of Scholars 258

G

Gaul Composition Contest, Harvey 259

Glad Music Co. 110

G Major Publishing 111

Gonzo! Records Inc. 145

Goodnight Kiss Music 111

Good Publishing, L.J. 112

Gotham Records 145

Great American Song Contest 259

Greater Grand Forks Symphony Orchestra 240

Guild of International Songwriters & Composers, The 275

Guthrie Centre, The Tyrone 302

H

Hailing Frequency Music Productions 176

Hambidge Center, The 302

Hammel Associates, Inc., R L 112

Hardison International Entertainment Corporation 194

Harrell & Associates, M. 194

Hawai'i Songwriters Association 276

Heart Consort Music 176

Heartland Men's Chorus 240

Heart Music, Inc. 145

Helena Symphony 241

Hendersonville Symphony Orchestra 241

Hershey Symphony Orchestra 241

Heuer Publishing Co. 229

Heupferd Musikverlag GmbH 112

Hollywood Reporter/Billboard Film & TV Music Conference 291

Home Town Hero's Publishing 113

Hottrax Records 146

Hudson Valley Philharmonic 242

I

IAMA (International Acoustic Music Awards) 259

IAMA (INTERNATIONAL ACOUSTIC MUSIC AWARDS) 113

Idol Publishing 113

Idol Records 146

Independent Music Conference 291

Indiana University New Music Ensemble 243

Integrated Entertainment 177

International Entertainment Bureau 195

International Songwriters Association Ltd. 276

Interscope/Geffen/A&M Records 147

Intoxygene Sarl 114

Island/Def Jam Music Group 147

Isle Royale National Park Artist-in-Residence Program 303

Ivory Pen Entertainment 114

J

Jae Enterprises, Jana 195

Jae Music, Jana 114

J Records 147

K

Kalani Oceanside Retreat 303

Kane Producer/Engineer, Karen 177

Kaysarah Music 115

Kentucky Opera 243

Kerrville Folk Festival 292

Kill Rock Stars 148

Kinley Memorial Fellowship, Kate Neal 260

Knoxville Songwriters Association 276

Kuper Personal Management/Recovery Recordings 195

L

L.A. Designers' Theatre Music Awards 260

L.A. Entertainment, Inc. 177

La Jolla Playhouse 220

Lamb's Retreat for Songwriters 292

Lark Record Productions, Inc. 148

Lark Talent & Advertising 178

Lennon Songwriting Contest, The John 261

Levy Management, Rick 196

Lexington Philharmonic Society 243

Lima Symphony Orchestra 243

Linear Cycle Productions 178

Lita Music 115

Loggins Promotion 196

Los Angeles Designers' Theatre 220

Los Angeles Music Network 277

Lyric Opera of Chicago 244

M

Mac-Attack Productions 179

MacDowell Colony, The 303

Magna Carta Records 148

Management by Jaffe 197

Management Trust Ltd., The 197

Manchester Music Festival 292

Manitoba Music 277

Marenco, Cookie 179

Martin, Pete/Vaam Music Productions 179

Martin Productions, Rick 197

Matador Records 148

Mathews, d/b/a Hit or Myth Productions Inc., Scott 180

Maui Arts & Music Association/Survivor Records/Ten of Diamonds Music 116

Mayo & Company, Phil 198

Mazumdar New Play Competition, Maxim 261

MCA Nashville 149

McClure & Trowbridge Publishing, Ltd. 116

McCoy Music, Jim 117

Meet the Composer 278

Megaforce Records 149

Memphis Songwriters' Association 278

Metal Blade Records 149

Mid-Atlantic Song Contest 262

MIDI Track Publishing 117

Milwaukee Youth Symphony Orchestra 244

Minnesota Association of Songwriters 278

Modal Music, Inc. 150

Monk International Jazz Composers Competition, Thelonious 262

Moores Opera Center 245

M & T Waldoch Publishing, Inc. 116

Music & Advertising Conference 293

Music BC Industry Association 279

Music Business Solutions/Career Building Workshops 293

MusicJones Records 181

Must Have Music 118

Mustrock Productionz Worldwide 181

N

Nashville Songwriters Association International 279

National Association of Composers/USA (NACUSA), The 279

NBT Records 150

Nervous Publishing 118

Nervous Records 151

Nestico Award, Sammy/USAF Band Airmen of Note 263

Neu Electro Productions 182

Newbraugh Brothers Music 119

New Experience Records/Faze 4 Records 182

New Harmony Project, The 293

Newport Folk Festival 294

Newport Jazz Festival 294

New Rap Jam Publishing, A 119

New York State Theatre Institute 221

Norfolk Chamber Music Festival 294

North by Northeast Music Festival and Conference 294

North Shore Music Theatre 221

North Star Music 151

Noteworthy Productions 198

Novus 214

NSAI Song Camps 295

NSAI Songwriters Songposium 295

O

Oglio Records 152

Omni Communications 214

On the Level Music! 198

Open Eye Theater, The 222

Opera America 280

Opera Memphis 245

Orchestra Seattle/Seattle Chamber Singers 245

Orford Festival 295

Outstanding Records 152

P

Pacific Northwest Songwriters Association 280

Palmetto Mastersingers 246

Panama Music Group of Companies, The 152

Paper + Plastick 153

Parliament Records 153

Pegasus Music 120

Perla Music 120

Peters Music, Justin 120

Piano Press 121

Piccolo Opera Company Inc. 246

Pioneer Drama Service 229

Pittsburgh Songwriters Association 281

Platinum Planet Music, Inc. 121

Playwrights Horizons 222

Pollybyrd Publications Limited 122

Primary Stages 222

Prime Time Entertainment 199

Prince Music Theater 223

Princeton Symphony Orchestra 247

Prism Saxophone Quartet 247

Pulitzer Prize in Music 263

Q

QUARK, Inc. 122

Quark Records 154

R

Rainbow Talent Agency 199

Ranco Music Publishing 123

Ranco Records 154

Raspberry Jam Music 199

RAVE Records, Inc. 154

RCA Records 155

Red Admiral Records, LLP 155

Redemption Records 155

Red Sundown Music 123

Reggae Sumfest 296

Reign Music and Media, LLC 200

Repertory Theatre of St. Louis, The 223

Reprise Records 156

Rhode Island Songwriters' Association 281

Riohcat Music 200

Rise Records 156

Roadrunner Records 156

Robbins Entertainment LLC 156

Robert Entertainment 201

Rocky Mountain Folks Festival Songwriter Showcase 264

Roll On Records 157

Rome Prize Competition Fellowship 264

Rotten Records 157

Rough Trade Records 158

Rustic Records 158

S

Sabteca Music Co. 123

Sacramento Master Singers 247

Sahara Records and Filmworks Entertainment 158

Sa'Mall Management 201

Sandalphon Management 201

Sandalphon Music Publishing 124

Sandalphon Records 159

San Diego Songwriters Guild 281

San Francisco Girls Chorus 248

Second Stage Theatre 223

SESAC Inc. 282

Shakespeare Santa Cruz 224

Siegel Entertainment Ltd. 202

Silver Bow Management 202

Simply Grand Music Inc 159

Singing Boys of Pennsylvania 249

Sinus Musik Produktion, Ulli Weigel 124

Sitka Center for Art & Ecology 304

Skeleton Crew 159

Skorman Productions, Inc., T. 203

SME Publishing Group 124

Smog Veil Records 160

SOCAN (Society of Composers, Authors, and Music Publishers of Canada) 282

Society of Composers & Lyricists 282

SODRAC Inc. 283

Songwriters Association of Washington 283

Songwriters Guild of America Foundation, The 296

Songwriters Guild of America, The 284

Songwriters Hall of Fame (SongHall) 284

Songwriters PlaygroundÆ 296

Songwriters Resource Network 285

Sony/ATV Music Publishing 125

Sony BMG 160

Sony Music Nashville 160

South by Southwest Music Conference 297

Southeastern Attractions 203

Southwest Virginia Songwriters Association 285

Starkravin' Management 203

St. John Artists 203

St. Louis Chamber Chorus 249

Sugar Hill Records 160

Susquehanna Symphony Orchestra 250

Swannanoa Gathering--Contemporary Folk Week, The 297

T

Tangent® Records 160

Tas Music Co./Dave Tasse Entertainment 204

Telluride Troubadour Contest 264

Ten-Minute Musicals Project, The 224, 265, 298

Texas Accountants & Lawyers for the Arts 285

Texas Rose Records 161

Thistle Hill 125

Thunder Bay Theatre 225

T.L.C. Booking Agency 204

Tommy Boy Entertainment LLC 161

Ton Records 162

Topcat Records 162

Toronto Mendelssohn Choir 250

Toronto Musicians' Association 286

Touch and Go/Quarterstick Records 162

Tourmaline Music, Inc. 125

Transamerika Musikverlag KG 126

Transdreamer Records 163

Transition Music Corporation 126

Trio Productions, Inc./Songscape Music, LLC 126

Tunesmith PRO 298

U

UAR Records 163
Umbrella Artists Management, Inc. 204
Undercurrents 298
Universal Music Marketing 205
Universal Music Publishing 127
Universal Records 164
U.S.A. Songwriting Competition 265

V

Vaam Music Group 127
Vagrant Recprds 164
Vancouver Chamber Choir 250
Vancouver Youth Symphony Orchestra Society 251
Verve Music Group, The 164
Victory Records 164
Virginia Center for the Creative Arts 304
Virginia Opera 251
Virgin Records 165
Volunteer Lawyers for the Arts 286

W

Warner Bros. Records 165
Warner/Chappell Music, Inc. 127
Warner Productions, Cheryl K. 205
Waterdog Music 165
Wemus Entertainment 205

West Coast Songwriters 286
West Coast Songwriters Conference 298
West End Artists 225
Western Wind Workshop in Ensemble Singing 299
Westwires Recording USA 183
Wheaton Symphony Orchestra 252
Wilcom Publishing 127
Winchester Records 166
Winterland Entertainment Management & Publishing 206
Winter Music Conference Inc. 299
WLM Music/Recording 183
World Beatnik Records 166
World Records 184
WorldSound, LLC 206

X

Xemu Records 167
XL Recordings 167

Y

Y.E.S. Festival of New Plays 265
Your Best Songs Publishing 128

Z

Zane Management, Inc. 206
Zig Productions 184